Seashore Life of the Northern Pacific Coast

*An illustrated guide
to Northern California, Oregon,
Washington, and British Columbia*

EUGENE N. KOZLOFF

UNIVERSITY OF WASHINGTON PRESS

Seattle and London

PHOTOGRAPHIC CREDITS

All photographs are by the author except those listed below.

COLOR PLATES

Charles Birkeland: 2, *Aglaophenia, Abietinaria*; 5, *Balanophyllia elegans* and *Didemnum, Ptilosarcus gurneyi*

K. Cameron Campbell: 14, *Triopha catalinae*; 15, *Triopha maculata* (mature), *Laila cockerelli, Flabellinopsis iodinea, Hopkinsia rosacea, Hypselodoris californiensis, Chromodoris macfarlandi*

Megan Dethier: 4, *Anthopleura artemisia*

David Duggins: 25, *Orthasterias koehleri*

Linda Price: 7, *Pista elongata*; 18, *Pollicipes polymerus*; 33, *Leathesia difformis*; 35, *Halosaccion glandiforme*

Gordon Robilliard: 3, *Metridium senile*; 25, *Pycnopodia helianthoides*

Ronald Shimek: 5, *Clavularia*; 28, *Perophora annectens* and *Balanophyllia elegans*; 29, *Aplidium* (left)

Hiroshi Watanabe: 29, *Aplidium* (right)

BLACK-AND-WHITE FIGURES

H. F. Dietrich: 17, *Bougainvillia principis*; 23, *Aequorea victoria*

Anne Hurst: 348, *Melibe leonina*

Claudia Mills: 18, *Polyorchis penicillatus*; 24, *Aglantha digitale*

Linda Price: 210, *Gigartina agardhii* (top)

Scott Smiley: 208, *Phragmatopoma californica* (left)

State of Washington, Department of Fisheries (through Cedric Lindsay): 259, *Siliqua patula*; 297, *Panopea generosa*

Copyright © 1973, 1983, 1993 by the University of Washington Press
Third printing (paper), with corrections, 1993
Fourth printing, 1996
Designed by Veronica Seyd
Text and black-and-white illustrations printed by Vail-Ballou Press,
    Binghamton, New York
Color inserts and cover printed by Dai Nippon Printing Co., Tokyo, Japan

Library of Congress Cataloging-in-Publication Data
Kozloff, Eugene N.
    Seashore life of the northern Pacific coast.
    Rev. ed. of: Seashore life of Puget Sound, the Strait of Georgia, and the
San Juan Archipelago. 1973.
    1. Seashore biology—Northwest, Pacific. 2. Marine biology—North Pacific
Ocean. I. Title
QH104.5.N6K7   1983   574.9795   83–1130
ISBN 0–295–96084–1

The paper used in this publication meets the minimum requirements of American National Standard for Information Sciences—Permanence of Paper for Printed Library Materials, ANSI Z39.48–1984. ∞

Preface

In *Seashore Life of Puget Sound, the Strait of Georgia, and the San Juan Archipelago* (1973), I included about 300 species of common plants and animals. When I started to revise and enlarge the work, I decided to extend its usefulness to the open coast, from Vancouver Island to northern California. This new volume deals with a wide geographic area, but the coverage of Puget Sound and adjacent regions has not been diluted. It has, in fact, been made more intensive than in the earlier study. As before, I have concentrated on invertebrates and seaweeds, but a few fishes are discussed, and most of the conspicuous flowering plants of sand dunes and salt marshes are mentioned. The result of my labors is a guide that will provide interested amateurs, students, and professional biologists with information about more than 650 species found in marine and maritime habitats from British Columbia to San Mateo County, California.

Some of the species described and illustrated occur in suitable habitats in all or much of the area under consideration. Others are decidedly northern or southern, and are found in only a small part of the region. This book will be useful as far south as Monterey County, but the reader will have to be charitable about the omission of a few rather important species that reach their northern limit in that part of California.

As in the 1973 publication of *Seashore Life*, the text is organized according to habitats. The user of this book will therefore be encouraged to associate certain animals and plants with a particular environment, such as a rocky shore or a mudflat, as well as with tide levels and with other organisms found in the same situation. For practical reasons, however, most of the pictures in the color plates are arranged according to the groups to which the subjects belong.

My debt to Alan Kohn and Robert Waaland, whose criticisms improved the manuscript of the original publication, still stands. In connection with this enlarged work, I am especially grateful to Lee Braithwaite, Megan Dethier, David Duggins, Robert Fernald, Lisbeth Francis, Larry Golden, Gayle Hansen, Paul Illg, Gretchen and Charles Lambert, Joyce Lewin, Thomas Mumford, Richard Norris, Carl Nyblade, Laura Richards, Ronald Shimek, George Shinn, Scott Smiley, Craig Staude, Richard Strathmann, Stephen Stricker, and Thomas Turner. Among those who provided me with specimens that I could study and photograph are Roger Eckert, Richard Emlet, Donna Koslowsky, Alison and Roger Longley, Norman McLean, and Craig Young. At the California Academy of Sciences I received generous help from Dustin Chivers, Welton Lee, Peter Rodda, and Barry Roth. At the Los Angeles County Museum of Natural History, James McLean and Gale Sphon were of much assistance.

Extensive portions of the manuscript were typed by Beverly Bergee and LaRena Christenson. It is a pleasure to remember their efficiency and good cheer. Estelle Johnson, Kathryn Lehde, and Dennis Willows, colleagues at Friday Harbor Laboratories, helped me solve a variety of logistic problems. Heidi Mercado, Thomas Moritz, Krispi Staude, and Adrienne Stevens located books and periodicals that I needed. My wife, Anne, read all proofs and participated in the preparation of the index.

I express my warmest thanks to Linda Price, who provided transportation for field trips in California, helped me search for specimens, and studied some of my problems of algal identification. She also let me use her patio for taking pictures and never complained about all the sea water I spilled on her tomatoes.

Some of the photographs in this book were supplied by persons I have already mentioned. Others were provided by K. Cameron Campbell, H. F. Dietrich, Charles Birkeland, Gordon Robilliard, Hiroshi Watanabe, Anne Hurst, and the Department of Fisheries, State of Washington (through the courtesy of Cedric Lindsay).

To the line drawings prepared by Catherine Eaton and Margaret Siebert for the 1973 edition of *Seashore Life*, Carol Noyes added a substantial number of new illustrations, and one figure was prepared by Carole Jerome. The careful work of all these artists is appreciated. I also thank Robert Scagel, University of British Columbia, and Yorke Edwards, Director of the British Columbia Provincial Museum, for allowing me to use drawings that had been made by Ernani Meñez for the *Guide to Common Seaweeds of British Columbia*, published by the Museum. Several of the line drawings were prepared by Jeanne R. Janish for *Vascular Plants of the Pacific Northwest* (University of Washington Press, 1976), and two illustrations she made for an article by Gilbert Smith were taken from *American Journal of Botany*. One figure was lent by William Newman.

Enlarging the scope of *Seashore Life* also increases the chance of inconsistencies. I welcome information that will enable me to make this guide as accurate as possible.

SEPTEMBER 1983

Contents

Changes in Scientific Names as of 1993

Since 1983, when *Seashore Life* was published, studies on marine organisms of the Pacific coast have led to replacement of some previously accepted scientific names. Many of the changes are minor, affecting only the genus or species, but others are more substantial. In the list that follows, most of the names in use at the present time agree with those given by Gabrielson, Scagel, and Widdowson in *Keys to the Benthic Marine Algae and Seagrasses of British Columbia, Southeast Alaska, Washington and Oregon* (Department of Botany, University of British Columbia, 1990) and by Kozloff in *Marine Invertebrates of the Pacific Northwest* (University of Washington Press, 1987).

NAMES USED IN *SEASHORE LIFE* (1983)	NAMES NOW GENERALLY ACCEPTED
Alia gouldi	*Alia gausapata*
Batillaria attramentaria	*Batillaria zonalis*
Botryoglossum farlowianum	*Cryptopleura ruprechtiana*
Chaetomorpha aerea	*Chaetomorpha linum*
Clavularia	*Alcyonium* sp. (not yet named) (*Clavularia* is a valid genus, but the intertidal species that has commonly been referred to it belongs in *Alcyonium*.)
Cnidopus ritteri	*Epiactis ritteri*
Collisella asmi	*Lottia asmi*
Collisella digitalis	*Lottia digitalis*
Collisella instabilis	*Lottia instabilis*
Collisella limatula	*Lottia limatula*
Collisella ochracea	*Lottia ochracea*
Collisella paradigitalis	*Lottia strigatella*
Collisella pelta	*Lottia pelta*
Collisella scabra	*Macclintockia scabra*
Convolvulus soldanella	*Calystegia soldanella*

Discodoris sandiegensis	*Diaulula sandiegensis*
Epitonium tinctum	*Nitidiscala tincta*
Flabellinopsis iodinea	*Flabellina iodinea*
Frankenia grandifolia	*Frankenia salina*
Fucus distichus	In some recent works on Pacific coast algae, our common *Fucus*, which closely resembles the Atlantic *F. distichus*, is designated *F. gardneri*.
Gastroclonium coulteri	*Gastroclonium subarticulatum*
Gersemia rubiformis	*Alcyonium* sp. (not yet named) (*Gersemia rubiformis* is a valid species, and occurs subtidally in our area, but most intertidal and subtidal specimens that have been referred to it belong to *Alcyonium*.)
Gigartina agardhii	*Mastocarpus jardinii*
Gigartina papillata	*Mastocarpus papillatus*
Gonatus fabricii	*Berryteuthis magister*
Gracilaria sjoestedtii	*Gracilariopsis lemaneiformis*
Gymnogongrus platyphyllus	*Gymnogongrus chiton*
Kellia laperousii	*Kellia suborbicularis*
Kornmannia zostericola	*Kornmannia leptoderma*
Leptochelia dubia	*Leptochelia savignyi*
Megatebennus bimaculatus	*Fissurellidea bimaculata*
Metridium senile	The large (commonly at least 25 cm tall) *Metridium* found on floating docks and in subtidal habitats is now called *M. giganteum*. It may have more than 200 tentacles, and its oral disk is prominently lobed. It does not reproduce by fragmentation of the pedal disk. The name *M. senile* is restricted to the smaller intertidal or subtidal species that has fewer than 100 tentacles. Its oral disk is only slightly lobed, and it reproduces rapidly by fragmentation of the pedal disk.
Mytilus edulis	The results of recent researches, concerned mostly with biochemical characteristics rather than with visible features, indicate that the common bay mussel of our region should be called *Mytilus trossulus*. True *M. edulis* is believed to be restricted to Atlantic shores. Another widely distributed species of the "*M. edulis complex*" is

	M. galloprovincialis, found on the Pacific coast from central California southward. It is being cultivated in Puget Sound, but the commercial stocks are derived from hatchery-reared "seed," and the species is not known to have become established.
Navicula	*Navicula pseudocomoides* (This is the common species that forms filaments of the type referred to as "Schizonema.")
Notoacmea fenestrata	*Tectura fenestrata*
Notoacmea insessa	*Discurria insessa*
Notoacmea paleacea	*Tectura paleacea*
Notoacmea persona	*Tectura persona*
Notoacmea scutum	*Tectura scutum*
Oenothera cheiranthifolia	*Camissonia cheiranthifolia*
Opalia chacei	*Opalia borealis*
Orobitella rugifera	*Pseudopythina rugifera*
Ovatella myosotis	*Phytia myosotis*
Pecten caurinus	*Patinopecten caurinus*
Phidiana crassicornis	*Hermissenda crassicornis*
Phidolopora pacifica	*Phidolopora labiata*
Rhodochorton purpureum	*Audouinella purpurea*
Rhodomela larix	*Neorhodomela larix*
Stichopus californicus	*Parastichopus californicus* (This species should probably be called *Stichopus californicus,* but the change has not been formally proposed in the scientific literature.)
Tapes japonica	*Tapes philippinarum*
Thymatoscyphus hexaradiatus	*Manania handi*
Ulvaria fusca	*Ulvaria obscura*
Zostera noltii	*Zostera japonica*

JANUARY 1996

Seashore Life of the
Northern Pacific Coast

1

Introduction

The rich variety of seashore life along the Pacific coast is due partly to the many different habitats that are represented. There are rocky shores with reefs, tide pools, and boulders; sandy beaches exposed to heavy surf; quiet bays in which the substratum ranges from nearly clean sand to smelly, blackish mud; and estuaries in which the salinity may fluctuate widely. Two other features are also of great importance. One of them is upwelling, the flow of cold water from the depths to replace the surface water that is driven away from nearshore areas by winds; the other is the drainage of numerous rivers into the sea. These phenomena replenish nutrients necessary for the photosynthetic activities of plants. As the plants flourish, animals prosper at their expense and may serve, in turn, as food for larger animals.

Each habitat has a characteristic assemblage of organisms. Some of the biological interactions that go on in a particular situation are obvious, as when a sea star attacks a mussel, or when a limpet grazes on seaweed. More often, however, the interactions are subtle, and most of them are still not understood. It is convenient, in any case, to discuss seashore animals and plants according to the situations where they occur. A brief introduction to the geological history of our region, and to the topographic features of a few specific areas, will be helpful in understanding why certain habitats are where they are.

A LITTLE GEOLOGY AND GEOGRAPHY

At one time, all of the earth's surface was covered by water. Buckling of the crust beneath the sea is believed to have produced the first land masses, to which much material was added through volcanic activity. There is now considerable evidence to support the idea that the continents as we know them are derived from a single supercontinent. After this broke up, some of its pieces slowly moved farther and farther apart. Thus Africa became widely separated from South America, and North America and Greenland became distinct from one another as well as from Europe. Antarctica and Australia were once closely associated with what are now South America, Africa, and India, but they wandered away. India, moreover, broke away from Africa and became incorporated into Asia.

The displacement of the continents has been brought about by movements of several huge plates of the earth's crust. The movements are still going on, largely as a result of volcanic activity on the sea floor. As volcanic ridges enlarge, the crustal plates are slowly pushed apart, so that the gap between certain continents is becoming wider, just as the gap between others is becoming narrower. When one continent presses against another, mountains are thrust up. The infinitesimally slow collision of India with Asia has produced the Himalayas, and the pressure of Africa against Europe has produced the Alps. Both of these mountain ranges are still growing.

North America was clearly distinct from Europe by about 250 million years ago. It has grown substantially, mostly as a result of uplift caused by folding of the earth's crust. The Pacific coast, about 25 million years old, is a relatively recent development. Although it originated to a large extent through uplift, it has also undergone localized sinking. The sea level of this region, moreover, has fluctuated considerably, as it has elsewhere around the world. Whenever there was an ice age, much of the water surrounding the earth became tied up in great continental ice sheets, and the sea level dropped. Whenever ice sheets melted, water returned to the sea, and the level therefore rose. The last ice age officially ended about 11,000 years ago. During the long period of thawing, enough water was returned to the sea to raise its level about 100 meters. The coastal portions of river valleys and glacial troughs were therefore "drowned." Most of our larger bays and fjords originated in this way.

Some of the geological formations at the shoreline of our region consist primarily of igneous rocks, such as basalt and granite. These were produced by the cooling of molten material coming from within the earth. Being hard, they resist erosion, and this explains why most of the prominent headlands along the coast are composed largely of igneous rocks. The sedimentary rocks at the shore are mostly sandstone, shale, conglomerate, or limestone. These, on the whole, are relatively soft, so they are subject to rapid erosion. Gravel, sand, and clay are sedimentary deposits, too, of course. They consist of progressively smaller fragments of rocks that have been worn away by the action of water, glaciers, wind, weather, and burrowing organisms.

The Puget Sound Region

Puget Sound proper spreads over the bottom of the trough that lies between the Olympic Mountains and the Cascade Mountains. It may be entered from the north by way of the channel between Port Townsend and Whidbey Island, through Deception Pass (between Whidbey and Fidalgo islands), or through the Swinomish Slough (which separates Fidalgo Island from the mainland). The main body of the sound extends southward past Seattle, Bremerton, and Tacoma to Olympia. A westerly offshoot, consisting of Hood Canal and Dabob Bay, runs between the Olympic and Kitsap peninsulas, and at two points it closely approaches the principal portion of the sound.

The large body of water between Vancouver Island and the mainland may be thought of as part of the "greater Puget Sound region." At least it occupies what is essentially a northward extension of the trough within which Puget Sound lies. The approximately 450 islands of the San Juan Archipelago represent the peaks of mountains that are now to a considerable extent submerged. The reefs, banks, channels, and straits reflect the nature of the land forms that were in the area before the sea level rose.

The principal channels of water circulation east and west of the San Juan Islands are called, respectively, Rosario Strait and Haro Strait. These channels connect the Strait of Georgia, north of the islands, with the Strait of Juan de Fuca. The name "Washington Sound," formerly applied to the water mass surrounding the San Juan Islands, is now obsolete and does not appear on official charts.

The Strait of Juan de Fuca runs almost directly westward between Vancouver Island and the Olympic Peninsula. Exchange of water between the open sea and the general area of Puget Sound, Strait of Georgia, and San Juan Islands is achieved by swift tidal currents. There are, however, many narrow passes between islands, and the entrances to Puget Sound proper are not especially large when one considers the size of this body of water. The character of the water in the region, in terms of salinity, temperature, organic nutrients, and other factors, is therefore not at all homogeneous. In some of the channels the tidal turbulence is violent, and mixing is rapid and complete; but in some of the bays removed from such channels, the interchange of water is relatively slight. Thus bays such as East Sound and West Sound, on the southern side of Orcas Island, are not immediately influenced by what goes on in San Juan Channel, just a few kilometers to the west.

The runoff of fresh water also contributes to the variety of water conditions. Puget Sound proper receives a number of small rivers draining the Cascade Mountains, and Hood Canal is entered by several rivers from the Olympic Mountains. Of the rivers draining into the Strait of Georgia and adjacent areas, the most important is the great Fraser River of southern British Columbia. When the runoff of the Fraser River is at its peak—usually in June, when the snows in the mountains melt away rapidly—the influence of the runoff in reducing the salinity of surface waters may be felt over a wide area.

San Francisco Bay

San Francisco Bay is a good example of a bay that was formed by the drowning of a large river valley. A number of streams run into it, but the Sacramento and San Joaquin rivers are the most important in terms of the volume of water carried. Thus the bay is viewed as the submerged coastal valley of the Sacramento–San Joaquin drainage system. The marvelous Golden Gate has been carved out of hard rock, mostly granite, so erosion here is slow. The powerful tidal currents that sweep into and out of the bay nevertheless scour the rock, even at the bottom, where the depth is about 100 meters. In most parts of the bay, the depth does not exceed 20 meters, for the rivers have brought down much sand and silt.

The bay is divided into three main portions. The largest, joined to the open ocean by the Golden Gate, is San Francisco Bay proper. It extends from near Palo Alto to Richmond, where Point San Pablo marks the beginning of San Pablo Bay. Carquinez Strait, running eastward for a distance of nearly 10 kilometers, connects San Pablo Bay with Suisun Bay. The latter receives the Sacramento and San Joaquin rivers, and its average salinity is low. Much of the marshland around Suisun Bay has been reclaimed for agriculture.

Some Other Important Bays

Coos Bay, Humboldt Bay, Grays Harbor, and a number of other bays along the Pacific coast are similar to San Francisco Bay in that they are drowned river valleys. In nearly all of them, the salinity varies to a considerable extent. When there is a great influx of fresh water from a river that enters a bay, then at least the upper reaches of the bay will have a salinity decidedly lower than that of full-strength sea water. If the influx of fresh water is small during a period when there are high tides flooding the bay, then the average salinity in the bay as a whole will be relatively high.

The origin of Tomales Bay, in Marin County, California, is different from that of bays of the type just discussed. It is the drowned portion of the trough that developed along the San Andreas fault. It does receive some small streams, so the salinity in its southern portion, far from its mouth, is low at certain seasons.

The mouths of many larger bays have been partly blocked by sandspits. Along the Pacific coast of North America, sand produced by erosion of rocks at the shore, and also that brought down to the sea by rivers, tends to move southward. This explains, in part, why a sandspit on the north side of some bays is more extensive than it is on the south side. One must also reckon, however, with the fact that storms that drive sand toward the shore of our region come largely from the southwest. In some bays, therefore, the sandspit on the south side is more extensive than it is on the north side. This is the case in Tillamook Bay and Willapa Bay. Certain bays, such as Grays Harbor, have substantial sandspits on both their north and south sides.

The presence of sandspits is by no means limited to the mouths of bays or estuaries along the open coast. A spit may appear in any situation where sand dropped by a prevailing current accumulates. Even within a relatively small bay, the circulation may be such that a sandspit develops. This often leads to the formation of a lagoon that is largely or completely separate from the rest of the bay.

TIDES

A brief explanation of tides is called for because the student of seashore life is going to think of many animals and plants at least partly in terms of where they live in relation to low tide or high tide. Both the sun and the moon exert a gravitational force on the earth and on the water that covers most of its surface. The moon, though smaller than the sun, has the greater effect because it is so much closer to the earth. The gravitational force of the passing moon pulls the water nearest it away from the earth, and at the same time pulls the earth away from the water farthest from it. Thus, where the water is heaped up, there will be high tides; but somewhere else the tides will have to be low. When the moon is between the sun and the earth (new moon), the gravitational effect of the sun reinforces that of the moon. When the moon is on the side of the earth opposite the sun (full moon), the gravitational pull of the moon opposes that of the sun; because the gravitational effects of sun and moon are exerted on the earth itself as well as on the water mass, however, there will in this case also be a heaping up of water on opposite sides of the earth. When the sun and moon are at right angles with respect to the earth (first quarter moon, last quarter moon), the tides are less well marked.

The moon orbits around the earth once each 27 days and 8 hours, making 13 lunar cycles a year. Since the earth rotates as it orbits around the sun, a particular longitudinal meridian comes under the influence of the moon each 24 hours and 50 minutes. Thus the daily tidal cycle is a bit longer than 24 hours. The maximum tidal effect does not coincide with the moment the moon passes over a given meridian; instead, there is a lag of several hours, which is constant for each location. Even this lag, however, cannot be used to predict the exact times of tides, because tides in particular ocean basins depend in large part upon conformations of the sea coast and ocean floor, and also because there are interactions between tidal patterns in contiguous ocean basins.

Along the Pacific coast of North America, a daily cycle typically has two unequal high tides and two unequal low tides. On the open coast, the higher of the high tides is usually succeeded by the lower of the low tides, and then the lower of the high tides is succeeded by the higher of the low tides. The overall pattern therefore looks like the one shown below:

At certain times in the tidal cycle, however, and rather regularly in Puget Sound, the San Juan Archipelago, and adjacent areas, the lower of the low tides succeeds the lower of the high tides, resulting in the pattern shown below:

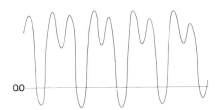

The average of the lower low tides (mean lower low water, or MLLW) of the annual cycle at a particular reference point is expressed as 0.0 feet or 0.0 meters.[1] So-called minus tides (–0.1 or lower) are therefore below the average of lower low tides. In Puget Sound proper an exceptionally high tide may reach a little above 13.0 feet, or 4.0 meters; an extremely low tide in the same daily cycle may bring the water level to below –3.0 feet (–0.9 meter). Thus the tidal amplitude—the difference between high and low tides—is slightly more than 16 feet, or about 5 meters. In the San Juan Archipelago and Strait of Juan de Fuca, the highest tides only occasionally reach 10.0 feet, or 3.0 meters, and the maximum amplitude is about 12.5 feet (3.8 meters). At Astoria and Aberdeen the amplitude is about the same, but along much of the open coast within the region covered by this book, it is decidedly smaller. At San Francisco, for instance, the amplitude is about 9 feet, or 2.7 meters.

About every two weeks, there is a period of several days in which the daily amplitude is decidedly greater than it is in intervening pe-

1. Tide tables for Victoria and Vancouver, British Columbia, are not reckoned on the same system as tables for the United States. To make these Canadian tables conform to the pattern in which 0.0 equals mean lower low water, subtract 2.5 feet (0.8 meter) from predictions for Victoria and 3.8 feet (1.1 meters) for Vancouver. Most predictions for various points along the open coast of Vancouver Island are based on those for Sitka, Alaska, and are on the United States system.

riods. The tidal graph below illustrates the way in which the amplitude gradually diminishes and then increases again.

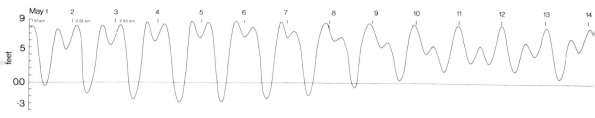

In a particular area, especially favorable low tides will come during the day in certain months. At other times of the year, however, the only really low tides are likely to be at night, or so early in the morning that all but the hardiest of naturalists will stay in bed. In planning field work, remember that a tide of 0.0 is at the average of the lower low tides for the year and exposes much of the intertidal region. Tides of −1.0, −2.0, and −3.0 feet (−0.3, −0.6, and −0.9 meter) expose progressively more of the intertidal area, and they are of progressively less frequent occurrence. There is much to observe, however, at tide levels between 0.0 and +3.0 feet (+0.9 meter). Even the higher reaches of the intertidal zone have some extremely interesting organisms, and certain of them show special adaptations to life on the fringes of the sea. A case in point is the big sow bug, *Ligia pallasii*, which, shunning water and yet requiring moisture, lives in crevices at levels normally reached only by spray.

Official tide tables for the Pacific coast are published by the United States Department of Commerce. These provide predictions, on standard time, for a number of principal stations (mostly port cities), with corrections for other localities near the reference stations. The information is reprinted, in one form or another, by gasoline companies, dealers in marine hardware, and other firms. Commercially produced tables are usually corrected to daylight saving time, for more convenient use in the late spring, summer, and early autumn.

Tides predicted for a given reference point, such as San Francisco, Astoria, or Seattle, have long been given in feet, with the feet divided into tenths instead of inches. The tables issued by the Department of Commerce now show tide levels in meters and tenths of meters as well as in feet. A meter is about 39⅓ inches, so a tenth of a meter is a much larger unit than a tenth of a foot. It is sufficiently precise for most purposes, however, especially when one appreciates that actual tides are affected by atmospheric conditions and do not necessarily agree with predictions. Low barometric pressure and winds from the ocean tend to raise the level of the water; high barometric pressure and winds from the continent tend to lower it. Thus some tides are less suitable for field work than predictions would indicate; others are slightly better than might be expected.

Many who are not biologists—and some biologists, too—may wonder about the wisdom of using scientific names in a book of this sort. Although names like "bent-nosed clam" and "clingfish" are nearly standardized by common usage, most of the animals and plants dealt with here just do not have dependable vernacular names. If you have no particular difficulty with *Geranium* and *Rhododendron,* you should be able to handle *Cadlina* and *Protothaca*—and probably even *Membranipora* and *Strongylocentrotus.* Latin names vary to some extent, as systematists revise their views on classification of certain organisms and reexamine the history of names applied to them. This is as it should be. Yet nothing could create more confusion for us than inventing a number of vernacular names or making use of names that have been indiscriminately applied to more than one kind of animal or plant. Perhaps someday we will be ready for what professional and amateur ornithologists almost take for granted: a set of common names that are standardized and just as precise as scientific names.

For our purposes a compromise can be worked out. Scientific names—at least the genus—will almost always be given. If the common name is generally accepted, it will be used more or less interchangeably with the scientific name. Scientific names usually consist of two parts: the first refers to the genus, the second to the species. There may be a third part, which refers to a subspecies, a variation— usually with a particular geographic distribution—of the species. A genus may consist of from one to many species, so in a sense the species name is like an adjective modifying a noun. For instance, on the Pacific coast there are four common species of clams of the genus *Macoma: M. nasuta, M. inquinata, M. secta,* and *M. balthica.* They are all rather closely related, hence they are all put into the same genus. They differ, however, at the species level, one having a bent shell, the others likewise having distinctive characteristics.

Scientific names of genera, species, and subspecies, as well as those applied to higher categories—classes, orders, families, and so on—are developed as Latin words. They do not have to be from the Latin language as spoken by the Romans, and just about anything goes, if it can be latinized—names of people (*lewisi, Smithora*), names of places (*pugettensis, oregonensis, sanjuanensis*), and even an allusion to a pleasant holiday on the links (*Golfingia*). The roots used in compounding scientific names are generally drawn from Latin or Greek; most Greek words have related Latin counterparts, anyway. If you enjoy words and language, you will probably find that understanding the roots of scientific names will help you to use them, at least in conversations with yourself.

Unrelated to the problem of scientific names versus common names, but something else that begs for justification here, is the use of the metric system instead of the so-called English system. Most of us think we can cope more easily with 4 inches than with 10 centimeters, or even with 3⅝ inches instead of 9 centimeters; but this is just a matter of tradition. In reckoning with money, we all understand very early in life that a dollar is worth 100 cents. We can certainly adapt, after a little habituation, to dealing with meters, centimeters, and millimeters. Nearly all nations except the United States use the metric system, and the United States is moving in that direction. There are two other reasons for using the metric system in this book, however; it is more suitable than the English system for giving precise measurements of small things, because it does not involve fractions; and other scientific works to which the reader may need to refer for further study will almost invariably use the metric system.

In the metric system, the meter (about 39⅓ inches in the English system) is divided into 100 centimeters, and each centimeter is divided into 10 units called millimeters (thousandths of a meter). If you must think in terms of inches and fractions of inches, you may find some comfort in the side-by-side comparison of metric and English scales given below. Note that 2.5 cm just about equals 1 inch, so 1 mm is ¹/₂₅ of an inch.

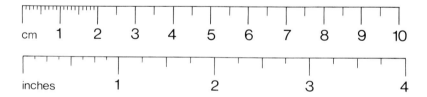

CARING FOR MARINE ANIMALS

Many who are excited by life at the shore may contemplate prospects for keeping a few animals alive in the living room. Unfortunately, the chances for their survival are slim, unless the aquarium into which they are placed is large and the water is kept cold and well aerated. Even in the summer, the temperature of sea water throughout most of our region is not likely to exceed 12° C (about 54° F). At this temperature, the water holds considerably more dissolved oxygen than it will at room temperature (20° C, or 68° F), so even those animals that can adjust to room temperature will not survive long unless they have a large volume of water in proportion to their size and number, or unless the water is aerated. In general, an aquarium for marine animals of temperate waters is not practical for most of us. If you insist on trying it, take care to select animals that are most likely to survive. Animals from sand or mud are hopelessly out of place, and those from the lower reaches of rocky intertidal habitats will require too much oxygen. Try a small crab or hermit crab from near the middle of the intertidal zone, and arrange some rocks so that it can hide among them, both above and below the surface. Small sea anemones from floating docks are sometimes hardy. It would be preferable to keep the aquarium on a shaded and cool porch rather than in the house. If the tank has a metal frame, the cement that holds the glass had better be of a type that effectively seals the metal from any contact with the sea water.

Remember that oxygen, temperature, and toxic metal ions are not the only problems these animals have to face in a container in which the sea water is not continually being renewed. Unless there is a large volume of water in proportion to the size and number of the animals, wastes will soon reach a toxic concentration. Overfeeding is another problem. A crab or sea anemone will relish a few bits of fish or clam; but if there are leftovers, the whole tank may soon turn putrid. To summarize, most animals one sees—even on floating docks, where there is pollution—will not survive in home aquariums. Even those that might are better left where one finds them. Few of our algae will live in water that is not cold and constantly moving; so if you think you can solve the problem of oxygen for the animals by putting in a little seaweed, after the fashion of a balanced, freshwater aquarium, you should be willing to accept defeat—and a stinking mess—graciously.

The transport of a few animals or plants for study in the laboratory requires care. From the standpoint of the collector, plastic pails and plastic bags are safer than glass; metal should be avoided for the sake of the organisms. Most animals and plants travel better if they are kept just wet rather than submerged, unless the volume of the container is very large and the water can be kept cold or agitated. In a small pail of water, a number of animals may quickly consume the available oxygen, whereas if these same animals are kept wet, as under a cover of paper towels or seaweed (but do not use any species of *Desmarestia*, because the sap that exudes from them is very acid), in a plastic bag or in a shallow layer of sloshing water, their moist surfaces will constantly be in contact with atmospheric oxygen. Besides, they are liable to be physiologically less active in this state than if they are submerged. Some animals and seaweeds, however, are so delicate that they must be transported in cold water in order to prevent them from rupturing, collapsing, or trapping air bubbles. Sponges, hydroids, and jellyfishes are among the more vulnerable animals, and most of these cannot be exposed to air for long. Sponges, especially those never uncovered by low tides, should not be lifted out of the water at all; they should be kept submerged while being transferred from their habitat to the container in which they are to be transported. Crabs, snails, clams, annelid worms, and most other animals travel well if they are kept wet as suggested above. Naturally, it will be essential to take back a supply of sea water in which to immerse the animals for observation or study with the microscope, and this water should be cooled before the animals are put into it. A refrigerator is a good place to store animals for a few hours.

A PLEA FOR CONSERVATION

This book has been written to help others enjoy the seashore life of the region. But what will happen if all the people who use this book go out and start turning over rocks and digging up the mud flats? Pollution, the pressure of increasing population, and the destruction or modification of natural areas are already bad enough.

It is probably true that wholesale destruction of certain kinds of habitats brings more animals and plants to extinction than picking common wildflowers or digging clams. However, our natural heritage needs all the protection it can get. Each of us, in his own personal involvement with the environment, should do everything he can to offset the greed and carelessness of others.

Those of us in educational work ought to be exemplary as conservationists. Unfortunately, we are the ones who know where the rarer animals are and are most likely to collect in quantity for class use. We also sometimes unleash classes on beaches without first providing proper instruction in matters of conservation. Clam diggers, fishermen, curio collectors, and divers with spears are often none too virtuous, either. Prizes for the biggest octopus—or for the biggest or most of anything, for that matter—are strictly out of the Dark Ages.

In California and Oregon, one must have a permit for collecting seashore animals or plants. (Most clams, crabs, and other animals that are taken for food are subject to fish and game laws, and the license that may be required for these is separate from a permit required to collect biological material.) There are, moreover, a number of state and county parks and preserves in which collecting or disturbing the fauna and flora is forbidden, except with special permission.

In Washington, the marine fauna and flora of San Juan County and some contiguous territory are protected by a law enacted in 1923. Permission to collect biological material from this area for other than food purposes must be obtained in advance from the Director of Friday Harbor Laboratories of the University of Washington. Of course, empty shells found on the beach can be taken home, but it is unlawful to make curios out of live animals.

For the benefit of those who use the seashore for recreation, gathering food, or learning, a few rules will be offered in the hope that our environment will get better before it gets worse.

1. Don't catch or dig up more than you really need or want. This idea should be extended to collecting for classroom study, too. One live specimen of a kind brought back to the laboratory may serve an entire class, especially if the class is not prepared to make detailed studies requiring several specimens.

2. Make as much use as you can of the fauna and flora of floating docks, thus taking some pressure off natural areas.

3. Avoid collecting altogether in unusual natural areas, because certain animals or plants that inhabit them are not often seen elsewhere in the same general region.

4. Don't collect or disturb animals and plants in areas designated by law as biological preserves. If you are a professional biologist and need to do some of your work in a preserve, apply to the appropriate state or county authorities for permission. (In California and Oregon, a state permit is required for collecting seashore life in any region, and special permission is required for work in areas designated as preserves.)

5. On a field trip, do as much studying as you can right at the shore, thereby sparing the animals unnecessary abuse.

6. If you bring animals back for study or for an aquarium, keep them cool and do not overcrowd them. It is better to transport them just wet than to crowd them in too little water.

7. If you cannot return animals to a habitat of the same type as that in which you found them, make all the use you can of them before they perish. Do not let the collection be an end in itself. Some animals can be preserved in such a way that their usefulness may be extended beyond the time they are studied alive.

8. When you turn over a rock, do it gently, being careful not to crush any animal that is beside the rock or that moves suddenly as its hiding place is uncovered. Always put the rock back the way it was, again being careful of animals underneath. It is generally better to move them aside before you turn the rock over again, as they will soon find cover; but if you do not think they will, put them under some seaweed or in a little puddle or channel, if there is one. When the tides comes back in, they will probably get along all right.

Leaving a rock "belly up" is an almost sure way to kill most of the animals that are living on its underside, and perhaps also the animals and plants on its upper side. It may be a long time before the same kinds of organisms can establish themselves on it again.

9. If you dig clams or other animals in a sand flat or mud flat, fill in the holes. By leaving unnatural piles of mud or sand next to the holes you have dug, you may kill many small clams or other animals whose burrows can no longer reach the surface.

10. Obey the fish and game laws with respect to open season, bag limits, and size and sex of the animals taken for food. These laws have been developed on the basis of what we know about the biology of the animals they are supposed to protect.

11. If you teach about animals and plants, teach also conservation and a reverence for life. Good citizenship and a love of nature will have much to do with what we leave to succeeding generations.

2

Some Instant Zoology and Botany

It is difficult to explain, in just a few words, why animals as different as clams, snails, and octopuses belong to a single major group. Oversimplifications are likely to be misleading, especially if they sidestep details of internal anatomy and embryology. If a few outstanding features of each major group are pointed out, however, the rest of this book will be more useful than it might otherwise be.

The cardinal groups of animals are called phyla. Most botanists refer to comparable categories in the plant kingdom as divisions, but the term phylum is also accepted and will be used here in order to be consistent.

Practically all of the phyla of animals, and the majority of plant phyla, are represented in the sea. Some of them, in fact, are limited to the marine environment. Even those phyla that are successful on land or in fresh water have certain subdivisions that are abundant in the sea. Therefore it seems best to provide a review of most of the phyla consisting of organisms that can be seen without the help of a microscope, and also some of the classes into which they are divided. As a rule, the strictly microscopic organisms and those groups that are not found intertidally or are composed entirely or largely of specialized internal parasites will be omitted. The vertebrates, represented in the sea by fishes, birds, and mammals, will also be excluded.

This chapter is intended to give the reader a general introduction to the names and characteristics of the phyla of invertebrates likely to be seen at the shore in the region covered by this book. A brief summary will be given of the salient features—especially the more obvious and externally visible ones—of each, with further discussion of any subdivisions significant to this guidebook. A subsequent synopsis with accompanying pictures will help the reader to associate quickly a particular animal with the phylum and class to which it belongs. After a little experience, one should be able to find his way around the synopsis with some speed and come up with the right identification most of the time—except, of course, for obscure or aberrant types that only an experienced zoologist could place. Finally, there will be a brief characterization of the important groups of marine algae. The sea-weeds may look simple enough, but their classification is based to a very large extent on microscopic details.

INVERTEBRATES

Phylum Porifera: The Sponges

Porifera is considered to be the simplest phylum of multicellular animals, so it should be easy to explain. Unfortunately, most sponges are vague as individuals because they just keep spreading, and this habit stands in the way of defining them cleanly. Basically, however, a sponge consists of a restricted variety of cells, not forming tissues or even definite layers, organized around a system of pores, canals, and chambers. The "body" of a sponge is to a large extent composed of inanimate material in the form of spicules of either calcium carbonate or silica; there may be a considerable accumulation of organic fibers as well. The spicules and fibers provide a framework over which and through which the living cells and water passages are arranged.

In the area dealt with in this book, we have nothing quite like bath sponges of the good old days, whose skeletons are composed entirely of fibrous material. There are, however, plenty of other sponges, mostly growing as thin or thick encrustations. A few are vaselike and thus are simpler to explain because their growth is not so indefinite. Over the entire outer surface of such a sponge are thousands of microscopic openings leading into canals through which water is moved by the action of flagella (vibratile projections) on certain cells. These particular cells function also in feeding, using a delicate collar to trap tiny food particles, including bacteria. After the water has passed through the system of canals, it enters a central cavity, then leaves the sponge by way of the single large opening at the top. The encrusting sponges follow the same general feeding process but they have many excurrent openings, often on little, volcanolike eminences, and the system of canals and chambers becomes very complicated.

The feltlike texture of many sponges, as well as the bristly margins of the excurrent apertures of some species, is caused by spicules sticking out through the surface. Some of our species are bright red, orange, or yellow; brown, tan, green, violet, amethyst, and off-white are other common colors. Certain species are inconsistent with respect to their coloration.

Phylum Cnidaria (Coelenterata): The Cnidarians or Coelenterates

This phylum includes jellyfishes and polyplike animals: hydroids, sea anemones, sea pens, corals, and related organisms. It is impossible to define the phylum honestly without going into the numerous variations of the basic body plan. Unlike sponges, the cnidarians have a true mouth and true digestive cavity, which is basically just a sac, but may be subdivided by partitions. In colonial types, the digestive cavities of the separate polyps are continuous.

A cnidarian has two definite layers of cells, one covering the body on the outside, the other forming the lining of the digestive cavity. Between these is a basically noncellular layer called the mesogloea ("middle jelly"); however, cells or muscle strands derived from the inner or outer layer may sink into the mesogloea, and the amount of jellylike material in the middle layer varies from practically none, as in hydroids, to a great deal, as in most jellyfishes.

Some other traits of cnidarians can be mentioned here to strengthen the characterization of this phylum. Tentacles situated around the mouths of feeding polyps (or around the margins of the bell, in the case of jellyfishes) are provided with little capsules (nematocysts) containing threads that are shot out when the capsules are properly stimulated. The threads act as lassos or as piercing and poisoning agents, mainly for the trapping of prey, but to some extent for self-protection. Cnidarians are routinely carnivores, feeding on crustaceans, molluscs, fishes, and various other animals. The prey is taken into the digestive cavity and indigestible residues are ejected through the mouth. Representatives of various subdivisions of this phylum, such as certain of our sea anemones, have symbiotic algae in their tissues; although they may benefit from the association, they remain basically carnivores.

Many cnidarians form colonies, frequently with more than one kind of polyp. Sea pens, for instance, which are closely related to sea anemones, consist of hundreds of polyps; some of the polyps resemble miniature anemones, others look more like tubes and serve as openings for sea water that "ventilates" the colony. In a colonial cnidarian there may also be polyps modified for reproduction, either sexual or asexual.

Finally, one other important characteristic of some cnidarians: alternation of two different phases in the life cycle. Most of our jellyfishes represent the sexual phase of a life cycle that also includes a polyp, or colony of polyps, which reproduces asexually.

Phylum Ctenophora: Comb Jellies

Comb jellies resemble jellyfishes because of their transparency and texture, for they are composed largely of jellylike material. They do not, however, move in the same way as jellyfishes, which pulsate to force water out of the cavity beneath the bell. Instead, comb jellies have eight meridional rows of little "combs" (ctenes), which are paddlelike aggregations of large cilia. These combs beat rhythmically to propel the animals steadily instead of jerkily through the water. There may be a pair of long and extensile tentacles that originate within deep sheaths on opposite sides of the body and have branches. They do not have stinging capsules, but are provided with sticky cells (colloblasts) that function in the capture of prey. Ctenophores, like cnidarians, are carnivores; they feed mainly on small crustaceans or upon one another.

Phylum Platyhelminthes: The Flatworms

The flatworms include the parasitic tapeworms and flukes, as well as the largely free-living turbellarians. They are not necessarily flattened, however; many of the smaller species, especially, are cylindrical. In flatworms, the digestive tract (unless it is absent altogether, as in tapeworms) is a simple or branched sac with a single opening, the mouth. Between the digestive tract and the outside epidermis is a cellular layer in which the organs of reproduction and much of the musculature are located. The reproductive system may be surprisingly complicated for animals that are otherwise so lowly.

Turbellarians are abundant in marine environments, especially in sediment, on growths of seaweeds and colonial animals, and on rocks; but the majority of them are microscopic. Some are herbivores, feeding mostly on diatoms; others are carnivores, feeding on crustaceans and other small animal organisms. They are characterized in part by being covered with cilia (flukes and tapeworms are not).

The only turbellarians likely to be seen with the naked eye belong to a group called polyclads. They are usually very flat and two or three times longer than wide. The digestive cavity is much branched, with the mouth being near the center of the lower surface, and they are strictly carnivorous. Polyclads are most likely to be found on the undersurfaces of rocks, but may be overlooked because they are so thin and may resemble a gelatinous coating unless they happen to move. They glide along by action of their cilia, but some can also swim by fluttering undulations of the margins of the body. These worms usually show several to many little pepper-dot eyespots near the anterior end or around part or much of the margin of the body. They may also have a pair of tentacles at the extreme anterior edge or a bit away from the anterior edge.

Phylum Nemertea: The Ribbon Worms or Nemerteans

In being soft and covered with cilia, nemerteans are much like turbellarian flatworms, but as a rule they are slender, highly contractile worms. Although some of them resemble rubber bands, they are not at all rubbery in texture—in fact, they are often fragile, breaking apart when handled or stretched. They are usually at least slightly flattened and may have eyespots on the anterior part of the body. They are considered to be more advanced than flatworms because they have a complete digestive tract, with a mouth at one end and anus at the other, and also a circulatory system consisting of definite blood vessels. The reproductive system of nemerteans, however, is simple compared to that of most flatworms.

A unique feature of nemerteans is the proboscis. When withdrawn, this is turned into itself, like the finger of a glove that has been poked in, and is contained in a fluid-filled cavity surrounded by a muscular sheath. When the muscles of the sheath contract, hydrostatic pressure within the cavity forces the proboscis out. Sometimes it emerges through its own pore at the tip of the head region, but in certain groups of nemerteans it comes out through the mouth, even though its origin is unrelated to that of the digestive system. The proboscis, being either sticky or provided with thornlike stylets and a venom gland, is used to capture prey, often swallowed whole.

Phylum Annelida: The Segmented Worms

The common earthworm belongs to the phylum Annelida and shows one of its cardinal characteristics: the division of the body into distinct segments. In some annelids, most or at least many of the segments may be essentially identical, even with respect to their internal organization. In others, segments in one region of the body may be quite different from those in another portion. Here again one faces the problem of trying to define a group of animals briefly, when the only way to understand them is to study representatives of many of the diverse groups.

The digestive tract of annelids is complete, with mouth and anus at opposite ends of the body, and there is a circulatory system. In addition, a feature not seen in the preceding groups shows up here: the body cavity, or coelom. The coelom is typically well developed and forms a fluid-filled space between the digestive tract and the outer body wall. Some of the organs—those concerned with reproduction, excretion, and regulation of water balance, for instance—lie in this cavity. Because it is lined by an epithelial layer, called the peritoneum, it is comparable to our own body cavity, through which the digestive tract runs and in which various other internal organs—liver, pancreas, lungs, and kidneys—are located. The body cavity in annelids also serves as a kind of skeleton against which muscles can operate, so it is important in burrowing, crawling, and swimming, as well as in extension and retraction of certain structures used in feeding.

Of the three classes of annelids, one—the Oligochaeta, which includes the earthworm—consists mostly of terrestrial and freshwater animals, although there are some marine species. The leeches, or Hirudinea, are best represented in fresh water, but there are some marine forms, and even a few on land. The Polychaeta constitute by far the largest group and are almost all marine, so they will serve as the primary representatives of the annelids in this book. There is much diversity within the Polychaeta. Burrowing types form a number of distinct groups, as do those that build tubes of one sort or another.

There are also many crawlers and swimmers. Structural specializations are especially evident in the anterior part of the body, where there may be tentacles, featherlike cirri, jaws, trap doors to close tubes, and so on. Most polychaetes have fleshy flaps of tissue on the sides of the segments; these flaps and the bristles that arise from them also show modifications that can be correlated with life styles. A number of entirely different types of polychaetes will be considered in this book, and the brief descriptions of their specializations for feeding, burrowing, and other functions will help one appreciate what a remarkably diversified group this is.

Phylum Sipuncula: The Peanut Worms

Sipunculans could be confused with certain polychaete annelids or with sea cucumbers. Unlike annelids, however, they show no signs of segmentation and have no bristles. They resemble certain sea cucumbers that lack tube feet, but these cucumbers at least have longitudinal lines indicating division of the body into five sectors. In annelids and most sea cucumbers, the anus is at the hind end; but in sipunculans it is on the dorsal side of the body, closer to the anterior end.

The body of a sipunculan is divided into two vaguely defined regions. The slender and mobile anterior portion, called the introvert or "neck," can be completely withdrawn into the more bulbous posterior part. The neck may have some denticles in the skin; and the mouth, at the anterior tip of the body, is encircled by tentacles, which are usually bushy, but in our most common intertidal species are inconspicuous and unbranched. The body wall is tough and rubbery, and when the animal is contracted, the strength of the wall coupled with the high hydrostatic pressure within it makes it almost impossible to squeeze the sipunculan.

In addition to being bent back on itself, the digestive tract is extensively coiled, so that its length greatly exceeds that of the body. Most sipunculans feed on detritus, using a coating of mucus on the tentacles to trap particles of organic matter.

Phylum Mollusca: The Molluscs

The phylum Mollusca is a very large group, successful in the sea, in fresh waters, and even on land. As a rule, the body of a mollusc is rather soft, and a portion of the body wall grows out around some or much of the rest of it as a sort of flap or tent, referred to as the mantle. When there are gills of the type peculiar to molluscs—called ctenidia—they are situated in the mantle cavity. The excretory organs and the anus also usually open into this cavity. A shell, two shells hinged together, or eight shells in a row may be present, and these are secreted by the mantle. In many molluscs, such as sea slugs, there is no shell, or there is only a remnant of a shell. Internally there is a body cavity, but it is much reduced, being restricted to the cavities of certain organs—the gonads, a sac (pericardium) around the heart, and the excretory organs. Now that molluscs have been defined as a group, the major subdivisions found at the seashore can be described.

The chitons (class Polyplacophora) are usually somewhat elongated, and their upper surface is covered by a series of eight separate, overlapping shells. Chitons cannot withdraw into their shells, but can only clamp down tightly to the rock, so that little of the body not protected by the shells is exposed. In the mantle cavity, on either side of the long, broad foot, is a series of gills. The head is not very distinct, but it is recognizable; there are no tentacles. The anus is at the end opposite the mouth. Most chitons feed by rasping with the radula, a structure that looks like a toothed ribbon, which when not in use is in a sac off the digestive tract, just behind the mouth.

The Gastropoda—the snails and slugs—have a more definite head than chitons and usually have tentacles of at least one kind. When they have a shell, it is single and either coiled, conical, or something like a cap. The body is generally thoroughly protected, although clamping to a rock may be necessary if the shell is not of a type into which the animal can withdraw completely. The foot is typically developed for crawling. The mantle cavity (which is missing or much reduced in some, such as the sea slugs) may have one or two gills, or none. Lunglike structures for breathing air are characteristic of most land snails and slugs, and of many freshwater snails that have apparently gone back to the water after a long period on land. Only a few seashore gastropods have the habit of breathing air.

Gastropods have varied food habits and mechanisms for feeding. Jaws and a scraping radula are characteristic of the herbivores, and specializations of these structures are used also by the carnivores and scavengers. A few gastropods are filter feeders, which sort out microscopic food from water entering the mantle cavity. The anus is not often at the posterior end, unless the mantle cavity is missing; it generally opens into the mantle cavity somewhere on the right side of the body.

In the Bivalvia—clams, mussels, and oysters—the head is much simplified, and the body is enclosed by two valves that usually protect it rather completely. There is ordinarily a large foot adapted for burrowing in softer substrata, and between it and the mantle, on both sides of the body, there is usually a large and elaborate gill. In most bivalves, the gills are not so much organs of respiration as organs of feeding. The activity of cilia on the gills causes water to be drawn into the mantle cavity and then moved out again, usually by way of two siphons that are extensions of the mantle cavity. As water passes over the gills, microscopic food is trapped in mucus and then moved along ciliary pathways to the mouth.

The modern Cephalopoda, which consists mostly of squids, octopuses, and their close allies, are remnants of a once magnificent group.

Only a few of the surviving members, such as the chambered nautilus of the Indo-Pacific region, have an external shell; cuttlefishes, not found along the Pacific coast of North America, have a rather strong internal plate useful to canaries for conditioning their beaks. Squids have a soft internal remnant of a shell, and octopuses do not have even that. The anterior part of the body of cephalopods is differentiated into eight muscular arms in octopuses, ten arms (two distinctly different from the other eight) in squids. The mantle cavity faces forward, and its wall is highly muscularized. By forcing water out of the mantle cavity, the animal can swim by jet propulsion. The jet emerges from a funnellike siphon on the ventral side of the mantle cavity, and as this siphon is mobile, the animal can control to some extent the direction in which it swims. There is a pair of large gills in the mantle cavity. The head is equipped with eyes that are remarkably well developed for an invertebrate. In octopuses, as a matter of fact, the eyes are similar to those of higher vertebrates in complexity and general organization. The nervous system as a whole is likewise very advanced. All squids and octopuses are carnivores, using a pair of jaws to subdue the prey that they capture.

Phylum Arthropoda: The Crustaceans, Insects, Spiders, and Their Allies

Arthropoda is the largest of all phyla, so it is naturally much diversified. The success of arthropods is evident not only from the fact that there must be over a million different kinds of them, but also because they have penetrated just about every habitat that supports life.

The more important characteristics of arthropods that are visible without dissection are the external skeleton, the tendency of the body to be divided into well-marked sections, and jointed appendages. The exoskeleton may be thin or thick—it may even be calcified, as in crabs—but it is in any case relatively firm, relatively impervious, and more or less unyielding. Thus, although it offers protection, it restricts growth; so in order for an arthropod to increase in size, it must shed its exoskeleton and secrete a new one.

The strong demarcation of the body into divisions, such as head, thorax, and abdomen, is generally accompanied by a loss, to at least some extent, of the identity of individual segments. Although it is true that segmentation is often indistinct in the head region of annelids, in arthropods the segments of the head are routinely run together, even though the appendages derived from them are perfectly clear. Another complication is that the exoskeleton may grow over a considerable part of the body as a carapace, as in certain crustaceans where the carapace forms an essentially continuous covering over both head and thorax.

The presence of jointed appendages is related to the existence of the exoskeleton. If the exoskeleton is firm, it follows that movement will be restricted unless the appendages are divided into articulating units. At the joints between the articles ("segments") of the appendages, as well as between segments or groups of segments of the body proper, the exoskeleton is thinner and more flexible than it is elsewhere, so that muscles can operate on them. The muscles, of course, are attached directly to the exoskeleton.

The three principal surviving groups of arthropods are the Crustacea, the Arachnida (spiders, ticks, mites, scorpions), and the Insecta. Most of the lesser groups—millipedes, centipedes, and so on—can be linked closely to one of these major assemblages.

Insects, which constitute the majority of known arthropods, are primarily terrestrial and freshwater organisms; those that can be said to be marine are mostly at the fringes of the intertidal zone. Arachnids, except for mites, are not abundant in the sea either, but there are a couple of odd arachnidlike groups—the so-called horseshoe crabs and the pycnogonids—that are strictly marine. The crustaceans, however, are well represented in the sea, as well as in fresh water, and some are found on land. Examples of most of the groups likely to be encountered in shore situations in our area are illustrated later in this chapter.

Phylum Bryozoa: The Bryozoans or Moss Animals

This phylum is large, and one of the more difficult ones for nonspecialists to deal with. Bryozoans form colonies of many essentially separate microscopic individuals and, although they are small, they are complicated.

Each member of a bryozoan colony is called a zooid, and the "house" that a zooid secretes around itself is termed the zooecium. Special muscles withdraw the animal into its house, and others operate to force it out again by increasing hydrostatic pressure around it.

Bryozoa reproduce asexually as well as sexually; asexual reproduction builds up the colonies, often in a nearly symmetrical pattern. The colonies may be in the form of thin crusts (sometimes heavily calcified); bushy growths; branching stolons; calcareous, staghornlike masses resembling corals; and various other configurations.

A circle of tentacles, called the lophophore, surrounds the mouth, and the action of the cilia on the tentacles drives food into a U-shaped digestive tract that loops back to the surface not far from the mouth, but outside the lophophore. Many bryozoans, especially those that form bushy colonies, superficially resemble certain hydroids, mostly because of their rings of tentacles and hyaline appearance. There are no nematocysts on the tentacles of bryozoans, however, and the level of complexity of these animals is much higher than that of hydroids. The way a feeding polyp of a hydroid reacts to touch is decidedly different from the way a bryozoan zooid reacts. It contracts, but it is not suddenly pulled down by strong muscles.

Although zooids concerned with feeding are the most conspicuous members of a bryozoan colony, there may be zooids specialized for

Haliclona (possibly *H. permollis*)

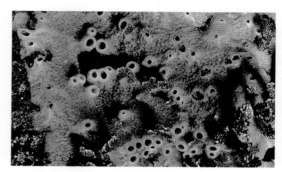

Haliclona (an undetermined species found on floats in San Francisco Bay)

Halichondria bowerbanki

Halichondria panicea

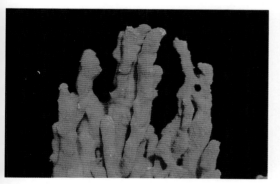

Microciona prolifera

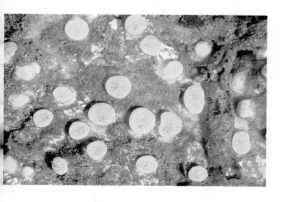

Ophlitaspongia pennata, with *Rostanga pulchra*, a sea slug that eats it; the coiled egg masses of *Rostanga* are also shown

Cliona celata, which bores into calcareous shells (in this case, the shell of the giant barnacle, *Balanus nubilus*)

Plate 1

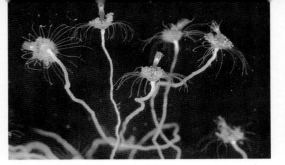

Tubularia crocea

Garveia annulata

Sertularia

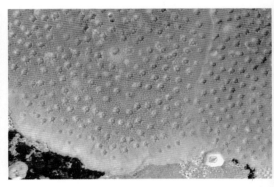

Sertularella

Plumularia setacea

Allopora porphyra, a hydrocoral. (The tentacles of the feeding polyps are retracted.)

Aglaophenia

Abietinaria

Plate 2

Cyanea capillata

Aurelia aurita

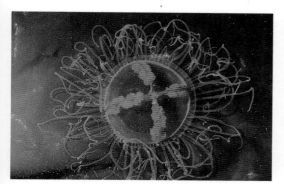

Gonionemus vertens

Velella velella

Diadumene franciscana

Haliplanella lineata

Metridium senile

Plate 3

Anthopleura elegantissima

Anthopleura artemisia

Anthopleura xanthogrammica, the green sea anemone

Cnidopus ritteri

Aulactinia incubans

Urticina crassicornis

Urticina coriacea

Urticina lofotensis

Plate 4

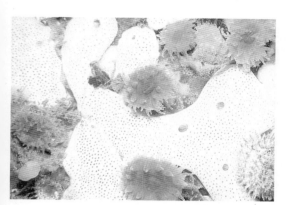

Balanophyllia elegans, the cup coral, and *Didemnum,* a compound ascidian

Epizoanthus scotinus, a zoanthid

Corynactis californica, a corallimorpharian

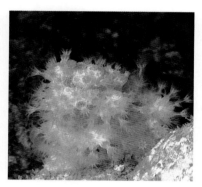

Gersemia rubiformis

Clavularia

Ptilosarcus gurneyi, the sea pen

Plate 5

Amphiporus imparispinosus

Notoplana acticola

Emplectonema gracile

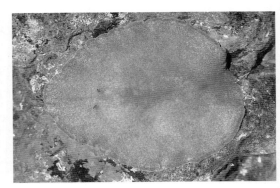

Kaburakia excelsa

Tubulanus polymorphus

Micrura verrilli

*Amphiporus
bimaculatus*

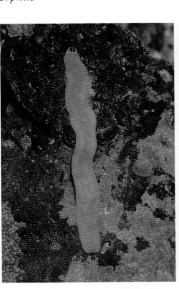

*Tubulanus
sexlineatus*

Plate 6

Eudistylia vancouveri

Eudistylia polymorpha

Schizobranchia insignis

Potamilla occelata

Serpula vermicularis

Spirorbis

Pista elongata (exposed portions of tubes among roots of *Phyllospadix*)

Plate 7

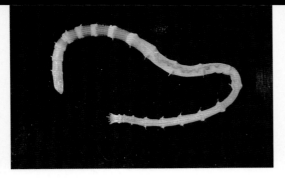

Axiothella rubrocincta, the bamboo worm

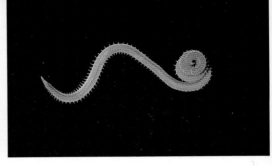

Hemipodus borealis

Notomastus tenuis

Abarenicola pacifica, a lugworm

Euzonus mucronatus

Euzonus dillonensis

Cirriformia spirabrancha

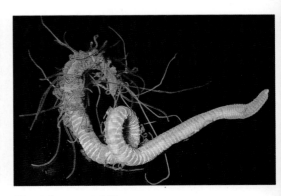

Cirratulus spectabilis

Plate 8

A typical spionid polychaete

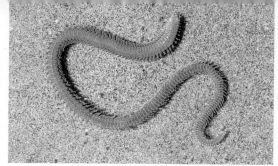

Nereis brandti

Sabellaria cementarium

Dodecaceria fewkesi

Nuttallina californica

Phascolosoma agassizii; the encrusting red alga is *Hildenbrandia*

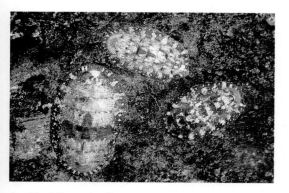

Lepidochitona dentiens

Plate 9

Cryptochiton stelleri

Stenoplax heathiana

Lepidozona mertensii

Lepidozona cooperi

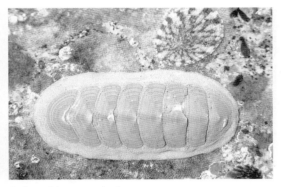
Ischnochiton regularis

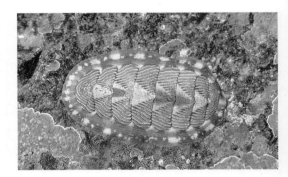
Tonicella lineata, the lined chiton; the encrusting coralline alga is *Lithothamnium*

Placiphorella velata

Plate 10

Littorina sitkana and *Balanus glandula*

Littorina keenae (L. planaxis)

Lottia gigantea, the owl limpet

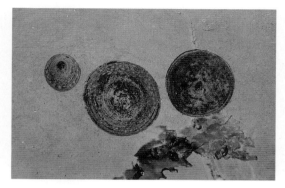

Notoacmea fenestrata

Surfgrass, *Phyllospadix torreyi*, with the encrusting coralline alga *Melobesia mediocris*, the limpet *Notoacmea paleacea*, and the snail *Lacuna marmorata*

Acmaea mitra, the whitecap limpet, overgrown by the coralline alga, *Lithothamnium*

Megatebennus bimaculatus

Haliotis kamtschatkana, the northern abalone

Plate 11

Tegula funebralis, the black turban, with (*left*) the limpet *Collisella asmi* and (*right*) the hooked slipper shell *Crepidula adunca*

Tegula brunnea, the brown turban, with its shell partly overgrown by the red alga *Peyssonellia meridionalis*

Tegula pulligo

Margarites helicinus, with the coralline alga *Lithothamnium*

Calliostoma ligatum, the topshell, with the coralline alga *Lithothamnium*

Calliostoma annulatum, the ringed topshell

Lirularia succincta, with two live specimens of *Spirorbis*

Lirularia succincta, with patches of the encrusting brown alga, *Ralfsia*

Plate 12

Petaloconchus compactus, the worm-shell

Olivella biplicata, the purple olive snail

Ocenebra lurida

Ceratostoma foliatum, the leafy hornmouth

Amphissa versicolor, with the coralline alga
Lithothamnium

Alia carinata, the keeled dove-shell

Octopus rubescens

Plate 13

Anisodoris nobilis

Cadlina luteomarginata

Archidoris montereyensis

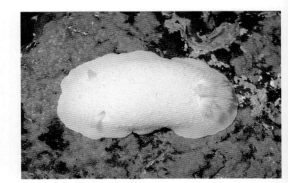

Archidoris odhneri

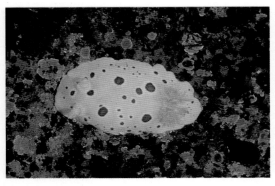

Discodoris sandiegensis

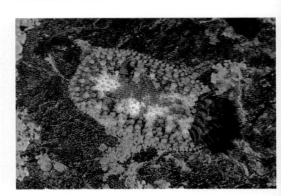

Onchidoris bilamellata

Triopha catalinae

Plate 14

Flabellinopsis iodinea

Hopkinsia rosacea

Hypselodoris californiensis

Chromodoris macfarlandi

Triopha maculata, a mature specimen

Triopha maculata, about half-grown

Laila cockerelli

Plate 15

Dendronotus frondosus

Dendronotus rufus

Aeolidia papillosa

Phidiana crassicornis

Dirona aurantia

Janolus fuscus

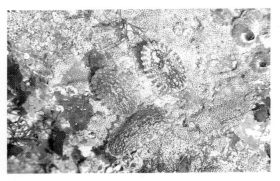

Onchidella borealis

Aplysia californica, the brown sea hare

Plate 16

other functions. Avicularia, which look like bird beaks on short stalks, help keep a colony clean by pinching strangers. Vibracula are essentially avicularia in which one jaw is drawn out into a long filament that sweeps back and forth; they also discourage unwelcome settlers. These two types of zooids must obtain their nourishment by way of delicate connections with feeding polyps, but in general the zooids of a bryozoan colony are more nearly separate and autonomous than the interconnected polyps of a hydroid colony.

Phylum Phoronida: The Phoronids

There are only a few species in the phylum Phoronida; these are assigned to just two genera, *Phoronis* and *Phoronopsis*. The phoronids live in tubes, and because they have a lophophore, they superficially resemble bryozoans. They are also superficially similar to sabellid polychaetes—the so-called feather-duster worms—but they are not segmented and have no bristles like those of polychaetes. Besides, the tentacles are never branched, and the way they are arranged, in a continuous double row having the general outline of a somewhat ornate horseshoe, is unlike anything seen in polychaetes. The digestive tract is U-shaped, so the anus is not at the end of the wormlike body; it is, in fact, close to the mouth, but outside the lophophore. There are a number of other peculiarities of internal anatomy and development that add to the distinctiveness of this phylum.

Phylum Brachiopoda: The Lamp Shells

Brachiopods look superficially like clams because they have a bivalved, calcareous shell. In brachiopods, however, the two valves are dorsal and ventral with respect to the rest of the animal, rather than being on the right and left sides of the body, as they are in a clam. In all of our local brachiopods, the valves are decidedly unequal; and a short, flexible stalk emerges through a hole or notch near the beak of the larger valve. (This is basically the ventral valve, though in nature the animal may be upside down.) The name "lamp shell" is given in allusion to the shape of many brachiopods, which resembles that of certain ancient oil lamps.

Brachiopods are close relatives of phoronids and bryozoans. They have a beautifully wrought lophophore, consisting of two diverging arms, each much coiled and with hundreds of tentacles used in trapping microscopic food in a mucous film. The food is then moved to the mouth by the action of cilia. Ciliary activity also brings water into the shell and then moves it out again by way of a gape at the broader end. The lophophore is usually supported by an exquisite little calcareous loop on the lower valve, which can be seen in some empty shells. The loop is so delicate, however, that it generally disappears before the shell as a whole shows signs of wear.

Phylum Chaetognatha: The Arrow Worms

The arrow worms constitute a small group of almost strictly planktonic marine animals. They are slender, slightly flattened, and almost transparent, and thus are difficult to see unless they are in just the right light and against a dark background. They are characterized externally by a group of bristlelike jaws on each side of the mouth, a pair of eyespots on the top of the head, a horizontal tail fin, and two pairs of lateral fins. The anus is at about the same level as the second pair of lateral fins. Most arrow worms are small, our only common species being about 2 cm long. They tend to lie motionless unless stimulated to move by being touched or by the prospect of something to eat nearby; swimming is accomplished by flexing the body as a whole. Copepods, fish larvae, and other small organisms are captured by the bristly jaws.

Phylum Echinodermata: The Echinoderms or Spiny-skinned Animals

This phylum can perhaps be most easily defined with reference to the characteristics of a sea star, a representative of the class Asteroidea. Attention is called, first of all, to its radial symmetry: a sea star with five rays can be cut into five essentially equal parts. Two other important features of echinoderms are their protruding, calcareous skeletal structures and mobile tube feet. The spines—sharp or blunt—that show on the upper and lower surfaces of most sea stars are not really external, for they are formed in the body wall, not on the outside of it. In a sense, they are like the tips of icebergs, because deeper in the body wall there are many skeletal elements that do not show.

The tube feet, arranged in one or more series on each side of the groove underneath each arm, are muscular and usually have tips something like suction cups. Their fluid-filled cores are continuous with a system of canals constituting what is called the water-vascular system. This, in terms of its origin during development of the animal, is related to the body cavity, but it eventually becomes almost wholly separate. When fluid is forced into a tube foot, by contraction of the muscular wall of a little internal reservoir, its tip becomes less cuplike. When fluid is withdrawn, it becomes more cuplike, and thus effective in clinging to a firm substratum. In any case, the locomotion of a sea star and its ability to hang on tightly to a rock or to open a clam enough to start feeding on it depend on the operation of its tube feet.

Another significant structural specialization found in certain sea stars is the pedicellaria. The pedicellariae, each consisting of a pair of calcareous jaws on a short stalk, are usually in clusters on the upper surface. They close in response to the stimulus of contact with foreign objects, including small animals, that might otherwise settle on the surface.

This description of a sea star will serve as a basis for comparison with the other three groups of echinoderms found at the shore. (One group, the crinoids, will be omitted, as these are found locally only in deep water.) Brittle stars (Ophiuroidea) are superficially like sea stars, but they move by the writhing of their snaky rays. There are tube feet along the undersides of the rays, but they are used for feeding, not attachment. Pedicellariae are absent. The rays are distinct from the central disk, rather than blending into it as in sea stars. Brittle stars, on the whole, feed principally on detritus and have a variety of methods for tangling food up in mucus before swallowing it.

Sea urchins (Echinoidea), like brittle stars and most sea stars, display a distinct, five-part radial symmetry. They are distinctive, however, in that they have an internal shell, or test. This is solid, though composed of many separate plates. The mobile spines, shaped like golf tees, are articulated to bumps on the test. The tube feet, emerging through pores in the test, are used for locomotion and for catching pieces of seaweed and detritus and passing them down to the mouth on the lower surface. A rather remarkable chewing apparatus is associated with the mouth. It is called Aristotle's lantern and consists of five teeth whose sharp tips converge. The teeth are used to chop up the food brought to the mouth. The pedicellariae of sea urchins, unlike those of sea stars, have three jaws instead of two.

Sand dollars also belong to the Echinoidea. They are aberrant sea urchins, being not only much flattened, but having the anus displaced from the top of the test to the lower surface just inside the margin; moreover, the spines and tube feet of sand dollars are small. These animals feed on small particles that are moved toward the mouth by action of cilia. Locomotion is effected by activity of the spines.

Sea cucumbers (Holothuroidea) are somehow more difficult to explain. They are basically radially symmetrical, but are elongated; and the five sectors are often unequal, either in actual size or in the extent to which the tube feet belonging to them are developed. Tube feet may be lacking altogether in certain sectors, so that the animal assumes a bilaterally symmetrical appearance. The featherlike or otherwise much-branched tentacles around the mouth of most sea cucumbers are tube feet specialized for feeding, serving mainly to trap relatively small detritus. In some burrowing sea cucumbers, these are the only tube feet. Sea cucumbers lack pedicellariae, and the skeletal elements tend to be isolated perforated plates in the body wall. In a few, some of these may protrude as tiny hooks or anchors that can catch one's skin; and in some others there is a definite coat of mail covering the body.

Phylum Urochordata: The Sea Squirts and Their Allies

In many systems of classification, the Urochordata are placed, along with the vertebrates and a small group of animals called cephalochordates, into a single phylum, Chordata. The three assemblages may appear to be unified because they share the following characteristics: a nerve cord that is dorsal (instead of ventral as it is in most other invertebrates that have a nerve cord); a notochord (at least during early stages of development); and pharyngeal perforations, or intimations of these. It is doubtful, however, that the urochordates, vertebrates, and cephalochordates are as closely related as has formerly been thought. Their notochords are certainly very different. It seems best to treat them as separate phyla.

Most members of the Urochordata belong to a group called ascidians, or "sea squirts." The definition of the phylum as a whole will be based on the structure and development of these animals. There are, however, some planktonic urochordates that deviate from the ascidian pattern.

Some ascidians are solitary, and most of the larger species to which the term "sea squirt" is applicable are of this type. Social ascidians are those connected, at least for a time, by creeping stolons. The stolons are essentially runners from which new individuals arise. Compound (or colonial) ascidians are those that form masses containing several to many specimens embedded in a continuous matrix that has the character of a stiff jelly. The matrix in which the separate, small individuals of a colony are embedded, and much of the body wall of solitary and social ascidians, is called the tunic. It consists largely of a carbohydrate substance called tunicin, which is chemically close to cellulose of plants, with which we are all familiar in the form of wood, cotton, and paper.

In its development, an ascidian goes through a tadpolelike stage that has a dorsal nerve cord and a fairly stiff yet flexible rod of cells called the notochord; the latter is limited to the tail region. The tadpole does not feed, but it nevertheless has a pharynx with perforations. After a very brief life on its own, the tadpole settles and metamorphoses into the attached adult phase, whereby the body becomes completely reorganized. The tail, together with its notochord, is resorbed. There is nothing now that can be called a head, though the cerebral ganglion survives in the upper part of the body, which ranges in shape from something like a low hemisphere to a cucumber. Two openings become obvious, and these may be on distinct elevations, rather like clam siphons. One of them brings water into the pharynx, where microscopic food is trapped in mucus. The water passes through the many perforations of the pharynx into a cavity called the atrium, and then leaves by way of the other opening. The intestine eventually opens into the atrium, so that residues from the digestive tract are carried out by the same stream of water. In some ascidians, the atrial cavity serves as a brood chamber for developing tadpoles, but in others the eggs and sperm liberated into the atrium leave the body and take their chances in the sea.

In compound ascidians, in which asexual reproduction is accompanied by deposition of additional matrix material, the incoming openings of the individuals are separate. The atrial openings may also be separate, but generally the atria of several individuals communicate first with a common chamber, which then has an aperture to the outside. When this is the case, the individuals are organized in circles around the common chamber.

ILLUSTRATED SYNOPSIS OF INVERTEBRATES
COMMONLY OBSERVED AT THE SHORE

This section is intended to help one quickly recognize the general groups to which most of our obvious seashore animals belong. It is organized primarily on the basis of superficial similarities and differences. Thus, some of the nine major categories outlined include animals that are not closely related; conversely, animals that are related may be found under two or more of these headings.

The novice is urged not to be too hasty in deciding into which phylum a particular animal fits best. He should read the descriptions of any primary and secondary categories that are reasonably good prospects, and at the same time scan the pictures for characteristics that agree with those of the specimen in hand. Some phyla are so diversified that a few illustrations cannot do them justice. As your understanding of important diagnostic features develops, you will find it increasingly easier to place almost any animal into the right group.

1. Thin crusts, feltlike patches, spongy masses, or gelatinous coatings of nearly uniform texture

A. If thick (up to about 2 cm), feels spongy; whether thick or thin, usually has a feltlike texture due at least in part to microscopic siliceous spicules sticking through the surface; generally with some distinct openings, these often on volcano-like elevations, scattered over the surface; color extremely variable: whitish, tan, brown, green, gray, lavender, or red

Phylum Porifera, Class Demospongiae

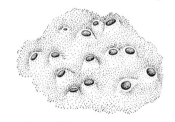

Encrusting siliceous sponge

B. Texture crusty, brittle, frequently partially or wholly calcified; under magnification, seen to consist of numerous tubular or boxlike units into which the living individuals, characterized by long, ciliated tentacles, can be withdrawn completely; color of colonies usually whitish or silvery, but sometimes orange, pinkish, or brown.

Phylum Bryozoa

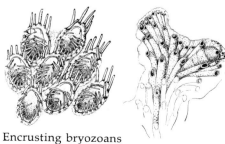

Encrusting bryozoans

C. Lumpy or stalked growths, or growths of nearly uniform thickness, usually with the texture of very firm jelly and with a slick surface; with regularly spaced internal bodies (often yellow or orange), which are the individual animals embedded in the matrix, generally arranged in circles around a common opening; color of colonies pinkish, purplish, or brownish, but sometimes nearly white

Phylum Urochordata, Class Ascidiacea

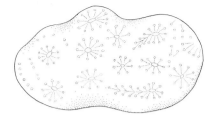

Compound ascidian

2. Fuzzy, featherlike, beardlike, or bushy colonies that are at least somewhat flexible; feeding individuals characterized by a circle of tentacles around the mouth

A. Branching slightly from a creeping stolon, or branching extensively into featherlike or bushy colonies; feeding polyps located at the tips of the branches or applied directly to one or both sides of the branches; tentacles not ciliated; in addition to feeding polyps, colonies may have polyps specialized for production of medusae

Phylum Cnidaria, Class Hydrozoa

Hydroid

B. Branching into bushy growths, sometimes with spiral tendencies, but never in the pattern of a feather; colonies consisting almost entirely of separate tubular or boxlike units, frequently with spiny elaborations, into which the tentaculate individuals can withdraw completely; tentacles ciliated; colonies may have scattered nontentaculate individuals, the most common type being that with two jaws resembling those of a bird's beak; an extremely varied group, impossible to define briefly

Phylum Bryozoa

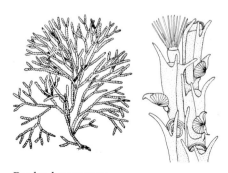

Bushy bryozoans

3. Fixed to the substratum, but not wormlike and not secreting tubes; appearing to be individuals rather than colonies (though they may aggregate, settle on one another, produce buds, or brood young at their bases)

A. Vaselike or elongated, with a single opening at the upper end; feltlike texture, due partly to calcareous spicules protruding through the surface; sometimes producing buds that eventually develop an opening like that of the parent; body as a whole not contractile, though the opening may close slowly if stimulated

Phylum Porifera, Class Calcarea

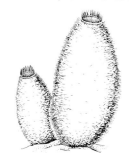

Calcareous sponge

B. Body with a cylindrical column, at the free end of which is a nearly flat disk bordered by a few to many tentacles; the tentacles and the rest of the body very reactive and contractile, so that the animal becomes approximately hemispherical when poked

Phylum Cnidaria, Class Anthozoa

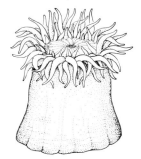

Sea anemone (cup corals similar, but have a column supported by an external calcareous skeleton)

C. Shape variable: hemispherical, more or less cylindrical and abruptly cut off, peanutlike, or globose and stalked; rather solid and firm; texture of surface variable: transparent and almost gelatinous, smooth and polished, translucent and like cartilage, or tough and leathery, sometimes with hairlike outgrowths; with two openings, either on distinct, siphonlike stalks or on little elevations of the surface, the size and shape of the openings and the siphons subject to muscular control

Phylum Urochordata, Class Ascidiacea

Solitary ascidian

D. With a volcanolike shell attached by its base to the substratum, or with a leathery stalk, at the top of which is a laterally flattened portion protected by five or many calcareous plates; when active, extending plumelike appendages

Phylum Arthropoda, Class Crustacea, Subclass Cirripedia

Acorn barnacle

Goose barnacle

4. Worms and wormlike animals

A. Very flat (usually only about 1 or 2 mm thick), and about two or three times as long as wide (length generally 1 to 3 cm); eyespots near the anterior end or around the margin of the body; sometimes with a pair of tentacles; glides over firm substrata, but may also swim by undulations of body margins

Phylum Platyhelminthes, Class Turbellaria, Order Polycladida

Polyclad flatworm

B. Usually at least slightly flattened; slender, many times longer than wide, something like a thin or thick rubber band, but very soft and very extensile; often with eyespots; no evidence of segmentation; sometimes fragile, breaking up into pieces while being disengaged from the substratum; glides over firm surfaces or through sediment, or burrows in sand or mud; may secrete a tube

Phylum Nemertea

Ribbon worm

C. Elongated (usually at least ten times as long as wide); soft or fairly muscular, divided into many distinct segments, mostly much like one another (but in some, the body may be differentiated into two or more somewhat separate regions); with fleshy flaps (parapodia), sometimes lobed, on either side of most segments, and with groups of bristles associated with them; may have simple or branched tentaclelike or gill-like structures associated with the head region or with other parts of the body; head region may also have enlarged bristles or other specializations; may crawl about freely, live in close association with other animals, burrow in sand or mud, or build a calcareous, muddy, parchmentlike, or concretelike tube

Phylum Annelida, Class Polychaeta

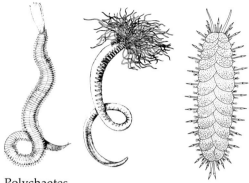

Polychaetes

D. Elongated, cylindrical body somewhat resembling that of many annelids; not segmented and without fleshy lateral flaps or bristles; delicate, unbranched tentacles arranged in the pattern of a horseshoe in which the free ends are spiraled; secretes a parchmentlike tube, generally with some foreign material adhering to it

Phylum Phoronida

Phoronid

E. Body divided into two somewhat distinct regions: a slender, mobile, necklike anterior portion and a more nearly bulbous posterior portion; anterior portion can be introverted, but when extended may show tentacles (very small and unbranched, or larger and bushy) surrounding the mouth; rubbery, firm, resisting pressure of the fingers when tightly contracted; skin tough, almost leathery; no segmentation

Phylum Sipuncula

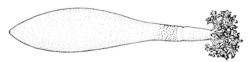

Peanut worm

F. Like a slender cucumber; soft, translucent, showing longitudinal lines indicating organization into five equal sectors; no segmentation; with ten tentacles, branched like feathers, around the mouth; clings to skin of fingers because of microscopic anchorlike spicules protruding from the body wall; burrows in sand

Phylum Echinodermata, Class Holothuroidea

Burrowing sea cucumber

G. Slender, transparent, looking like a sliver of ice; about 2 cm long; horizontal tail fin and two pairs of lateral fins; two eyespots on head; jaws consisting of a number of stiff bristles; in plankton, generally motionless, but capable of rapid flexing movements

Phylum Chaetognatha

Arrow worm

5. Jellyfishes or jellyfishlike animals, transparent or translucent, swimming free

A. Shaped like a saucer, bowl, or tall bell; moving by pulsations; with unbranched tentacles arising at or near the margin

With a shelflike rim (velum) inside margin of bell; mouth (which may be on a long stalk) without large, frilly lobes; diameter generally less than 10 cm

Phylum Cnidaria, Class Hydrozoa

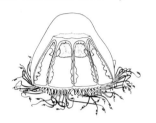

Hydromedusae

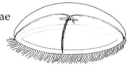

Without a shelflike rim inside margin of bell; mouth with large, frilly lobes; diameter regularly exceeding 10 cm

Phylum Cnidaria, Class Scyphozoa

Scyphomedusa

B. Globular to cucumber-shaped; not moving by pulsations; with eight meridional rows of glassy aggregates of thick cilia that propel the animal slowly and steadily; long tentacles, if present, only two in number, branched and retractable into sheaths

Phylum Ctenophora

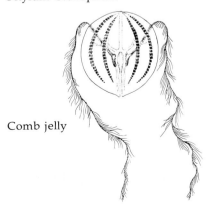

Comb jelly

6. Sea stars ("starfishes"), brittle stars, sea urchins, and sand dollars—animals with radial symmetry (usually five-parted) and with externally evident calcareous spines, tubercles, or scales

A. With from five (the usual number) to over twenty rays, these neither jointed nor sharply demarcated from the central disk; tube feet on lower surface of rays generally with suckerlike tips that can adhere tightly to firm surfaces and therefore are useful in locomotion; arms themselves not capable of rapid movements

Phylum Echinodermata, Class Asteroidea

Sea star

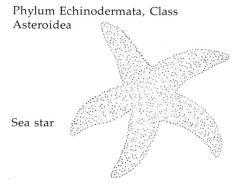

B. With five rays that are jointed and rather sharply demarcated from the central disk; tube feet fingerlike and not capable of adhering to firm substrata; locomotion by relatively rapid movements of the rays themselves

Phylum Echinodermata, Class Ophiuroidea

Brittle star

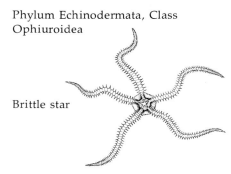

C. With long, sharp, movable calcareous spines sticking out from a nearly globular test; tube feet slender when extended and with suckerlike tips; mouth, in center of lower surface, surrounded by five sharp-tipped jaws arranged something like those of a pin vise (but only the tips can be seen in an intact animal); anus in the center of the upper surface

Phylum Echinodermata, Class Echinoidea

Sea urchin

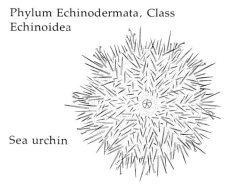

D. Test disk-shaped, with short spines and small tube feet (at least some of which are tipped with suckers); radial pattern on upper surface of test eccentric and not perfectly symmetrical; jaws similar to those of a sea urchin, but very small; anus displaced to the lower surface, near the margin

Phylum Echinodermata, Class Echinoidea

Sand dollar

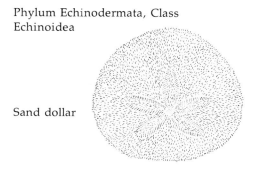

7. Shaped like a cucumber, with branched (bushy or moplike) tentacles around the mouth, capable of being completely retracted; tube feet (those functioning in locomotion and attachment have suckerlike tips) may be in five equally developed and equally spaced longitudinal sets, or in unequally developed and unequally spaced sets, in which case the division of the body into five sectors is not clear externally; calcareous skeletal elements embedded in the tissue of the body wall and not evident externally (exceptions: burrowing sea cucumbers, which have tiny anchorlike spicules sticking out of the surface of the body wall, but no tube feet; certain bizarre types in which the lower surface of the body is flattened and the upper surface is covered by scalelike calcareous plates)

Phylum Echinodermata, Class Holothuroidea

Sea cucumber

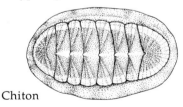

Burrowing sea cucumber

8. Molluscs and mollusclike animals (such as snails, slugs, clams, squids, and octopuses)

A. Body protected dorsally by a series of eight calcareous plates bordered by a margin of tough flesh that may be scaly or bristly (in one species, it completely covers the plates)

Phylum Mollusca, Class Polyplacophora

Chiton

B. With a coiled, conical, or cap-shaped shell into which the animal can generally withdraw at least partially

Phylum Mollusca, Class Gastropoda

Snail   Limpet

C. Sluglike, without a shell (or with a shell that is strictly or largely internal, and in any case much too small for the animal to withdraw into)

Phylum Mollusca, Class Gastropoda

Sea slug

D. With a shell of two calcareous valves hinged together; generally burrowing in sand, mud, clay, rock, or wood, but may be attached to a firm substratum by threads of organic material or permanently attached by one valve (this valve may or may not have a hole in it, but it remains stationary)

Phylum Mollusca, Class Bivalvia

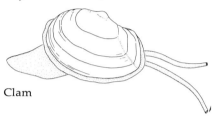

Clam

E. With a shell of two calcareous valves hinged together; attached to rock or shell by a tough but flexible and movable stalk emerging through a hole in one valve near the hinge

Phylum Brachiopoda

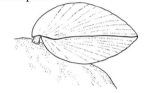

Lamp shell

F. Octopuses (with eight more or less equal arms) and squids (with ten arms, of which two are longer than and different from the others)

Phylum Mollusca, Class Cephalopoda

Octopus

Squid

9. Shrimps, crabs, hermit crabs, and other animals sharing at least some of the same traits: jointed legs and jointed antennae; a body showing evidence of segmentation (usually at least in the abdominal region); a stiff or hard external skeleton

Phylum Arthropoda, Class Crustacea

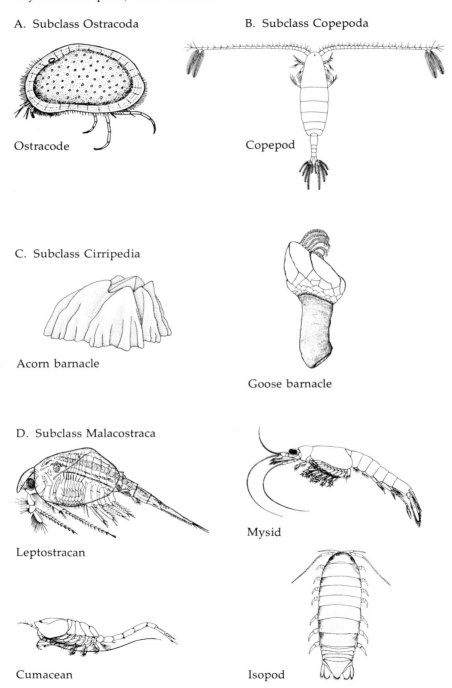

A. Subclass Ostracoda

Ostracode

B. Subclass Copepoda

Copepod

C. Subclass Cirripedia

Acorn barnacle

Goose barnacle

D. Subclass Malacostraca

Leptostracan

Mysid

Cumacean

Isopod

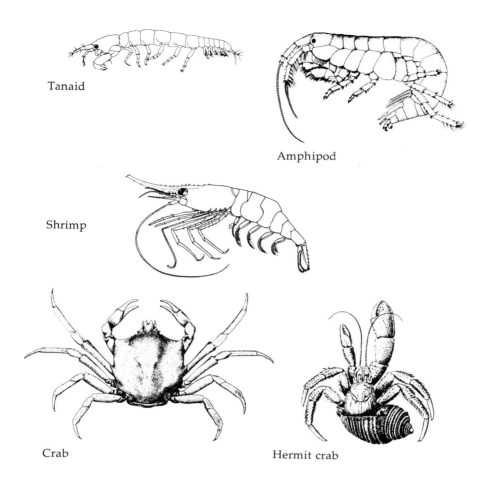

Tanaid

Amphipod

Shrimp

Crab

Hermit crab

ALGAE

Not all algae represented in marine habitats can be called seaweeds. The diatoms, for instance, are one-celled, even though their scummy or filamentous growths may be visible to the unaided eye. They will be considered briefly in this review, but other strictly microscopic groups will be excluded.

The classification of algae is based to some extent on pigmentation, hence the names blue-green, green, brown, and red algae. On the other hand, general structure, patterns of reproduction, and food storage products are also important. Many of the seaweeds this book will help you to identify have alternate stages that are different from those described and illustrated. These alternate stages are often microscopic, or at least not easily noticed, and may be short-lived. There are a number of basic life histories and many variations on these themes. Although they are fundamental to the classification of algae, they will not be discussed here.

Phylum Cyanophyta: The Blue-Green Algae

Most blue-green algae are colonial, forming scummy growths or slick coatings over wet soil, seepage areas, and at the bottoms of shallow pools; a few are free-floating. The colonies are generally composed either of more or less single cells scattered through a gelatinous matrix or as masses of filaments, each of which consists of a row of cells surrounded by a gelatinous sheath. In either case, the individual cells are routinely smaller than those of most other algae. When viewed under a microscope with transmitted light, they are usually blue-green in color, since the chief pigments are chlorophyll (green) and phycocyanin (blue). However, other pigments—even the red phycoerythrin, which we think of as being the property of the Rhodophyta—are present in varying amounts, and sometimes to a degree that the coloration is decidedly something other than blue-green. The colonies as a whole show considerable variation in color, too, partly on account of the actual pigmentation, but also because of contamination by other algae or physical attributes such as the amount of secreted matrix material. Dark blue-green, olive, brown, and nearly black are common colors.

Blue-green algae are very simple organisms in terms of the structure of their cells. They have nuclear material, but not definite nuclei, and this is one reason why some specialists think of them as being more closely related to certain bacteria than to other algae.

Blue-green algae are better represented in fresh water and in wet terrestrial situations than in marine environments. They should be mentioned in this guide, however, because they are a regular feature of cliffside seepage areas just above the high-tide line; and in estuarine situations and salt marshes, they may coat the bottoms of shallow pools. One genus, *Calothrix*, is abundant in the upper reaches of rocky intertidal areas, where it forms very thin patches that dry out to a dull black.

Phylum Chlorophyta: The Green Algae

Interpreted broadly, this group includes many one-celled species as well as others forming fuzzy, ropy, or stringy growths that cannot really be identified without the help of a microscope. In marine habitats, however, there are a number of distinctive larger types.

The green algae are indeed usually green, for their chlorophyll is not normally masked by other pigments. Some species, however, are distinctly yellowish or brownish. Most of the green seaweeds of the region fall into three general categories with respect to superficial appearance. Some grow as flexible or stiff filaments, often just one cell thick, and sometimes not even divided into cells; these are the ones most nearly like the filamentous algae of freshwater habitats. *Cladophora*, *Acrosiphonia*, and *Derbesia* fit into this category. Then there are types like *Ulva* and *Kornmannia*, which form extensive thin sheets one or two cell-layers thick, and *Enteromorpha*, in which the microscopic appearance is about the same, though the thalli are in the form of hollow tubes instead of sheets. Finally, there are a few, such as *Codium*, that are thick, almost spongy growths consisting of many fine filaments woven together.

One odd alga common in salt marshes and on wet soil in terrestrial situations should probably be mentioned here, though it is not one of the Chlorophyta. This is *Vaucheria*, which forms feltlike mats of fine filaments that are not divided up into cells. In this respect, as well as in general color, it resembles certain green algae. When its pigments and storage products are analyzed, however, and when details of the structure of its reproductive cells are considered, it appears to be more closely related to a small group called the yellow-green algae.

Phylum Bacillariophyta: The Diatoms

As individual plants, the diatoms are one-celled, but some form filamentous colonies that may be confused with small brown seaweeds. Generally, they make a thin, scummy brown growth, often quite cohesive, over the surfaces of rocks, shells, wood, mud, other algae, and even on animals that are sessile. There are also many planktonic species. In short, one finds diatoms just about everywhere in seashore situations, and commonly in freshwater habitats as well.

The two outstanding characteristics of the diatoms are a cell wall composed largely of silica and an olive or yellow-brown coloration. The chlorophylls are masked to some extent by various other pigments, including fucoxanthin, which is found also in the brown algae.

Diatoms are extremely important as food for many animals, large and small. They are beautiful when studied under a microscope, because of the way in which the silica shell is sculptured with ribs, pits, pores, tubercles, spines, and other elaborations. The gliding style of locomotion of many diatoms is also engaging.

Phylum Phaeophyta: The Brown Algae

The brown algae predominate in the intertidal region, and are also plentiful below the low-tide line. Most of the coarser seaweeds that we call kelps belong to this group. The presence of the pigment fucoxanthin, in addition to chlorophylls, usually results in a brown, golden brown, or olive coloration; a few encrusting species are nearly black, especially after they have dried out a bit.

The brown algae are highly varied in form. Some grow as essentially microscopic filaments just one cell thick. Others may have a fleshy stalk from which one or more broad blades arise. There is about every imaginable form in between: thin hollow sacs, compact brainlike masses, feathery growths, and so on. A feature of many kelps is a holdfast consisting of a mass of stubby, rootlike structures. This type of holdfast, looking like something fished out of a jar of mixed pickles, is limited to the brown algae. Float bladders are another distinctive characteristic of many representatives of this group.

Phylum Rhodophyta: The Red Algae

In terms of numbers of species, there are more red algae than brown algae. A large proportion of them are small and delicate, and may go unnoticed; few red algae begin to approach the larger brown kelps in size. In addition, red algae become progressively more abundant in the lower intertidal region and subtidally until they dominate the algal flora of deeper water. Their red pigment, phycoerythrin, functions together with chlorophyll in photosynthesis and absorbs green and blue components of the spectrum. Since light of these shorter wave lengths is more effective than light of longer wave lengths in penetrating water, some red algae can live at depths where no other kinds of algae can survive.

If green algae are green and brown algae are at least close to brown, then one might hope that the Rhodophyta will be red. Usually they are. They not only have phycoerythrin, however, but also a variety of other pigments, including chlorophylls. The mixtures of these pigments, coupled with physical structure of the surface, result in a variety of colors, including pinkish red, brownish red, purplish red, and olive. Some red algae are so dark as to be nearly black, especially if they have dried out appreciably. Species that are olive or very dark might easily be mistaken for brown algae.

The red algae come in many shapes and styles of organization. Some grow as simple or branched filaments, perhaps just one cell thick, often with a feathery pattern of branching. Other red algae form broad thalli ranging in texture from thin membranes to thick, rubbery, and sometimes warty sheets. One important group found in the lower zones of rocky intertidal areas consists of coralline types. These are impregnated with calcareous material to the point that they are rather hard. Some coralline algae spread out as thin coatings, others form jointed, branching growths.

3

On and Around
Floating Docks and Pilings

The immense interest in boating and related recreational activities has brought on the development of yacht clubs and public and private marinas in nearly all protected harbors of our region. The docking facilities are usually constructed of heavy planking supported by floats of wood, Styrofoam, fiberglass, or concrete. Though man-made, and sometimes constructed partly of synthetic products, the floats are favorable environments for many kinds of seaweeds and invertebrate animals, especially after certain pioneering organisms have colonized them.

Nearly all extensive docking facilities have sections that have not been in the water long enough to be heavily populated by marine organisms. Floats that have been in place for at least a few months will almost certainly have a characteristic fauna and flora, depending on a number of variable conditions. Certain sections may be roofed over and thus shaded; others may be exposed to direct sunlight much of the time. The salinity may be equal to that of the open sea, or it may be much reduced, at least at certain seasons of the year, by the influx of fresh water from a river or large streams. In any case, considerable variation may be expected in different portions of one set of docking facilities, and certainly between docks placed in ecologically different situations.

Generally speaking, floats exposed to considerable illumination tend to be monopolized by diatoms and by a few species of seaweeds. Partly or completely shaded areas are apt to have more interesting assemblages of animals and of certain delicate algae. Any group of floating docks, however, should have portions that offer an excellent introduction to the animal and plant life of the sea. As these docks are built to rise and fall with the tide—a matter of considerable importance in a region where the tidal amplitude is large—study and collection of material may be made at almost any time. This is a distinct convenience, especially during those times of the year when the only very low tides come well after dark. Moreover, many of the animals and plants on floats are those normally found at lower levels of the intertidal zone, or even subtidally. They can live close to the surface, yet not be in danger of exposure.

Anyone who has been given permission to use floating docks to indulge his enthusiasm for study of marine life is expected to treat the facilities with respect. It is one thing to scrape off carefully a few organisms, and something else to rip out pieces of Styrofoam, pull on hoses that may be functioning as a system of water pipes, clamber over boats, and make a mess on the planking. Many marinas employ caretakers to minimize vandalism, or exclude non-members, and the amateur or professional biologist may have to make a convincing case for permission to use the floats.

Floating docks are usually placed in protected situations. During much of the year, especially from late spring to early autumn, there is little wave action and only slight turbidity. The visibility is sometimes excellent, facilitating observation of animals and plants on the floats themselves, as well as jellyfishes and other animals swimming near the surface. The planking is not often more than a foot or two above the water line. If you find it easier to get a good look at the sides of the floats by lying on your belly, wear old clothes and watch out for splinters. If you wear glasses, it is a good idea to equip them with something that will keep them from falling off when your head is down.

A thin film of oil is frequently present on the surface of the water. Much of this unfortunate nuisance is due to carelessness in handling fuel and crankcase oil, but some of it results from the operation of two-cycle engines, which always leak a little fuel. It may be impossible to lift animals into a bucket without bringing up some of the oil with them. Although the toxicity of certain components of the film of oil may discourage some animals from settling permanently on the floats, species that luxuriate are evidently little affected.

The more obvious elements in the complex embroidery of attached organisms on floats are certain seaweeds, sponges, hydroids, sea anemones, tube-dwelling polychaete annelids, barnacles, mussels, and ascidians. Slow-moving animals may be represented, at least in some areas, by sea urchins, sea cucumbers, and sea stars. Shrimps, certain other crustaceans, and small fishes may dart in and out of the heavy growths. But these are just the organisms that can be seen in a quick reconnaissance. Sharp eyes—and eyes that are trained—will soon discover many other creatures, and a hand lens or low-power dissecting microscope will reveal an astonishing variety of animals and plants in a colony of hydroids or in a small clump of worm tubes. Some of the organisms are so dependent upon others that they form constant associations with them.

When it comes to truly microscopic organisms, the variety becomes frustrating. Even a specialist on protozoans or small turbellarians would find species that he could not identify and that have never been described or given names, although they may have been seen many times before by other professional biologists. Many kinds of bacteria are present. Even though the variety of life on floats may seem to be relatively restricted when compared with that on a rocky coast exposed at low tide, the number of kinds of animals, plants, and microorganisms is enormous and the web of life is exceedingly complex. Moreover, there are seasonal changes, variations in annual cycles and patterns of succession, and occasional surprises. A dock that a biologist has visited regularly for years may suddenly show a good growth of some species never noted there before.

This chapter will cover most of the conspicuous animals and seaweeds that colonize floats, as well as some of the animals that can be seen swimming near the surface at certain times of the year. Attention will also be called to related species that, though they may not be common, may be noted by the more careful or experienced observer. Finally, it will be useful to mention some of the animals that live in tight associations with other animals, in what may be called symbiotic relationships or specialized predatory relationships. Thus there will be times when a particular animal is discussed out of order with respect to its position in the system of classification, simply because it is more appropriately considered in connection with the animal on which it is somehow dependent.

PUGET SOUND, THE SAN JUAN ARCHIPELAGO, AND ADJACENT AREAS

The floating docks within the "greater Puget Sound region"—this includes Puget Sound proper, the Strait of Georgia, and the waters around the San Juan Archipelago—have a more diversified fauna and flora than do those in San Francisco Bay, Coos Bay, and most other protected harbors within the geographic area covered by this book. It seems best, therefore, to deal first and most extensively with the Puget Sound region. A discussion of organisms found on floats in San Francisco Bay will follow. Most of the conspicuous and common animals and seaweeds found in marinas from British Columbia to central California will be mentioned in one or the other of these two sections.

Protozoans

In the film of microscopic organisms and detritus that coats the substratum and also the surfaces of some of the algae and sessile animals, protozoans of various sorts are usually abundant. Although they are important constituents of the fauna, it is impossible to discuss them exhaustively in this book because they are so diversified and cannot really be appreciated without extensive study. Moreover, microscopes of high quality, capable of magnifications of one hundred to one thousand diameters, are required for serious work with protozoans. There are a few types, however, that can be recognized with the aid of a hand lens and can be more fully appreciated with the help of a low-power microscope.

Ephelota (fig. 1) is common on stalks of hydroids such as *Obelia* and *Tubularia,* but it will grow on a variety of other substrata, such as worm tubes, ascidians, wood, and occasionally even on planktonic crustaceans. *Ephelota* belongs to a group of protozoans called suctorians, whose adult stage is characterized by tentacles that make contact with delicate prey organisms, usually other protozoans, and withdraw their juices. Most suctorians are sessile, secreting stalks by which they are permanently attached. The tough stalk of *Ephelota* may reach a length of nearly 1 mm, so the bulbous tentaculate portion is elevated well above the substratum. Large specimens often show a number of elongated buds on their upper surface. These buds sprout cilia, become detached, and swim around until they find a suitable place to settle. They then lose their cilia, start to secrete a stalk, and develop tentacles. *Ephelota* is sometimes so numerous that it forms a rather conspicuous whitish fuzz. When first seen with a low-power microscope, this protozoan may be mistaken for a small hydroid because of its general shape and its tentacles.

Foraminiferans are generally abundant wherever detritus accumulates. Most of them are truly microscopic, but some can be seen with a hand lens or even by the unaided eye. There are many kinds of foraminiferans in shore situations. The majority have calcareous tests, often resembling snail shells because of the way they are coiled (fig. 2). The tests are partitioned into chambers connected by openings, so the protoplasmic mass of a foraminiferan is continuous from chamber to chamber. Perforations of the test permit the long, slender extensions of protoplasm, called pseudopodia, to emerge through almost all parts of the test, as well as from the principal aperture of the largest and newest chamber. The pseudopodia, which unite to form complex networks, trap very small organisms, including bacteria, and carry them by protoplasmic streaming into the main body.

Gromia oviformis (fig. 3), formerly classified as a foraminiferan, is now placed in a separate small group. It is almost always present on wood, worm tubes, and other firm substrata. The light brown test of *Gromia* consists of an organic material, and is usually shiny. The shape is ovoid or spherical, and the diameter may reach 5 mm, although it is usually from 1 to 3 mm. Under favorable conditions (cool water is essential), the animal may extend its numerous slender pseudopodia, which it uses to trap bacteria, small diatoms, and other microscopic organisms. The pseudopodia radiate widely from the protoplasm that emerges from the aperture at one end of the test. Unlike those of foraminiferans, they tend to remain single, although they may occasionally join one another.

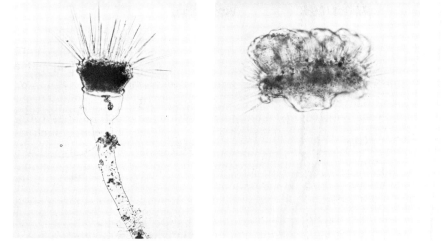

1. *Ephelota gemmipara,* a suctorian; photomicrographs. The specimen on the right is in the process of producing ciliated buds. These will swim away, settle, and become transformed into stalked individuals.

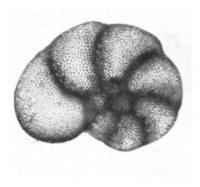

2. The chambered test of a common type of foraminiferan; photomicrograph

3. Tests of four specimens of *Gromia oviformis* on wood tunneled by the gribble, *Limnoria lignorum*

4. *Scypha,* a vaselike calcareous sponge

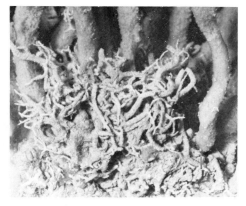

5. *Leucosolenia,* a simple calcareous sponge that forms a mat of branching tubes

Sponges

The identification of sponges is usually difficult and depends to a considerable extent on microscopic examination of the spicules. On floating docks, however, only a few kinds are likely to be encountered. One of them, *Scypha* (fig. 4), is distinctive because of its whitish, vaselike growths that are attached by their bases to the substratum. It is a relatively simple sponge, and much used for instructional purposes. All over its surface are microscopic pores that lead into a complex system of canals and chambers. The chambers are lined by peculiar little "collar cells," so named because each has a ring of fingerlike projections that looks (under the highest magnification possible with a light microscope) like a transparent collar. These cells also have flagella, which create the currents that move water into and through the sponge until it finally enters a central cavity and then goes out by way of the single large opening (osculum) at the top. The collar cells are also the principal feeding cells of the sponge, trapping microscopic food on their collars and ingesting the particles after the fashion of amoebae. The constant movement of water through the sponge not only brings in food but also supplies oxygen to cells remote from the surface and carries away waste products. The body wall of *Scypha* is supported in part by calcareous spicules. Some of these are like needles; others are three- and four-rayed structures. The needles or rays that protrude to the outside give the sponge a bristly appearance.

Leucosolenia (fig. 5), with calcareous spicules much like those of *Scypha*, forms a low mat of branched, whitish tubes that are about 2 or 3 mm in diameter. The branches may unite where they touch, so the mat becomes a network. The collar cells line the central cavity of each tube, and the pores on the outside lead directly into the cavity. For this reason, *Leucosolenia* is considered to be even simpler than *Scypha*. The species of *Leucosolenia* that occurs on floats in the Puget Sound region, San Francisco Bay, and other bays within the range covered by this book has not been positively identified. It is thought to have been introduced to this region.

Leucilla nuttingi (fig. 228) looks much like *Scypha*, but it is smoother and is attached to the substratum by a slender, almost wiry stalk. This sponge, which is slightly more complex internally than *Scypha*, generally grows in clusters. It will be mentioned again in Chapter 5, for although it is sometimes found on floats in the San Juan Archipelago, it is common at low tide levels of rocky shores of the open coast.

Two sponges that are almost invariably found on floats are *Halichondria bowerbanki* and a species of *Haliclona* that is close to, but not certainly identical with, *H. permollis*. Both have needlelike spicules that consist of silica, rather than of calcium carbonate, and both are encrusting types that may form extensive patches. They are complicated sponges that have many oscula scattered over their exposed surfaces, and thousands upon thousands of microscopic incurrent pores obscured by the felt of protruding spicules.

Haliclona (pl. 1) is usually gray, pale amethyst, or lavender, sometimes drab brown. Its oscula are on definite, volcanolike elevations.

Halichondria bowerbanki (pl. 1) is generally tan or yellowish. It makes a mass up to about 3 cm thick, but the form varies. Portions of the mass may be raised up into slightly flattened lobes, but the oscula are not prominent. *Halichondria* often grows up over stubs of algae or over worm tubes. It is called the crumb-of-bread sponge, in allusion to its texture when it is squeezed or broken. It has a strong odor, similar to that of exploded gunpowder.

To get a clear look at the spicules of a sponge under the microscope, place a bit of the sponge in a commercial bleaching preparation consisting of sodium hypochlorite. The solution will destroy all of the organic matter, leaving a debris of spicules that can be washed in water and then mounted on a slide for examination. To determine whether a sponge has calcareous or siliceous spicules, place a bit of it into a drop or two of strong hydrochloric acid: siliceous spicules resist the acid, but calcareous spicules will be destroyed and bubbles of carbon dioxide will be given off.

Cnidarians

Hydroids. Among the invertebrates that form a conspicuous part of the fauna of floating docks are the hydroids. The more common types belong to the genus *Obelia,* several species of which are found in this region. At least two are regularly found on floats: *O. dichotoma* (*O. longissima*) (fig. 6), which forms beardlike colonies 20 or 30 cm long, or sometimes even longer; and *O. geniculata* (figs. 7 and 8) grows as a delicate whitish fuzz about 2 cm high. In both species, and others that may occasionally be present, the colonies are branched; but the branching of *O. dichotoma* is of course very extensive. The feeding polyps have a crown of tentacles provided with stinging capsules, called nematocysts. These are formed within certain cells and explode when they are contacted by a small crustacean or other prey organism. The trapped prey is then brought by the tentacles to the mouth.

Hydroids, being cnidarians, have basically only two cellular layers, one lining the digestive cavity, the other lining the outside of the body. The jellylike layer between these definitely cellular layers is not as extensive as it is in some other cnidarians, especially jellyfishes. In *Obelia* the digestive cavity of one feeding polyp continues down the stalk to join that of others. The outer cellular layer secretes a thin, hyaline covering, called the perisarc, which in *Obelia* and other hydroids of the same general type envelops not only the stalks but also the feeding polyp.

At various points along the stalks are found club-shaped structures within which asexual reproduction takes place (fig. 8). The products of this budding process are little medusae (jellyfish), which eventually escape from the reproductive polyp by way of an opening at the top. When first set free, the medusae are only about 0.5 mm in diameter. They start to feed on small crustaceans and grow until they reach a diameter of nearly 5 mm. On their four radial canals they develop gonads—either ovaries or testes—and the eggs or sperm are released into the sea water. Eggs that happen to be fertilized develop into ciliated larvae called planulae. If a planula succeeds in settling on a suitable substratum, it is transformed into a polyp. This is the first stage, then, of the hydroid generation. As the young polyp grows, it puts out branches that terminate in new polyps. Eventually, reproductive polyps appear and another generation of medusae is produced.

A number of organisms from both the plant and animal kingdoms live on the stalks of colonies of *Obelia*, especially in the older and essentially dead portions. Diatoms, the suctorian *Ephelota,* and even other small hydroids may be among the adherent or tightly attached guests. Various kinds of small worms and crustaceans may wander in and out, or they may remain in the coating of diatoms and sediment that sticks to them. There are two distinctive types of organisms, however, that are present in nearly every *Obelia* colony: the caprellid amphipods and a little yellowish green sea slug, *Eubranchus olivaceus.* Both will be mentioned again later on in this chapter, in connection with some of their relatives. It should be pointed out here, however, that caprellids (fig. 47) scarcely resemble typical amphipods. The abdomen is reduced nearly to the point of disappearance, and the thoracic region resembles a stick. The way the thoracic appendages are modified and arranged makes a caprellid look something like a praying mantis. Certain species feed mostly on detritus and diatoms; others are carnivores, and polyps of *Obelia* and other hydroids may constitute much of their diet. *Eubranchus* (fig. 6) has a benign appearance, but it is in fact a predator that nips off the polyps of *Obelia.*

Gonothyraea (fig. 9) is a genus that closely resembles *Obelia.* Its medusae, after coming out of the reproductive polyp in which they are formed, remain attached to the opening. They reproduce sexually, but the eggs are retained by the female medusae until they have been fertilized and have developed into planulae. The planulae finally escape, settle, and become transformed into polyps. *Gonothyraea clarki* is the common species in this region; it is most likely to be found in situations where the salinity is a little lower than that of full-strength sea water.

Two featherlike thecate hydroids, *Plumularia* (pl. 2) and *Aglaophenia* (pl. 2), are sometimes found on floats. They are much more common on rocky shores, however, so they will be dealt with in Chapters 4 and 5.

6. Portion of a colony of *Obelia dichotoma*, with two specimens of *Eubranchus olivaceus*, a sea slug that eats the polyps

7. Feeding polyps of *Obelia geniculata*; photomicrograph

8. Reproductive polyps (*left*) of *Obelia geniculata*, and a recently-released medusa (*above*); photomicrographs. (The medusa of *O. dichotoma* is similar to that of *O. geniculata*.)

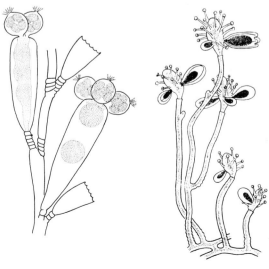

9. (*Far left*) Portion of a colony of *Gonothyraea clarki*, as seen with a microscope, showing sessile medusae attached to the reproductive polyps that produced them. The feeding polyps, which resemble those of *Obelia*, are omitted.

10. (*Left*) *Sarsia tubulosa*, as seen with a microscope. Some of the feeding polyps are in the process of budding off the characteristic four-tentacled medusae.

In a different group of hydroids, the perisarc—if this protective covering is present at all—does not extend to the feeding polyps. These are called athecate (*a* = without, *theca* = covering) hydroids, differentiated from the thecate types discussed above. Two athecate hydroids are more or less regularly encountered. *Sarsia* (fig. 10) is small—only about 1 cm high. The upper portion of each club-shaped polyp bears a number of scattered, knobbed tentacles, the knobs being batteries of stinging capsules used in the capture of prey. Just below their tentacles, the polyps produce buds that develop into medusae. The medusae of the two more common species of *Sarsia* found in the Puget Sound region will be described a little farther on in this chapter. Hydroids that look just like those of *Sarsia* but that do not release their medusae are placed in a separate genus, *Coryne*. There is at least one species of *Coryne* in the region covered by this book.

The largest athecate hydroid on floats in the Puget Sound region is *Tubularia marina* (fig. 11). Its pale, orange-pink polyps, on unbranched but generally crooked stalks up to 5 cm long, may be 1 cm in diameter when they are expanded.

Careful examination of a polyp of *Tubularia* will reveal two entirely different sets of tentacles. One set forms a whorl around the mouth; the other set is at the base of the mouth cone. Between these rings of tentacles are stalked clusters of fruitlike bodies, which are comparable to the medusa-forming reproductive polyps of *Obelia* and *Gonothyraea*. The medusae produced by *Tubularia*, however, are buried in the tissue, and only a detailed study of cross sections of the reproductive polyps will show that the medusae have a plan of construction similar to that of typical free medusae. These medusae, abortive as they are, do produce either eggs or sperm, and the eggs are fertilized within the female medusae. There they develop into planulae, which work their way to the outside but remain in close association with the polyp. They metamorphose into little polyps that already show the two rings of tentacles characteristic of mature polyps. This stage is called the actinula. When it is ready, the actinula drops away from the "parent" (remember that it is not produced directly by the hydroid stage, but indirectly by way of the abortive medusa generation) and settles on the substratum, generally in the same vicinity, and starts to grow into a mature hydroid.

On floats in San Francisco Bay, *T. marina* is replaced by *T. crocea* (pl. 2), introduced from the Atlantic coast. This species may reach a height of 15 cm and branches from the base to the extent that it forms large clumps. It will be discussed again in connection with the fauna of floats in San Francisco Bay. A *Tubularia* that occurs on floats in Coos Bay forms large clumps, too, but it seems not to be *T. crocea*.

On the lips of the tubes of two polychaetes—*Schizobranchia insignis* and *Potamilla occelata*, both of a type called plume worms—is found an unusual little athecate hydroid called *Proboscidactyla flavicirrata*. Its feeding polyps have only two tentacles, and the integrity of the colony depends very much on its close association with the living plume worm. *Proboscidactyla* is dealt with later in this chapter, in connection with its polychaete hosts.

Garveia annulata (pl. 2), with attractive orange polyps, is sometimes found on floats in the San Juan Archipelago. It is discussed more fully in Chapter 5, for it is common at low tide levels on rocky shores of the open coast.

The genus *Bougainvillia* (fig. 12) is represented by at least one species. This forms rather flexible, much-branched tufts that are usually 3 or 4 cm high and of a brownish gray color. Medusae are produced singly along the branches that bear the feeding polyps. The hydroid stage of *Bougainvillia* may not be impressive, but the medusae have great beauty. One species, *B. principis* (fig. 17), will be described in the section "Jellyfishes" in this chapter.

Jellyfishes. The quiet waters of Puget Sound, the Strait of Georgia, and the San Juan Archipelago have a superb fauna of jellyfishes. More than forty species are known to occur in this general region, and about twenty of them are encountered frequently. One can expect to see about ten species in Coos Bay, at least near its mouth. San Francisco Bay, Tomales Bay, and Bodega Bay have fewer. Some of the jellyfishes one observes in a particular place may have originated in the vicinity, whereas others are there only because they have been carried in with currents. Many of our species are small, no more than 5 mm in diameter. One, however, may be large enough to fill a washtub. The majority fall into the range between 1 and 5 cm.

The more common or conspicuous jellyfishes of Oregon and central and northern California are among those found in Puget Sound and adjacent areas. Thus an account of the species of the Puget Sound region will be useful throughout the range covered by this book. It is important to point out, however, that although most of the jellyfishes of the Puget Sound region are likely to be seen only between April and October, this is not necessarily true of the few species that are abundant in California.

The animals called jellyfishes belong to two separate groups of cnidarians, the Hydrozoa and Scyphozoa. Hydrozoan medusae are regularly characterized by the presence of a membrane (velum) extending for some distance inward from the margin of the bell. The mouth may be on a rather long stalk (manubrium), but it is not provided with extensive lobes. The gonads are usually either on canals that extend radially from the central stomach or on the manubrium. Our largest hydrozoan medusae may come close to being 10 cm in diameter, but most species are much smaller than this.

The scyphozoan medusae of this region, when mature or approaching maturity, are relatively large—generally at least 10 cm in diameter.

They have no velum, and the corners of the mouth are extended into long, frilly lobes ("oral arms"). The gonads lie in pouches off the stomach and are horseshoe-shaped in our more common species. There are other structural differences between medusae of the two groups, but the above should suffice for our purposes.

Hydrozoan medusae represent the sexual phase of the life cycle, and as a rule they are produced asexually by hydroids. There are exceptions to this rule, and the eggs of some hydrozoan medusae, after fertilization, develop directly into another generation of medusae. Scyphozoan medusae never come from hydroids, though most of them do have a polyp phase of a type called the scyphistoma (fig. 13). The scyphistoma resembles a little vase, but is provided with tentacles that enable it to trap small crustaceans and perhaps other animal organisms. Under certain conditions the scyphistoma divides transversely into a number of lobed, saucer-shaped individuals, each a prospective jellyfish. In the Puget Sound region, scyphistomae are sometimes found attached to rocks, shells, or floats—especially old and decaying floats of wood. Once in awhile, a float will have what must be millions of scyphistomae on its shaded underside. These are judged, on the basis of the types of stinging capsules they have, to belong to *Aurelia*.

As might be expected, there are some scyphozoans in which the scyphistoma stage is obviated; sexual reproduction leads directly to another generation of medusae. The more common scyphozoan jellyfishes found in the area do go through the scyphistoma stage, however.

Of the three or four species likely to be seen in this region, the largest is *Cyanea capillata* (pl. 3). It may be more than 50 cm in diameter and seems to be most abundant in the late summer. Specimens seen bobbing about in shallow water are often headed for disaster, being left high and dry when the tide recedes. The big blobs of jelly provide interesting conversation pieces. *Cyanea* is generally yellowish brown, though the coloration is sometimes absent and the animal just looks milky. There are eight groups of tentacles arising near the margin of the bell. Each group is approximately crescent-shaped, with its seventy or more tentacles arranged in four rather distinct rows. The tentacles are very extensile: in a medusa 50 cm in diameter, they may trail for 2 m or more. The margin of the bell is scalloped into eight notched lappets, and in the notch of each is a little sense organ called a rhopalium. The rhopalium is an organ of balance: it contains a crystalline mass, which gives it some weight, so that depending on the orientation of the jellyfish at the moment, the rhopalium either is or is not weighing down on the cilia of some sensory cells located on a little lobe beneath it. Information fed into the nervous system of the medusa from the various groups of sensory cells around the animal leads to appropriate righting reflexes. The frilly oral lobes are large and capable of great extension, and they are also richly provided with

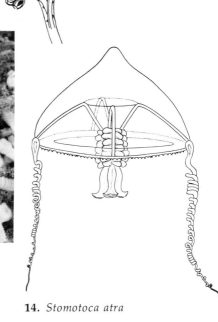

11. (*Above*) *Tubularia marina*

12. (*Right*) *Bougainvillia,* the hydroid stage producing medusae, as seen with a microscope

13. Scyphistomas of *Aurelia,* attached to wood; some are in the process of dividing transversely to form medusae

14. *Stomotoca atra*

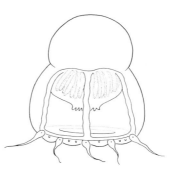

15. *Sarsia tubulosa*   **16.** *Catablema nodulosa*

stinging capsules. Contact with either the oral lobes or marginal tentacles is not recommended. *Cyanea* seems to be the only reasonably common jellyfish in this area that can give a nasty sting. Some persons are more seriously affected by it than others.

A scyphozoan that may occasionally be abundant in certain localities is *Aurelia aurita* (pl. 3). The huge populations are not surprising after one has seen the sheets of scyphistomae, thought to belong to this species, on floating docks in certain marinas. In some years, however, few medusae of *Aurelia* are seen by jellyfish watchers. *Aurelia* is generally from about 10 to 15 cm in diameter, but it can be larger. The bell is rather shallow, at least when expanded, and nearly colorless, except for the horseshoe-shaped gonads, which may be tinged with violet, pink, or yellow. The margin of the bell is divided into eight lobes, each with numerous short and delicate tentacles. Sense organs of the rhopalial type, bordered on either side by small lappets, are located between the marginal lobes. The radial canals of the digestive tract are easily seen: they branch repeatedly as they move outward toward the margin, and some of the branches anastomose. The oral lobes are fairly large, but much less frilly than those of *Cyanea*.

The methods by which *Cyanea* and *Aurelia* feed are distinctly different. The former, using potent nematocysts on its tentacles and oral lobes, can capture shrimps and fishes. The latter, however, consumes only small organisms, such as copepods; these stick to mucus produced by the jellyfish and are moved to the mouth by the action of cilia.

Most of our hydromedusae fall into two rather distinct categories with respect to the shape of the bell, location of the gonads, nature of the marginal sense organs, and parentage—that is, whether they are derived from thecate or athecate hydroids. To put the matter as simply as possible, medusae with bells that are as tall or taller than they are wide, with pigmented eyespots near the bases of the tentacles, and with gonads borne on the manubrium, are usually derived from athecate hydroids, such as *Sarsia*. Medusae with bells wider than tall, with marginal balance organs (statocysts) but no eyespots, and with gonads borne on the radial canals are usually derived from thecate hydroids, such as *Obelia*. The least reliable character is that of the shape of the bell. Moreover, some jellyfishes do not fit into either of these categories.

Of the species belonging to the first group, one is unusual because it has only two tentacles. This is *Stomotoca atra* (fig. 14). Its gonads are organized into eight series of cross foldings on the manubrium. There are four radial canals. The bell, up to 1.5 cm in diameter, is about as high as wide, and somewhat pointed at the tip.

Species of *Sarsia* have decidedly tall bells and typically four tentacles, each with an eyespot at its base. *Sarsia tubulosa* (fig. 15) is especially common in the Puget Sound region. The bell of a mature specimen is only a little more than 1 cm high, but the manubrium, when fully extended, may be more than twice as long as this. *Sarsia rosaria* is similar to *S. tubulosa*, although its manubrium rarely reaches beyond the edge of the bell. *Euphysa flammea* is in the same general group. It lacks eyespots at the bases of the tentacles, however. Its rather short manubrium is sometimes carmine red throughout, sometimes red around the mouth and pink higher up.

Jellyfishes of the genus *Bougainvillia* are distinctive in that their tentacles are concentrated into four clusters. Of the species known to occur in this area, *B. principis* (fig. 17) is probably the most common. It reaches a diameter of about 1.5 cm and has up to forty tentacles in each cluster. There may be eight gonads in some large specimens, four in others.

A number of tall-belled species are unusual in having an apical projection or thickening; this may be pinched off slightly from the rest of the bell. *Catablema nodulosa* (fig. 16) is the one most likely to be seen.

Polyorchis penicillatus (fig. 18) is one of our more beautiful hydromedusae. Its attractiveness is related to a considerable extent to the intricacies of its structure. The bell, shaped almost like a hen's egg that has been opened at one end, may reach a height of 5 cm. Each of the four radial canals has many blind side branches, and each of the numerous tentacles has a conspicuous reddish eyespot at its base. The gonads hang down like sausages between the bell and the tube on which the mouth is located. Although often seen from floats, this jellyfish is inclined to stay close to bottom, especially where there are extensive beds of eelgrass populated by caprellid amphipods and other small crustaceans upon which *Polyorchis* feeds.

Of the jellyfishes that have gonads on the radial canals, statocysts instead of eyespots, and usually shallow bells, the more common of the readily visible species in the Puget Sound area are *Phialidium gregarium*, *Mitrocoma cellularia*, and *Aequorea victoria*. All of these have numerous marginal tentacles. *Phialidium* (fig. 19) is the smallest of them, its bell being not quite 1.5 cm in diameter. The gonads are restricted to the outer portions of the four radial canals, and there are about sixty tentacles. The mouth opens directly into the stomach. This particular species of *Phialidium* is produced by a hydroid that is referred to the genus *Clytia*. Ideally, the medusa and hydroid should have the same name, but zoologists concerned with nomenclature of these animals have not decided which name is the better one.

Mitrocoma (fig. 20) resembles *Phialidium*, partly because the mouth is not on a stalk. It is larger, however, frequently exceeding a diameter of 5 cm. It also has many more tentacles—at least 250—and the gonads are wavy and run the entire length of the four radial canals.

Aequorea (fig. 23) is our largest common jellyfish. It frequently attains a diameter of about 7 cm, and still larger specimens have been reported. In comparison with the other species just described, it has a

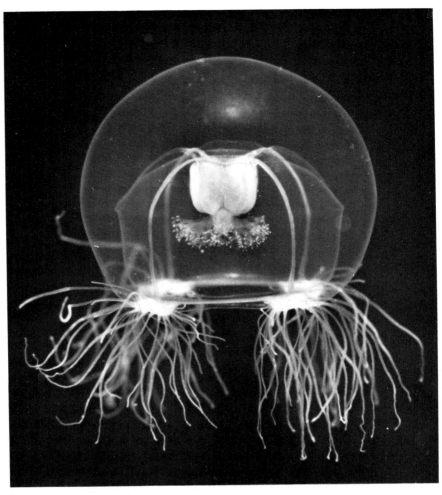

17. *Bougainvillia principis*

very thick, gelatinous bell. There are about sixty radial canals, and the delicate gonads are under these. The tentacles, numbering over fifty in large specimens, are capable of great extension.

Melicertum octocostatum (fig. 21) belongs to the same general group as the three species just described, although it has a relatively tall bell. There are eight radial canals, each with a conspicuous wavy gonad. All around the margin, small tentacles alternate more or less regularly with about sixty larger ones, and the manubrium is proportionately stout. The diameter reaches 1 cm.

The next two jellyfishes—one tall-belled, the other shallow-belled—do not have a hydroid stage. Their fertilized eggs, in other words, develop into planulae that gradually change into medusae. For this reason, both genera are placed in a group separate from those to which most of our hydromedusae belong.

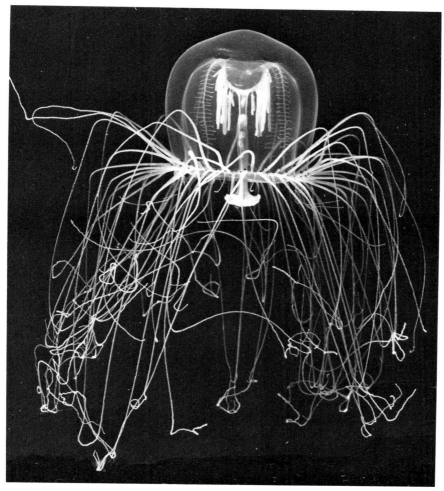

18. *Polyorchis penicillatus*

Aglantha digitale (fig. 24), with a tall bell up to 1.5 cm high, has about one hundred tentacles. There are eight radial canals and eight gonads that hang down like sausages inside the bell. Unlike most of our jellyfishes, which move rather slowly and by regular pulsations, *Aglantha* may appear to be motionless much of the time; but when it does go into action, it almost leaps.

Solmissus (fig. 22) is up to about 5 cm in diameter and something like *Aequorea* in profile and consistency, but there is little similarity otherwise. The margin is scalloped into about eighteen or twenty lappets, and the relatively stiff tentacles arise between these, well above the edge of the bell. The mouth is very wide and opens directly into a large stomach with a number of side pockets in which the gonads are located; there are no radial canals. Developing medusae of the next generation are sometimes found on the floor of the stomach.

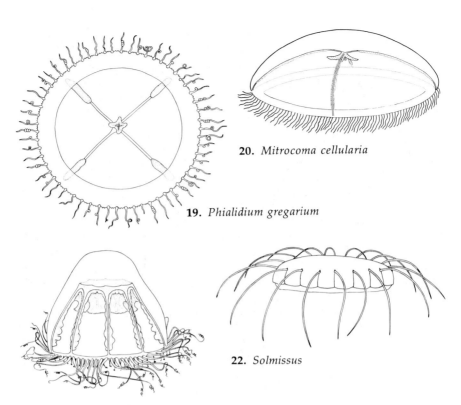

20. *Mitrocoma cellularia*

19. *Phialidium gregarium*

22. *Solmissus*

21. *Melicertum octocostatum*

Most of our larger hydrozoan medusae are luminescent. If it is dark, and if one's eyes are adapted to the darkness, flashes of light emitted by jellyfishes and certain other animals bobbing near the surface will probably be seen. The best way to observe luminescence at close range is to take a jellyfish into an absolutely dark room, allow a little time for your eyes to become accustomed to the darkness, then touch or rub the animal. *Aequorea* is a good one to use for this purpose; its luminescent material is especially concentrated around the margin of the bell. *Aequorea*, by the way, is an important resource to biologists concerned with the physiology of nerves and muscles. The luminescent substance, called aequorin, will not produce light unless free calcium ions are present. This makes purified aequorin useful for monitoring certain reactions in which calcium ions are taken up or released.

Sea Anemones. The most common sea anemone attached to floats is *Metridium senile* (fig. 25; pl. 3). In many situations, especially in estuaries where the salinity is reduced, it is the only one to be found. This species, which sometimes attains a height of 25 cm or more, may be white, tan, brownish orange, or related colors. Unlike most other sea anemones, which have rather thick tentacles, *Metridium* usually has hundreds of relatively small tentacles, arranged in lappetlike groups,

23. *Aequorea victoria*

24. *Aglantha digitale*

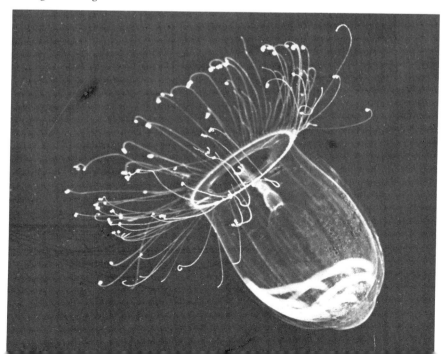

and the number continues to increase as the animal grows. The majority of our sea anemones feed upon small fishes, crabs, shrimps, and other prey of considerable size, but *Metridium* feeds primarily upon small organisms. It is nonetheless a carnivore.

Metridium occasionally reproduces asexually as well as sexually. In sexual reproduction, it discharges eggs or sperm (depending on its sex) into the sea by way of its mouth. The eggs, once fertilized, develop into planula larvae, which settle and metamorphose into little anemones. Asexual reproduction, when it occurs, may be accomplished by fragmentation of the basal disk, with the pieces differentiating into small but complete anemones, or by an anemone pulling itself into two parts. It is not unusual to find specimens in which the basal disk is elongated and in which the column is already reorganizing with the prospect of forming two complete individuals.

Metridium senile varies in certain respects other than size and color. Some specimens, for instance, have fewer and proportionately longer tentacles than most specimens do. Others have "catch tentacles." These are provided with a particular type of nematocyst, fired as part of a pattern of aggressive behavior when one anemone encroaches on another's territory.

An anemone that fits under *M. senile,* as this species is interpreted broadly, is locally common on floats, and is sometimes found intertidally on wood, shells, or rocks in muddy bays. The prevailing color of its column and oral disk is brown or tan, but the tentacles are grayish or whitish, and there is often a white ring around the mouth (fig. 26). The height of larger individuals, when fully extended, is about 5 cm. This variant is less inclined to divide than to produce young by budding from the base. The buds generally have some tentacles and show other signs of being little anemones before they become detached. In any case, large aggregations are often formed by this method of asexual reproduction.

Experts concerned with *Metridium* are not in agreement as to whether *M. senile* is a polymorphic species, or whether it should be broken up into several species, or at least into subspecies. Much research must be done before the situation is clarified.

An entirely different type of sea anemone, *Urticina crassicornis (Tealia crassicornis)* (pl. 4), is usually common, provided that the salinity is nearly the same as that of full-strength sea water. The column and thick tentacles are usually greenish gray or olive gray, but diffuse red tints are often strong; in addition, the tentacles have some light bands. The column can be an audacious mixture of red streaks and a light, olive-green background, or it may be uniformly red or pale tan.

Ctenophores, or Comb Jellies

The comb jellies resemble jellyfishes because of their texture and transparency, but they are really quite different. Instead of pulsating, comb

25. *Metridium senile*

26. A variant of *Metridium senile;* the prevailing color is brown, but the tentacles are whitish or grayish, and there is often a light ring around the mouth

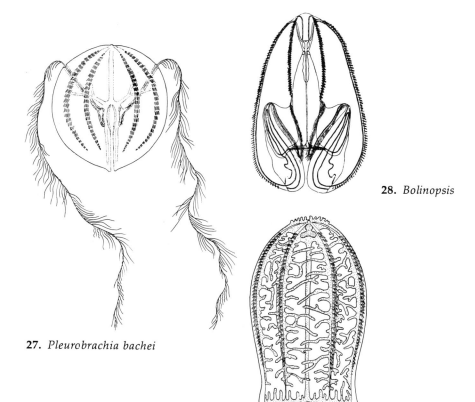

27. *Pleurobrachia bachei*

28. *Bolinopsis*

29. *Beroe*

jellies propel themselves by the action of large cilia. The cilia are arranged in paddlelike aggregations (ctenes, or "combs"), disposed in eight meridional rows, called comb rows. (The phylum name, Ctenophora, means "comb-bearing.") Comb jellies are not strong swimmers and are therefore not really independent of currents. When observed in quiet water, they can be seen to make forward progress; if they happen to be of a type that has long tentacles, the tentacles will be trailing behind them. Although the unaided eye cannot distinguish the individual cilia, the cilia of a comb row collectively have a shimmering opalescence that is sometimes readily apparent.

Our most common comb jelly is the "sea gooseberry," *Pleurobrachia bachei* (fig. 27). It is probably present throughout the year in the Puget Sound area, but is rare in winter and not likely to be seen unless the plankton is sampled thoroughly. It begins to become common in the spring and generally reaches a peak of abundance in summer. Specimens are often washed up on beaches. If they have not been out of the water long, and if the day is cool, some of them will revive if put into a jar of sea water.

Pleurobrachia is approximately egg-shaped, and a large specimen is about 1.5 cm long. The mouth is situated at one end—the oral end—and opens into what can be called a stomach, from which a number of canals constituting the rest of the digestive tract arise. At the end opposite the mouth—the aboral end—there is a complicated little organ of balance, in which a crystalline mass rests on sensory cilia and is roofed over by a transparent dome also consisting of cilia. Closer to the aboral end than to the oral end are the sheaths in which the two tentacles originate and into which they can be retracted. When the tentacles are extended, they may be nearly 15 cm long, and their numerous fine side branches confer a cobwebby appearance on the tentacles as a whole. As these tentacles are dragged through the water, adhesive "glue cells" (colloblasts) on them become discharged when they touch prospective prey organisms, such as copepods and other small crustaceans. The tentacles then contract, bringing the trapped prey to the mouth. *Pleurobrachia* will usually survive for a number of days in a large jar of cool sea water and is uninhibited about extending its tentacles. If some copepods are added, it may eventually trap some of these and push them into the mouth.

Although *Pleurobrachia* is decidedly our most common ctenophore, a species of *Bolinopsis* is sometimes abundant, and *Beroe* is a pleasant surprise on occasion. *Bolinopsis* (fig. 28) is distinctive because of its slightly compressed, helmet-shaped body, much of which consists of two oral lobes. The principal tentacles, comparable to those of *Pleurobrachia*, are short and originate close to the mouth; some other small tentacles lie in grooves leading toward the mouth. The comb rows are conspicuous, but four are shorter than the rest; none of them runs the full length of the body. *Bolinopsis* is beautifully luminescent. A large specimen is about 3 cm tall.

Beroe (fig. 29) is not often brought in by prevailing currents, but it is an impressive ctenophore. It is shaped something like a cucumber and may be 7 or 8 cm long. The mouth and pharynx are capacious and can take in crustaceans of considerable size, as well as its own relative, *Pleurobrachia*. A striking feature is the honeycombed appearance of the body which results from the division of the eight main branches of the digestive cavity into numerous ramifying and interdigitating diverticula. *Beroe* is another of the marvelously luminescent ctenophores.

Flatworms

There are many kinds of turbellarian flatworms crawling over seaweeds and over clumps of mussels, hydroids, and other animals attached to floats. Most of these turbellarians are less than a millimeter long and are not likely to be observed except with the aid of a low-power microscope. Some of them are herbivores grazing principally on diatoms, others are carnivores feeding on small crustaceans or other invertebrates. They fall into several rather separate groups, and our fauna of small turbellarians is essentially unknown. Few of the many species in this area have been named and described, and their habits and ecological relationships with other organisms are also in need of study.

Occasionally, a large turbellarian, belonging to the group called polyclads, will be found crawling over the surface of a float or will emerge from material brought back to the laboratory for sorting. Our largest species, not really characteristic of the fauna of floats but sometimes found on them, is *Kaburakia excelsa* (pl. 6). It reaches a length of more than 5 cm, but is only about 2 or 3 mm thick when extended and in tight contact with the substratum. Its usual color is tan or grayish brown. It has little black spots, consisting of pigment associated with its light-receptor organs, along the entire margin of the body, as well as on a pair of short tentacles situated near the anterior end, at the base of these tentacles, and in the region of the brain. Other polyclads that may be encountered on floats are about 1 or 2 cm long. Most of them do not have tentacles, and the pigmented eyespots are generally restricted to the region of the brain. A species of *Notoplana*, shown in Plate 6, is typical of the group.

All polyclads are carnivores, feeding on crustaceans, molluscs, worms, ascidians, and other invertebrates. They have a much-branched digestive tract, to which the name polyclad alludes. The mouth is usually near the middle of the ventral surface, and in most species there is a large, eversible, ruffled pharynx which can be extended like an umbrella over the prey. Digestion is generally begun while the pharynx is out, and a combination of ciliary and muscular activity brings partly digested food into the branched digestive tract, where digestion is completed. As the digestive system of polyclads, like that of other turbellarians, is just an elaborately branched sac, indigestible residues must be voided through the mouth.

Nemerteans

It is unusual to find nemerteans just crawling around on exposed surfaces of floats. However, careful examination of clumps of algae, ascidians, mussels, tube-dwelling polychaetes, and other invertebrates may reveal one or more small species, mostly under 2 cm long. Occasionally a large nemertean may turn up in a bucket of material scraped off the floats. The most common large species encountered in this situation in our area seems to be *Tubulanus sexlineatus* (pl. 6). This worm may be about 50 cm long when fully extended, and its thickness is about a quarter of that of a pencil. Its background color of chocolate brown is interrupted by evenly spaced white rings and five or six longitudinal white lines (the specific name, *sexlineatus*, means "six-lined"), one of which runs right down the middle of the upper surface. *Tubulanus sexlineatus* inhabits a parchmentlike tube, and specimens in captivity soon secrete new tubes around themselves. Like nearly all nemerteans, this species is a predator, using its eversible proboscis to trap polychaetes and perhaps other animals.

Polychaete Annelids

Of the more obvious polychaetes, representatives of the two families of plume worms—the sabellids and the serpulids—are especially prominent. The sabellids generally construct leathery tubes, and the anteriormost part of the body (prostomium) is modified into a number of featherlike cirri ("tentacles" is a less desirable term for them) which, when they are expanded, collectively resemble a feather duster. On the inner face of the main stem and on each fine side branch of a cirrus is a broad tract of crowded, short cilia. Currents of water set up by some larger cilia bring tiny particles of food into the crown of cirri, and mucus on the ciliated tracts traps particles that are in a suitable size range. The film of mucus and food is moved down the side branches and then down the main stems of the cirri to a right and a left collecting groove that direct the film to the mouth.

As the tubes of sabellids are blind at their lower ends, these worms must have some kind of a system for transporting digestive wastes and reproductive cells out through the mouths of the tubes. Sabellids have ciliated tracts that move fecal material from the posterior end of the body forward to the open end of the tube. Eggs and sperm released into the space around the animal by sexually ripe segments are likewise carried forward by these ciliary tracts.

At least four species of sabellids are encountered on floats, but only two of them are apt to be common and regularly present. The most abundant species is invariably *Schizobranchia insignis* (pl. 7), whose cirri—colored red, orange, brown, gray, or greenish—fork dichotomously several times and thus are like branched feathers. Its tubes are up to about 20 cm long, and their diameter may exceed that of a pencil. *Schizobranchia* sometimes forms huge masses and thus provides a hiding place for some animals and a substratum to which others can become attached. This polychaete is abundant, in nearly all harbors of the Northwest.

Potamilla occelata (pl. 7) is a little smaller than *Schizobranchia*. Its cirri are characteristically a light tan color, though they may be banded with brown, and they have conspicuous, darkly pigmented eyespots. In structure, the cirri of *Potamilla* are distinctly different from those of *Schizobranchia* because they are simply featherlike; the main stems do not fork.

On the outside of tubes of *Schizobranchia* and *Potamilla*, right at the edge of the opening, there is generally a growth of a small hydroid, *Proboscidactyla flavicirrata* (fig. 30), in which the feeding polyps have only two tentacles. To really appreciate this little gem, one has to examine it with a low-power microscope. The feeding polyps, connected together by a stolon creeping over the surface of the tube, have their tall mouth cones raised well above the bases of the tentacles. Collectively they may resemble circles of ballet dancers in various poses. Also arising from the stolon are some simple, fingerlike polyps and reproductive polyps that bud off medusae from near their free ends. The medusae, as in other hydroids, represent the sexual generation. They mature after being set free, gradually developing about sixty tentacles, but are only about 1 cm in diameter when full grown. They are unusual because the four radial canals they start out with branch repeatedly, and the number of ultimate branches coincides with the number of tentacles.

Proboscidactyla may for the moment be considered a commensal symbiont, profiting by living in a situation where food of appropriate types is brought within its grasp by currents of water set up by its hosts. As the tube of *Schizobranchia* or *Potamilla* is enlarged, the hydroid keeps propagating itself to keep up with the edge, and the older part of the colony dies away. Experimental work on *Proboscidactyla* has demonstrated that close contact of the feeding polyps with the cirri of the sabellid host is essential to maintain a differentiated colony. In the absence of such contact, the colony deteriorates.

Two other sabellids likely to be found on floats are *Eudistylia vancouveri* and *Myxicola infundibulum*. *Eudistylia* (pl. 7) is larger than *Schizobranchia*, with tubes reaching a diameter of more than 1 cm. The cirri are simply pinnate, like those of *Potamilla*, and are richly colored by alternating bands of maroon and dark green.

Myxicola (fig. 31) is an unusual sabellid because its tubes consist of a transparent mucus and its cirri, which are practically colorless, are united for more than half their length by delicate membranes, thus forming a funnel. On floats, *Myxicola* tends to be scattered and solitary, and is most often found as a stranger among other sabellids or in clumps of ascidians.

The other group of tube-dwelling worms that invariably catches one's attention in visits to floating docks is the serpulids. They secrete calcareous tubes about themselves; and although they have featherlike cirri similar to those of sabellids, they also have a device for closing the tube after withdrawing. This soft structure, called the operculum, is shaped something like a golf tee; it is, in fact, a striking specialization of prostomial outgrowths comparable to those that develop into cirri. Serpulids feed in much the same way as sabellids, trapping microscopic food on ciliary-mucous tracts and conveying it to the mouth.

Our only large serpulid is *Serpula vermicularis* (pl. 7). Its coiled or rambling white tubes, up to about 10 cm long, are readily recognized if they are not overgrown by other organisms. The cirri and operculum are usually red. It is common to find specimens that have two opercula functioning together to close the tube.

There may be several tiny serpulids of the genus *Spirorbis* (pls. 7 and 12) in a single square centimeter of a hard substratum such as fiberglass or concrete, unless this happens to be heavily overgrown by other colonizers. *Spirorbis* is also common on shells of mussels and other molluscs. There are several species in our area, but they all look very much alike except to a specialist. The coils of their tubes are rarely more than 2 or 3 mm in diameter, but their cirri are usually reddish, so they look like miniature *Serpula*.

All serpulids and sabellids react quickly to touch, and sometimes also to sudden agitation of the water near them. They withdraw their cirri with great haste; but left alone, they will soon expand their flowerlike crowns and resume feeding.

When the holdfasts of seaweeds or clumps of worm tubes or other animals are detached, several species of polychaetes may be encountered. Two that are nearly ubiquitous in such situations—*Halosydna brevisetosa* and *Harmothoe imbricata*—are members of a group called scaleworms (family Polynoidae). They are carnivores, feeding on a variety of invertebrates, including other polychaetes.

Halosydna brevisetosa (fig. 32) is the larger of the two scaleworms, attaining a length of up to 5 cm. Its color varies, but it is generally gray or brownish gray, often with rather strong transverse bands. There are eighteen pairs of scales covering its dorsal surface. This species is often involved in commensal relationships, especially with polychaetes of the family Terebellidae, but most specimens found on floats are probably free-living.

Harmothoe imbricata (fig. 33) is slightly smaller, rarely reaching 3 cm, and has only fifteen pairs of scales. It tends to be rather dark green

30. *Proboscidactyla flavicirrata,* a group of feeding polyps (*left*) and a reproductive polyp producing medusae (*right*); photomicrographs

31. *Myxicola infundibulum*

32. *Halosydna brevisetosa,* a scaleworm

33. *Harmothoe imbricata*

or brown for the first few segments of the dorsal surface; behind this region, the coloration is generally a little lighter, with mottling of the scales, but without any distinct transverse banding. *Harmothoe* is one of the scaleworms known to brood its eggs under the scales, releasing its young in a free-swimming larval stage called the trochophore.

Bryozoans

Some bryozoans may be confused with hydroids because they form branching colonies in which the individual animals have circles of delicate tentacles. Bryozoans, however, are much higher than hydroids on the evolutionary scale. Together with the phoronids and brachiopods, they constitute the lophophorate phyla (the term "lophophore" applies to the group of tentacles). There are a number of reasons, based on our understanding of the internal and external anatomy of the animals in these phyla, for considering them to be closely related.

A close look at a bryozoan should dispel any illusions about its kinship to the hydroids. First of all, each individual, called a zooid, is enclosed within a separate "house," or zooecium. As the colony is built up by asexual reproduction, protoplasmic connections between zooids may persist, but these connections are at best tenuous. Recall that in hydroid colonies, the tissues and digestive cavity of one polyp are fully continuous with those of neighboring polyps. Also, when the zooid of a bryozoan is retracted, the entire animal is withdrawn into its zooecium by special muscles. In hydroids, the tentacles shorten and may bend inward—and in some species the whole polyp may contract until it is out of sight—but there are no special muscles for pulling it down into the theca. Other mechanisms are also involved in the withdrawal of a bryozoan. If the zooecium has an operculum for complete closure, as it often does, a special set of muscles operates this movement. In addition, there may be muscles that pull on the wall of the zooecium, or that operate in other ways, to effect an increase in hydrostatic pressure sufficient to force the lophophoral portion of the zooid out again.

Of course, bryozoans have no stinging capsules, and they are basically filter feeders, not carnivores. Ciliary activity moves water through the lophophore, and particles of appropriate size and character are driven by cilia into the mouth. The digestive tract is U-shaped and complete, leading to an anus located to one side of the lophophore.

The bryozoans discussed so far have been only feeding individuals. The colonies of many bryozoans are polymorphic, with some individuals specialized for functions other than feeding and reproduction. For instance, a type of individual called the avicularium resembles the beak of a bird, with muscles for closing one jaw against the other. A vibraculum is an individual in which the structure that corresponds to the movable jaw of an avicularium is drawn out into a vibratile process.

Both avicularia and vibracula are supposed to discourage unwelcome settlers.

Bryozoan colonies come in many different forms. A few branching types that look something like hydroids have already been mentioned. Some species form flat, encrusting growths or leaflike colonies that are connected to the substratum only at one point. Others form branching calcareous masses that superficially resemble certain corals, and one group has brownish cartilaginous colonies that may be mistaken for seaweeds. The classification of bryozoans is so complicated that a superficial review of it would be worse than none.

On the floats, the arborescent type is regularly represented by *Bugula* (figs. 34, 35, and 36). It looks lacy and soft, but its actual texture is brittle and gritty, for it is to some extent calcified. The pattern of branching is such that a colony of any size—a large one is about 4 or 5 cm high—exhibits a distinctly spiral configuration. Much of the colony consists of zooecia that no longer contain living zooids; but the upper portions should show plenty of active tentaculate individuals as well as the beaked avicularia. The dark brown bodies found in many of the zooecia are the remains of disintegrated organs.

Growing over the flat blades of brown algae, such as *Laminaria saccharina*, are silvery patches of an encrusting species, *Membranipora membranacea* (figs. 37 and 38). It is common only during the late spring, summer, and early autumn. The colonies are often nearly circular. The orderly asexual reproduction by the peripheral zooids arranges the zooids in radiating series that branch and rebranch. The opaque white lines (marking the thin, calcified walls of the zooecia) and more nearly translucent areas occupied by the polypides themselves form a pattern resembling fine lacework.

Some colonies of *Membranipora*, after being taken out of the water, have what look like little lumps of jelly of about the same color as the colony. If the colony is submerged in clean sea water and examined with a strong hand lens or a low-power microscope, the little blobs may prove to be one of the marine zoologist's delights, *Doridella steinbergae* (fig. 37). This is a tiny, flattened sea slug whose length does not quite reach 1 cm. Its color pattern—white lines on a translucent and nearly colorless background—almost perfectly matches that of *Membranipora*. A close look at an active *Doridella* will reveal the two to four pairs of branched gills on either side of the anus at the posterior end. *Doridella* is specialized for grazing on the extended lophophores of *Membranipora* and rarely ventures off its pastureland. Its eggs are laid in little crescentic masses.

Corambe pacifica is also sometimes found on *Membranipora* in this area. It has more gills on both sides of the anus than *Doridella* does, and there is a distinct notch at the posterior end of the dorsal surface. Both *Doridella* and *Corambe* belong to a group of sea slugs called dor-

34. *Bugula*

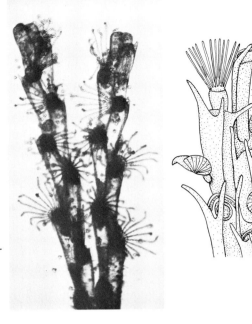

35. (*Right*) Portion of a colony of *Bugula*, showing zooids with lophophores extended; photomicrograph

36. (*Far right*) Portion of a colony of *Bugula*, showing avicularia

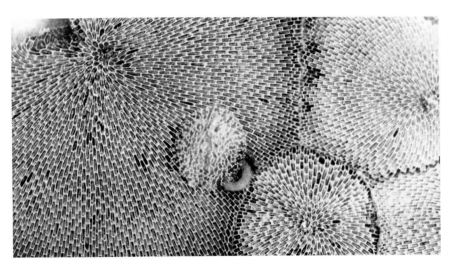

37. Contiguous colonies of *Membranipora membranacea*, with the sea slug *Doridella steinbergae* and its egg mass

38. Extended zooids of *Membranipora membranacea*

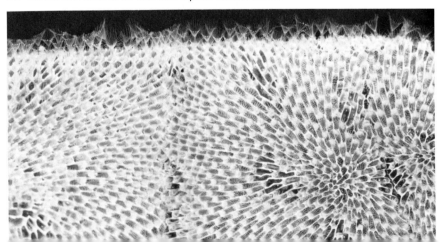

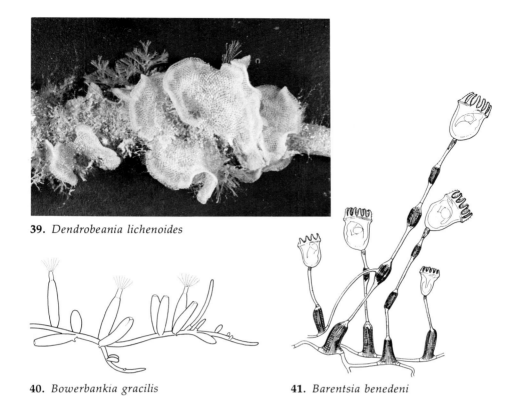

39. *Dendrobeania lichenoides*

40. *Bowerbankia gracilis*

41. *Barentsia benedeni*

ids, which typically have a circle of gills around the anus situated on the dorsal surface in the posterior part of the body.

Another encrusting bryozoan, found at all seasons, is *Schizoporella unicornis* (pl. 23). Colored a dingy orange, it grows on shells of mussels and barnacles as well as concrete and fiberglass. Its colonies are much less regular and also thicker than those of *Membranipora.* This species of *Schizoporella* was almost certainly introduced to this area with oyster spat from Japan.

Dendrobeania lichenoides (fig. 39) forms a flexible growth that is somewhat leaflike. The older portion of the colony develops in tight contact with the substratum, so there is a little stalk from which the free foliar portion spreads out. *Dendrobeania* is usually pale brownish white or tan, and on floats it seems generally to prefer to settle on tubes of sabellid polychaetes. It is often mixed with *Bugula,* hydroids, sponges, and other organisms that have a liking for the same type of situation.

Much of the fuzzy stuff that coats worm tubes, mussels, hydroids, and seaweeds consists of *Bowerbankia.* Bryozoans of this genus spread by a stolon from which the slender zooids, each less than 1 mm long, arise. *Bowerbankia gracilis* (fig. 40) is the most common species on the Pacific coast. It is particularly abundant on floats and pilings in harbors, but it is also found at low tide levels on rocky shores.

An Entoproct

Members of the phylum Entoprocta resemble certain bryozoans in general appearance and also because they have a circle of ciliated tentacles around the mouth. The anus is also within the circle, however, and this is one of several reasons why zoologists keep entoprocts separate from bryozoans, in which the anus is outside the circle. The only entoproct that will be dealt with in this book is *Barentsia benedeni* (fig. 41). It is often common on mussels, worm tubes, ropes, and other firm substrata. There is a basal stolon, much like that of the bryozoan *Bowerbankia*, and the upright zooids, up to about 4 mm tall, arise from this. The stolon may branch, and the zooids may also start new stolons, so the colony eventually becomes a dense, fuzzy growth. The zooids of this species are especially interesting because each one sooner or later develops a muscular swelling at its base, and it may add up to three more of these swellings along its stalk. There are places where the zooid can quickly bend. A colony of *Barentsia* is always a busy place, with some members bending while others are unbending. The tentacles, whose cilia create currents that bring food particles to the mouth, border the cup-shaped upper part of each zooid. They cannot be withdrawn, for there is no "house" such as a bryozoan zooid has. They can only be turned inward if the zooid is disturbed.

Crustaceans

Among crustaceans that live in close contact with the substratum but are not permanently cemented to it, the copepods, amphipods, isopods, and certain shrimps are the more common. The copepods are mostly of a type called harpacticoids, which grub about for detritus and microscopic algae. They are small—generally under 1 mm long—and there are numerous species about which we know all too little. A picture of one of them (fig. 42) will show their general appearance.

Ostracodes have a bivalve shell, and thus may resemble tiny clams. Their jointed appendages, however, which typically include two pairs of antennae, mouth parts, and two or three pairs of legs, show that they are crustaceans. Most ostracodes are under 2 mm long. The shells are often sculptured or studded with bristles, and sometimes are opaque. Figure 43 shows a relatively delicate, transparent species common on floats. There are many others in the sediment on worm tubes, colonies of barnacles, and similar situations.

Planktonic Copepods. A variety of smaller crustaceans may be seen swimming near the surface. Some of them are large-eyed, truly planktonic amphipods, or amphipods that have briefly cut themselves loose from the bottom or from the mat of vegetation on the floats. During late spring, summer, and early autumn, however, planktonic copepods are abundant. These belong to a group called calanoid copepods (fig. 44), characterized by first antennae that are long and have more than twenty articles, and by a body in which the posterior portion is distinctly set apart from the larger, anterior portion. In both these respects they are quite different from the harpacticoids found grubbing in sediment. Calanoids move jerkily, using the first antennae and thoracic limbs for propulsion. The mouth parts and second antennae create currents from which microscopic food is strained. Calanoids are extremely important in the food chain, for they are herbivores, feeding on diatoms and other photosynthetic primary producers, and are in turn eaten by small fishes or by other organisms eventually eaten by fishes. Most calanoids are under 2 mm long, and when they are colorless they may be overlooked. Those that store up red and orange carotenoid pigments from the plant food they consume are easily visible.

Amphipods. Amphipods (fig. 45) are plentiful among algae and other growths. Some actually feed on algae, and certain species may even build little nests from pieces of seaweed that they stick together. Those closely associated with seaweeds are often the same color: for instance, there are some on *Ulva* that are bright green. Most of the amphipods in shore situations are somewhat compressed laterally and have long first and second antennae. The last three pairs of abdominal appendages are nearly as conspicuous as the seven pairs of legs. (The name Amphipoda was given to the group in allusion to the "legs" at both ends of the body.) No attempt will be made to characterize any particular species found on floats. The larger ones, about 3 cm long, are mostly species of *Ampithoe*.

Where silt and detritus accumulate, as among growths of other organisms, some small amphipods of the genus *Corophium* (fig. 46) may form masses of soft, muddy tubes. The distinctive characteristics of *Corophium* include a body that is slightly flattened dorsoventrally instead of laterally, and proportionately stout second antennae. Our species rarely exceed 1 cm in length, including the antennae. *Corophium* feeds by filtering out detritus. Certain of the abdominal appendages create currents, and the fringes of fine hairs on the legs farther forward strain out the food, which is then scraped off by the mouth parts. Although *Corophium* is found on floats almost everywhere, it is particularly abundant in estuarine situations where the salinity is reduced and silting is heavy.

Some strange amphipods of a totally different group, the suborder Caprellidea, have already been mentioned in connection with *Obelia* and other hydroids. Caprellids (fig. 47) have no abdomen to speak of. The thoracic segments are long and slender, and as a result the legs are widely spaced. In some caprellids, certain legs are missing altogether, although the gills that typically grow from the bases of the legs survive as little fleshy pads or clubs. As in typical amphipods, however, the female has a thoracic pouch, covered by some large, overlapping plates, in which the young develop. Because the body of a caprellid is so slender and the legs are so far apart, a brood pouch full of eggs or young is more noticeable than it is in most amphipods.

Caprellids are sometimes called skeleton shrimps, a name that suits them well. They remind one of a praying mantis, partly because of their general form and partly because of the appearance of their prehensile first and second legs. It is interesting to watch their looping movements: they attach themselves by their more anterior legs as they let go with the legs that are in the rear portion of the body; then, after bringing the hind end forward, they attach themselves by the rear legs again. They may remain motionless much of the time, however. Some of the caprellids associated with hydroids nip off the polyps and eat them; others feed mostly on diatoms and detritus.

Isopods. The most common and conspicuous isopod is *Idotea wosnesenskii* (pl. 19). It is about 3 or 4 cm long, and the color of specimens found on floats is generally olive green, but varies from rather bright green through brown to nearly black. (When found among coralline algae on rocky shores, this species may be mostly pink.) The posterior quarter of the body (the abdominal region) is mostly unsegmented; its terminal portion is rather smoothly rounded, except for a tiny blunt tooth at the tip. When picked up, it may almost reflexly cling to a finger with its seven pairs of claw-tipped legs. On floats, *Idotea* hangs onto holdfasts, stalks, and blades of seaweeds, and to worm tubes and other objects. Although it is often abundant in this general situation, it is still more common under rocks on the shore.

Wooden floats and pilings that have been in the water for a few years are usually riddled by burrows of a tiny isopod, *Limnoria lignorum* (the "gribble") (fig. 48) and those of a clam, *Bankia setacea* (the "shipworm"). Together or separately, the gribble and the shipworm cause an enormous amount of damage and could be called the "termites of the sea." (The shipworm is discussed more fully later in this chapter.)

The burrows of the gribble are small, as the animal itself, looking like a miniature sow bug, is only about 3 mm long. However, by the time a piece of wood has been worked over by a thriving population, it will be a spongy mess. The gribble's mouth parts rasp away the wood, and the small particles pass rather quickly through the digestive tract. Exactly how the cellulose is degraded into simpler compounds which might be of use to the animal, and how proteins and other essential foods are obtained, has never been satisfactorily explained. In any case, the burrows of the gribble expose more of the wood's surface to destructive bacteria and fungi.

An isopod sometimes found on floats and pilings is *Gnorimosphaeroma oregonense* (fig. 118). It is a small species, only about 1 cm long, and is similar to the terrestrial pill bug in form and in its ability to roll up into a ball. Its color is basically a drab, mottled gray. *Gnorimo-*

42. A harpacticoid copepod; photomicrograph

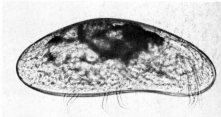

43. An ostracode; photomicrograph

44. A calanoid copepod; photomicrograph

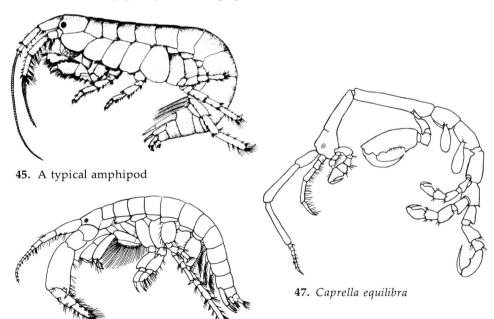

45. A typical amphipod

47. *Caprella equilibra*

46. *Corophium,* an amphipod characterized by stout antennae

sphaeroma is most likely to be found living under mussels, among barnacles, or in cavities in wood mined by shipworms and the gribble, *Limnoria*. Large populations of it are usually an indication that the salinity is at least a little below that of full-strength sea water.

Shrimps.   Clinging to seaweeds, and generally going unnoticed until they flop off when a bunch of weed is lifted, are the "broken-back" shrimps of the genus *Heptacarpus* (fig. 49). They range from about 2 to 3 cm in length and are characterized by a sharp bend in the region of the third abdominal segment. Like some other shrimps, and also crayfishes, they propel themselves backward by rapidly flexing their tails forward, so that they are momentarily almost U-shaped. Most broken-back shrimps have a translucent look and generally are colored green, olive, brown, or reddish brown, often with some opaque white markings or darker streaks, especially on the thorax.

Once in awhile, the relatively large, nearly straight-bodied shrimps of the genus *Pandalus* are seen gingerly poised on the floats or swimming by. These are the commercially important shrimps of our region and may reach a length of 15 cm or more. The dock shrimp or coon-stripe shrimp, *P. danae* (fig. 50), with rather strong brown, red, and nearly white markings, is perhaps the one most likely to occur around floats.

Crabs.   The crabs on floats are chiefly those that look something like spiders, because of their proportionately long and slender legs. The kelp crab, *Pugettia producta* (fig. 191), is the largest of these, its carapace attaining a length of 5 cm or more. Its coloration is on the whole olive or olive brown, but there may be some attractive red or orange tones on the lower surface. The upper side of the carapace is smooth and does not normally accumulate growths of small seaweeds or sessile animals such as sponges or bryozoans.

Pugettia gracilis (fig. 358) is a smaller cousin of *P. producta*. Unlike the latter, its upper surface is somewhat roughened and almost always has some algae and animals growing on it, so that its reddish brown color may be almost completely obscured. Crabs that allow other organisms to grow on them, or that actually stick these organisms on their carapaces, are called decorator crabs. Even more inclined to be decorated is *Oregonia gracilis* (fig. 192). This species has a carapace that is almost triangular in shape, with its narrowed anterior end prolonged into two long, nearly parallel rostral horns. The color is mostly light tan, and is just about matched by the color of the sponges, hydroids, and bryozoans that are usually found on the carapace and frequently on the legs as well.

Barnacles.   Three species of barnacles are common on floats and pilings. One of them, *Balanus glandula* (fig. 99; pl. 11) is the most nearly

48. *Limnoria lignorum*

49. *Heptacarpus*

50. *Pandalus danae*

51. *Balanus crenatus*

ubiquitous barnacle on the Pacific coast. It is characteristic of the upper reaches of the rocky intertidal region, so more will be said about it in Chapter 4. On pilings, nearly all of the barnacles at levels reached only by higher tides are *B. glandula*, unless *Chthamalus dalli* (fig. 98) is present. (The latter is almost strictly limited to rocks.) On floats, *B. glandula* is likely to be concentrated at the waterline, or just slightly above it. The individuals above the surface, of course, are able to feed only when the water is sufficiently agitated that waves splash over them.

A distinctive feature of *Balanus glandula* is the way the plates in the "crater" fit together when the animal is inactive. The line separating the two smaller plates from the two larger plates is markedly sinuous. Large specimens are about 1.5 cm in diameter. The height is about equal to the diameter, except in the case of individuals that are crowded together; these tend to be nearly columnar. The shell, unless covered by diatoms or otherwise overgrown, is generally grayish white and rather smooth.

Balanus crenatus (fig. 51) is similar to *B. glandula*, but even more smooth and almost pure white. The line between the smaller and larger plates of the closing apparatus is much less sinuous than it is in *B. glandula*. *Balanus crenatus* is basically a subtidal species, and is not so likely as *B. glandula* to be found at or above the waterline. It sometimes forms dense aggregations, but even then it tends to remain broader than tall. The diameter reaches 2 cm.

Semibalanus cariosus (fig. 108), like *B. glandula*, is common on rocky shores. Specimens growing singly may reach a diameter of 5 cm, and they show clearly the characteristic ridges and furrows of the shell. The ridges actually consist of spinelike outgrowths that point downward and that are often fused together. When *S. cariosus* forms dense masses, it is forced to grow in a nearly columnar shape, and the ridges may then be scarcely evident. On floats, however, *S. cariosus* does not often become crowded the way *B. glandula* does, and it is usually distinctly below the waterline. On pilings as on rocks, its vertical distribution is on the whole lower than that of *B. glandula*.

Barnacles are remarkably specialized crustaceans. In the so-called acorn barnacles, such as *Balanus*, the shell consists of a number of overlapping plates, and some other plates, controlled by muscles, close the opening at the top of the shell. All of the plates are secreted by a sort of mantle that surrounds the soft parts of the animal. The barnacle's counterparts of a crab's legs are six pairs of what look like rather soft, branched feathers, called cirri. As the cirri are rhythmically extended and retracted, they quite literally comb the water for microscopic food. The mouth parts collect the material strained out by the cirri and move it to the mouth.

Although adult barnacles might not easily be accepted as crustaceans, their life history includes certain developmental stages that pos-

itively establish the relationship. The first larval stage, called a nauplius, is similar to the nauplius of other groups of crustaceans in having three pairs of appendages: the first and second antennae and mandibles of later stages. But, the barnacle nauplius is unique in having a
pair of extensions, resembling handlebars, arising laterally from the
anterior part of the carapace. After some changes and additions, accomplished between several molts, the developing barnacle arrives at
the cypris stage. This has the appendages of the nauplius, some additional mouth parts, and six pairs of thoracic limbs. If this cypris
settles on a suitable substratum, it fastens itself with the help of a
cement produced by glands associated with the first antennae. The
bivalve shell of the cypris is lost, and the complex metamorphosis into
a barnacle is completed. The limbs of the cypris survive as the food-
catching cirri.

Molluscs

Chitons. The chitons most likely to be found on floats are *Tonicella
lineata* (pl. 10) and any of the three species of *Mopalia* of the Puget
Sound region: *M. muscosa* (fig. 172), *M. ciliata* (fig. 173), and *M. lignosa*
(fig. 174). All of these species are described in the section on rocky
shores, as they are not often encountered on floats.

Limpets. *Collisella pelta* (*Acmaea pelta*) (fig. 110) is the only limpet
one is likely to find on floats. It has a rather tall shell, in which the
apex is nearer the middle than the anterior edge. The length reaches
about 4 cm. As this species is typical of rocky shores, it is discussed
in more detail in Chapter 5.

Sea Slugs. Many species of nudibranch gastropods ("sea slugs") are
known to occur on floats in the region, but only a few of these are
"regulars." Some are inseparably linked to other invertebrates. Two of
them, *Doridella* and *Corambe,* have been discussed in connection with
the bryozoan *Membranipora. Eubranchus,* which lives on *Obelia,* will
be mentioned shortly.
  Phidiana crassicornis (Hermissenda crassicornis) (pl. 16) is perhaps the
most nearly ubiquitous of the nudibranchs. It is found in beds of eelgrass and in rocky intertidal areas, and is sometimes the prevailing
larger species on floats. It belongs to a group of nudibranchs called
eolids (or aeolids), characterized by the presence of numerous fleshy
dorsal processes termed cerata (in addition to the pair of clubshaped
tentacles called rhinophores, on the head) and also by the absence of
any plumelike gills around the anus. In *Phidiana* the cerata, set on a
translucent and nearly white body, have an orange band close to their
ends and are finally capped with white. The brown cores of the cerata
are actually branches of the liverlike digestive gland, which go up into

them. The coloration displays some other distinctive features. An orange band runs some distance backward from between the rhinophores, and there is frequently a similar band farther posteriorly. These orange bands are bordered by opaque white or electric blue lines which begin on the tentacles and run to the tip of the tail. A large *Phidiana* is about 5 cm long when it is stretched out.

Although most nudibranchs are rather particular about what they eat, *Phidiana* is not fussy. It consumes, among other things, hydroids, ascidians, other molluscs, eggs of various sorts, and pieces of fish. Some of the stinging capsules it ingests with hydroids end up in the tips of the cerata, where they are stored in an unexploded state. By pulling off a ceras, mounting it under a coverglass, and examining it with a microscope, one can observe the concentration of stinging capsules. Many eolid nudibranchs store these structures, and they probably have a protective function.

Aeolidia papillosa (pl. 16) is an eolid just a little larger than *Phidiana* and about as adaptable as far as habitats are concerned. It is considerably more choosy about food, however, and apparently eats anemones almost exclusively. On floats, of course, the variety of anemones available to it is restricted, but it will take both *Metridium* and *Tealia*. The body of *Aeolidia* is whitish and translucent, with some gray or brown spots, and usually has a large, triangular white patch, devoid of cerata, in the area in front of the rhinophores. The cerata are typically grayish brown, sometimes with white tips, but they can be almost colorless. They are so numerous and so crowded that *Aeolidia* looks like a shaggy little mouse.

Colonies of *Obelia* (especially *O. dichotoma*) are generally inhabited by the tiny eolid, *Eubranchus olivaceus* (fig. 6). It is pale yellowish green and has both dark and light flecks. Its relatively few cerata are swollen and bumpy to the point of nearly branching. Mature specimens are about 6 or 7 mm long. *Eubranchus* is a predator on *Obelia* and nips off the polyps as it wanders through its horn of plenty. Its little egg masses are regularly found along with it.

A rather different group of nudibranchs, called dendronotids, are represented in our area by several species of *Dendronotus*. In dendronotids, the cerata are branched; and as the ultimate branches have sharp tips, the cerata in some species look a bit like thorny bushes. Around the rhinophores are sheaths with extensions in the form of simple or branched papillae. Unfortunately, only two species of these beautiful animals, *D. frondosus* and *D. rufus*, are found on floats; the rest are subtidal. *Dendronotus frondosus* (pl. 16) is generally not over 4 cm long. Its color varies immensely, and specimens taken on floats are usually quite different from those collected in deeper water. The body as a whole may be almost completely white, with just some pinkish brown spots; it may be pale brown with yellow or white on the cerata and elsewhere; or it may be dark reddish brown with white or yellow markings. *D. frondosus* eats a variety of hydroids, including *Tubularia* and *Sarsia* among the athecate types and *Obelia* among the thecate types. On floats it seems to prefer the latter, of which there is no shortage.

Dendronotus rufus (pl. 16) is a large species, attaining a length of nearly 30 cm. It has from six to nine pairs of bushy cerata and several smaller cerata as well. The background color of the upper surface is usually white, with the branches of the cerata and of the rhinophores being dark reddish brown or dull magenta. In most specimens, there is a magenta line around the upper part of the foot. *Dendronotus rufus* feeds to a large extent on the scyphistomae of jellyfishes, and its presence on floats is a good indication that these little polyps are plentiful.

The dorid nudibranchs, another large category, do not have true cerata into which branches of the digestive gland ascend. They may, however, have dorsal tubercles and other fleshy processes. Their hallmark is a circle of featherlike gills surrounding the anus, which is located on the dorsal surface in the posterior region of the body. A common and sometimes beautiful dorid found on floats, as well as in rocky intertidal situations, is *Archidoris montereyensis,* the sea lemon (pl. 14). Its color is basically yellow, but the exact shade and intensity vary. There are patches of black pigment on the tubercles as well as on the areas between them. *A. montereyensis* commonly reaches a length of about 5 cm. Its diet consists entirely of sponges, especially *Halichondria*.

Anisodoris nobilis (pl. 14), which reaches a length of about 10 cm, resembles *Archidoris montereyensis* and has the same food preferences. It has much less black pigment, however, and the pigment rarely touches the tubercles. The basic color, which ranges from pale yellow to bright orange-yellow, is clear, whereas in *A. montereyensis* it is often dingy.

Archidoris odhneri (pl. 14), another sponge eater, looks as though it might be an albino version of either of the two species just discussed, for it is absolutely white. Large specimens are about 5 or 6 cm long.

Discodoris sandiegensis (Diaulula sandiegensis) (pl. 14) feeds on both *Halichondria* and *Haliclona*. Its basic color is generally pale gray, with several conspicuous rings or blotches of blackish brown superimposed on it. The dorsal surface is very firm and feels almost gritty because of the many small, hairlike projections of the skin. The six gills can be completely retracted. Large specimens may be nearly 8 cm long, but most fall into the range of 4 to 5 cm.

Mussels, Scallops, and Other Bivalves.   Most of the bivalves found on floats and pilings are firmly attached to the substratum by a byssus, secreted by a gland at the base of the foot. The foot of such bivalves is much reduced when compared with that of clams that burrow in mud or sand.

The prevailing bivalve on floats and pilings is *Mytilus edulis,* the bay mussel or edible mussel (pl. 17). Its byssus is composed of many brownish threads—looking more vegetable than animal in texture—extending out ventrally between the valves. The byssus threads are somewhat elastic, but hold the animal firmly to the substratum. The shell of *M. edulis* reaches a length of about 6 cm and varies considerably in color. Typically, it is dark blue-black or brownish black, but young specimens are often brown. Like almost all bivalves, *Mytilus* is a filter feeder. In an animal that is actively processing water from which the ctenidia, or gills, collect microscopic food, the exhalant siphon is just evident at the rounded, posterior end. There is no real inhalant siphon, as water enters by a rather broad gape on the ventral side, between the right and left folds of the mantle.

The dense masses formed by *M. edulis* provide protection and other biological necessities for many other organisms. The shells themselves serve as a substratum to which a variety of animals, such as barnacles, hydroids, bryozoans, and ascidians, may become attached. On pilings, this mussel has a wide vertical range, and some populations are so high that they are out of water much of the time.

The jingle shell, or rock oyster, *Pododesmus cepio* (fig. 52), is tightly stuck to the substratum by a heavy, hard byssus that emerges through a hole in one of the valves. The valves are nearly circular, sometimes 10 cm in diameter. If the animal happens to have settled on a substratum that is not flat, the shells will be deformed to follow its contour; some are bent nearly to a ninety-degree angle. The flesh of the jingle shell, which can be seen if the animal is actively pumping water and the valves are separated slightly, is bright orange.

Scallops (*Chlamys*) are primarily animals of deeper water and tend to be concentrated on substrata in which gravel and shells predominate. They lie with the right valve against the substratum and may be cemented down to this by a byssus secreted by a gland on the much-reduced foot. There are no siphons, as the mantle margins are separate all the way around. When the shell is agape and the animal is actively processing water from which its ctenidia collect microscopic food, the sensitive tentacles projecting from the edge of the mantle will be evident, and the shining blue-green ocelli (simple eyes) may also be seen just inside the edge. The ocelli are sensitive to changes in light intensity and are rather complicated, but they do not form images. When stimulated by certain predators, such as a sea star whose tube feet have contacted the mantle, the scallop claps its valves together repeatedly and may succeed in propelling itself away from danger. Of the species of scallops in Puget Sound and the San Juan Archipelago, one— *Chlamys hastata,* the pink scallop (figs. 187 and 188)—is rather frequently seen in intertidal areas and on floats. Its shell is about 6 cm high. It differs from *C. rubida,* with which it is mixed subtidally, in

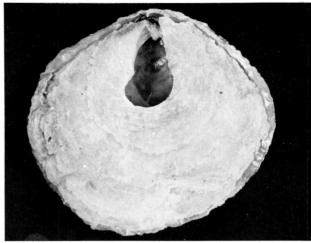

52. *Pododesmus cepio,* the jingle shell. The byssus by which the animal is attached to the substratum emerges through a hole in one valve (*right*).

53. Burrows of the shipworm, *Bankia setacea,* in an old piling. The pallets of a deceased inhabitant are shown in one of the burrows.

having its radiating ribs roughened by small, arched spines, and also in having rougher margins.

The destruction of wooden timbers by the gribble, a small isopod, was discussed in the section on Crustacea. The gribble is often joined in this enterprise by the shipworm, *Bankia setacea*, a decidedly bizarre bivalve mollusc. It is often referred to as *Teredo*, but genuine teredos are rarely reported in the Puget Sound area.

The shipworm's burrows (fig. 53) may be large enough to take a pencil comfortably. Unlike those of the gribble, which are concentrated in the superficial layers of a timber, they go very deep. When the microscopic planktonic larva of *Bankia* settles on a suitable substratum and metamorphoses into a tiny clam, it commences working its way into the timber. It digs by rocking its roughened shell with respect to its foot, rotating on the foot periodically, and thus carves out a neat, tubular burrow. The wood it rasps away goes into the digestive tract. At least some of the cellulose is converted by an enzyme (cellulase) into simpler carbohydrates that the shipworm can use as food. Much of what it swallows, however, seems to be undigested and passes out the anus, to be carried away by the current of water moving out of the exhalant siphon. *Bankia*, although adapted to a way of life quite different from that of most clams, has preserved the system of filter feeding characteristic of its relatives. Its ctenidia process water by ciliary action, and food, in the form of microscopic organisms and other particulate material, is moved to the mouth by ciliary-mucous tracts.

When a timber burrowed by *Bankia* is cracked open, a number of live animals may be found in the deeper portions. (Even timbers that have been lying on the beach for a few days may have live shipworms inside.) Note that the burrows generally follow the grain and do not break into one another. The shells of *Bankia* are small in proportion to the rest of the body and resemble little shields with a filelike decoration. They abut the head of the burrow where they can do the most good (or the most harm, depending on how one looks at it). The odd, calcareous, featherlike structures, called pallets, often found even in inactive burrows, serve to close the burrow when the siphons are retracted. Like the thin, calcareous film lining the burrow, the pallets are secreted by the mantle.

Squids. Squids are almost never seen at floats during the daytime, and it is unusual for them to show up at night. Specimens that do come into the range of dock lights are usually immature, but almost all of them can be referred to one or the other of two species, *Loligo opalescens* and *Gonatus fabricii*. In both, the mantle (the conical part of the body behind the head) reaches a length of about 15 cm. In *L. opalescens* (fig. 54), however, the eight arms and two specialized tentacles

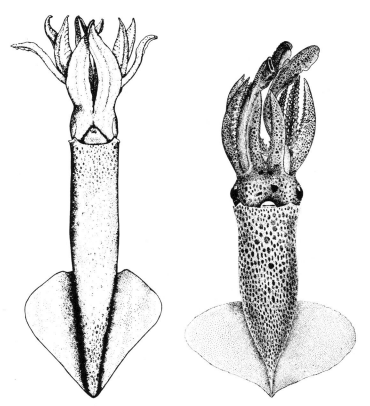

54. *Loligo opalescens* **55.** *Gonatus fabricii*

are shorter in proportion to the length of the mantle than they are in *G. fabricii* (fig. 55). The tail fins of *Loligo* are also less ample than those of *Gonatus*. Most squids, including our species, feed on small fishes, shrimps, and some other swimming invertebrates. They use their tentacles for capturing prey, the arms for holding it securely, and the beaklike jaws for biting it until it is quiet and can be swallowed. Squids swim backward by jet propulsion, forcing water out of the mantle cavity through a funnellike extension of the latter.

Just about everything squids do is interesting, but the way they can change their pattern of pigmentation with respect to the substratum is particularly striking. When on a light background, a squid tends to contract its pigment-containing cells so that the pigment becomes concentrated in tiny, widely spaced flecks; the body as a whole thus becomes lighter. On a dark background, the pigment cells expand, diffusing the pigment over a larger area and making the body darker.

Once in a rare while, a giant squid, with a total length of 2 m or more, is washed up. It is usually dead for all practical purposes, but the pigment cells of the skin may still be reactive. This large species invariably proves to be *Moroteuthis robusta*.

Echinoderms

The fauna of echinoderms in the Puget Sound area is astonishingly rich, but little of it will be seen on the floats. At best, there are usually only two species of sea stars, two sea cucumbers, and one sea urchin.

Sea Stars. The sea stars found on floating docks and pilings are generally either *Pisaster ochraceus* (fig. 124; pl. 25) or *Evasterias troschelii* (pl. 25). Both are large: *Pisaster* regularly reaches a diameter of about 25 cm; larger specimens of *Evasterias* are usually in the range of 25 to 30 cm, but this species looks more graceful because its disk is smaller and its arms more slender. Within Puget Sound and the San Juan Archipelago, *Pisaster* belies its species name because it is represented almost exclusively by a vivid purple phase. The coloration of *Evasterias* is variable—it may be gray, gray-green, brown, or nearly red. It is never really purple, however. Both these sea stars are discussed in connection with rocky shores, but it is important to point out here that they are among the chief predators of the float fauna, taking a steady toll of mussels, other bivalves, and barnacles.

Solaster stimpsoni (pl. 26) has been seen on floats, but it is uncommon. It is usually found in the lower intertidal region of rocky shores and is therefore described in Chapter 4.

Sea Cucumbers. The principal cucumber on floats is *Eupentacta quinquesemita* (fig. 56), which is basically cream-colored and faintly tinged with orange or apricot. It attains a length of about 10 cm, but is usually hidden among masses of worm tubes or mussels. The tube feet are crowded and rather slender when fully extended; all five sets of them are well developed. The bushy tentacles around the mouth are modified tube feet and are interesting to watch. After an oral tentacle becomes more or less "saturated" with detritus and miscroscopic food organisms, it bends into the mouth as the accumulated material is licked off. Then another tentacle will do the same thing.

Eupentacta is among the many sea cucumbers that may become eviscerated when handled roughly or subjected to other forms of stress. A portion of the digestive tract and some other internal organs are simply ejected following a rupture of the body wall usually at one end or the other. The missing parts are eventually regenerated. The eviscerative habit of *Eupentacta* (and of some of the other sea cucumbers in the area) works to the good fortune of a group of strange snails that live in the body cavity. These are modified to the extreme: they have no shells and look like soft, white worms. However, their affinities are betrayed by certain stages in their development, and especially by a type of larva called the veliger. The larvae would have no avenue of escape from the body cavity, and thus could not infect other sea cucumbers, if it were not for an occasional evisceration by the host.

Cucumaria miniata is a larger, reddish or reddish brown sea cucumber found on floats in some places. It is not common, so its description can be deferred until its typical habitat, the lowermost zone of the rocky intertidal region, is discussed in Chapter 4.

Sea Urchins.   Of the several sea urchins in our area, the only one that seems able to survive on floats is *Strongylocentrotus droebachiensis*, the green sea urchin (pl. 24). It is abundant in rocky intertidal areas, as well as subtidally on various substrata. In favorable situations its test reaches a diameter of about 8 cm; on floats, where it is a bit out of place, it is rarely larger than 5 or 6 cm. This urchin feeds largely on algal growths, which it chews up with the aid of five sharp-toothed jaws. These jaws are organized into a beautifully unified structure that is commonly called Aristotle's lantern. It is only fair to point out, however, that this term was first applied to the test of sea urchins, not to the jaw complex.

In all of the echinoderms mentioned above, the eggs and sperm are discharged into the sea. If the eggs are fertilized, they develop into a distinctive planktonic stage that has bilateral symmetry instead of the radial symmetry characteristic of adult echinoderms. Presumably the animals on floats are derived from larvae that have merely settled and metamorphosed in this situation. These larvae, then, could have been derived from eggs shed by individuals living in completely different habitats many miles away.

Chaetognaths

If the water surface is very quiet and the sun is shining brightly, you may see what looks like a sliver of ice, up to about 2 cm long, seemingly just suspended in the water. If you can capture it, you will probably find it to be an arrow worm, a member of the phylum Chaetognatha. *Sagitta elegans* (fig. 57) is the only species of this interesting group of marine animals found within our area, though others will be encountered in the open ocean. With few exceptions, they are strictly planktonic. Arrow worms are almost completely transparent, except for a pair of little black eyespots on the head, so they are next to impossible to see unless brightly illuminated from one side. However, they can be very numerous; and if a net is towed through the water for a few minutes, it may pick up many more than one might have expected on the basis of seeing a single specimen free in the water.

Arrow worms are an important link in the food chain, for they eat small crustaceans and fish larvae, and serve in turn as food for other animals, especially fishes. *Sagitta elegans* is more or less cosmopolitan and, along with some other organisms, has proved to be valuable for identifying water masses. In this respect it has helped researchers attempting to predict runs of herring.

Although much of an arrow worm's time is spent lying motionless, the prospect of a meal may cause it quite literally to spring into action.

With powerful strokes of its finned tail, it quickly leaps a few lengths to where its sensory receptors indicate the prey is located, and its jaws, composed of stiff, sharp bristles, snap shut on the victim.

Ascidians

Ascidians are filter-feeding animals that process sea water for the microscopic food it contains. By the activity of cilia, ascidians bring water through an incurrent opening (often on a siphonlike eminence) into a large perforated pharynx which functions as a kind of mechanical sieve. Fine particles and small microorganisms are trapped in mucus. Cilia then move the mucus containing the food to one side of the pharynx, and there the mucus is compacted into a string, which is directed by cilia into the digestive tract proper.

Around the pharynx is a cavity called the atrium, and the water entering the atrium from the pharynx leaves by way of a second opening, the excurrent (atrial) pore. The anus and ducts from the gonads (both testis and ovary are usually present in each individual) enter the atrium also, so wastes and gametes leave by the same pore as water that has been processed by the pharynx for the food it may have contained.

The nature of an ascidian cannot be understood without an appreciation of its development. A larval stage, called the "tadpole," shows certain features that are lost or at least so much changed in the adult that they cannot readily be recognized. Some ascidians release their eggs and sperm into the sea as soon as they are ripe, and in these species the development of the tadpole takes place outside the body; others retain their eggs in the atrial cavity or in a pocket of the atrium that serves as a brood pouch, so that the tadpole develops there. In any case, the tadpole shows certain structures more clearly than the adult does. These structures are the notochord, a rodlike organ consisting of large cells, running most of the length of the tail; and the nerve cord, which extends from the swollen anterior portion of the body into the tail, where it is dorsal to the notochord. The gut is blind and nonfunctional; and the pharynx, although it has a few perforations already, is simple compared to what it will become after proliferation of many more openings. There are other complications of anatomy that need not be dealt with here. The main point is that the tadpole shows a plan of structure—pharyngeal slits, a notochord, and a dorsal nerve cord—somewhat like that in amphioxus and lampreys, and at least in embryos of other fishes and higher vertebrates. For this reason, ascidians have long been considered to be close relatives of vertebrates. The relationship has been questioned, however, and we really do not know how close ascidians are to vertebrates.

The ascidian tadpole, when ready to develop further, usually has only a few hours to find a suitable substratum and to settle and metamorphose; otherwise it will die. By muscular activity of its tail, used in the fashion of a sculling oar, it drives its anterior end against the substratum. If it manages to stick in a favorable place (the adhesion is facilitated by some glandular papillae), the tail is resorbed and the body becomes completely reorganized. A tunic of a carbohydrate chemically related to cellulose is laid down around the animal. This tunic, although essentially a secreted layer, does have some living tissue and even blood vessels in it.

The heart of an ascidian has the curious ability to pump blood in either direction. It is a thin but muscular sac, which in the case of species with a transparent tunic may readily be seen without dissection. *Corella* is an admirable subject in which to observe the activity of the heart, whose contractions resemble the wringing out of a wet rag.

The ascidians found on floats can be divided into two groups: those that live singly (solitary ascidians) and those that form colonies consisting of several to many individuals embedded in a common matrix (compound ascidians). The colony of a compound ascidian is built up by asexual reproduction and coincident secretion of additional tunic material.

Solitary Ascidians. Of the five solitary ascidians to be considered here, two are particularly undistinguished in appearance. In both, the tunic is a translucent dingy brown and often supports a coating of diatoms and other small organisms. One species, *Ascidia callosa* (fig. 58), is more or less hemispherical, with its flattened lower side in tight contact with the substratum. The upper side shows two small elevations marking the incurrent and excurrent siphons. Larger specimens are about 3 cm in diameter. The other species, *Chelyosoma productum* (fig. 59), is firm in texture and sharply truncate. The flat upper surface, on which both siphons are situated, is composed of thin, horny plates which are generally evident without magnification. Its diameter does not often exceed 2 cm.

Pyura haustor (fig. 60), like the two preceding ascidians, is broadly attached to the substratum, sometimes to another member of its own species. When extended, however, it is quite tall, reaching a height of about 5 cm. Its siphons are pronounced, smooth, and of a gorgeous pinkish red color. Over the rest of its body the tunic, usually brown or reddish brown, is thick, tough, and wrinkled. Bits of shell or other hard material may be embedded in it, and it may be colonized by various small organisms.

Boltenia villosa (fig. 61) is a pale orange-brown color and is distinctly stalked, though the length of the stalk in proportion to the size of the body as a whole is variable. The most unusual characteristic of *Boltenia* is the presence of numerous hairlike outgrowths of the tunic. On floats, this species rarely approaches the maximum height (about 5 cm) attained by specimens found on rocky coasts, especially subtidally, but specimens up to 3 cm high are fairly common.

The most beautiful solitary ascidian on the floats is *Corella willmeriana* (fig. 62). Its tunic looks like ice, being colorless and generally free of encrusting organisms. Some of the internal organs—pharynx, digestive tract, and heart—can be recognized without having to be exposed by dissection. *Corella* may be attached to mussels or tubes of sabellids, but it is more often stuck to the float itself. It lives only about a year. Very large specimens, around 3 cm tall, are most likely to be found during the winter months. It is most striking when hundreds of individuals form tightly packed clusters, which resemble confections or sheets of lumpy ice. Such aggregations are more apt to be seen on the lower reaches of pilings exposed by very low tides than on floats.

Styela montereyensis (pl. 28), primarily found in rocky intertidal habitats of the open coast, is abundant on floats and pilings in the harbor at Neah Bay, Washington, and also at Bamfield, on the west coast of Vancouver Island. It is a tough-bodied ascidian with a long stalk and prominent lengthwise ridges and grooves. The color is mostly light tan. Large individuals are about 15 cm tall. This species often has hydroids, small bryozoans, and other organisms growing on it. More will be said about it in Chapter 5.

Compound Ascidians. Of the compound ascidians found in the area, only two are regularly associated with floats. *Distaplia occidentalis* (fig. 59; pl. 29) is more or less ubiquitous. Its colonies range from orange to purple in color, and are generally about the size of an olive, though they may be several times as big. Most colonies are shaped something like a mushroom. The individual zooids are small, but as they are of a light yellowish or orange color, they can usually be distinguished within the common tunic. Each zooid has its own incurrent siphon, but a single excurrent opening serves a circle of several zooids; the atrial cavities of these zooids are therefore continuous.

Distaplia reproduces sexually during the spring or summer. Each zooid produces only a few eggs at a time. The eggs are not released into the sea, but are retained in a sort of brood pouch derived from the atrial cavity, where they develop into the tadpole stage. Colonies of *Distaplia* are therefore useful sources of essentially typical ascidian tadpoles for class study.

Diplosoma macdonaldi (pl. 29) will occasionally be noted by the sharp-eyed observer. It forms rather thin, gelatinous encrustations on floats, seaweeds, and worm tubes. (It also lives on rocks that are continually submerged.) The color is grayish or brownish, but the colonies are translucent and nearly homogeneous even though they contain hundreds or thousands of zooids. The excurrent openings, each serving several zooids, are often on prominent elevations.

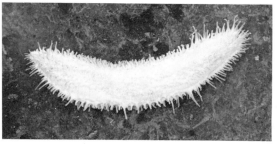

56. *Eupentacta quinquesemita*

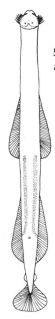

57. *Sagitta elegans,* an arrow worm

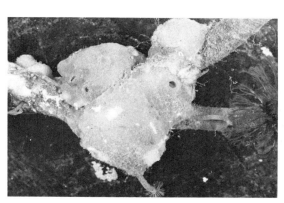

58. *Ascidia callosa*

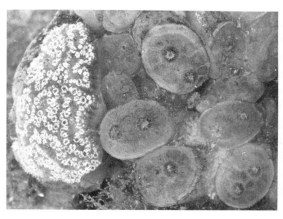

59. *Chelyosoma productum* (*right*) and *Distaplia occidentalis,* a compound ascidian (*left*)

60. *Pyura haustor*

61. *Boltenia villosa*

62. *Corella willmeriana*

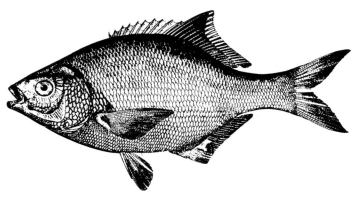

63. *Rhacochilus vacca,* the pile perch

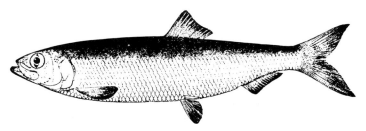

64. *Clupea harengus pallasi,* the Pacific herring

65. *Ammodytes hexapterus,* the sand lance

Fishes

The most common of the larger, deep-bodied fishes seen around docks is the pile perch *Rhacochilus vacca* (fig. 63). It belongs to the family Embiotocidae, which includes the surfperches that anglers try to catch with hook and line on sandy beaches of the open coast. These fishes are like guppies in that the females, instead of laying eggs, bear their young alive. The pile perch reaches a length of about 40 cm and resembles a freshwater perch or sunfish in having a dorsal fin that consists of a spiny-rayed anterior portion and a soft posterior portion. The color is mostly silvery, but the back is dark and there are blackish blotches on the sides. Young specimens usually have dark vertical bars. This species eats a variety of animals, and small mussels make up much of its diet. It swallows these whole, crushes them, and eliminates the shell fragments with other fecal matter.

The only fishes likely to be seen swimming in large schools around the docks are the Pacific herring (*Clupea harengus pallasi*) (fig. 64) and the Pacific sand lance (*Ammodytes hexapterus*) (fig. 65). They are about the same color—silvery on the sides, dark above—but are otherwise so different that they can be identified without being taken out of the water. The herring, which may reach a length of more than 25 cm, but which is generally under 20 cm, has about the same proportions as a trout. The dorsal fin is short—only about one-eighth the length of the body.

The sand lance, usually less than 20 cm long, is more slender than the herring, and its dorsal fin is about three-fourths the length of the body. The common name refers to the fact that this fish can bury itself in sand, and it will do this even on wave-swept beaches of the open coast.

Both the herring and sand lance feed on various small organisms, especially crustaceans and fish larvae, that are in the plankton. The herring is gathered commercially for food, for the production of oil and fish meal, and for bait. The sand lance, though tasty, is of no commercial importance.

Algae

The algal flora on floating docks is not as varied as it is on rocky coasts, but it has some interesting surprises. A number of species found on floats are characteristically either subtidal or found only at lower levels of the intertidal region. Just a few species that are regularly encountered will be dealt with here, however. In addition to the algae large enough to be called seaweeds, there are many microscopic plants. Among these are diatoms (fig. 66), which are well represented on floats, generally forming scummy brownish growths over the primary substratum and over other organisms.

Some diatoms form filamentous colonies that might be confused with small brown algae. At least one of the species of *Navicula* common on floats in the Puget Sound region produces filaments that are somewhat flattened and dichotomously branched (fig. 67). When examined with a microscope, the filaments are seen to consist of separate diatom cells embedded in a transparent matrix (fig. 68). The name *Schizonema* has, in the past, been applied to filamentous colonies of *Navicula*.

Green Algae. The green algae on floats range from semimicroscopic filamentous types to larger forms that can confidently be assigned to the right genus in the field. In many harbors, the sea lettuce, *Ulva* (pls. 32 and 35), is decidedly the dominant alga. On floats exposed to considerable sunlight, *Ulva* grows so luxuriantly that there is little room for anything else. The thalli are thin, transparent sheets, bright green in color, and often rather crinkly. They are two cell-layers thick, a point that has to be established by microscopic examination of thin slices. Experts have disagreed with respect to the names that should be applied to the broad-bladed species of *Ulva* on the Pacific coast of North America. These algae are extremely variable, and their habit of growth is affected by water temperature and other environmental cir-

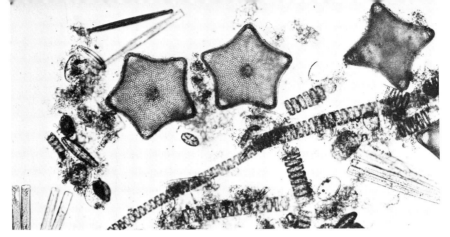

66. A variety of diatoms; photomicrograph

67. Branching filamentous colonies of a species of *Navicula* ("*Schizonema*")

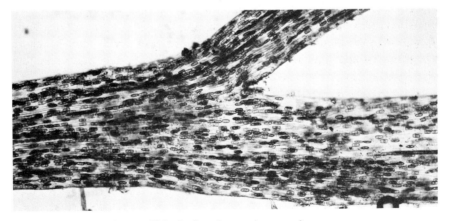

68. Portion of a colony of *Navicula;* photomicrograph

96 / On and Around Floating Docks and Pilings

cumstances. At the present time, it appears likely that the common *Ulva* on floats in the Puget Sound region is *U. fenestrata*. On sand and mud in quiet bays, this species is often perforated (see pl. 32); in other habitats, however, it may have no perforations at all, except for those made by grazing animals.

An alga similar to *Ulva*, and often mixed with it on floats and in other habitats, is *Ulvaria*, chiefly represented in this region by *U. fusca* (*Monostroma fuscum*). Its thalli are only one cell-layer thick. When young, it forms a bright green sac, but this breaks open into a flat sheet, and as the thallus ages it may become more nearly olive. If dried, this seaweed will almost invariably turn brown or olive brown.

Enteromorpha linza (fig. 69) is of the same general color as *Ulva*, but it grows in the form of flattened tubes. It is tolerant of rather low salinities and is therefore the principal alga in some estuarine situations.

Blidingia minima (fig. 70) could be confused with *Enteromorpha linza* or with other species of this genus, because of its bright green, basically tubular thalli. In *Enteromorpha*, however, each thallus is separate, and its lowermost portion, where it is attached, produces little rootlike outgrowths; in *Blidingia* several thalli arise from one basal "cushion," and the individual thalli lack rootlike processes. *Blidingia minima* is more likely to be found on pilings or on rocks that are uncovered by the tide than on floats or other situations where it is continually submerged. A closely related species, *B. subsalsa* (fig. 71), is characteristic of brackish water. It occasionally grows on floats, or accumulates next to them after floating in from a mudflat, salt marsh, or slough nearby. The thalli of *B. subsalsa*, often tangled together, have slender branches, and are generally detached from the basal cushions that produced them. It should be mentioned that *B. subsalsa* is sometimes common in freshwater ditches, including many that run into San Francisco Bay. A complication one should be aware of is that *Enteromorpha clathrata*, extensively branched in much the same way as *B. subsalsa*, is also found in brackish-water habitats. The *Ulva-Ulvaria-Enteromorpha-Blidingia* complex is difficult because the species in these genera vary a great deal, and certain species of one genus may closely resemble those in another genus. If positive identification is necessary, one will have to turn to specialized references.

Bryopsis corticulans (fig. 72) is often found on floats, and also at low-tide levels on pilings. The many main stems that come from the holdfast are slender and cylindrical. They reach a length of about 15 cm and branch in a nearly featherlike pattern. In spite of its delicate nature, this alga tends to have a deep green color.

Codium fragile (pl. 31), often abundant at lower levels of the intertidal zone, is sometimes seen on floats in the San Juan Archipelago. There is no other alga that can be confused with it. Its nearly cylindrical branches commonly reach a diameter of 5 or 6 cm, and are sometimes of such a dark green color that they are nearly black. This species is more fully described in Chapter 4. It is, in any case, not common enough on floats to be considered characteristic of this habitat.

A semimicroscopic green alga sometimes common on floats is the spore-producing generation of *Derbesia marina* (fig. 73). It grows as rather stiff, blunt-tipped filaments that branch periodically. Here and there one may find the little ovoid structures within which the spores are produced. The spores, under appropriate circumstances, develop into the sexual stage, which was called *Halicystis ovalis* before its relationship with *Derbesia* was established. "*Halicystis*" forms little greenish globules, about 1 cm high, in the lower reaches of rocky intertidal areas, especially where there is an encrustation of coralline red algae. It liberates gametes, and the products of the union of these develop into the filamentous stage.

Brown Algae. In terms of total mass, the most conspicuous seaweed on floats is usually *Laminaria saccharina* (fig. 74). It merits being called a kelp, a term applicable to any large brown alga. The holdfast consists of a number of branching, rootlike structures and may provide a home or hiding place for a variety of worms and other invertebrates. The cylindrical stipe, which may be very short or more than 20 cm long, widens out gradually into the blade. This is usually several times longer than wide and is characterized by two series of blisterlike areas (bullations) running most of its length. (Very young plants, and some older ones as well, lack bullations.) The blades of large specimens may be over a meter long, but they are often badly torn.

A handsome kelp often growing with *Laminaria* is *Costaria costata* (fig. 75). Its broad blade has several strong ribs, but these are raised only on one side. The bullations between the ribs are conspicuous. The stipe is short, and the part that fans out into the blade is usually furrowed.

Quite a different sort of brown alga is *Desmarestia viridis* (*D. media*) (fig. 76). The thickest part of its main stalk is usually no more than about 5 mm in diameter, and the many side branches are very slender. Large plants are about 50 cm long. Like all desmarestias, it cannot be trusted in a pail with other plants and animals because the cell sap that exudes from bruised tissue is strongly acid.

Red Algae. The more common red algae on floats are types that are small and finely branched. Members of one particular complex of genera—*Antithamnion, Antithamnionella, Hollenbergia,* and *Scagelia*—predominate. They are all similar and, for our purposes, an illustration of one species of *Scagelia* (fig. 77) will suffice. A strong hand lens, at least, will be necessary to appreciate the beauty of these delicate algae, which branch so frequently that it is difficult to trace the main axes of the colony. The branches consist of single rows of cells.

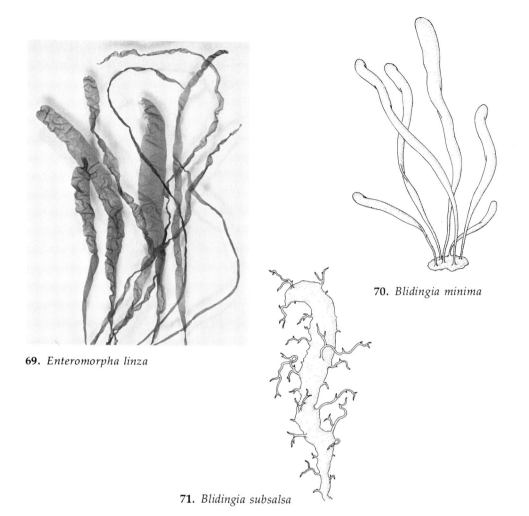

69. *Enteromorpha linza*

70. *Blidingia minima*

71. *Blidingia subsalsa*

72. *Bryopsis corticulans*

73. (*Right*) *Derbesia marina*, filamentous stage; photomicrograph

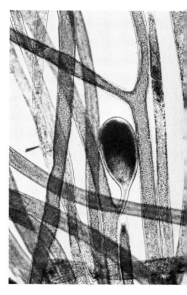

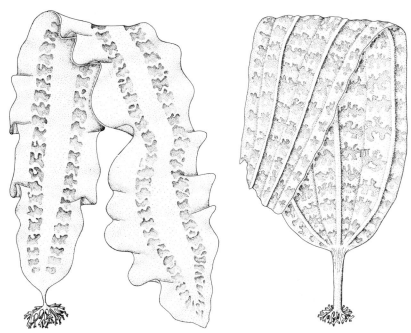

74. *Laminaria saccharina*　　　　　　**75.** *Costaria costata*

Polysiphonia (fig. 78), which forms reddish tufts somewhat similar to those of *Antithamnion* and its allies, is fairly easy to recognize when it is examined with a microscope. The tiered arrangement of the cells is characteristic. Each tier consists of a central cell and an outer circle of about a dozen cells. Slender, colorless filaments called trichoblasts arise between the tiers near the tips of the branches. There are many species of *Polysiphonia* on the Pacific coast, and they live in a variety of habitats. In mud flats, for instance, *Polysiphonia* commonly grows on pebbles or shells, and is often found on the tips of the siphons of gaper clams. The genus will be discussed again briefly in Chapter 7.

The larger red algae that may be expected are species found at low tide levels on rocky shores. *Polyneura latissima* (fig. 79) is often common. The broad primary blades coming from its holdfast may remain more or less entire, or they may branch once or twice; the branches often look as if they had been torn apart, and their tips frequently show some signs of wear. Considering the limited variety of red algae on floats, *Polyneura* is usually unmistakable because of its form and rich pink coloration. When a blade is viewed with light coming from behind it, however, a characteristic network of veins shows up. The blades routinely reach a length of about 10 or 15 cm, but are occasionally a bit larger.

Iridaea cordata (fig. 147) grows to a much larger size than *Polyneura*. Its broad blades, deep purplish red and iridescent when under water,

76. *Desmarestia viridis*

77. *Scagelia;* photomicrograph

78. *Polysiphonia;* photomicrograph

may reach a length of 1 m. This species and some of its close relatives will be discussed in more detail in Chapter 4.

Delesseria decipiens (fig. 80) is distinctive because of the way its primary and subsidiary blades arise from the thickened midrib. The plant grows from a rather concentrated, buttonlike holdfast, and the broader portions of the original blade or its branches may slightly exceed 1 cm. The color ranges from dark pink to purplish red. This seaweed is common on floating docks in the Northwest, but all along the coast from Alaska to central California it is also found on rocks at very low tide levels. In rocky situations, however, it is among so many other algae that it is less noticeable than it is on floats. Most plants are under 20 cm long, but the species is capable of growing to 40 or 50 cm.

Membranoptera platyphylla (fig. 81) is similar to *Delesseria* in color and general appearance, but its blades are rarely more than 10 cm long and they show no tendency to send out branches from the midrib. The midrib is fairly prominent, though not as stout as that of *Delesseria*, and it gives rise to many delicate "veins."

Callophyllis edentata (fig. 82) is primarily a subtidal alga that is often common on floats. Its thin, pinkish-red blades, which branch dichotomously, reach a length of about 20 cm. There is no midrib, and the plant tends to spread out more from near its base than does *Membranoptera*. The branching is nevertheless in one plane, just as it is in *Membranoptera*, and essentially also in *Delesseria*.

Pilings in the Puget Sound Region

In central and southern California, where long piers have been built right on the open coast, the pilings support marvelous faunas and floras that can be studied at low tide. In the Northwest, however, there are few pilings except in relatively calm waters, and just about everything that grows on them can be found on floats. They are nevertheless useful in showing us which animals and plants are successful at higher levels of the tidal range, and something of the mobility of predators that rise with the tide to feed on them.

Floating docks are generally linked to wharves or are at least connected to a set of pilings that provides stability. Thus where there are floats, there will probably be pilings close by, perhaps within arm's length. If this is the case, one can see, during an extremely low tide, a ten- or twelve-foot stretch of piling that was submerged a few hours before.

Nowadays, wooden pilings are subjected to a rather strict prophylaxis before they are pounded into place. Treatment with creosote and other preservatives, or ensheathment with metal or plastic, discourages destructive fungi, other microorganisms, shipworms, and *Limnoria*. It may be some time before a few hardy first settlers can stake out their claims and put the welcome mat out for their friends.

It is not necessary to review in any detail the animals and plants

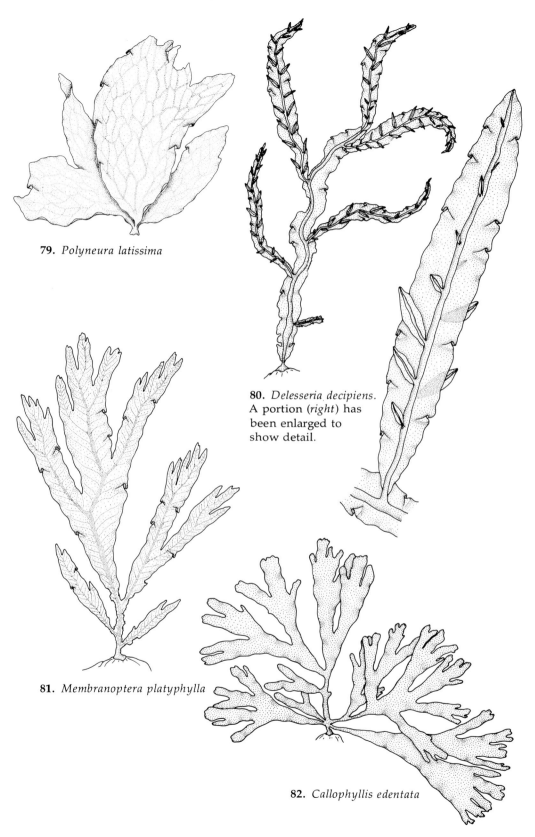

79. *Polyneura latissima*

80. *Delesseria decipiens.*
A portion (*right*) has
been enlarged to
show detail.

81. *Membranoptera platyphylla*

82. *Callophyllis edentata*

103 / On and Around Floating Docks and Pilings

likely to be seen on pilings at the level of very low tides—those below about 0.0—because the fauna and flora on almost continuously submerged portions of piling are essentially the same as those found on floats. Above 0.0, however, the organisms that cannot stand much exposure are quickly thinned out. In the upper five or six feet of the tidal range one generally finds little in the way of seaweeds, and the more obvious animals are *Collisella digitalis, C. paradigitalis, Balanus glandula, Semibalanus cariosus,* and *Mytilus edulis.* Zonation is not likely to be very distinct, but *C. digitalis* and *B. glandula* will probably reach upward farther than *C. paradigitalis, S. cariosus,* or *M. edulis.*

In the middle and lower portions of the barnacle-mussel association, the limpet *Collisella pelta* is sometimes abundant. The sea stars *Pisaster* and *Evasterias,* if they have climbed the pilings to feed on the barnacles and mussels, may remain there after the ebbing tide has left them behind.

Nearer the low-water line, *B. glandula* and *S. cariosus,* as well as *Mytilus,* may still be successful, though their exposure to predation by sea stars is increased. Seaweeds, *Ulva* in particular, become more abundant close to the 0.0 level, and may practically cover the other organisms. In any case, most of the available space will be occupied. Between about 0.0 or –1.0 foot and the low-water line, *Metridium,* hydroids, *Serpula, Schizobranchia,* solitary ascidians, the compound ascidian *Distaplia,* and other sessile animals, together with seaweeds, usually luxuriate, especially during the summer months. As stated previously, just about anything that will grow on floats can be expected on pilings within a foot or two of the low-water line.

San Francisco Bay

Floating docks and pilings in San Francisco Bay have a rich fauna, but there is a higher proportion of introduced species to native species than is the case in Puget Sound and Coos Bay. The algal flora is not as diversified as it is in the Puget Sound region. *Ulva, Enteromorpha linza, Blidingia subsalsa,* and *Bryopsis corticulans* are the prominent green algae.

Unless the water is too brackish, some of the delicate red algae such as *Polysiphonia* and *Antithamnion* are likely to be present. There may also be a few larger red algae. On floating docks close to the Golden Gate, for instance, *Prionitis lanceolata, Polyneura latissima, Gigartina exasperata,* and a species of *Cryptopleura* (probably *C. violacea,* which is similar to *C. lobulifera,* shown in fig. 154), are abundant. Of these, *Cryptopleura* is the one most likely to be found at Alameda and other places where the salinity is moderately high but where the daily exchange of water is not so active as it is near the mouth of the bay. It is rare to find any brown algae that may be called kelps, although there are small, filamentous genera. Diatoms are plentiful on almost all surfaces where they can form their coatings or fuzzy growths.

Sponges

Microciona prolifera (pl. 1) is easily recognized because it is usually bright red, orange, or orange-brown. It produces firm, fingerlike outgrowths that become fused together where they contact one another, so generally at least part of the colony is in the form of a network. The height of a large mass may exceed 10 cm. This species, introduced from the Atlantic coast, is now widespread in the bay and provides most of the bright color one sees at lower tide levels on shaded pilings and rocks, as well as on floats.

Halichondria bowerbanki (pl. 1) has been described in connection with the fauna of floats in the Puget Sound region. As in more northern waters, it generally forms lumpy growths that have short, flattened lobes, and the color is commonly dingy yellow. When crushed between one's fingers, it gives off a strong odor that is much like that of exploded gunpowder.

A still-unidentified *Haliclona* (fig. 83; pl. 1) found in San Francisco Bay forms tubular lobes, each with an opening at its tip. It is from these openings that water being processed by the sponge leaves the colony. There is much variation in the form and size of the tubes, and also their color. In general, however, the tubes are about 3 to 5 mm wide and up to 5 or 6 cm high, and the color is whitish to tan.

The three common and obvious sponges just mentioned have siliceous spicules. The next two, which are on the whole much smaller, have calcareous spicules. They have been dealt with in the section on the fauna of floats in Puget Sound, so only a few words need to be said about them here. Both are dingy white. *Scypha* (fig. 4) is vaselike, up to about 5 cm high. The tubes of *Leucosolenia* (fig. 5) are about 1 mm in diameter and are to a large extent organized into a network that hugs the substratum rather closely.

Cnidarians

Hydroids. *Obelia dichotoma* (fig. 6) and *O. geniculata* (figs. 7 and 8) are abundant, and *Gonothyraea clarki* (fig. 9) is much more common in San Francisco Bay than it is in the Puget Sound region. The medusae of *Gonothyraea*, as explained earlier in this chapter, do not swim. After emerging from the opening at the tip of a reproductive polyp, they remain stuck to this; the female medusae eventually release planulae. A number of other genera of thecate hydroids, similar to *Obelia* and *Gonothyraea*, may be expected on floats in the bay, but most of them are small and inconspicuous.

Tubularia crocea (pl. 2), an athecate type, is an estuarine species that almost certainly was introduced into California during the nineteenth century. It is similar to *T. marina*, found on floats in the Puget Sound region and at lower tide levels on rocky shores all along our coast, but it is much larger. Individual polyps sometimes reach a length of 15 cm. This hydroid branches extensively from the base—a feature that distinguishes it from *T. marina*—and thus forms impressive clusters. Some of the better places to look for it—and don't give up too soon!—are in the marinas that line the channel between Oakland and Alameda.

Jellyfishes. Considering the quantity of *Obelia dichotoma* and *O. geniculata* growing on the floats, one may expect plenty of *Obelia* medusae to be in the plankton. These are so small, however, that they are not likely to be noted in the field. The only reasonably common medusae of moderate size are *Polyorchis penicillatus* (fig. 18), *Sarsia tubulosa* (fig. 15), and *Eutonina indicans*. The first two have been described in the section dealing with jellyfishes of Puget Sound. *Eutonina indicans,* about 1 cm in diameter, looks much like *Phialidium* (fig. 19), but its manubrium is on a conical projection hanging down from the underside of the bell. *Eutonina* occurs in Coos Bay, but it is only occasionally seen in the Puget Sound area, where *Phialidium* is so common.

Sea Anemones. *Metridium senile* (fig. 25; pl. 3) is abundant in San Francisco Bay, but it does not often grow as large as it does on floats in the Puget Sound area. *Urticina crassicornis* seems to be absent altogether.

Haliplanella lineata (*Haliplanella luciae*) (pl. 3), a small, olive-green anemone with lengthwise stripes of pale orange or yellow, will be discussed in connection with the fauna found on rocks in the Puget Sound region (Chapter 7). In San Francisco Bay, it occurs on floats to some extent, but is more abundant on pilings and pieces of waterlogged wood that are lying on mud. A large specimen, when fully extended, is about 3 cm high.

Diadumene franciscana (pl. 3) is about the same size as *Haliplanella lineata* and could be confused with it. It is a little more translucent, and although its column may be pale green, any vertical stripes that are present (they may be lacking) are white, never orange. Another point of distinction is the fact that two of the tentacles—those nearest opposite ends of the elongated mouth slit—have yellowish bases. Unlike *Haliplanella*, *D. franciscana* does not necessarily have greenish tints; its column is often gray or cream. It is known only from San Francisco Bay, where it lives mostly on floats and pilings in places where the salinity is not normally up to that of full-strength sea water.

Diadumene leucolena also occurs in San Francisco Bay, as well as in parts of Tomales Bay and other quiet-water situations where the salinity is reduced. Though small, it is more slender than either *D. francis-cana* or *H. lineata*. Its prevailing color is usually the palest pink or salmon; the upper portion of the column is sometimes faintly green-ish. There are, however, no vertical stripes.

Polychaete Annelids

There are many kinds of polychaetes, but most of them are small. Only a few of the readily recognizable types will be mentioned. Among these is the scaleworm *Harmothoe imbricata* (fig. 33). It is about 2 cm long, pale brownish gray, and will be found in almost any sponge mass or clump of hydroids or mussels. It is fragile, and usually sheds its scale-like elytra if it is handled.

The sabellids *Eudistylia vancouveri* (pl. 7) and *Schizobranchia insignis* (pl. 7), common on floats and pilings in the Puget Sound region and in Coos Bay, and also occurring on rocky shores along much of the Pacific coast, are not often seen on floats in San Francisco Bay. One or both may be present in some places, however. *Eudistylia polymorpha* (pl. 7) seems to be the most abundant large sabellid in the bay. It is slightly smaller than *E. vancouveri* and is less inclined than the latter to form large colonies. Its prostomial cirri are usually reddish brown or nearly maroon, and are tipped with orange. An even more reliable distinguishing feature of *E. polymorpha* is a deep cleft in each of the two spiraled bases from which the cirri arise. The clefts can be seen when the animal is viewed with its dorsal side uppermost. (The dorsal side is easy to recognize, because its anterior portion has a conspicu-ous longitudinal groove. For most of the length of the worm, this groove, which carries fecal wastes and gametes to the mouth of the tube, is on the ventral surface, but as it nears the anterior end it curves around the body and becomes dorsal.)

Serpula vermicularis (pl. 7) and serpulids of the genus *Spirorbis* (pls. 7 and 12), are present, but seem not to be as abundant in San Fran-cisco Bay as in the Puget Sound region. The bay does, however, have a serpulid whose success is phenomenal. This is *Mercierella enigmatica* (fig. 84), introduced sometime before 1920 by ships coming from the Australian region. It is found mostly in water of low salinity, and is especially common on rock, concrete, and wood in Oakland's Lake Merritt and Berkeley's Aquatic Park. Its calcareous tubes, about 2 mm in diameter, form large and fairly compact aggregations that slightly remind one of certain corals. The tubes are nearly chalk white, flared a little at the open end, and have conspicuous annulations along the way. The tentacles are grayish and the free end of the operculum that closes the tube when the animal withdraws is rimmed by small spines. Although *M. enigmatica* now has a wide distribution, its occurrence on the Pacific coast of the United States seems to be limited to the San Francisco Bay area.

Bryozoans and Entoprocts

The bryozoans that stand out in San Francisco Bay are two species of *Bugula*. Neither is native to the region. One of them, *B. stolonifera* (pl. 23), comes from the Atlantic. It forms whitish or grayish colonies up to 5 cm high, and resembles the common *Bugula* of the Puget Sound region except for the fact that its pattern of branching is less markedly spiral. The other species, *B. neritina* (pl. 23), widely distributed in warmer parts of the world, is purplish brown and much more robust than *B. stolonifera*. The height of large colonies may exceed 8 cm. It is an unusual *Bugula* in that it lacks avicularia. The caprellid amphipod, *Caprella californica*, is almost invariably abundant on both bugulas of San Francisco Bay (fig. 91).

The most common encrusting bryozoan in the bay is the dingy orange *Schizoporella unicornis* (pl. 23). On floats and pilings, mussel shells provide it with an especially favorable substratum, but it occurs on other hard surfaces, including rocks along the shore. Earlier in this chapter, it was explained that this widespread species is believed to have been introduced to the Pacific coast of North America. There seem to be no records of its occurrence until Japanese oysters were first imported.

Bowerbankia gracilis (fig. 40) is plentiful, but may not be noticed unless one looks with a magnifier at worm tubes, mussel shells, ascidians, seaweeds, and other firm objects. There is also likely to be the entoproct *Barentsia benedeni* (fig. 41), engaging because of the way its zooids bend sharply at the muscular swellings located along the stalks and at their bases.

Sea Spiders

"Sea spiders" are not true spiders. They belong to an allied group called the Pycnogonida, and they resemble spiders in having four pairs of legs for walking or clinging. In males, these are preceded by another pair of small legs used for carrying eggs. A male sea spider collects eggs from a female as she lays them, cements them to his specialized limbs, and takes care of them until they hatch into six-legged larvae. These extra legs are present in females of some species, but they do not function as egg-carrying devices.

The layout of the body is unusual for an arthropod in that the abdominal region is practically nonexistent. In front of the portion that bears the legs, the body is drawn out into a proboscis that is used for sucking juices from other animals, mostly hydroids and anemones. The two pairs of appendages near the base of the proboscis are comparable to those called chelicerae and pedipalps in a spider. The chelicerae may be tipped by a claw or pincer, or they may be much reduced or even absent. The pedipalps may also be lacking, so there is much variation among sea spiders as far as appendages are concerned.

A common sea spider in San Francisco Bay is *Achelia nudiuscula* (pl.

83. A species of *Haliclona* with slender, tubular lobes

84. *Mercierella enigmatica*

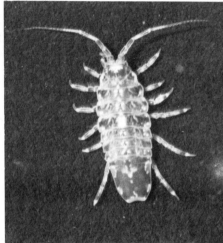

85. *Synidotea laticauda*

86. *Limnoria tripunctata*

87. *Limnoria quadripunctata,* posteriormost portion of the abdomen

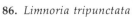

109 / On and Around Floating Docks and Pilings

18). This species tolerates a little pollution and survives in situations where the salinity is decidedly lower than that of full-strength sea water. It is generally found where there are dense growths of hydroids, sponges, mussels, and barnacles, and it occurs on rocks and concrete at the shore as well as on floats and pilings. It is especially abundant in the channel between Oakland and Alameda. A large specimen, with legs spread, is about 2 cm across.

Crustaceans

Isopods. *Gnorimosphaeroma oregonense* (fig. 118) is more common on floats and pilings in San Francisco Bay than it is in the Puget Sound area. It often lives in places where the salinity is extremely low. A specialty of San Francisco Bay is *Synidotea laticauda* (fig. 85). Some think it was introduced, but if this is so, no one knows where it came from. Others believe it is a native. In any case, it seems not to have been found anywhere else. It is less common than *Gnorimosphaeroma*, but one should watch for it when sorting out the smaller animals that occur among mussels, ascidians, hydroids, and sponges. *Synidotea* is about 2 cm long and slightly resembles certain species of *Idotea*, one of which (*I. wosnesenskii*) is abundant on floats in the Puget Sound region. If you look closely at it, however, you will notice that none of the leg-bearing segments have little side plates of the sort characteristic of idoteas.

Limnoria lignorum, so common in the Puget Sound region and in other harbors of the Northwest, is not found in San Francisco Bay. Two other gribbles, however, are plentiful wherever there is old wood for them to attack. These are *L. tripunctata* (fig. 86) and *L. quadripunctata* (fig. 87). Their species names allude to the presence of either three or four little wartlike bumps on the platelike terminal piece of the abdomen. (*Limnoria lignorum* lacks these bumps; in their place it has some little ridges that form a Y.) Both *L. tripunctata* and *L. quadripunctata* reach a length of approximately 4 mm.

Amphipods. As in the Puget Sound area, there are a number of species of amphipods on floats, but most of them cannot be distinguished without recourse to the microscope and specialized treatises. Only some of the more distinctive genera will be mentioned. One of them is *Corophium* (fig. 46), almost ubiquitous where there is enough silt for it to form the tubes from which it extends the anterior part of its body in order to collect the detritus it eats. Slightly similar to *Corophium*, of which there are several species in San Francisco Bay, is *Chelura terebrans* (fig. 88). It lives in wood that has been riddled by gribbles of the genus *Limnoria*. It probably does not eat wood, but only profits by having the burrows of *Limnoria* to live in. It is about the same size as *Limnoria* and *Corophium*, and one of its distinctive features is the rel-

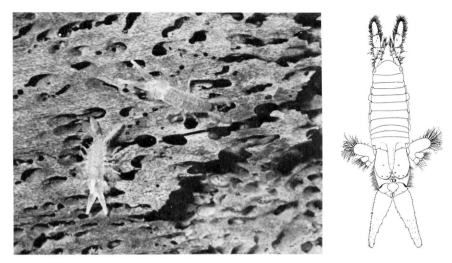

88. *Chelura terebrans*

89. *Palaemon macrodactylus*

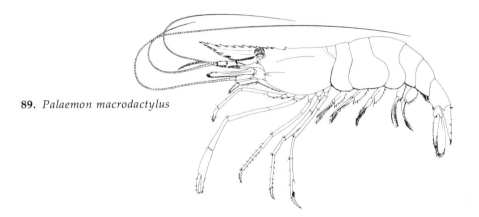

90. *Pyromaia tuberculata*

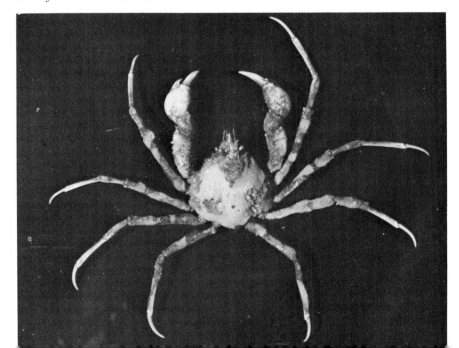

atively long appendages of the next to last pair. These extend well behind the rest of the body and together form what looks like a tail.

Shrimps and Crabs. In general, shrimps are less abundant on floats in San Francisco Bay than they are in the Puget Sound region. "Broken-back" shrimps of the genus *Heptacarpus* (fig. 49) are found, however, in some places. Where the water is of low salinity, one should watch for *Palaemon macrodactylus* (fig. 89), introduced some years ago from the Orient.

The only crab likely to be found on floats in the bay is *Pyromaia tuberculata* (fig. 90), which is basically a subtidal species. Its range on the Pacific coast extends from northern California to South America. *Pyromaia* is one of the spider crabs that decorates itself with sponges, compound ascidians, and seaweeds. Underneath all of the encrusting organisms, its body is pale tan. The legs are very slender, and the almost pear-shaped cephalothorax reaches a length of about 2.5 cm. *Pyromaia* differs from all other spider crabs found within the range covered by this book in that its rostrum is not deeply divided into two parallel projections.

Barnacles. The more common barnacles on wood, mussel shells, and other hard substrata are *Balanus crenatus* (fig. 51), *B. amphitrite* (pl. 18), and *B. improvisus*. *Balanus crenatus* has been discussed earlier in this chapter, for it occurs in the Puget Sound region and Coos Bay, where the problem is to distinguish it from *B. glandula*. Unfortunately, *B. crenatus* and *B. improvisus* are rather similar, too, and the latter is in turn closely related to *B. amphitrite*, so barnacle identification in San Francisco Bay is an especially delicate matter.

Balanus amphitrite is the easiest to describe concisely. Each of the plates making up its wall is typically marked with purplish gray vertical lines; the spaces between these lines become wider toward the base. Neither *B. improvisus* nor *B. crenatus* has colored, vertical lines, although the former often shows hyaline lines in its wall plates. The two species can be positively distinguished only by careful study of the plates that close the opening when the animal withdraws. The plates must be removed and the soft tissue separated from them. Among the differences, one in particular stands out: in *B. improvisus*, the narrow end of each of the two smaller plates, called terga, is prolonged as a fingernail-like lobe that is nearly twice as long as wide; in *B. crenatus*, this lobe is only half as wide as long. *Balanus improvisus* is generally restricted to water of low salinity. Both *B. crenatus* and *B. amphitrite* can live where the water is less salty than it is outside the bay, but neither is likely to be found where the salinity is extremely low.

Molluscs

Snails.   Few shelled gastropods are found on floats and pilings in San Francisco Bay. The slipper shell, *Crepidula convexa* (fig. 312), is about the only one. This species has a shell about 2 cm long, and the external surface of this (unless overgrown by encrusting organisms) usually has reddish brown streaks. The apex of the shell is not turned to one side as it is in *C. fornicata*, which should probably be expected on floats and pilings once in a while, for it is common in some places where oysters are being cultivated. Both of the crepidulas just mentioned were introduced; *C. fornicata* is discussed at greater length in Chapter 7.

Sea Slugs.   The most abundant nudibranch is almost certainly *Eubranchus olivaceus* (fig. 6), which lives on colonies of *Obelia*, eating the polyps. It is such a small sea slug that it may not be noted in the field. *Eubranchus* is described and discussed earlier in this chapter, in connection with the fauna of floats in the Puget Sound region. There are some other small species associated with hydroids in San Francisco Bay. Most of them, such as *Tenellia pallida*, a predator of *Tubularia crocea*, are relatively scarce.
   Phidiana crassicornis (pl. 16) is the only large nudibranch that is abundant. In spite of the prevalence of sponges on the floats and pilings, dorids are rarely noted within the bay.

Bivalves.   *Mytilus edulis* (pl. 17) is common on floats almost throughout the bay. *Geukensia demissa* (*Ischadium demissum*), the ribbed horse mussel (fig. 307), is not often found on floats, but it is sometimes seen on pilings. Its usual habitat is a firm substratum, such as a rock or piece of wood, set in mud, and it will be discussed in more detail in Chapter 7. *Ostrea lurida*, the native oyster (fig. 309), is common in some places. A few facts about it are found in Chapter 7.
   Bankia setacea, the so-called shipworm, destroys wooden structures in San Francisco Bay with as much of a vengeance as it does farther north. There is also its more famous cousin, *Teredo navalis*, although this species is not particularly abundant. Its pallets are one-piece, nearly paddle-shaped structures, not divided up into many more or less separate units as they are in *Bankia*.

Ascidians
   The ascidian fauna of floats and pilings in San Francisco Bay is decidedly different from that of comparable situations in the Puget Sound region. There is, in fact, no overlap. The largest species in the bay is *Ciona intestinalis* (pl. 28); it sometimes reaches a height of 15 cm. There may be almost no color to this nearly translucent animal, but generally a yellowish green tint is perceptible. Unless considerable debris has accumulated on the outside of the almost gelatinous tunic, the gut and

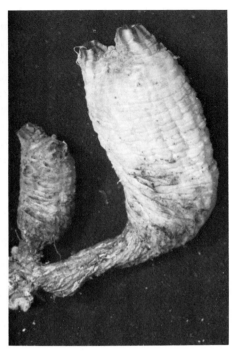

91. *Caprella californica*
on *Bugula neritina*

92. *Styela clava*

certain other internal structures can usually be seen. Even the heart may be observed working in typically ascidian fashion: a few beats forcing blood in one direction, then a few beats driving it in the opposite direction. The siphons, delicate when fully expanded, are always clean. This species has a wide distribution, for it is found in Europe and on the Atlantic coast of North America. On the Pacific coast it ranges from southern California at least to British Columbia, but it is not common anywhere north of California. It prefers quiet water and is extremely abundant on floats and pilings in San Francisco Bay, as well as in marinas farther south.

Styela clava (fig. 92), abundant on floats and pilings in San Francisco Bay and also in protected situations farther south in California, is an Asiatic species that has been carried to many parts of the world on ship bottoms. It resembles *S. montereyensis* of the open coast (see Chapter 5), but is wartier and stouter, and its inhalant siphon does not bend downward. The height of *S. clava* commonly reaches 8 cm, but some specimens are considerably larger.

Ascidia ceratodes (pl. 28) resembles, in size and appearance, *A. callosa* of the Puget Sound region. Its eggs, however, are red or pink, rather than white, and there are some other subtle differences. It is not likely to be found where the salinity is significantly lower than that of full-strength sea water, and it is not of general occurrence in San Francisco Bay, although it is found there to some extent. At Monterey, it is extremely abundant, colonizing floats and pilings as well as the seaweeds and worm tubes that are attached to them.

Molgula manhattensis (pl. 28), introduced from the Atlantic coast, is now firmly established in San Francisco Bay, Tomales Bay, and a few other calm, slightly brackish situations. It is nearly globular, up to about 2 cm in diameter, and generally forms dense clusters. The color is usually dingy gray. There may be considerable sediment accumulating on the surface, but when the tunic is brushed clean it is rather shiny.

The principal compound ascidians are *Botryllus* (pl. 29) and *Botrylloides* (pl. 29). In some places, one or both of them are found growing over mussels, worm tubes, and solitary ascidians, as well as over the surfaces of the floats and pilings. Both are gelatinous in texture and vary considerably in color, ranging from nearly white to yellow, orange, reddish brown, bluish, and nearly black. *Botryllus* is characterized by having its zooids arranged in rather neat systems that have a circular, oval, or star-shaped configuration. In *Botrylloides* the systems tend to be elongated, and they are often irregular. Experts are reluctant to state firmly which species of *Botryllus* and *Botrylloides* predominate within the bay.

4

Rocky Shores of the Puget Sound Region

Within the rather extensive region covered by this book, the character of rocky shores varies greatly. There are differences in the rock itself. Sandstone, shale, and limestone are relatively soft rocks of sedimentary origin. Granite and basalt are of igneous origin—they result from the action of heat within the earth—and they are hard. In many places, moreover, there are igneous intrusions into sedimentary deposits.

Rocky shores also vary in topography and their situation with respect to climate, currents, and wave action. Some shores are steep cliffs; others have a gentle slope. The substratum may be a massive, projecting reef or it may consist to a large extent of separate boulders. The physical characteristics of the shore are very important. Some organisms can live only on exposed surfaces; others inhabit crevices or live beneath ledges or under rocks.

Much of the Pacific coast of North America is subject to relatively strong wave action even in calm weather. The height of a wave that reaches the shore depends largely on two factors: the velocity of the wind that has propagated it and the distance over which it has moved. The Pacific Ocean is so vast that it offers great possibilities for the development of huge waves. The higher the wave, of course, the greater the force with which it falls.

Wherever there are offshore islands, submarine ridges, and projecting headlands, the coast will enjoy at least some protection from the aggressive wave action that is typical of areas where such barriers are absent. The barriers need not be parallel to the coast to be effective, because the direction of prevailing winds may be such that waves move obliquely toward shore. In some places, large beds of kelp offshore act as wave retardants.

Within Puget Sound and San Francisco Bay, wave action is usually negligible. On the more exposed shores of the San Juan Archipelago, which face the Strait of Juan de Fuca, the normally slight wave action is intensified during storms. The fact that the islands of the archipelago are in a large body of water confluent with the open ocean means that there will be swift tidal currents running around them and between them.

Many animals and plants of the intertidal zone thrive only where the wave action is strong. The purple sea urchin, *Strongylocentrotus purpuratus*, is almost never encountered except on shores that are somewhat exposed. The same may be said of surfgrasses of the genus *Phyllospadix*. Quiet waters, on the other hand, provide the right physical and biological environments for many organisms.

The natural history of rocky shores will be dealt with in two chapters. The first of these will be concerned primarily with Puget Sound, the San Juan Archipelago, and the Strait of Georgia; the second will be devoted to the open coast. Some overlap should be expected, for many of the organisms characteristic of the open coast are found also in relatively protected situations. There is no fully satisfactory way to divide up the material, but it makes sense to deal with the relatively protected shores of Puget Sound and adjacent areas before going on to the open coast, where the fauna and flora are appreciably different and substantially richer.

The Strait of Juan de Fuca, which connects the open ocean with Puget Sound, the Strait of Georgia, and the waters surrounding the San Juan Archipelago, deserves special mention. Some of its shorelines, especially along the southwest coast of Vancouver Island, sustain considerable wave action. Elsewhere, however, the water is relatively quiet. Within the Strait, in other words, one sees a gradual change from open-coast conditions to those characteristic of the inland waters.

Relatively little of the shoreline of Coos Bay and San Francisco Bay consists of natural rock formations. Some of the rocky areas may have swift currents running past them, but they do not get much wave action except during storms, and in this respect they are similar to rocky shores in the Puget Sound region. They do have some distinctive features, however, and most of these are related to the nature of the rock. For instance, at Fossil Point, in Coos Bay, the sedimentary rock is soft, and is a perfect substratum for rock-boring bivalves and the nestlers that fill up the burrows after the original inhabitants die. There are many situations comparable to this on the open coast, but not in the Puget Sound region, where the rock, in general, is hard. It is impossible to deal separately with every kind of rocky habitat one may encounter. Most of the conspicuous and common plants and animals of rocky shores within the range of this book will be mentioned in this chapter or the next. The illustrations, moreover, should enable one quickly to find the right page.

As you work your way down a rocky shore from the high-tide line to the low-tide line, you will observe that the distribution of most of the more obvious animals and plants is not at all general. Even organisms that have a wide vertical distribution tend to be concentrated at certain levels. This phenomenon, called intertidal zonation, is due partly to the influence of physical conditions on each species. Animals and plants in the higher reaches of the intertidal zone must be able to withstand exposure for long periods. In winter they may be subjected to rain and to temperatures decidedly below that of the sea water; in summer they may be exposed to bright sunlight and warm air, and some of them will lose water by evaporation. Among the intertidal organisms that are adapted to a nearly terrestrial existence are the periwinkles, little snails of the genus *Littorina*. If put into a jar of sea water, they promptly crawl out and remain well above the water line. Few animals and plants from lower levels of the intertidal zone can survive prolonged exposure, especially during warm and dry weather.

Zonation is not, however, entirely the result of adaptations to physical conditions. There are biological factors, especially competition and predation, that have to be considered. If a particular predator, for instance, can live comfortably at certain tide levels, then the population of a species on which it feeds will be kept in check. If the prey species can flourish at higher levels than the predator can, then it may become abundant at those levels. Well-documented cases of this sort involve snails of the genus *Nucella* and certain barnacles belonging to the genera *Balanus* and *Chthamalus*. The barnacles are capable of living over a rather wide vertical range, but predation by *Nucella* keeps them in check over most of it. At higher levels, where *Nucella* drops out, the barnacles grow thickly.

The vertical distribution of these barnacles is also affected by competition for space. Although *Chthamalus* can live at levels lower than those at which it is normally abundant, it does not compete well with *Balanus*. The fact that it can prosper at levels too high for *Balanus* gives it an advantage in the uppermost part of the intertidal region. So, the distribution of both *Chthamalus* and *Balanus* results from the combined effect of the competition between the two barnacles, the predation by *Nucella*, and the ability to survive at progressively higher levels.

Discussion of the fauna and flora of rocky shores will be based to a large extent on the zonation shown by some of the more conspicuous organisms. But since the intertidal region is not one continuous, smooth sheet of solid rock, there will be sections dealing with life in crevices, in tide pools, and other specific situations. Some of the trophic relationships, such as those of prey to predator, and various kinds of symbiotic associations, will also be pointed out.

To follow this basic framework it will be convenient to divide the

93. A rocky shore exposed to a moderate amount of wave action (west side of San Juan Island)

intertidal region into four numbered zones: "1" will indicate the uppermost zone, "4" the lowermost. In many treatments of the subject of intertidal zonation, the term "supralittoral fringe" applies to our zone 1, and "infralittoral fringe" to our zone 4. The midlittoral zone, then, corresponds to our zones 2 and 3. For this introduction to rocky intertidal areas, it will be most instructive to use one in which the substratum is composed to a large extent of massive and more or less coherent rock formations (not just an accumulation of small rocks or boulders), and one that sustains at least a little wave action. Rocky shores of this type (the one shown in Figure 93 is a good example) are found on the west and south side of San Juan Island and elsewhere in the San Juan Archipelago. What one learns from such a shore can be adapted to various other kinds of situations. One can expect, however, that generalizations formulated on the basis of observations of one particular area will be violated elsewhere. Moreover, in many places zonation is simply not well marked. Almost any exposed rocky shore on the open coasts of Oregon, Washington, or Vancouver Island will exhibit zonation that is more dramatic than that shown by any topographically similar situations within Puget Sound or the San Juan Archipelago. Nevertheless, a good many characteristics of the zonation on the open coast will be seen in even relatively protected areas (pl. 30). Vertical bulkheads and sea walls generally show more pronounced zonation than is evident on slopes.

No matter how strong the zonation may be, two features found on most rocky shores will tend to blur it to some extent. Permanent tide pools, especially larger ones, and gullies in which water sloshes up and down after waves break make it possible for certain organisms to live at appreciably higher levels than they would be able to do otherwise. Thus, although surfgrass (*Phyllospadix*) and coralline red algae are considered typical of the lowermost zone of the intertidal region, in tide pools and gullies they may be found well above this zone.

ZONE 1: THE SUPRALITTORAL FRINGE

This zone is affected only by higher tides, and its uppermost portion may not often be wet except from spray or rain. To relate it to data given in a tide table, in the San Juan Archipelago its lower limit is usually about 7 feet (2.1 m) above 0.0 (mean lower low water); in much of Puget Sound, its lower limit is about 9 feet (2.7 m) above 0.0. Of course, it passes rather imperceptibly into the next zone below. Remember that a zone is characterized by an assemblage of organisms, not by the finite distribution of one species. In any case, zone 1 has relatively few conspicuous species, but those that do occur here may be present in large numbers.

Of the plants that are obvious, some are lichens—symbiotic associations of microscopic algae with fungi. Most lichens are strictly terrestrial, but certain of them are especially abundant at the fringes of the sea, and a few are truly marine. *Verrucaria* (pl. 30) is generally prominent in the splash zone, where it forms a thin, black coating on the rocks. The band of *Verrucaria*, often a meter in vertical height, is usually more distinct if viewed from a distance than at close range.

Mixing to some extent with *Verrucaria*, but mostly at slightly higher levels and therefore not often affected by spray, are some other lichens. *Caloplaca* (pl. 30), resembling weathered orange paint, is the most prominent. The sharply defined disks on its surface are the reproductive structures of its fungal component. *Xanthoria* (pl. 30) has crowded, nearly leaflike lobes. When dry, it is mostly yellow or yellow-orange; when wet, it becomes more greenish. *Physcia caesia* (pl. 30), which has close allies in situations remote from the shore, forms lobed patches of a grayish white color, and has disks or shallow cups of a pale brown color. There are other lichens in the region sometimes affected by spray, but the ones that have just been discussed are the more easily identified species.

Two flowering plants will be mentioned in connection with the spray zone. One of these is the seaside plantain, *Plantago maritima* (pl. 30), a fleshy-leaved relative of the weedy plantains of lawns and gardens. Its flowering spikes reach a height of about 20 cm. This perennial plant commonly grows out of pockets of soil in rock crevices.

Thrift, *Armeria maritima* (pl. 30), is the only member of the leadwort family (Plumbaginaceae) found north of the Oregon-California border. It forms evergreen tufts in which there are many slender basal leaves, and its small rose-pink flowers are concentrated in dense heads lifted 10 to 30 cm above the ground. When in bloom, on seaside bluffs and

Tresus nuttallii, a gaper clam

Macoma balthica

Mytilus edulis, the bay mussel or edible mussel

Modiolus modiolus, the horse mussel

Mytilus californianus, the California mussel, and *Pollicipes polymerus,* the goose barnacle

Mytilimeria nuttallii, the sea-bottle clam, encrusted by the compound ascidian *Cystodytes lobatus*

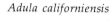

Adula californiensis

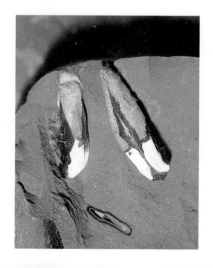

Plate 17

Achelia nudiuscula, a pycnogonid common in San Francisco Bay; the barnacle is *Balanus amphitrite*

Lepas fascicularis, a pelagic goose barnacle

Balanus amphitrite

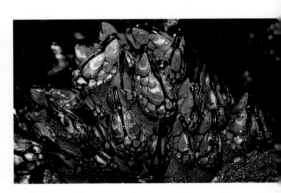

Pollicipes polymerus, the goose barnacle

Balanus nubilus, the giant barnacle

Tetraclita rubescens

Plate 18

Megalorchestia californiana

Traskorchestia traskiana

dotea wosnesenskii (*above and right*), two color phases

dotea stenops; the encrusting red alga is *Hilden-randia*

Crangon. The lump on the right side is due to the presence, under the carapace, of a parasitic isopod, *Argeia pugettensis*.

allianassa californiensis, the ghost shrimp

Plate 19

Pagurus hirsutiusculus

Pagurus samuelis

Petrolisthes eriomerus

Petrolisthes cinctipes

Pachycheles pubescens

Oedignathus inermis

Hapalogaster mertensii

Plate 20

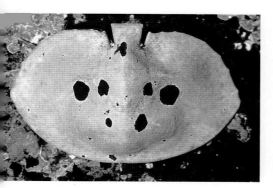

ryptolithodes sitchensis, the turtle crab

Cryptolithodes typicus, with the social ascidian *Metandrocarpa taylori*

achygrapsus crassipes, the lined shore crab

Emerita analoga, the mole crab

'emigrapsus oregonensis

Hemigrapsus nudus

Plate 21

Lophopanopeus bellus, the black-clawed crab

Telmessus cheiragonus, the helmet crab

Mimulus foliatus

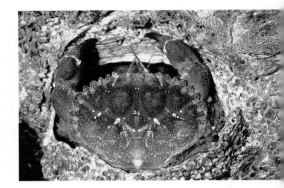

Cancer oregonensis

Cancer antennarius

Cancer antennarius

Cancer gracilis, the graceful crab

Plate 22

Schizoporella unicornis

Eurystomella bilabiata

Phidolopora pacifica

Heteropora magna

Bugula stolonifera

Bugula neritina

Flustrellidra corniculata

Plate 23

Phoronopsis viridis

Phoronis vancouverensis

Strongylocentrotus droebachiensis, the green sea urchin

Strongylocentrotus franciscanus, the red sea urchin

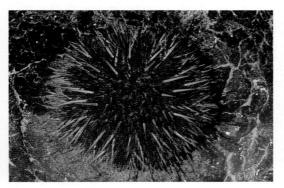

Strongylocentrotus purpuratus, the purple sea urchin

Oligocottus maculosus, the tidepool sculpin

Anoplarchus purpurescens, the cockscomb prickleback

Gobiesox maeandricus, the clingfish

Plate 24

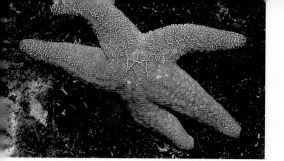

Pisaster ochraceus

Pisaster brevispinus

Evasterias troschelii

Orthasterias koehleri

Pycnopodia helianthoides, the sunflower star

Leptasterias hexactis, the six-rayed sea star

Patiria miniata, the bat star

Plate 25

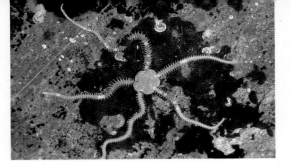
Amphipholis squamata

Ophiothrix spiculata

Ophiopholis aculeata

Solaster stimpsoni

Henricia leviuscula, the blood star

Mediaster aequalis

Dermasterias imbricata, the leather star

Plate 26

Stichopus californicus

Lissothuria nutriens

Cucumaria pseudocurata

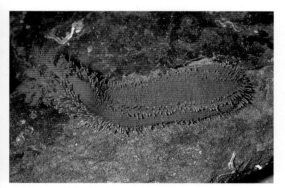

Cucumaria lubrica

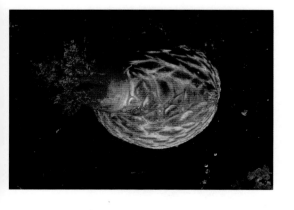

Cucumaria miniata

Cucumaria miniata, extended oral tentacles

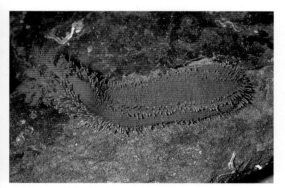

Psolus chitonoides

Plate 27

Cnemidocarpa finmarkiensis

Molgula manhattensis

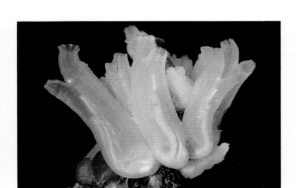

Ciona intestinalis

Metandrocarpa taylori

Clavelina huntsmani

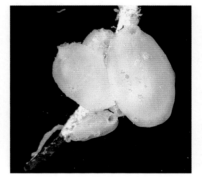

Ascidia ceratodes

Perophora annectens and *Balanophyllia elegans*, the cup coral (*right*)

Plate 28

Styela montereyensis

Aplidium (*above and right*), two species

Distaplia occidentalis

Ritterella pulchra

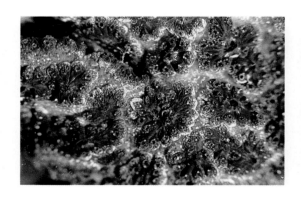

Botryllus (*above and right*), two color phases

Botrylloides

Diplosoma macdonaldi

Plate 29

Verrucaria

Caloplaca

Xanthoria candelaria (yellow) and Physcia caesia (light gray)

Armeria maritima, thrift

Plantago maritima, the seaside plantain

Prasiola meridionalis

Neomolgus littoralis, a mite that feeds on small flies

Plate 30

Intertidal zonation in a somewhat protected bay on the west side of San Juan Island. Just above the black band formed by Verrucaria, a few orange patches of Caloplaca can be seen.

Verrucaria

Caloplaca

Xanthoria candelaria (yellow) and *Physcia caesia* (light gray)

Armeria maritima, thrift

Plantago maritima, the seaside plantain

Prasiola meridionalis

Neomolgus littoralis, a mite that feeds on small flies

Plate 30

Intertidal zonation in a somewhat protected bay on the west side of San Juan Island. Just above the black band formed by *Verrucaria*, a few orange patches of *Caloplaca* can be seen.

Aplidium (*above and right*), two species

Distaplia occidentalis

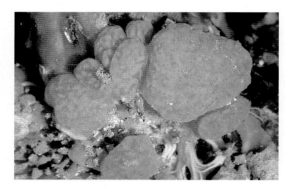

Ritterella pulchra

Botryllus (*above and right*), two color phases

Botrylloides

Diplosoma macdonaldi

Plate 29

lysia hedgpethi, a sacoglossan that feeds on *Codium fragile*

Placida dendritica, a sacoglossan on *Codium fragile*

Acrosiphonia coalita

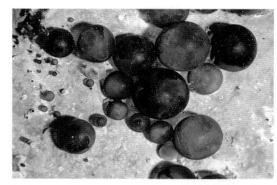

Derbesia marina (the "Halicystis" stage), growing on an encrusting coralline alga

Codium fragile

Codium setchellii

Enteromorpha intestinalis in a cliffside seepage area

Urospora penicilliformis

Plate 31

A luxuriant growth of green algae, mostly *Ulva* and *Enteromorpha,* on muddy sand in Tomales Bay, Marin County, California

False Bay, San Juan Island, Washington. The bright green algae are mostly *Ulva fenestrata* and species of *Enteromorpha;* the nearly black patches consist of *Vaucheria.*

Ulva (center) and *Enteromorpha* growing on gravelly mud

Ulva fenestrata, the perforated form

Filamentous green algae (mostly *Percursaria percursa*) in a pool in muddy sand

Chaetomorpha aerea

Vaucheria

Alderia modesta, a sacoglossan that feeds on *Vaucheria*

Plate 32

Aplysiopsis smithi, a sacoglossan that feeds on filamentous green algae

among rocks covered by *Caloplaca* and other lichens, it is a lovely sight. Unfortunately, it is not of general occurrence in the Puget Sound region. In the San Juan Archipelago, for instance, it is more likely to be seen on some of the smaller islands than on the major islands. The same species of *Armeria* is found on the Atlantic coast of North America and in Europe. In England, it has served as a symbol of thrift and has even been featured on postage stamps.

Prasiola meridionalis (pl. 30) is a green alga that grows as little blades about 1 cm high. In Puget Sound and the San Juan Archipelago, it seems to be rather regularly present and may form extensive patches, generally just below the black band of *Verrucaria*. On the open coast, it is often more or less restricted to rocks where there are colonies of sea birds and plenty of droppings.

Crawling around on *Prasiola*, lichens, and rock surfaces in the uppermost part of the intertidal region is a bright red mite, *Neomolgus littoralis* (pl. 30). Mites are like spiders and ticks in that they have four pairs of legs, instead of three as is characteristic of insects. *Neomolgus*, which has a wide distribution in the northern hemisphere, reaches a length of about 3 mm. It moves actively and responds very negatively to the approach of a human finger. It uses its long snout for piercing small flies and sucking out their juices. Other kinds of mites are found in the uppermost zone, too, and some of them form dense aggregations in crevices and depressions. They are small, however, and not sufficiently distinctive to be identified except by an expert. Finding an expert on seacoast mites is not easy, either.

Where there is seepage of fresh water onto the vertical face of a rock or out through a fissure, there will almost certainly be a growth of the bright yellowish green *Enteromorpha intestinalis* (pl. 31). As it dies, it turns white, so large splashes of this alga are often varicolored.

Red algae are not characteristic of the upper reaches of the intertidal region. One species, however, should be expected in caves or in places where rocks are continuously shaded. This is *Rhodochorton purpureum* (pl. 35), which forms what looks like pinkish purple felt. The short filaments that make up the mat are about 20 micrometers (0.02 mm) wide.

In depressions in rock that serve as miniature tide pools, there may be a bloom of various microscopic green algae and diatoms that makes the water look like thin pea soup. In this situation, look for a reddish harpacticoid copepod, *Tigriopus californicus* (fig. 94). Members of the genus *Tigriopus* are found in various parts of the world, almost always in this kind of place—pools that may not be refreshed for several days, or even several weeks. Such pools may become brackish during periods of rain and hypersaline during warm summer weather.

One or both kinds of little snails called periwinkles will certainly be found in zone 1. *Littorina sitkana*, the Sitka periwinkle (fig. 95; pl. 11) commonly has a fat, almost globose shell which reaches a height of a little more than 1.5 cm. It generally has some strong spiral sculpturing in the form of continuous ridges and furrows. The color is variable: some specimens are monotonously brown or gray, but others have lighter bands, especially on the upper sides of the whorls. The lighter areas, and occasionally much of the body whorl, may be a rather pretty yellow or orange. *Littorina scutulata,* the checkered periwinkle (figs. 96 and 103; pl. 33), rarely exceeds a height of about 1 cm, and its shell is more slender than that of *L. sitkana.* It does not have any significant spiral sculpturing. The color is brown to bluish black, usually mixed with some white in a checkerboard pattern.

Recently, zoologists who have studied *L. scutulata* intensively have come to the conclusion that there are two closely related species, one that can be called the "true" *L. scutulata* and another to which the name *L. plena* has been given. The differences between these "sibling species" are subtle and involve internal anatomy, composition of proteins, and the appearance of the egg capsules. Shell characters by themselves are insufficient for positive determination. In this book, therefore, only one name—*L. scutulata*—will be used. Similar cases of sibling species have been reported in certain groups of polychaetes, barnacles, and other organisms.

Of the limpets, *Collisella digitalis* (fig. 97) is the one most likely to be found with the periwinkles. Its shell has distinct "ribs," an undulating margin, and an apex that is displaced so far anteriorly that it is nearly or fully as far forward as the edge of the shell. This species reaches a length of about 2 cm.

Both of the periwinkles and *C. digitalis* are herbivores that scrape small algae from the rocks. They are often found clustered along cracks in which moisture collects and which therefore may support a growth of algae a little less depauperate than that on relatively smooth surfaces.

Two species of barnacles are characteristic of this zone. *Chthamalus dalli* (fig. 98) is a small species, its diameter at the base not often exceeding 5 or 6 mm. It is rather easy to recognize because of the way the contiguous margins of the four cover plates, when closed, form a cross-shaped configuration. Its color is characteristically brownish. The more nearly ubiquitous *Balanus glandula* (fig. 99; pl. 11) reaches a diameter of about 1.5 cm and tends to be white.

In some rocky areas, the larger specimens are more abundant in zone 1 than elsewhere because snails of the genus *Nucella,* which prey heavily on *B. glandula,* are mostly active at lower levels. Since the barnacles are filter feeders, using their thoracic appendages to comb the water for microscopic food, those in the uppermost part of the intertidal region can feed only when the tide is high. Some are left high and dry for longer periods than others, and may not be wet except by spray for several days at a time.

In deep crevices and under ledges, generally so high that it is only

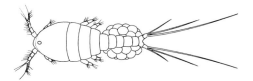

94. *Tigriopus californicus*

95. *Littorina sitkana*

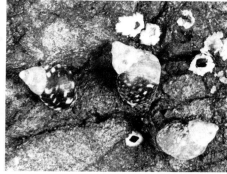

96. *Littorina scutulata*

97. *Collisella digitalis,* with *Chthamalus dalli* (*left*) and with *Littorina scutulata* (*below*)

rarely drenched directly by sea water, is the isopod *Ligia pallasii* (fig. 100). Squeezing into cracks, so that it is sometimes almost impossible to extract in one piece, it behaves much like a cockroach. The female is larger and proportionately wider than the male, attaining a length of about 3 cm. As in other isopods, overlapping plates on the underside of the thoracic region of the female form a brood pouch in which the young develop. *Ligia* is a scavenger, feeding mostly on decaying algal material.

Hiding under the lower edges of boulders is a large limpet that has an almost inflated look because the posterior and lateral slopes of its shell are so distinctly convex. *Notoacmea persona* (fig. 101) sometimes reaches a length of about 5 cm and may be abundant in both zone 1 and zone 2, providing it has the habitat it likes. In any case, it tends to be somewhat gregarious, except at night, when it wanders to feed on the thin surface film of algae and diatoms.

ZONE 2: THE UPPER MIDLITTORAL ZONE

In the San Juan Archipelago, this part of the intertidal region ranges from about 7 feet (2.1 m) down to about 4 feet (1.2 m); in most portions of Puget Sound that are characterized by rocky shores, it is a little higher. Among the brown algae, *Fucus distichus*, the rockweed (pl. 33), stands out. It is a substantial seaweed with a flattened thallus that keeps branching dichotomously until it reaches a length of about 30 cm. The midribs of the branches are continuous and prominently raised. The holdfast is not much more than a thickened button. At least some of the terminal branches become swollen and warty; these are the sites of egg and sperm production. *Fucus* luxuriates in late spring and summer, and where it grows well, it may cover just about everything else.

In some places in the San Juan Archipelago, on the west side of Vancouver Island, and probably elsewhere in the same general region, there is also *Fucus spiralis* (pl. 33). As its species name suggests, its thalli tend to twist a little, especially as they dry out. Two other features will help you recognize this seaweed: the terminal swellings are more nearly spherical than those of *F. distichus*, and there are tufts of hairs that emerge from pits on the surfaces of the thalli. These hairs are especially prominent in specimens that have been exposed to air for a time. *Fucus spiralis* usually occurs with *F. distichus*, but tends to be concentrated in a narrow vertical band above the latter, as shown in one of the illustrations on Plate 33.

Scytosiphon lomentaria (fig. 102), also a brown alga, is easy to recognize because its flabby, tubular growths, generally about 20 cm long and 3 or 4 mm thick, are pinched into sausage-shaped segments. The color is usually light olive. *Scytosiphon* is most common at the edges

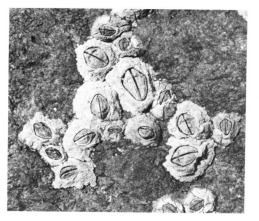

98. *Chthamalus dalli*

99. *Balanus glandula*

100. *Ligia pallasii,* adult (*left*) and immature specimen (*above*)

101. *Notoacmea persona*

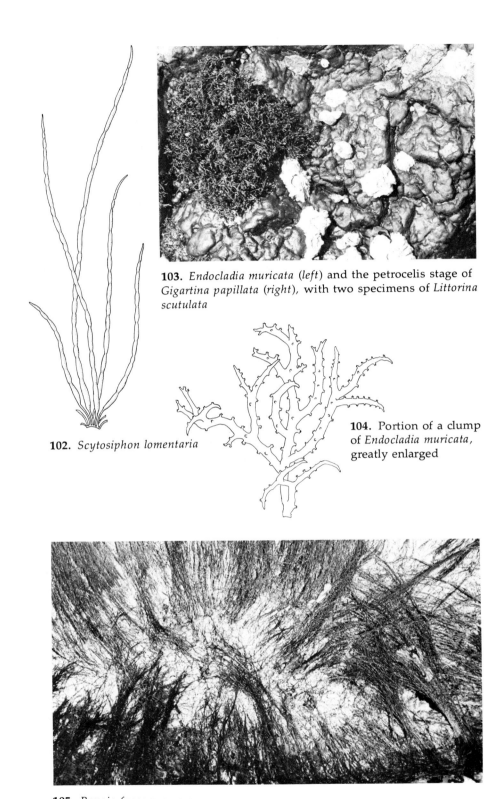

103. *Endocladia muricata* (*left*) and the petrocelis stage of *Gigartina papillata* (*right*), with two specimens of *Littorina scutulata*

102. *Scytosiphon lomentaria*

104. Portion of a clump of *Endocladia muricata*, greatly enlarged

105. *Bangia fuscopurpurea*

of shallow pools and is sometimes found when there is a substantial amount of fresh water seeping down onto the rocks.

A red alga especially characteristic of this zone is *Endocladia muricata* (figs. 103 and 104; pl. 35). It is small and rather delicate, forming tufts not often more than 3 cm high. The branches are cylindrical and studded with short tubercles crowned by a number of tiny spines. The color of the tufts ranges from dark brownish red to greenish brown or blackish brown; they become almost black when they dry out during summer low tides.

A common red alga that is especially noticeable on the upper surfaces of smooth boulders is *Bangia fuscopurpurea* (fig. 105). It is not at all pretty, growing as rather thin filaments of a rusty, purplish brown, or blackish color. Younger portions of these filaments are just one cell thick. As the tide ebbs, the filaments spread out over the rock in a way much too reminiscent of a few hairs artfully plastered down on a nearly bald head. Is *Bangia* making fun of some of us?

The several species of *Porphyra* found in zone 2 consist of single, thin blades. They are sometimes gray, sometimes brownish purple, and so iridescent as to appear oiled. *Porphyra perforata* (figs. 106 and 107) is a distinctive kind, ruffled and perforated, especially near the edges. It is abundant in late spring and summer. A really large thallus, if carefully spread out, may be nearly 1 m in diameter. *Porphyra torta* is the prevailing species in winter and early spring. It is nearly impossible, even for an expert, to differentiate the various local species of *Porphyra* without studying microscopic details.

Gigartina papillata (pl. 33) is dark, brownish red. Its thin but tough blades, which arise in clusters from a small holdfast, may reach a length of about 15 cm, and are usually split dichotomously two or three times. They are studded with small warts. There is much variation in the size and wartiness of this common species.

Wherever there are plants of *G. papillata,* there are also likely to be encrustations of an alga that has long been called *Petrocelis franciscana* (fig. 103). Its coatings, about 2 mm thick, are generally purplish black or purplish gray when dry, brownish red when wet. They are sometimes extensive, being interrupted only by barnacles, *Endocladia,* and other attached organisms. Recent studies have shown that *Petrocelis* is just a stage in the life history of *Gigartina papillata.* It reproduces by spores, whereas the *Gigartina* stage reproduces sexually. In any case, the name *Gigartina papillata* should be used to cover both stages.

Two other dark crusts could be confused with the petrocelis phase of *G. papillata.* These are *Hildenbrandia* (pl. 35), a red alga, and *Ralfsia* (pl. 12), a brown alga. Both of these are thinner than petrocelis, however. *Hildenbrandia,* moreover, comes much closer to being red than petrocelis does. Its favored habitats are tide pools and wet crevices. The coatings of *Ralfsia* are so thin that they cannot easily be separated

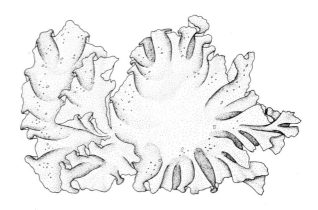

106. *Porphyra perforata*

107. *Porphyra perforata*

108. *Semibalanus cariosus;* the dark patches on the rock in the left-hand figure consist of a lichen, *Arthopyrenia*

from the rock with a fingernail. The color is usually olive or brown, and the patches tend to be small.

All three of the encrusting algae just mentioned are sometimes called "tar spots." The petrocelis phase of *Gigartina* comes closest to looking like a deposit of tar.

A black lichen, *Arthopyrenia orustensis* (figs. 108, 110, and 112), is often abundant in this zone, occupying much of the space not taken up by barnacles or other organisms. It resembles *Verrucaria*, but usually forms more distinct patches. Other lichens have been reported to occur at about the same level, so one's identification of *Arthopyrenia* should be tentative.

A common green alga in zone 2 is *Cladophora columbiana* (pl. 35), which forms clumps that resemble the tufted growths of certain mosses. When young, they are almost perfectly hemispherical, but as they spread out they tend to become more irregular. *Cladophora* generally hugs crevices, and considerable sand may become trapped between its branching filaments. Each filament, with a diameter of about 0.2 mm, consists of a series of large cells. This species is found from British Columbia to Baja California, and is not restricted to the open coast. It is abundant in the Puget Sound region, not only on rocks but also on pilings and bulkheads.

Ulva, or sea lettuce (pls. 32 and 35), is generally present, but is likely to be more prevalent at slightly lower levels. Any other green alga occasionally found in zone 2 will probably be one of those described later in connection with zone 3.

Among the barnacles, *Chthamalus*, for all practical purposes, is out of the picture here. *Balanus glandula* (fig. 99), however, is abundant in zone 2, and so is *Semibalanus cariosus* (fig. 108). The shell of the latter has very prominent ridges, which give rise, especially near the base, to downward-directed projections. When *S. cariosus* is broken off the rock, it leaves soft tissue instead of the calcareous scar left by *B. glandula*. Large specimens have a basal diameter of about 5 cm. Intertidally, *S. cariosus* becomes the prevailing acorn barnacle at levels below zone 2. Once it has grown to a size exceeding that attained by *B. glandula*, it becomes less subject than the latter to predation by *Nucella* and sea stars.

Of the limpets, a few *Collisella digitalis* may be present, but *C. paradigitalis*, *C. pelta*, and *Notoacmea scutum* are more typical of this zone. *Collisella paradigitalis* (fig. 109) resembles *C. digitalis* and *C. pelta*, and it could be confused with either of these. The length of its shell does not often exceed 1.5 cm, however. The exterior is usually grayish and pitted, but sometimes it is olive green with bluish white markings. The interior is white to bluish white, with some irregular dark markings, especially at the edges, but there is no prominent dark blotch. *Collisella paradigitalis* is common in the mid-intertidal region from Brit-

109. *Collisella paradigitalis*

110. *Collisella pelta* and the black lichen *Arthopyrenia*

111. (*Above and right*) *Notoacmea scutum*

ish Columbia to Baja California, and is mixed with both C. *digitalis* and C. *pelta*.

Collisella pelta (fig. 110) is an extremely variable species. It may be strongly ribbed and have a wavy margin, but even with these features it differs from C. *digitalis* in having its apex some distance back of the anterior edge. Other specimens may have a smooth margin and no ribs. Large specimens attain a length of about 4 cm.

Notoacmea scutum (fig. 111) also grows to a length of about 4 cm, but its shell is low and shieldlike. It is never strongly ribbed, though it may be marked with fine radiating lines.

The periwinkles so characteristic of zone 1 may be fairly abundant in zone 2, but some larger snails become conspicuous here. *Nucella emarginata* (figs. 112 and 114) gets to be about 2.5 cm long and has strongly developed spiral ribs; as a rule, heavier ribs alternate with more delicate ones. The ribs themselves are usually white, and the furrows between them are yellow, orange, brown, gray, or almost black. *Nucella canaliculata* (figs. 113 and 114) is on the average a little larger and a little more slender, reaching a length of about 3 or 4 cm. The spiral ridges are all much alike in caliber and distinctly set off from one another by deep furrows. The coloration on the whole is light, generally whitish gray. *Nucella lamellosa* (fig. 116), with a shell that often exceeds a length of 5 cm, may be common, although it is more typical of zone 3. Specimens from protected situations usually have attractive axial frills, but those from exposed areas tend to be nearly smooth. The color is almost uniform, ranging from white to pale brown or gray.

All of the species of *Nucella*, unlike the limpets and periwinkles, are carnivores and are the most important predators on intertidal barnacles. The interactions between these two groups of organisms have been the subject of a number of studies in Europe and America. In our region, *Balanus glandula* is preferred over B. *cariosus* as food, and the usual relative scarcity of the former, except at higher levels, is definitely related to the abundance of *Nucella*. In situations where there are few or no *Nucella*, B. *glandula* can enjoy a much wider vertical distribution.

Nucella drills a small hole into the shell of a barnacle where two wall plates meet, at the base of one of these plates, or at the edge of one of the valves that cover the animal when it is withdrawn. The proboscis, however, is too large to go through the hole, so probably some toxic substance is introduced through the hole in order to relax the muscles that close the valves.

The peculiar stalked egg cases of *Nucella* (fig. 116), laid in large clusters on the undersides of rocks, are abundant in the spring and summer. Each pale translucent yellow case is about the size of a large oat. These cases are useful sources of developmental stages.

Another fairly large snail may show up in zone 2, at least in its lower portion. This is the spindle shell, *Searlesia dira* (fig. 115). On rocky shores it reaches a length of about 3 cm. (It grows larger in bays, where it lives at the lower edges of rocks set on gravel or mud.) The shell is gray on the whole, but a close inspection will reveal that most of the color is concentrated in the furrows between the rather fine spiral ridges. The dark pigment in the furrows that reach the lip of the aperture is visible within the aperture as a series of dark streaks. There are some low axial ribs on the upper whorls, but these are not continued on the body whorl. *Searlesia* has rather catholic carnivorous tastes, eating periwinkles, barnacles, worms, and other animals, and is said to specialize on animals debilitated by injuries or other misfortunes.

The hermit crabs must be close to the top of everyone's list of favorite seashore animals. The idea of living in an empty snail shell has been explored by several groups of invertebrates, including some other crustaceans, but hermit crabs have made a real success of it. As a hermit crab outgrows one shell, it must find another, sometimes running into serious competition for available homes in the right size range. Once the crab has solved its housing problem and has safely tucked away its soft, coiled abdomen, it will not look again for some time. On the whole, unoccupied shells, especially larger ones, are in short supply wherever hermit crabs are found, but the intensity of competition varies depending on circumstances. In any case, hermit crabs will fight for exclusive rights to empty shells, and this behavior can be observed in aquaria as well as in tide pools.

Of the approximately twenty species of hermit crabs known to occur in the Puget Sound region, only three are regularly found intertidally. Some of the more peculiar species from deeper water just have to be mentioned, however. One of them, *Discorsopagurus schmitti*, has a straight abdomen and lives in empty tubes of two kinds of polychaete annelids, *Sabellaria cementarium* and *Serpula vermicularis*. At least three other species sometimes live in masses of a hard-textured sponge, *Suberites*. They start out as juveniles in empty snail shells, but these become overgrown, except at the aperture, by the sponge. The shells eventually dissolve, and the hermit crabs live out the rest of their lives in lumps of *Suberites* many times larger than they are.

Getting back to zone 2, the only hermit crab likely to be found here is *Pagurus hirsutiusculus* (fig. 117; pl. 20). The name alludes to its general hairiness, but other good characteristics by which most larger specimens can be recognized are the white spots on the antennae and the white or pale blue band around the base of the next to last article (the "segment" just before the claw) of the second and third legs. In any case, *P. hirsutiusculus* is usually abundant in tide pools between and under rocks (especially those resting on coarse gravel), and under masses of seaweed. Larger specimens, with a body length of up to about 3 cm, prefer the shells of *Nucella emarginata* and *Searlesia dira*; small specimens are most often found in shells of one or the other of

112. *Nucella emarginata* and the black lichen
Arthopyrenia

113. *Nucella canaliculata*

114. *Nucella emarginata* (*right*) and *Nucella
canaliculata* (*left*)

115. *Searlesia dira*

116. *Nucella lamellosa*. The specimen shown with its egg cases (*left*) is from
quiet water; the other two specimens (*right*) are from a situation exposed to
considerable wave action.

133 / Rocky Shores of the Puget Sound Region

our two species of *Littorina*. Too frequently, the fit seems much tighter than it should be, so the little hermit cannot get its head under cover. This situation is typical for large males of *P. hirsutiusculus*. The majority of hermit crabs, including *P. hirsutiusculus,* feed largely on detritus, but they may scavenge on dead animal and plant material to some extent.

Where rocks lie on a gravelly or sandy substratum, and where decaying seaweed accumulates under their edges, two species of isopods are abundant. *Idotea wosnesenskii* (pl. 19) has already been mentioned in connection with the fauna of floats, but it prefers under-rock situations with plenty of vegetable debris. The coloration is generally uniform and ranges from brown through olive green to nearly black; dark olive green seems to be the most common shade. (Specimens associated with coralline algae, however, may be partly or almost wholly pink.) The length of large specimens is about 4 cm. *Idotea wosnesenskii* can cling tightly to rough rock—and to one's fingers—by its seven pairs of clawed legs. It does not look like much of a swimmer, but it is remarkably agile and graceful when it does swim; the paddlelike appendages on the underside of the abdomen propel the animal, and the legs are kept spread as if to take hold of any firm object that comes along.

Gnorimosphaeroma oregonense (fig. 118) is smaller, only about 1 cm long. It is not much for looks, being pudgy and of a drab, mottled gray color; but it is rather distinctive among marine isopods because of its ability to roll up into a ball, like its garden cousin, the pill bug. *Gnorimosphaeroma* seems generally to be most abundant where there is considerable seepage of fresh water onto the shore.

When the intertidal region is submerged, many kinds of fishes move in and out of it. As stated in the Preface, this book is not meant to deal in detail with fishes, for there are other references that cover the species found in the area. It is not fair, however, to neglect completely a few that are encountered regularly in the course of field work. At this particular point only the tidepool sculpin, *Oligocottus maculosus* (pl. 24), need be mentioned. It is abundant in tide pools of zones 2 and 3, where other fishes are not so likely to be found. It is a typical sculpin, with a big head, large pectoral fins, and a tapering posterior portion. *Oligocottus maculosus* reaches a length of 10 cm. The coloration is extremely variable, but greenish black tones predominate. Younger specimens are particularly undependable with respect to color, but as a rule they are more sharply marked—especially with white areas—than adults.

Mussels and Goose Barnacles

Between about 4 feet (1.2 m) and 0.0, the flora and fauna show some distinctive components. Where there is some real wave action—as is typical of the west side of San Juan Island and the southern part of Lopez Island—there will be beds of the California mussel, *Mytilus californianus*, and of the goose barnacle, *Pollicipes polymerus*. Neither of these will be found in Puget Sound proper, and they are absent from most islands of the San Juan Archipelago. Thus only the more exposed shores in the archipelago can come close to showing a lower midlittoral zone of the sort seen on the outer coast.

The California mussel (fig. 119; pl. 17) sometimes attains a length of about 20 cm, but specimens 15 cm long can be considered large. Like the edible mussel prevalent in quiet waters, it is tightly attached to the rock by means of a byssus and tends to be aggregated. The masses are sometimes several feet across. The California mussel has a good flavor when it is cooked by boiling or roasting, but it can be very poisonous. "Mussel poisoning" is caused by a toxin derived from a microscopic organism, a dinoflagellate called *Gonyaulax catenella*. When *Gonyaulax* is abundant in the plankton, it is ingested along with other organisms, and the toxin accumulates in the tissues of *Mytilus*. The paralyzing effect of this substance is somewhat similar to that of curare, which has long been used on darts and arrows by certain South American Indians. In California the beaches are routinely posted from late spring to early autumn to warn of the danger. The summer months are apt to be the only really dangerous ones, although the poison stored in the tissues may remain for some time after the *Gonyaulax* has disappeared from the diet of mussels. In any case, one should avoid gathering the California mussel for food in the summer months. Toxicity can be established by injecting laboratory mice with an extract of mussel tissue, but this is obviously not practicable for every lover of seafood. Cooking does gradually destroy the toxin, but even high heat over a long period cannot be trusted to do the job thoroughly. Other bivalves, including the littleneck clam of protected situations, store up the toxin at dangerous levels, but the California mussel is the worst offender on the open coast.

The beds of the California mussel accumulate a gritty mixture of sand and bits of shell. In this, and elsewhere among the tightly packed mussels, an interesting assemblage of other organisms is usually found. A little blackish sea cucumber, *Cucumaria pseudocurata* (pl. 27), only about 2 cm long, is more or less completely restricted to this situation. Then there are a number of polychaete annelids, including *Nereis vexillosa* (fig. 120). This reaches a length of about 15 cm, and its color is mostly a mixture of leaden grays with iridescent greens and blues and some reddish tones. If picked up, it wriggles to get away and may be

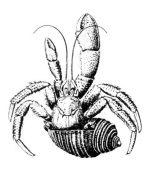

117. *Pagurus hirsutiusculus*   **118.** *Gnorimosphaeroma oregonense*

119. *Mytilus californianus,* the California mussel

120. *Nereis vexillosa*

excited enough to protrude its eversible pharynx, which is armed with a pair of blackish, pincerlike jaws and studded with numerous small denticles. If the worm does not spontaneously extrude its pharynx, try pressing gently, between thumb and forefinger, just behind the head. Nereids, as a group, are herbivores, and their big jaws are handy for tearing off pieces of algae.

The tight colonies of *Pollicipes* (fig. 121; pls. 17 and 18) generally alternate with beds of the California mussel, but the two species mix to some extent. The tough stalk of *Pollicipes* is generally about 2 cm long and contains the gonads and an adhesive gland. The upper portion of the body includes most of the rest of the viscera and the appendages. It is protected by a kind of coat of mail consisting of a number of essentially separate calcareous plates of varying size.

The feeding of *Pollicipes* differs from that of most acorn barnacles, such as the species of *Balanus*. The cirri do not beat regularly and rhythmically, but instead are spread so that water can rush through them. The catch includes small crustaceans and other planktonic organisms whose size on the average is larger than that combed out of the water by acorn barnacles. When sufficient food has accumulated on the cirri, they withdraw and the catch is transferred to the mouth parts.

If *Pollicipes* feeds by spreading its cirri to form a net, one might expect the cirri to face the incoming wave. This barnacle, however, typically takes advantage of the water running *off* the rock. For this reason, the specimens in a colony on one part of a large rock mass may be oriented in one direction, whereas some others not too far away may be oriented in a completely different direction. Those situated in definite channels, regardless of which way these run, characteristically face the down-rushing water. Because *Pollicipes* feeds the way it does, some colonies are found much higher than the typical *Mytilus-Pollicipes* association. These colonies will almost invariably be in gulleys in which water breaking on the shore surges upward for some distance before it falls back.

Mytilus edulis, the edible mussel (pl. 17), is characteristic of quiet waters and of estuaries where the salinity is relatively low. Over most of the area with which we are concerned, it is the only mussel found intertidally. It is not often observed on the exposed outer coast, where *M. californianus* is in its element, but one has only to locate a protected harbor and it will be present if there is rock or wood for it to settle on. In the San Juan Archipelago, in those few places where the California mussel does occur, the rocky habitat is not quite comparable to that on the open coast and the edible mussel is generally found along with it. It can easily be separated from the California mussel by its smaller size (the maximum length rarely exceeds 6 cm) and its relatively smooth shell; the California mussel typically has several strong ribs.

Chitons

Even if *Pollicipes* and *M. californianus* are absent, other animals help to define this zone. The black chiton, *Katharina tunicata* (fig. 122) is rather regularly present. It is up to about 7 cm long, and its eight shell plates are very nearly covered by the mantle. If you detach it (you may have to use the blade of a pocket knife or putty knife, so be careful with the animal), you will see that the undersurface is mostly a dull yellowish orange. The numerous separate gills characteristic of a chiton are arranged in a single row on each side of the broad clinging foot. Water enters the mantle cavity anteriorly, passes over the gills, then exits posteriorly. Like almost all chitons, *Katharina* is an herbivore, grazing on the film of diatoms and on other algae that coat the rocks.

Lepidochitona dentiens (*Cyanoplax dentiens*) (pl. 9) is often abundant in this zone, at least at lower levels. It is small—up to about 2 cm long—and is therefore likely to be overlooked or mistaken for the young of some other species. The upper side of the girdle has a finely granular appearance when magnified. The color of *L. dentiens* varies; on the whole, it is usually brown, brown with tints of green, or reddish brown. The girdle often has light specks, however, and some of these may be organized into a distinct pattern. The valves, except for the first and last, are rather strongly beaked, and their internal surfaces are almost always bluish green.

Snails, Limpets, and a Sluglike Mollusc

Nucella lamellosa is common in zone 3; *N. emarginata* and *N. canaliculata* are also present, along with *Searlesia dira*. *Collisella digitalis* will not be found here, and *C. pelta*, *C. paradigitalis*, and *Notoacmea scutum* are generally less abundant than they are in zone 2.

Granulina margaritula (fig. 123), up to about 3 mm long, looks like a tiny cowrie, because its shell consists almost entirely of the body whorl; the spire is hidden. The animal itself is attractively spotted and moves about rapidly in a businesslike manner. This little snail has a wide range, being found from Alaska to Panama. It usually lives in the gritty sediment among algal holdfasts.

Onchidella borealis (pl. 16), a sluglike animal that reaches a length of about 1.5 cm, is an oddity in that it has a cavity similar to the lung of land snails and slugs. It does not seem to be as closely related to these gastropods, however, as it is to opisthobranchs, the varied group that includes sea slugs. The general color ranges from yellowish green or olive to reddish brown or brownish black, but there is a pattern of mottling and sometimes there are white spots. The eyes are at the tips of distinct stalks, and the margin of the body is studded with little tubercles. This species feeds largely on diatoms, and its usual habitat is among seaweed holdfasts.

Crabs and Hermit Crabs

Under loose rocks and in cracks, the crabs *Hemigrapsus nudus* (pl. 21) and *H. oregonensis* (pl. 21) will be found. Sometimes these two species occur together, but more often there is only one or the other. *Hemigrapsus nudus* is most likely to be present in exposed rocky situations, whereas *H. oregonensis* is typical of quiet water and of rocky habitats within estuaries. Both species of *Hemigrapsus* have a nearly rectangular carapace. *Hemigrapsus nudus* is usually rather reddish and has a number of distinct purple spots on the pincers of its first pair of legs; its legs in general are not particularly hairy. *Hemigrapsus oregonensis* tends to be grayish green and lacks purple spots on the pincers; its legs have conspicuous fringes of hairs. These crabs can pinch hard if they have to, but their food consists to a large extent of seaweed, especially *Ulva*.

Although *Pagurus hirsutiusculus* (fig. 117; pl. 20), common in zone 2, is also found in zone 3, most of the hermit crabs one finds here belong to *P. granosimanus*. This species is about the same size as *P. hirsutiusculus*, but is almost hairless, and its antennae do not have white spots. The shells used by larger individuals are mostly those of *Searlesia dira*, *Nucella emarginata*, and sometimes *N. canaliculata*. Small specimens use periwinkles. *Pagurus granosimanus* generally manages to find shells into which it can withdraw completely.

Where loose rocks rest tightly on an accumulation of sand or rather fine gravel, there will probably be porcelain crabs, *Petrolisthes eriomerus* (pl. 20). These are much flattened, sometimes blue, sometimes purplish red, with a nearly circular body up to about 2 cm across. The second antennae, which are longer than the first antennae, are widely spaced and are lateral to the eyes. This characteristic, together with the fact that the fifth pair of legs is small and tucked under the body, sets these crabs apart from "true" crabs such as *Hemigrapsus*. They are actually more closely related to hermit crabs. When a rock hiding some *Petrolisthes* is lifted, they scurry wildly for cover. A curious trait of this crab and some of its relatives is the ease with which it can autotomize a leg that happens to be immobilized. Near the base of each leg is a groovelike ring that marks a feature quite comparable to the abscission layer between a stem and a leaf that is about to fall away. Thus if the leg is pinned down, the crab simply parts company with it and walks away, as a lizard might from a tail caught in the mouth of a predator. The wound does not bleed long, and within a few weeks the lost portion of the limb will be regenerated from the stub.

Lophopanopeus bellus (pl. 22), the black-clawed crab, is sometimes common under rocks, especially those set on muddy gravel. This species is often mixed with *Petrolisthes*. The black-tipped claws constitute a reliable characteristic for identification, since the only other intertidal crabs with claws so marked are *Cancer oregonensis* (pl. 22) and *C. productus* (fig. 357); both have a number of almost equal and evenly spaced teeth between the eyes and widest part of the carapace, whereas

L. bellus has just three teeth, all close to the widest part. The carapaces of large specimens of *L. bellus*, moreover, rarely reach a width much greater than 2.5 cm. This species varies a great deal in color, some specimens being red or nearly red and others ranging through browns and grays to almost white. Unfortunately, the coloration of most specimens taken within Puget Sound and the San Juan Archipelago could not be much duller, so they look like little gray or brownish gray stones. The hardness of the carapace and the tendency of *Lophopanopeus* to go into a state of "rigor mortis" when handled adds to the illusion.

Sea Stars

The most conspicuous sea star of rocky intertidal areas is *Pisaster ochraceus* (fig. 124; pl. 25). It is most appropriately considered at this point in our survey of the beach because its food consists to a large extent of the California mussel, when available. It also preys, however, on the edible mussel, acorn barnacles, limpets, and other snails. It may even move into zone 2 with the rising tide and not move back down as fast as the tide ebbs. In any case, it shows a rather wide vertical distribution.

Pisaster ochraceus is a very stiff sea star, harsh to the touch, which commonly attains a diameter of about 25 or 30 cm. Its specific name implies that the color should be close to ochre, and it sometimes is. The ochraceous phase can better be described as being orange-ochre, but some specimens are brown. On the open coast, individuals having the orange-ochre color are mixed with those of a deep purple phase. In Puget Sound and in the San Juan Archipelago, almost all specimens are purple.

Like many other sea stars, *P. ochraceus* vanquishes its prey by a combination of the holding and pulling action of hundreds of tube feet, the ability to hump and pull with its arms in more than one direction, and mobility of its stomach. Part of the stomach can actually be extruded and spread over the prey or inserted into a crack between its shells. Among the clusters of spines that stand out on the upper surface are numerous microscopic, stalked pincers, called pedicellariae, which discourage settlement of other organisms. If you let the inner side of your forearm rest in solid contact with the upper surface of a *Pisaster* for a half minute or so, then draw it away, you may be able to feel that the pedicellariae have engaged the skin or some of the hairs.

Sea Anemones

The sea anemone *Anthopleura elegantissima* (pl. 4) is almost ubiquitous in zone 3 up and down much of the Pacific coast. It may range upward on the shore, however, if there are tide pools and depressions that hold water. It is typically found in situations where the rock to which it is attached accumulates some sand and fragments of shell; or per-

121. *Pollicipes polymerus,* the goose barnacle

122. *Katharina tunicata,* the black chiton

123. *Granulina margaritula*

124. *Pisaster ochraceus*

125. A bed of *Anthopleura elegantissima* attached to rock that is covered by sand

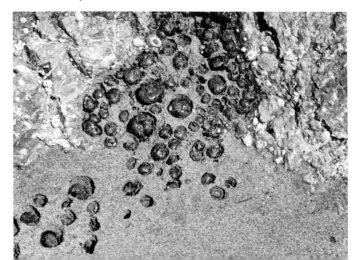

haps it is fairer to say that where *A. elegantissima* colonizes rock, sand and shell will accumulate. The column of this anemone is studded with little tubercles, to which foreign particles adhere. When it is submerged, *A. elegantissima* stands about 4 or 5 cm high, so its tentacles are spread well above the sand that may be covering its lower portion. When the tide ebbs, the animals not in pools contract into gritty blobs (fig. 125); but the beds are still plenty wet, and if sat on or walked on, the anemones exude water through the mouth and through pores on the column. The coloration of this species is subdued, but nevertheless beautiful. The tubercles and some of the rest of the column are green or olive green, and the tentacles are generally a delicate pink. Algal cells in the tissues contribute much of the green and olive color. There are, in fact, two kinds of unicellular algae in *A. elegantissima*. One kind is green; the other, a type of dinoflagellate, is olive. Both may be present in the same anemone. In any case, the color of the animal as a whole depends to some extent on the proportions of the two species of algae, as well as on pigments produced by the anemone itself. A discussion of the symbiotic relationship between the algae and *A. elegantissima* will be postponed until the section on a related species, *A. xanthogrammica* (pl. 4), which is found in zone 4. It should be pointed out, however, that in spite of its capacity to grow algae, *A. elegantissima* is a carnivore that feeds primarily on small crustaceans and other animals, including some that have been dislodged from rocks.

In a particular tight colony of *A. elegantissima*, all of the individuals will have originated by asexual multiplication: the founder divides, its progeny divide, and so on. Thus the colony is a clone of anemones that can be traced back to a single individual, and they are genetically identical. When one clone begins to encroach on the territory occupied by another, the clones engage in warfare. At the bases of the tentacles of *A. elegantissima* there are little bulbous structures where certain types of stinging capsules are concentrated. The anemones along the line of aggression fire these at one another, and soon a clear boundary is established between the clones.

Seaweeds

In covering the algae of zone 3, attention will have to be restricted to species that are either very common or very distinctive. Among the green algae, *Ulva* is routinely abundant; and where it grows profusely, its thin, bright green sheets may cover large surfaces. *Acrosiphonia coalita* (*Spongomorpha coalita*) (fig. 126; pl. 31) is quite a different type, composed of branching filaments of single cells. Some of the branches curve near their tips and hook onto other filaments, so that a plant of *Spongomorpha* forms almost ropelike complexes up to about 20 or 30 cm long.

There are a few conspicuous brown algae. *Fucus distichus* (pl. 33), already mentioned in connection with zone 2, may be present, but it is not likely to be as important as it is higher up. *Hedophyllum sessile* (pl. 33) is almost always dominant in zone 3. It looks something like a low-grade cabbage, but is composed actually of just one large, thick blade that becomes partly wrapped around itself. Most specimens are badly torn, in places almost all the way up to the base. Plants growing on the open coast are generally rather smooth, but those in sheltered areas usually have a blistered look. Large specimens are about 50 cm long.

Leathesia difformis (pl. 33) is an interesting brown alga—its color is actually more olive than brown—which appears in the late spring and hangs on until early autumn. It forms hemispherical or globular masses somewhat resembling a brain because of the convolutions of its surface. Most specimens are 4 or 5 cm across. *Leathesia* is sometimes attached to other algae, but usually it prefers rocks that have a coating of other small species.

Halosaccion glandiforme (pl. 35) is certainly one of the more distinctive red algae of zone 3. The major part of its thallus consists of one to several hollow sacs growing out of a disklike holdfast. The sacs sometimes exceed a length of 10 cm, but they are generally smaller than this. As they are filled completely or nearly completely with water, desiccation of the alga is minimized when low tides coincide with warm, dry weather. Perhaps, by keeping the sacs turgid and erect, this internal water also helps to prevent mechanical abrasion. Although *Halosaccion* is a red alga, its color is more often yellowish brown or olive; some specimens are reddish purple, at least at the base.

The flat fronds of *Microcladia borealis* (fig. 127; pl. 35), another kind of red alga common in this zone, reach a length of about 15 cm. The major divisions of the fronds are branched only on one side, and the tips of the ultimate branches curve toward one another, forming little pincers. *Microcladia* is usually dark brownish red. Its holdfast consists of a number of rootlike growths that cling to the rock.

ZONE 4: THE INFRALITTORAL FRINGE

This part of the intertidal region is exposed only by very low tides—those that bring the water level down into the range between about 0.0 and −3.5 feet (−1.1 m). The fauna and flora of zone 4 are apt to be frustratingly rich for a beginner, so they will have to be approached selectively, with a view to laying a solid foundation on which one can continue to build as his background and interest deepen.

Surfgrass and Seaweeds

Some plants that are characteristic of this zone will be discussed first. The surfgrass, *Phyllospadix scouleri* (fig. 215; pl. 34), is not a true grass, but it does have flowers, and the family to which it belongs (Zosteraceae) is not far from the grasses. Its bright green leaves are narrow (generally under 3 mm wide) and usually about 30 to 50 cm long. They arise from short stalks produced by a fuzzy, creeping stem. The flowers are borne in tight, caterpillarlike clusters, and pollination takes place under water. When *Phyllospadix* grows in pools, or in channels that retain at least a little water, it may occur considerably higher than 0.0, but when it is at the mercy of the tide, its upper limit is generally close to 0.0.

A narrow-leaved form of eelgrass, *Zostera* (discussed more fully in Chap. 7), is occasionally found in pools and channels on rocky shores, especially where there is relatively little wave action. It can easily be confused with *Phyllospadix*. The two genera may be positively distinguished during the summer by the arrangement of their flowers. In *Phyllospadix*, the pollen-bearing ("male") flowers and the flowers that ultimately produce seed ("female") are not only in separate clusters, but on separate plants. In *Zostera* (pl. 35), both types of flowers occur in the same cluster.

In late spring and summer, both *Phyllospadix* and *Zostera* frequently have a red alga, *Smithora naiadum* (pl. 35), attached to the leaves. *Smithora* grows as thin, purplish red sheets up to several centimeters long. It is a close relative of *Porphyra*, discussed in connection with zone 2. A green alga, *Kornmannia zostericola* (*Monostroma zostericola*) (pl. 35), is also likely to be present. It is about the same size as *Smithora*.

At about 0.0 and lower, there is typically an assemblage of brown algae of the type called laminarians—members of the genus *Laminaria* and some of its close relatives. When the tide drops to about −1.5 or −2.0 feet (−0.5 or −0.6 m), a forest of these is exposed. One species, *Laminaria saccharina* (fig. 74) has been described in Chapter 3, for it is common on floating docks. *Laminaria groenlandica* (fig. 128) is larger. Its blades, often more than 1 m long, are generally divided into three lobes (as a rule, one can tell the true lobes from strips that develop as the blades become lacerated). The stalk between the blade and holdfast is short, which will help differentiate *L. groenlandica* from *L. setchellii* when the two species occur together, as they do on the open coast (see Chapter 5).

Another large laminarian, *Costaria costata* (fig. 75), has also been discussed in connection with the algae of floating docks. Its great blades, with five parallel ribs and a blistery texture, are truly handsome.

Agarum fimbriatum (fig. 129) resembles *Costaria* in that its blade is much blistered, but there is only one lengthwise rib. The blade, moreover, is generally at least half as wide as long, and there is a slight concavity in its margin where the stalk joins it. The blade commonly has holes, and its margin has serrations or fingerlike outgrowths of unequal size. The stalk has even more prominent outgrowths. The blade is almost always worn off at its free end. The color is usually

127. *Microcladia borealis*

126. Portion of a growth of *Acrosiphonia coalita,* as seen with the aid of a microscope

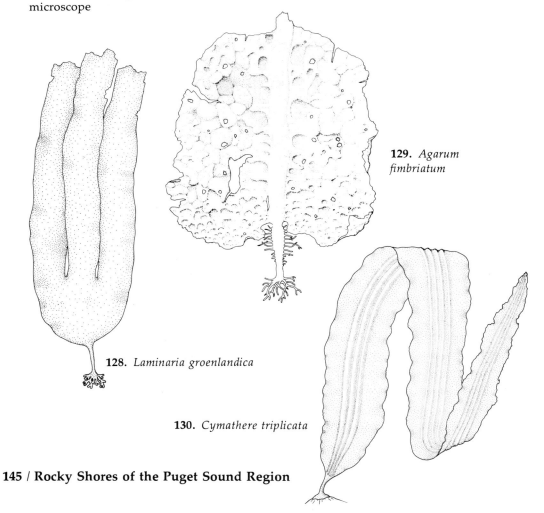

129. *Agarum fimbriatum*

128. *Laminaria groenlandica*

130. *Cymathere triplicata*

dark olive brown. *Agarum* is more common subtidally than inter-tidally.

Cymathere triplicata (fig. 130) is distinctive because its blades, which are generally about 1 m long and 6 to 8 cm wide, have three to five conspicuous longitudinal folds. The holdfast is buttonlike and the stalk is not often more than 10 cm long. The color of the plant is usually light olive.

Egregia menziesii (fig. 131; pl. 33), the feather boa kelp (the common name alludes to a once-fashionable scarf made of feathers), is as easy to recognize as it is common and luxuriant. It has branching stipes about 2 or 3 cm wide and 5 cm or more in length, which are rather strongly flattened, tough, and covered with little bumps. From either side arise numerous crowded blades of various lengths up to about 5 or 6 cm; some of the blades are swollen into floats about the size of a large olive. On the whole, *Egregia* is more or less olive or olive brown, but the stipe is sometimes very dark. On the open coast, this species is regularly found in what would correspond to zone 3; but its presence at this higher level on the more protected shores of the San Juan Archipelago is unusual.

A coarse, hard brown alga that is mostly subtidal is *Pterygophora californica* (fig. 132). Its stalk, arising from a holdfast of the type generally found in kelps, is almost woody; the plant lives for a number of years and the stalk forms growth rings much like the annual rings found in the trunks and branches of trees. The stalk is continued apically into a blade, below which several other broad blades branch off on opposite sides. The lower portion of the stalk, at least in older plants, is devoid of any such branches. Large specimens of *Pterygophora* may reach a length of about 2 m, of which about half is taken up by the stalk.

Alaria marginata (fig. 133) is closely related to *Pterygophora*, and also to *Egregia*. Its stalk is short and is continued as the midrib of the long, wavy-edged blade, which may be 2 or 3 m long. On either side of the stalk are a number of small, oval blades which are specialized for the production of spores.

Desmarestia ligulata (figs. 134 and 135) grows to a fairly good size—up to about 3 m long—but it is comparatively delicate for a kelp as large as this. The growth form shown in Figure 134 has a broad main axis, generally 2 or 3 cm wide, from the edges of which arise numerous pairs of almost perfectly opposite branches that resemble elongated leaves; these usually branch again. The main axis and branches have slender marginal teeth. This is a variable species, and younger stages and certain growth forms have in the past been accorded separate names. Desmarestias that fit the description just given were called *D. munda* and *D. herbacea*. The type of plant shown in Figure 135, with a more delicate and nearly featherlike pattern of branching, is what algologists have identified as *D. ligulata*. It is apparently just a younger

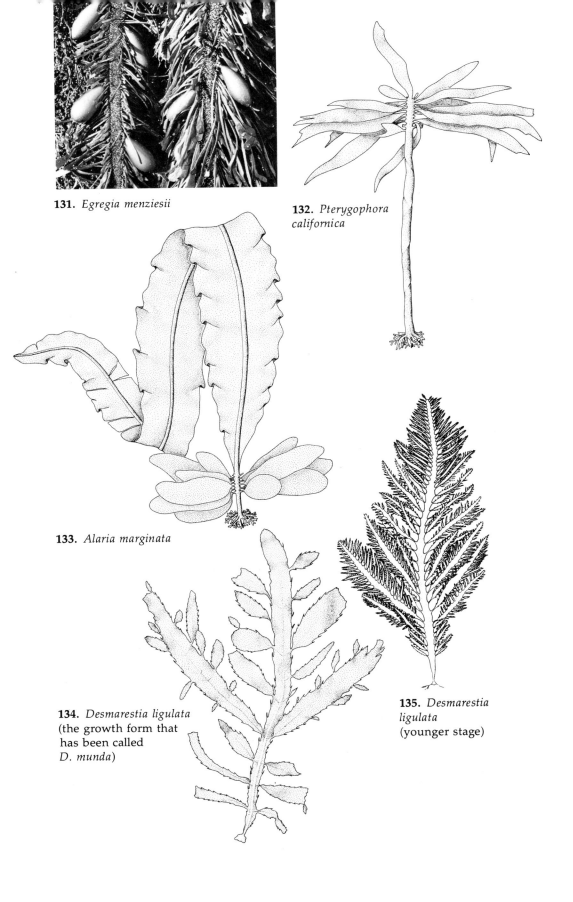

131. *Egregia menziesii*

132. *Pterygophora californica*

133. *Alaria marginata*

134. *Desmarestia ligulata* (the growth form that has been called *D. munda*)

135. *Desmarestia ligulata* (younger stage)

stage of D. *"munda"* and D. *"herbacea,"* but its name has priority and now serves for the whole complex.

Desmarestia viridis (fig. 76) is not at all like D. *ligulata,* for its branches are wirelike and generally cylindrical or only slightly flattened. It grows up to about 50 cm long.

Species of *Desmarestia,* as a group, have a very acid cell sap. After they have been bruised, the sap that oozes out of them is a menace to other organisms. Therefore, members of this genus must not be used as packing material to keep animals and delicate algae wet during the trip home.

The most talked-about kelp occurring in the Puget Sound region is *Nereocystis luetkeana* (figs. 136 and 137). It is both large and curiously wrought. From a branching holdfast much like that of laminarians, a long stalk leads to a bulbous float, from which four groups of broad, flat blades arise. The stalk of a large specimen may be 20 m long, the float may be over 12 cm in diameter, and the blades may attain a length of 3 m. The gas in the cavity of the float, which is continuous with a cavity in the thicker upper portion of the stalk, contains a considerable proportion of carbon monoxide. But perhaps the most astonishing fact about this huge kelp is that it is an annual and makes all of its growth during part of one year. Plants that develop in the spring and summer die off the next winter and accumulate on the beaches. They are tough, however, and the stalks are especially durable, resisting decay and fragmentation for weeks. Even during the growing season specimens come loose and wind up on the beach, providing temporary cover and food for scavenging amphipods and other organisms. On almost any rocky shore, great beds of *Nereocystis* can usually be seen, but the holdfasts are below the level reached by low tides.

The kelp phase of *Nereocystis* reproduces asexually by microscopic motile spores. The sexual generation that develops from these spores is very small and filamentous. It lives through the winter to produce the next kelp generation. This same general type of life history is followed by laminarians and some other brown algae.

Sargassum muticum (fig. 138) is a newcomer, having been introduced to the Northwest from Japan, and has become well established in some places. Large plants are over 1 m long, and the color is usually yellowish brown. There is typically a short stalk, from which arise some flat outgrowths that look like long leaves and a number of branches that divide again several times. The younger portions of the branches develop either into flattened, irregularly toothed structures that look like leaves; into swollen, club-shaped bodies in which the reproductive organs are concentrated; or into almost spherical floats.

Cystoseira geminata (fig. 139) is much like *Sargassum,* but grows larger—up to 4 or 5 m long. Also, its floats usually consist of two to several vesicles in a series, the terminal one being sharply pointed.

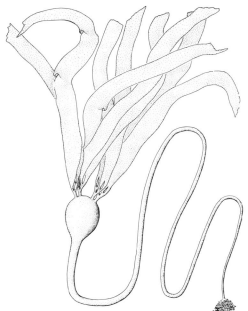

136. *Nereocystis luetkeana*, the bladder kelp

137. *Nereocystis luetkeana*, forming a kelp bed just offshore

The species frequently serves as host to another brown alga, *Coilo-desme californica* (fig. 140), which forms delicate, easily collapsible sacs up to about 20 cm long.

Analipus japonicus (fig. 141) produces one to several cylindrical stems from its encrusting holdfast. The stems have many side branches,

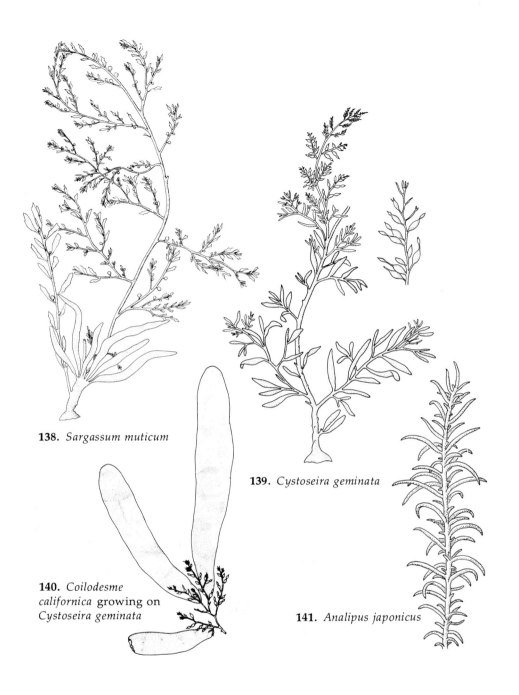

138. *Sargassum muticum*

139. *Cystoseira geminata*

140. *Coilodesme californica* growing on *Cystoseira geminata*

141. *Analipus japonicus*

mostly 1 or 2 cm long, and some of these are appreciably flattened so that they resemble needles on a twig of a fir tree. The color of *Analipus* ranges from olive tan to dark olive brown.

For a green alga, *Codium fragile* (pl. 31) is decidedly unusual in texture and habit of growth. The branches, which fork dichotomously, are solid and cylindrical, almost as thick as a pencil. The tips are blunt and the surface is velvety and soft, so *Codium* is often mistaken for a sponge. The plant is actually composed of separate filaments all woven together. The color is such a dark green as to be nearly black. Young specimens of *Codium* may stand almost upright, but as they get longer they start to droop. In large plants, the length of the fronds may exceed 30 cm. The holdfast disk is thin, but it may spread out irregularly over the rock to cover an area perhaps 5 cm in diameter.

There are two sea slugs that feed on *Codium fragile*. One of them, *Placida dendritica* (pl. 31) is characterized by numerous dorsal outgrowths. These structures are comparable to the cerata of eolid nudibranchs, because each one contains a branch of the digestive gland. The color of the animal is mostly olive green, but there are numerous white spots on the cerata and on the tentacles of the head. The length is usually about 1 cm. The other species, *Elysia hedgpethi* (pl. 31), lacks cerata, but both sides of its body are drawn out into flaps that can be spread laterally or pulled together dorsally until their edges touch. Branches of the digestive gland go out into the flaps. The color of *Elysia* is olive green, but the flaps have tiny white spots and also some larger blue spots. The length sometimes exceeds 5 cm, but is generally closer to 2 or 3 cm.

Placida and *Elysia* belong to a group of herbivorous gastropods called sacoglossans. The radula typically has an enlarged, sharp tooth that is used to slitting open algal cells. The animal can then suck out the protoplasm. After a tooth wears out, it is replaced. The name sacoglossan means "sac tongue," and refers to the fact that there is a little sac at the base of the radula, close to the mouth, where discarded teeth accumulate.

A remarkable feature of *Elysia* is that many of the chloroplasts it sucks in continue to carry on photosynthesis for several days after they have been taken up by cells of the digestive gland. In a European species of the same genus, the chloroplasts may function for about three months, provided that the animal is not deprived of light. In *Placida*, however, the chloroplasts are digested soon after they have been eaten. Both *Elysia* and *Placida*, by the way, also feed on *Bryopsis corticulans*, and are sometimes found on this green alga on floats and in quiet bays.

Codium setchellii (pl. 31) has the same texture and blackish green color as *C. fragile*, but it does not develop branches. It simply forms a thick encrustation on rocks, and it may overlap the holdfasts of laminarians and other kelps.

Among the red algae that stand out in this zone, the coralline species just about have to be mentioned first, since they are so abundant and so distinctive. Like *Phyllospadix*, the coralline red algae may occur at tide levels well above 0.0, but then they are mostly in pools, gullies, or at the edges of cracks that hold water. In the infralittoral fringe, they are just about everywhere.

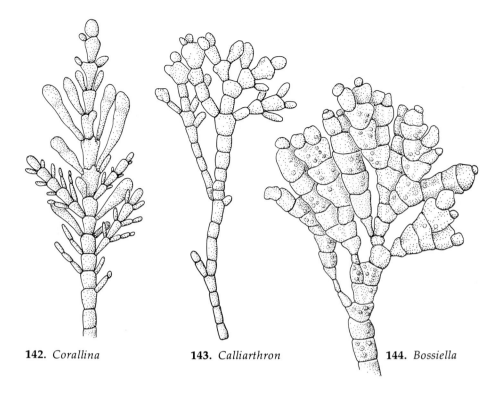

142. *Corallina*   **143.** *Calliarthron*   **144.** *Bossiella*

The coralline red algae are rendered hard and gritty by large amounts of calcium carbonate. They are reddish pink to purplish pink, but as they die they turn white. One genus, *Lithothamnium* (pls. 10, 11, and 12), forms encrusting growths resembling lichens. Other genera in our area produce tufts of articulated, branching stems, although a part of the thallus may have the encrusting habit; some that are reluctant to develop articulated growths are difficult to distinguish from *Lithothamnium*. The technical differences between them are complicated. On the basis of superficial features, however, a partial differentiation of three common genera in the region can be provided. In *Corallina* (fig. 142), the branching produces, in general, nearly featherlike growths, and the segments are usually decidedly longer than wide; in the upper part, the segments are cylindrical or only slightly flattened. More importantly, the reproductive structures are concentrated only at the tips of branches, and these tips become swollen. In *Calliarthron* (fig. 143; pl. 34) and *Bossiella* (fig. 144; pl. 34), the reproductive structures are located in elevations on the surfaces of some of the segments. It is almost impossible to distinguish between these two genera without recourse to microscopic characters. In *Bossiella*, the segments are regularly flattened, as they are in the species illustrated, whereas in *Calliarthron* they may be flattened or cylindrical. Thus a *Calliarthron* with cylindrical segments can be distinguished from a *Corallina* on the basis of the arrangement of its reproductive structures, but one with flattened segments will be difficult to tell apart from a *Bossiella*. A species of *Lithothrix* (pl. 34), slender and with short, curved branches, also occurs in our region.

Some clumps of jointed coralline algae may have a nonjointed species growing on them. The thalli of these are tightly attached, but their edges are free, so that they form irregular, wavy-edged disks. *Mesophyllum conchatum* (pl. 34) is one of several similar species found on the Pacific coast. The distinctions between these epiphytic coralline algae are based on details that require microscopic study.

Many of the noncoralline red algae of the infralittoral fringe are relatively small. Delicate types such as *Hollenbergia* (fig. 77) and *Antithamnion*, mentioned in Chapter 3, are abundant on rocks and on the stipes and fronds of other algae. There is, however, a large assortment of medium-sized species and a few larger ones; those described here will include a selected few that are more or less unmistakable.

A real oddity is *Constantinea simplex* (fig. 145), which looks a bit like certain terrestrial cup fungi. It has a short stalk which ordinarily does not branch but expands into a saucerlike blade. Sometimes there are additional blades encircling the stalk below the primary cup. Any or all of the blades may be frayed or split. The color is usually a dark purplish red. The stalks are not often more than 2 or 3 cm long, and the primary blade is generally under 5 or 6 cm in diameter; but larger specimens are occasionally found. The closely related *C. subulifera* may branch several times, and each branch may have a terminal blade as well as subsidiary ones below it. The most distinctive feature of this species is a fingerlike extension of the stalk coming up through each primary blade.

Gigartina exasperata (fig. 146) forms one or more broad, thick blades up to about 30 or 40 cm long, and the edges and flat surfaces of these are roughened by hundreds of tall, stiff outgrowths. The specific name is fully appropriate, as it refers to the rasplike character of the blades. The color of *G. exasperata* is usually a purplish brick red, and the surface is often somewhat iridescent when it is wet.

Iridaea cordata (fig. 147; pl. 35) is much like *G. exasperata* in overall form, thickness, and color. However, its blades are on the whole darker and much more iridescent, portions of them appearing purple or blue; they are also very slick, for they lack the outgrowths that roughen the blades of *Gigartina*.

Gigartina exasperata and *I. cordata* are perennials, but they die back in winter to a sort of crust. The little blades that start to grow out in early spring enlarge quickly. Both of these seaweeds are good sources of carrageenin (or carrageenan), a substance used as a stabilizer in many products ranging from cottage cheese to printer's ink. They have been "farmed" in an experimental way by attaching young plants to racks or lines of nylon rope kept submerged below the low-tide mark.

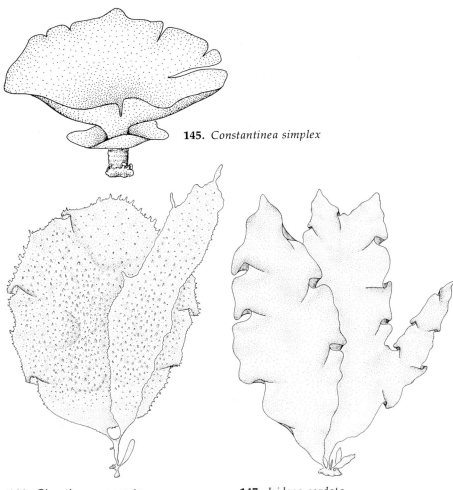

145. *Constantinea simplex*

146. *Gigartina exasperata*

147. *Iridaea cordata*

The crops have been good enough to encourage exploration of prospects for commercial production of carrageenin in Pacific Northwest waters.

Odonthalia floccosa (fig. 148) is common in zone 4 and is also abundant in tide pools at appreciably higher levels. It is not easily recognized as a red alga, for it is usually dark, blackish brown. It grows to a length of about 30 or 40 cm and is much branched. The branching tends to be in the same plane, and the final branches are sharply pointed, unless the tips have been worn off or eaten off.

Odonthalia washingtoniensis (fig. 149) is not likely to be confused with *O. floccosa* because its main stems and branches are strongly flattened. The color varies from brownish red to blackish brown. Although this species occurs from British Columbia to northern California, it is almost strictly subtidal south of Washington.

148. *Odonthalia floccosa*

149. *Odonthalia washingtoniensis*

150. *Rhodomela larix*

Rhodomela larix (fig. 150), like *O. floccosa*, is often common in tide pools at levels higher than zone 4. It, too, is dark blackish brown, and is about the same size as *O. floccosa*. It is, however, more firm than the latter. The generic name of larches, *Larix*, was adopted as its specific name because its clustered short branches are arranged after the fashion of the needles of this tree. Both *Rhodomela* and *Odonthalia* provide shelter for a variety of small animal organisms, especially amphipod crustaceans, and both may have an interesting brown alga, *Soranthera ulvoidea* (fig. 151), attached to them. *Soranthera* develops from a solid mass into a more or less egg-shaped hollow sac about 5 cm long. The darker bumps all over the sac mark the location of reproductive structures and some accessory hairlike outgrowths.

Colpomenia peregrina, another saclike brown alga, could be confused with *Soranthera*, as well as with *Coilodesme*, which was described in connection with the kelp *Cystoseira geminata*. Its thalli, which reach a length of about 6 cm, differ from those of *Coilodesme* in being less regular and less elongate; they differ from those of *Soranthera* in lacking warts. This species often grows on other algae, but it is just as likely to be attached directly to rock. *Colpomenia bullosa*, which forms a cluster of fingerlike sacs that may be up to 10 cm long, almost always grows on rock. It has been proposed that *C. bullosa* and *C. peregrina* are merely forms of one species, and if this is the case the former name has priority.

Large plants of *Hymenena flabelligera* (fig. 152) are easy to recognize when they show the prominent dark lines that characterize the blades. These mark the places where certain reproductive cells, called tetraspores because they develop in groups of four, originate. The lines are nearly parallel, but they diverge to some extent and one line may divide into two. They are generally less prominent on the younger portions of a plant than on older parts. The width of the blades may exceed 1 cm, and the height of well-developed specimens is usually about 15 or 20 cm. The color is pinkish red or brownish red.

Botryoglossum farlowianum (fig. 153) is similar to the preceding species in color and general appearance, but the edges of its blades have crowded ruffles and outgrowths that contain patches of tissue where tetraspores are formed. These patches correspond, therefore, to the dark lines on the blades of *Hymenena*. *Botryoglossum* may grow to a height of 50 cm, but most plants are not over 25 cm high.

Cryptopleura lobulifera (fig. 154) is a close relative of both *Hymenena* and *Botryoglossum*. It is difficult to describe concisely because it is so variable. Its blades, up to about 1.5 cm wide, are ruffled at the tips as well as along the margins, but do not have distinct outgrowths such as are characteristic of *Botryoglossum*. The patches of tissue that produce tetraspores are located in or beside the ruffles.

The three red algae that have just been described are probably the most commonly-encountered intertidal representatives of the genera

151. *Soranthera ulvoidea* growing on *Odonthalia floccosa*

152. *Hymenena flabelligera*

153. *Botryoglossum farlowianum*

154. *Cryptopleura lobulifera*

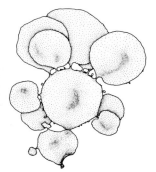

155. *Erythrophyllum delesserioides*   156. *Opuntiella californica*

to which they belong. There are additional species in these genera, however, as well as some look-alikes in other genera. An expert will study a variety of microscopic details before rendering an opinion about the identity of a particular specimen, and may not wish to decide at all if the material in hand does not show certain diagnostic features. A novice need not feel badly about remaining noncommittal.

Erythrophyllum delesserioides (fig. 155) is one of our larger and more vivid red algae. To be fully appreciated, it must be seen spread out in a tide pool or in a pan of water. The elongated blades, of which there may be several arising from the same basal stalk, reach a length of 50 cm or more, and have a prominent midrib that sends off lateral branches. This species is an annual, and in late winter or early spring, when the plants are young, the blades are more or less intact. By midsummer, they become deeply lacerated, and the branch veins develop secondary branches. Wartlike protuberances, within which reproductive cells develop, gradually become more numerous. In late autumn, little is left of the blade except the midrib, branch veins, and warts. The range of *E. delesserioides* is from Alaska to San Luis Obispo County, California. In spite of its delicate appearance, this species is found only in relatively exposed situations.

Opuntiella californica (fig. 156) is found intertidally in British Columbia and Washington, but becomes strictly subtidal farther south. It is a distinctive and easily recognized seaweed. The nearly circular blade that develops when the plant is young produces secondary blades at its edges, and these blades may produce more. The genus name means "little *Opuntia*," and alludes to the fact that the plant slightly resembles a prickly pear cactus. Robust specimens reach a height of 30 cm, and one of the larger blades may be more than 5 cm in diameter.

Several species of *Prionitis* occur along the Pacific coast, but only two are common in the Puget Sound region. Both are variable, but both smell like laundry bleach, and this helps to place them in the right genus. In *P. lyallii* (fig. 157), the secondary blades, which are usually

157. (*Above and right*) *Prionitis lyallii*

158. (*Above and right*) *Prionitis lanceolata*

between 1 and 3 cm wide, are broader than the main blades, and they are often fringed by crowded, small outgrowths. Although the branching is basically in one plane, the blades may curl to some extent, so the plant as a whole is not flat. The color varies; it may be brick red, brown, or greenish brown. Tide pools and tidal channels, especially those in which the bottom is sandy, are its preferred habitats.

In *Prionitis lanceolata* (fig. 158), the secondary blades, mostly under 1 cm wide, are not significantly broader than the primary blades, and they may even be narrower. In at least some part of the plant, the branching will probably be more clearly dichotomous than in *P. lyallii*, and there is little tendency for the blades to curl. This species is found in a wide variety of habitats, including tide pools that are small enough and high enough to be warmed by the sun. The color of intertidal plants is generally brownish red, but in certain situations *P. lanceolata* may be blackish brown or nearly purple.

The presence of *Laurencia spectabilis* (fig. 159) may be detected before the plants are seen. This is because of the pungent odor they give off when they are bruised. *Laurencia* has a peppery taste, and most of us cannot resist nipping off a tiny piece now and then. The flattened fronds, purplish red in color and mostly about 10 or 15 cm long, have a rather tough texture. Most of the divisions of the primary branches on each side are short and blunt-tipped.

Plocamium cartilagineum (fig. 160) is one of the more attractive red algae. Its flattened fronds are deep pinkish red, and the smaller divisions resemble little combs because of the way they are branched on one side only. Large plants reach a height of more than 20 cm.

The genus *Ceramium* is represented by a number of species. These are delicate, deep red algae whose dichotomous branches do not often exceed a diameter of 0.1 mm. A feature common to most of them is the way the tips of the ultimate branches curve toward one another to form little "pincers." A banded appearance, due to the fact that the branches are encircled by more or less regularly spaced rings of cells, is typical of certain species, such as *Ceramium californicum* (fig. 161), which grows to a height of about 8 cm and is of a deep rose color. It has a look-alike, *C. gardneri*. *Ceramium pacificum* is taller—up to about 15 cm high. It does not show prominent cross-banding, but it is distinctive in having short, almost hairlike outgrowths coming off most of its branches.

Pterochondria woodii (fig. 162) grows on various species of larger brown algae, such as *Cystoseira geminata*. It looks a little like *Ceramium pacificum*, but its stems are decidedly flattened rather than cylindrical, and the branching is not obviously dichotomous. The banding is not very distinct and there are no "pincers." The height is usually about 10 cm, and the color ranges from greenish brown to reddish brown.

Microcladia coulteri (fig. 163) does not closely resemble *M. borealis* (fig. 127), which is common in zone 3. It is, in fact, more likely to be

159. *Laurencia spectabilis*

160. *Plocamium cartilagineum*

161. *Ceramium californicum*, and a photomicrograph of its branches

162. *Pterochondria woodii*

163. *Microcladia coulteri*

164. *Callithamnion pikeanum*

confused with *Odonthalia washingtoniensis* than with *M. borealis*, partly because it produces branches on both sides of its main stems. A characteristic that may be helpful in narrowing down the list of prospects is the tendency of *M. coulteri* to grow on other red algae, especially species of *Prionitis*. The color is usually deep rose, and the height may reach 40 cm, but most plants are much smaller than this.

In *Callithamnion pikeanum* (fig. 164), each of the several main stems, which are about 1 or 2 mm in diameter, produces many extremely fine branches, whose tips are curved to the extent that they may interlock. Because of this, and also because diatoms and other microorganisms grow luxuriantly on the branches, a plant of *Callithamnion* does not readily flatten out or shrivel up when it is exposed to air; it tends to hold water, much like a sponge does. The color is typically purplish brown, and the height of a robust specimen may reach 30 or 40 cm.

The remaining red algae that will be discussed in this chapter typically grow in situations where sand swirls about, and certain of them are attached to rocks that are embedded in sand. *Ahnfeltiopsis pacifica* (*Ahnfeltia gigartinoides*) (fig. 165) is usually partly buried. It is a stiff plant whose branches, nearly cylindrical and about 1 mm thick, divide dichotomously. Large growths reach a height of more than 20 cm. The color is brownish red to dark, purplish brown. Older portions of the plant are darker than the younger parts. *Ahnfeltia plicata* is similar, but smaller and more compact; its branches are only about 0.5 mm thick. This species is almost always about half covered by sand, and may survive long periods of being nearly completely buried.

Gymnogongrus linearis (fig. 166) is another tough, stiff seaweed that is densely branched in a dichotomous pattern. As a rule, the branches are widest near their tips, where they are usually 5 or 6 mm across. The color is dark, brownish red, but varies considerably. The warty protuberances that are often prominent in *Gymnogongrus* are the sites of spore formation. The plants may be partly covered by sand, but are not likely to be deeply buried.

Two other species of *Gymnogongrus* are fairly common along the Pacific coast. *Gymnogongrus leptophyllus* is more slender than *G. linearis*, its widest branches being less than 2 mm broad. In *G. platyphyllus* the branches are about the same width as those of *G. linearis*, but they are much thinner.

Gracilaria sjoestedtii (fig. 167) and *Sarcodiotheca gaudichaudii* (fig. 168) form trailing growths that are in constant motion when water is sloshing past them. *Gracilaria* is commonly found on rather smooth rocks that are not quite buried. It is brownish red and sometimes reaches a length of 2 m. There are several to many main stems coming from the holdfast, and these have side branches. Neither the main stems nor the branches are likely to be more than 2 mm thick.

Sarcodiotheca, also brownish red, is up to about 40 cm long. It is more fleshy and more densely branched than *Gracilaria*. A character-

165. *Ahnfeltiopsis pacifica*

166. *Gymnogongrus linearis*

167. (*Above*) *Gracilaria sjoestedtii*   **168.** (*Below*) *Sarcodiotheca gaudichaudii*

istic feature of this species is the way the ultimate branches, mostly 2 or 3 mm thick, are tapered to sharp tips. Warts that develop on the branches are places where reproductive bodies are produced. In some works on Pacific coast algae, *S. gaudichaudii* is called *Neoagardhiella baileyi*.

Sponges

Both *Haliclona* and *Halichondria* are likely to be abundant. The *Haliclona* that grows on rocks, and sometimes over seaweed holdfasts, is similar to the one found on floats (pl. 1) and it is perhaps the same species—possibly *H. permollis*. Its color is usually gray or pale violet. The *Halichondria*, tentatively assigned to *H. panicea* (pl. 1) is decidedly different from the type seen on floats. It forms rather "tight" encrustations characterized by prominent oscula; the oscula are generally situated along distinct ridges. The color ranges from yellow to dull green. Bright red or orange-red patches, much thinner than typical growths of *Haliclona* or *Halichondria*, belong mostly to *Ophlitaspongia pennata* (pl. 1); but some other red sponges look much like it. Microscopic analysis of the spicule complements is necessary before positive identification is possible.

Ophlitaspongia is pretty enough by itself, but it will often provide the more observant student with a delightful surprise. A small, orange-red sea slug, *Rostanga pulchra* (pl. 1), generally only about 1 cm long, grazes on this sponge. This sea slug not only matches the color of the sponge it eats, but it also lays coiled egg masses of the same color. *Rostanga* is not often found far from *Ophlitaspongia* and can distinguish between it and other sponges if given a choice.

Hydroids

Hydroids are usually abundant in the lower part of the intertidal region, where they are attached to rocks, kelps, carapaces of certain crabs, worm tubes, and other firm substrata. Unfortunately, the very small species are likely to escape notice in the field, and the delicate beauty of larger hydroids cannot be appreciated when they are out of water. If you can get a few pieces back to the laboratory in plenty of cold sea water, then set them in a dish under a dissection microscope, you will probably be able to observe the polyps in an expanded state.

Among the hydroids on fairly exposed rocky shores, some, such as *Obelia*, *Sarsia*, and *Tubularia*, are of the general types discussed in connection with the fauna characteristic of floating docks. Many others, however, are not likely to be found anywhere except on rocks where there is wave action, or in certain subtidal situations. Most of these have a stiff texture because the perisarc is thick. One of the more distinctive genera in this category of hydroids is *Aglaophenia* (pl. 2), in which the main stem and branches collectively form a featherlike pattern. The individual feeding polyps are arranged in a row on just one side of each branch, and on some branches there may be basketlike structures, called corbulae, which contain the reproductive polyps comparable to those of *Obelia*. The medusa stage produced by these structures is not readily recognizable as such and never leaves the tissue in which it is formed. The abortive medusae do produce eggs and sperm, however, and the fertilized eggs develop into planulae which escape, settle, and start new colonies. Another firm-textured hydroid likely to be encountered at very low tide is *Abietinaria* (pl. 2). Its polyps are arranged on both sides of the branches, which, as in *Aglaophenia*, come off the main stems in a featherlike pattern.

Sea Anemones and Their Allies

In this lowermost part of the intertidal zone, several species of anemones stand out. *Anthopleura xanthogrammica* (pl. 4), the green anemone, is characterized by a broad, flat oral disk; the color of the disk and tentacles is typically a beautiful muted emerald green. The diameter of the tentacular crown in a fully expanded specimen may reach 15 cm. The column is nothing special to look at, being a rather drab olive or brownish color. If a finger is placed on the tentacles of this or most other anemones of reasonable size, the tentacles will cling weakly to the skin, in part because of the discharge of nematocysts whose extruded microscopic threads engage the skin. A kind of suction also seems to be involved. In any case, the tentacles function effectively in trapping prey animals—mostly mussels that have somehow come loose—and pushing them into the mouth.

Although *A. xanthogrammica* is a carnivore, it normally supports a large population of microscopic algae, which are responsible for much of the green color. *A. elegantissima* (already discussed under zone 3) also has symbiotic algae, though its tentacles are not often really green. Two distinctly different types of algal cells are known to occur in both of these anemones. Zooxanthellae, characteristically yellow brown because of the presence of pigments that partially mask the chlorophyll, are dinoflagellates which have no flagella in the symbiotic phase. The other algae, called zoochlorellae, are bright green. The two types may be mixed in one specimen—even in the same tissue—or separate anemones may have only one type or the other. The algae are concentrated in the gastrodermal layer, that is, in the tissue that lines the digestive tract. Since the core of each tentacle is a branch of the digestive tract, the green color shows through the overlying tissue.

The biological relationship of the algae to their anemone hosts has been studied to some extent. It appears that the value of the association to the anemone is at least partly a nutritional one. Organic compounds synthesized by the algae move into the tissues of the anemone. When starved, anemones without algae lose weight more rapidly than anemones of the same species that have a normal complement of algae.

Two other large anemones need to be mentioned here. *Urticina cras-sicornis* (pl. 4) is about the same size as *A. xanthogrammica* (the disk of a large specimen is about 15 cm in diameter), but its tentacles are proportionately longer and thicker. The prevailing color of the disk and tentacles is usually greenish gray or olive gray, but the tentacles typically have lighter cross bands and may also have a reddish suffusion. The column, not the prettiest part of most anemones, is very striking because of the way the light olive green ground color is streaked with red. (In Puget Sound, the column of most specimens is entirely red.) *Urticina crassicornis* is commonly found on the under-sides of ledges, and the way it hangs down limply when the tide is out is fascinatingly obscene.

Urticina coriacea (pl. 4) is a less common species, except in certain places. It favors situations where its column can be partly covered by fine gravel or bits of shell. The upper part of the column, which is bright red, regularly has particles from the substratum sticking to it. The prevailing coloration of the disk and tentacles is a mixture of red and gray; the tentacles, which are stubbier than those of *U. crassicor-nis,* have some ill-defined lighter bands.

Metridium senile (fig. 25; pl. 3) may be abundant, especially in rela-tively protected situations where there is not much wave action. Inter-tidally, however, it does not often make a showing as impressive as it does subtidally or on floats (see Chap. 3). It is usually hidden away under ledges and in caves, and large specimens are uncommon.

Epiactis prolifera, the brooding anemone (fig. 346) is a small species. The height of an expanded specimen does not often exceed about 3 cm. The basic color is ordinarily brown to greenish brown, but it is sometimes red, pinkish red, or dull green. The oral disk is generally marked with radially arranged white lines; the pedal disk and column have similar lines, though they may not be as sharp. The numerous young regularly found on the pedal disk do not originate there by asexual budding, but are derived from eggs fertilized in the digestive cavity. The motile larvae, after swimming out of the mouth, migrate down to the disk and become installed there until they become little anemones ready to move off.

Aulactinia incubans (pl. 4) slightly resembles *Epiactis* because its oral disk has radiating white lines. Most of these lines begin some distance away from the mouth, but two of them, opposite one another, origi-nate at the lips of the mouth. The rest of the animal is usually dark gray or gray green, but some specimens are brick red, pale orange, or cream colored. The column is studded with small warts. Large speci-mens are about 3 cm in diameter at the base, and when fully extended they reach a height of about 1.5 cm. This anemone, which has been found in some of the more exposed situations in the San Juan Archi-pelago, as well as on the open coast, broods its young internally until they are fully formed. It then releases them through pores at the tip of the tentacles. A similar species, *Cnidopus ritteri* (pl. 4), is rather common on the open coast, and perhaps should be expected in the San Juan Archipelago, too. It is described in Chapter 5.

One of the real gems of this lowest zone is the cup coral, *Balanophyllia elegans* (pl. 5). Its disk and column are bright orange; the tentacles are barely tinged with orange and almost transparent. Though it looks like a squat little sea anemone, about 1 cm in height and in diameter, the cup coral has a strong calcareous skeleton; this not only supports the body wall but also the partitions in the digestive cavity. Dead specimens, of which only the skeleton remains, look something like short lengths of dry bone, though the inner portion, because of the centripetal partitions, does not really resemble a marrow cavity. *Balanophyllia* is not often found in really exposed situations. It seems to prefer dark places, and in the intertidal region it is generally restricted to caves and the undersides of ledges.

Epizoanthus scotinus (pl. 5) is our only representative of a group of anemonelike anthozoans called the zoanthids. There is no calcareous skeleton in *Epizoanthus*, but sand grains, bits of shell, and diatoms become incorporated into the body wall. Foreign material of this sort is also embedded in the surface of the tan or flesh-colored column, so that the animal has a gritty texture. The tentacles are much paler than the column. If they are caused to contract, it may take them several hours to become extended again, especially if the animal has been detached from the rock on which it has been living. *Epizoanthus* can reproduce asexually by budding and thus may form clumps of several to many individuals. Large polyps reach a height of about 7 cm, but most specimens are not over 3 cm tall. Although the coloration of *Epizoanthus* is undistinguished, a colony of expanded animals is a beautiful sight.

Flatworms

In the Pacific Northwest, the only free-living flatworms large enough to see without the help of a microscope are the polyclads, so-called because of their much-branched digestive tracts. Most are about 1 to 3 cm long. *Kaburakia excelsa* (pl. 6) is about the only common large species, reaching a length of 5 cm or even more, and has already been mentioned in connection with the fauna of floating docks. It is occasionally seen clinging to the undersides of rocks, to rocks exposed when other rocks are lifted off, or under clumps of mussels.

Most of the polyclads are relatively nondescript. Their classification is based largely on details of the reproductive system, and cannot be understood without a lot of microscopic work and preparation of sections. Patterns of eyespot arrangement, coloration, and general shape are helpful, but it would be misleading to attempt to help the user of this book to identify even a few species on the basis of superficial characteristics alone. The more common polyclads seem to be *Free-*

mania litoricola and several species of *Notoplana*. One of the latter, *N. sanguinea*, is distinctive enough to be recognized in the field because of a dark red saddlelike blotch on the central part of its dorsal surface.

Nemerteans

Members of the phylum Nemertea are represented by several easily recognized species and by some others better omitted here, as they cannot be identified without recourse to microscopic characters. *Tubulanus polymorphus* (pl. 6) is large, up to about 1 m long when fully extended; however, when it is uncovered by lifting up seaweed or turning a rock, it is usually at least partly contracted, and then parts of it may be nearly as thick as a pencil. *Emplectonema gracile* (pl. 6) is as slender as a thin rubber band, dark green above and whitish or yellowish below; it reaches a length of about 7 or 8 cm, and is sometimes abundant higher up, especially in beds of the California mussel.

The most beautiful of our nemerteans is *Micrura verrilli* (pl. 6). It secretes almost papery tubes on the undersides of rocks and thus may be overlooked. The undersurface of *M. verrilli* is ivory white; the upper surface is dark, purplish brown, crossed transversely by regularly spaced white lines, and the head is bright orange.

The slender, pale pink or nearly white nemertean found crawling around among algal holdfasts, barnacles, and mussels usually turns out to be *Amphiporus imparispinosus* (pl. 6). Among the features that characterize it are the numerous little eyespots on both sides of the head. It feeds at least to some extent on barnacles, and it reaches a length of about 6 or 7 cm. It is common throughout the range of this book. *Amphiporus formidabilis* is similar in general appearance, but it grows to a length of about 30 cm. To be certain about the identification, it is essential to make a sandwich of the specimen between two glass slides or glass plates so that the proboscis can be examined with a microscope. The proboscis of both species has a single main stylet, a spinelike structure that is used to impale the prey. There is an important difference, however, in the number of little side sacs where replacement stylets are produced. In *A. imparispinosus* there are only a few (generally 2 or 3) sacs of developing replacement stylets; in *A. formidabilis* there are generally eight to twelve of them.

Amphiporus bimaculatus (pl. 6) does not closely resemble its kin. Although its length does not often exceed 12 cm, it is stouter and proportionately much broader than most nemerteans. The upper surface is mostly brownish red or brownish orange, but the head is light, with a pair of nearly triangular dark markings. None of our other nemerteans has these distinctive spots. *Amphiporus bimaculatus* is most likely to be found beneath rocks or hidden away in crevices, but it occasionally occurs on pilings. Its range extends from Alaska to central California.

Nearly all nemerteans are predators. They feed on worms (especially polychaete annelids), small molluscs, crustaceans (including barnacles), and other animals. They use their eversible proboscis, which may be sticky or armed with stylets that operate in conjunction with a venom gland, to capture and quiet the prey. Some nemerteans swallow their prey whole; others suck out their juices.

Polychaetes

Most of the many polychaete annelids are hidden away in crevices, in holdfasts of large seaweeds, and in the sediment that accumulates between and under rocks. Those in the open secrete tubes as personal hiding places. Among these the serpulids stand out because they are so abundant and because their tubes, even when tiny, are white and calcareous. The common species found in the lowermost reaches of the intertidal region are the ones whose characteristics and life styles have been discussed in connection with the fauna of floats. *Serpula vermicularis* (pl. 7) can be a gorgeous sight when all of the specimens in a group have their bright red tentacular crowns extended. They are likely to be seen this way only in a tide pool, of course. The various species of *Spirorbis* (pls. 7 and 12), with their tubes generally coiled like snail shells, are so small and so ubiquitous that study with a low-power microscope is necessary to make one appreciate that they are as beautiful as *Serpula* in form if not in coloring.

The principal sabellid in rocky situations is generally *Eudistylia vancouveri* (pl. 7), which builds leathery tubes about 1 cm wide and sometimes 20 to 25 cm long, and is characteristically aggregated in large clumps. The crown of featherlike tentacles at the anterior end is deep maroon, banded with green, and may be 5 cm in diameter when expanded. Occasionally *Eudistylia* is found in zone 3, especially if it can establish itself in a deep fissure.

In crevices, between rocks that fit tightly together, and under rocks lying on sand or gravel, there will probably be a variety of polychaete annelids. Some of these may seem nondescript unless they are examined carefully with a low-power microscope. Be on the lookout, however, for the larger terebellids, which are rather distinctive. The terebellids are characterized by numerous, very extensile tentacles arising from the extreme anterior end of the body, and two or three pairs of gills arising from the dorsal surface of certain of the segments just a little farther back. These gills may be bushy or they may consist of clusters of unbranched filaments. The bodies of terebellids tend to be pudgy, especially when they are contracted, and often have a flabby look. The anterior portion is usually somewhat swollen, and the bristles on the segments of this region are specialized as short, thickened hooks. These hooks are often arranged in such a way that they resemble one row or both rows of teeth in a zipper.

Most terebellids form parchmentlike tubes or thin muddy tubes around themselves. From the mouth of the tube, their tentacles range widely over and through the substratum, trapping microscopic food and passing it, in a film of mucus, down a ciliated groove toward the mouth. As food accumulates near the base of a tentacle, it is rubbed off onto a sort of lip near the mouth, from which food is driven by cilia into the mouth itself.

In rocky intertidal areas, *Thelepus crispus* (fig. 169) is usually the prevailing terebellid. A large specimen, fully extended, is about the diameter of a pencil and about 10 cm long. Its gills, in three pairs, consist of clusters of unbranched filaments. The body color is a sort of brownish pink, and the tentacles are whitish and translucent. When broken-off tentacles of *Thelepus* and its relatives are found crawling around by themselves, they are apt to be taken for delicate little nemerteans. Along with some other things seen out of context, like chopped-off clam siphons, they provide some embarrassing levity to laboratory sessions devoted to identification of the morning's catch.

Two members of the family Cirratulidae are likely to be common. Cirratulids, as a group, are characterized by threadlike filaments that arise from several to many segments behind the head region. On a particular segment, the filaments may consist of a pair of gills, a pair of gills plus a pair of grooved tentacles, or a pair of gills plus clusters of grooved tentacles. Some cirratulids also have a pair of stout grooved palps at the back of the head region. In any case, the exact format varies.

Cirratulus spectabilis (pl. 8), which reaches a length of about 8 cm, is most likely to be in crevices filled with muddy sand, or beneath rocks set in muddy sand. It has gills coming off most of its body segments, and there are two sets of grooved tentacles originating on the dorsal side of a segment close to the head. The general color is brownish, brownish yellow, or orange yellow, but the gills and tentacles are red. Some specialists consider *C. spectabilis* to be a subspecies of *C. cirratus*, a smaller worm—its length does not exceed 4 cm—that is found on both sides of the Atlantic Ocean and along much of the Pacific coast from California southward.

Dodecaceria fewkesi (pl. 9) constructs calcareous tubes, crowded together in tangled masses and usually mixed with encrusting coralline algae of the genus *Lithothamnium*. The worms, when sticking out of their tubes, are easily recognized because they are dark, brownish black. In *Dodecaceria*, the palps of the head region are prominent, and they are succeeded by several pairs of gills. There are no grooved tentacles comparable to those found on most segments of *Cirratulus*, however. Large specimens of *Dodecaceria* reach a length of about 3 cm.

Sipunculans

Under rocks and in tight crevices between rocks, especially where some muddy sand or gravel has accumulated, one may frequently find a rubbery worm so firm when it is contracted that it resists being squeezed. This is *Phascolosoma agassizii* (pl. 9), a member of the small phylum Sipuncula. Its firmness is due in part to its strong, muscular, and rather inelastic body wall, and in part to a high hydrostatic pressure within its body cavity. If put back into sea water, it will soon extend its more slender anterior portion by turning it inside out; it will then probably alternately withdraw and extend this part more or less indefinitely. There are a few very short tentacles around the mouth, which are used for feeding on detritus at the surface of the substratum where the worms peek out from under or between rocks. The digestive tracts of sipunculans are almost U-shaped, so the anus is not at the posterior tip of the body, but on the dorsal side, and is rather far forward. The length of a large *Phascolosoma*, when stretched out, is about 6 or 7 cm. The plump posterior part of the body is tan or greenish tan; the introvertible anterior portion is basically paler, but it has a number of black lines and blotches.

Some types of intertidal animals, while in the larval stage, settle in small holes or in burrows made in rock by other animals, and then just stay there for the rest of their lives. Many of these animals, called nestlers, grow to a point where they fit tightly in their little abodes. Chief among them are certain clams and sipunculans. One of the sipunculans, *Phascolosoma agassizii,* has just been mentioned; it is not at all limited to holes, for it is fairly abundant between or under rocks, but it does often qualify as a nestler. A different sipunculan, *Themiste pyroides* (fig. 170), is almost strictly a nestler. It is more plump than *P. agassizii,* lacks the dark markings on the introvertible anterior portion, and has bushy tentacles. *Themiste* favors burrows excavated by rock-boring bivalve molluscs, and it fits these about as snugly as possible. It is only occasionally found in the Puget Sound region, where rock borers are scarce, but it is fairly common on the open coast.

Sea Stars

Pisaster (fig. 124; pl. 25) has already been discussed because of its prevalence in zone 3, into which it ascends to feed. Somewhat similar to *Pisaster* and often needlessly confused with it is *Evasterias troschelii* (pl. 25). Its diameter may reach 50 cm, but most specimens fall into the range of 25 to 30 cm. The arms are long in proportion to the size of the disk, so *Evasterias* is more graceful than *Pisaster*. Its pattern of white spines is much like that of *Pisaster;* but its ground color is never really purple nor often as close to orange as is characteristic of some specimens of the latter. The color nevertheless varies greatly, ranging from gray to gray green to brown and nearly red.

Orthasterias koehleri (pl. 25) is a long-rayed sea star that is occasionally encountered intertidally in the San Juan Archipelago. The spread of a large specimen may exceed 50 cm. The color is mostly pinkish red, sometimes mixed with brick red, but many individuals show dull yellow or tan markings. The prominent, rather sharp spines are often almost white, and many of those on the arms fit into meandering rows. *Orthasterias* consumes a wide variety of invertebrates, including chitons, gastropods, bivalves, barnacles, and ascidians.

The leather star, *Dermasterias imbricata* (pl. 26), has short, thick arms, and the texture of its upper surface is soft and slippery. This species, which reaches a diameter in excess of 20 cm, smells much like exploded gunpowder. The coloration of the upper surface is blotchy, but is predominantly reddish brown, mixed with a sort of leaden gray; nearly purple patches are mixed into the coloration of some specimens. This species feeds primarily on sea anemones.

Perhaps our most beautiful intertidal sea star is the sun star, *Solaster stimpsoni* (pl. 26). Typically, it has ten graceful even if somewhat gritty rays, and it attains a diameter of about 25 cm. The background color of the upper surface of most specimens is usually either orange or rose, and wide streaks of grayish blue or grayish purple run from the center of the disk to the tip of each arm. The food of this *Solaster* consists mostly of small sea cucumbers.

Leptasterias hexactis (pl. 25) is the least conspicuous of our intertidal sea stars, and it is also the most common. It is especially abundant on beaches where there are a lot of loose rocks resting on one another. The diet of this species, which has six rays and which reaches a maximum diameter of about 9 cm, includes limpets and other snails, chitons, mussels, and barnacles. The color of *Leptasterias* is characteristically drab—leaden, gray, greenish gray, or occasionally nearly black. Once in a rare while a brightly colored specimen with some orange or pink tones shows up. *Leptasterias* compensates for its lack of physical attractiveness by some interesting habits connected with reproduction. Between about December and March, mature individuals congregate, in groups of a dozen or more, under rocks. Both sexes spawn more or less simultaneously. As each female liberates her eggs from pores on the upper surface, she collects those that do not slip away into a cluster, which she holds with her tube feet and over which she humps her body, remaining attached to the rock only by the tips of her arms. When the tube feet of the young have developed to the point where they can cling to the rock—after a period of about forty days—the mother finally can flatten out. The brooding period continues for approximately twenty days more. By this time the young are a little more than 1 mm in diameter, but they are essentially fully formed and the female leaves them.

During the period she is looking after her young, the female evidently does not eat. She pays close attention to her brood, cleaning the eggs as they develop and in some way helping them to escape from the thin membrane that surrounds them for the first three weeks or so.

The most brightly colored sea star in the intertidal zone is *Henricia leviuscula* (pl. 26), the blood star. The upper surface is typically a brilliant orange red, but the color may range from tan to nearly purple, and some specimens are mottled. This species is relatively small, its diameter rarely exceeding 12 cm. The graceful appearance and smooth texture of *Henricia* are due to the absence of pedicellariae and spines from the upper surface. *Henricia* feeds chiefly on sponges.

A thoroughly astonishing sea star is the sunflower star, *Pycnopodia helianthoides* (pl. 25). It is common in certain situations on rocky shores, but is probably even more abundant on sandy or gravelly substrata in deeper water. A large specimen may attain a diameter of nearly 1 m. The number of rays varies, as do their lengths, because some may be regenerating in the place of rays that have been lost. The color also varies extensively, but *Pycnopodia* is characteristically more or less orange, with violet or purple tufts where the pedicellariae and dermal branchiae are concentrated. Some specimens are a purplish color almost throughout. Although *Pycnopodia* is spiny, its rays are rather soft and flabby. They are also so fragile that specimens clinging tightly to rocks may part with a ray or two if they are pulled too roughly from the substratum. The helpless appearance of a sunflower star draped over the palm of one's hand is misleading. For a sea star, this species moves rapidly, especially when submerged, and it is a powerful predator. It feeds on a wide variety of organisms, but concentrates on bivalve molluscs; it will also scavenge on dead fish. *Pycnopodia* is definitely feared by other invertebrates. The large sea cucumber, *Parastichopus californicus,* which is about as lethargic as any of our animals, will work itself into a writhing gallop if the tube feet of a *Pycnopodia* make contact with its skin. Some bivalves, stimulated by the prospect of being eaten, go into violent activity in order to escape. Scallops, for instance, clap their valves together to swim out of danger, and the common cockle extends its foot and pushes it against the substratum to get away. Sea urchins respond to *Pycnopodia* by extending their pedicellariae.

Brittle Stars

On really rocky shores (as opposed to situations where rocks are scattered over muddy sand or gravel), only one brittle star, *Ophiopholis aculeata* (pl. 26), is common. It is, however, our most beautiful species. The coloration is generally a mixture of brown or buff and either bright red or dark red; on the upper side of the disk, the brown and red markings are often in bold juxtaposition. On the whole, reddish tones seem to predominate. The prickly look of this species is due to the prominence of the arm spines. *Ophiopholis* can be very abundant in the lower part of the intertidal region, where it prefers crevices, especially those between rather tight-fitting rocks. The maximum diameter of this species is about 8 cm.

Amphipholis squamata (pl. 26), usually plentiful under rocks that are set on sand or gravel, is our smallest common brittle star. The diameter of a large specimen is about 3 cm. The color is generally uninteresting: gray above, whitish below. This species does, however, have the engaging feature of brooding its young. Most brittle stars release their eggs and sperm into the water, where the fertilized eggs develop into free-swimming larvae quite different from the adults. *Amphipholis* holds its eggs in little pockets that open to the outside near the bases of the arms, and there they develop directly into little brittle stars. The food of *Amphipholis* consists of diatoms and detritus.

Sea Urchins

Of the several species of sea urchins occurring in the Puget Sound region, three may be found in the lower part of the intertidal region. One of them, the green sea urchin, *Strongylocentrotus droebachiensis* (pl. 24), has a wide distribution in northern waters. (It was originally described from specimens collected at Drobak, Norway.) Its spines are crowded, short, and rather fine. The color of the animal as a whole is decidedly greenish, but there are reddish brown tones here and there, especially near the top. The test of a large specimen is about 8 cm in diameter.

The red sea urchin, *S. franciscanus* (pl. 24), is one of the giants of the group. Its test may be more than 12 cm in diameter, and the spines may be more than 5 cm long. It is typically a kind of acid red, though the tube feet tend to be darker. This species, which has a range from Alaska to Lower California, inhabits relatively quiet shores as well as those where there is considerable wave action, and it is common subtidally.

The purple sea urchin, *S. purpuratus* (pl. 24), has a geographic range comparable to that of *S. franciscanus*, but is decidedly partial to shores having strong wave action. It is therefore common on the open coast, but will not be found in Puget Sound, and only a few restricted populations of it are known in the San Juan Archipelago. It is apparently even more dependent than the California mussel on wave action. The test of the purple urchin may be up to about 8 cm in diameter. The spines are short, like those of the green urchin, but they are much stouter. The color of the spines is such a rich purple that one almost expects a dye to start dripping from the animal as soon as it is picked up. In situations on the open coast where this species is abundant and the substratum is of relatively soft rock, the urchins work themselves into hollows that may eventually become deep enough to enclose them completely. Just how they do this is not fully understood, but the abrasive action of the movable spines is suspected to be the primary cause. The spines are covered by living tissue which continues to deposit calcareous material. The rock, however, cannot restore itself, so the holes get deeper.

The food of all of our sea urchins consists largely of pieces of seaweed. Whatever lands on them or under them is passed to the mouth with the aid of the tube feet. The sharp tips of the five jaws that make up a structure called Aristotle's lantern chop the food into tiny fragments which can be swallowed and digested for whatever nutritional value they have. *S. franciscanus* is known to use its jaws to scrape off small barnacles.

If you have a strong hand lens or a microscope, you may wish to compare the pedicellariae of an urchin with those of a sea star. The former have three jaws, the latter have two.

The digestive tracts of most sea urchins support an astonishing assortment of ciliated protozoans, most of which seem to be commensals feeding on bacteria in the gut. Then there is a pretty, reddish rhabdocoel turbellarian, about 4 or 5 mm long, called *Syndisyrinx franciscanus*. Just what it lives on is still uncertain. Mature worms usually contain a conspicuous golden egg capsule with a long, threadlike extension. After a capsule is laid and finally escapes with the feces of the urchin, the thread probably gets tangled up with a piece of seaweed and the capsule thus has a chance to enter another host. Sometimes as many as 30 or 40 worms will be found in one urchin. Rarely another worm of the same general type, but brown rather than reddish, occurs along with *Syndisyrinx*. This other species seems to belong to the genus *Syndesmis*.

Sea Cucumbers

The largest of our sea cucumbers is *Stichopus californicus* (pl. 27). It regularly attains a length of about 40 cm, and may be even larger. It cannot be said to be beautiful, or even typical, but it is interesting. The body is limp when extended, but firm and fully packed when contracted. The coloration is dark reddish brown above, somewhat lighter below, and all over the upper surface and sides are pointed, fleshy warts. The tube feet are crowded together on the lower side, and only three of the five pairs of rows are distinct; the others have essentially abortive tube feet. The tentacles around the mouth, which are specialized tube feet, look something like mops, and the tips of their branches are elaborated into little disks. After some detritus has accumulated on a tentacle, it is inserted into the mouth and licked clean.

Next in order of size is *Cucumaria miniata* (pl. 27), which grows to a length of about 20 cm. It lives in crevices or between rocks piled one on top of the other, and normally only the crown of bright orange oral tentacles (pl. 27) is visible. Most of the rest of the body is reddish brown or pinkish brown. It is, on the whole, an attractive cucumber. The oral tentacles are much branched and trap particles of detritus suspended in the water. After a tentacle is "saturated" with food material, it is pushed into the mouth and cleaned off.

Cucumaria lubrica (pl. 27), abundant subtidally, is occasionally encountered in the lowermost portion of the intertidal region. Its color ranges from dirty white to nearly black, but the side that is habitually applied to the rock is generally at least a little lighter than the rest of the body. This species could be confused with the appreciably smaller *C. pseudocurata*, discussed earlier in this chapter, in connection with beds of the California mussel. It is different, however, in that many of its tube feet, especially on the lower surface, do not fit into such distinct double rows as are characteristic of *C. pseudocurata*.

Eupentacta quinquesemita (fig. 56) has already been dealt with in connection with the fauna on floating docks, where it is the predominant cucumber. In rocky habitats it occupies the same general situations as *Cucumaria*, living in crevices and between rocks. Its color ranges from nearly white to very pale orange, and its maximum length is usually about 8 or 9 cm. The five sets of tube feet are almost evenly spaced around the body, and the individual tube feet are distinctive because when they contract to the fullest extent possible, they are still obvious. In most sea cucumbers, they practically disappear.

Psolus chitonoides (the species name means "resembling a chiton") is odd enough not to be even recognized as a holothurian by many who encounter it for the first time. *Psolus* (pl. 27) has the shape of a short cucumber sliced lengthwise, for one side of it—the side with the tube feet—is almost perfectly flat. It clings tightly to rock and is essentially sedentary. The upper surface is covered with overlapping calcareous plates, and the mouth is situated on this surface some distance from the anterior end. When the bright red oral tentacles are extended, *Psolus* is a gorgeous sight. Unfortunately, it is not often encountered in shore collecting. It is abundant in deeper water, however, and it is joined there by a smaller species, more or less purplish pink in color, called *Psolidium bullatum*. *Psolus* reaches a length of about 5 cm, and *Psolidium* a length of about 3 cm.

Brachiopods

There are several species of brachiopods in the Puget Sound area, but only one of them, *Terebratalia transversa* (fig. 171), is regularly seen intertidally. On the open coast *T. transversa* is not often observed except at very low tide levels, and even then it is rare. In the San Juan Archipelago, however, it may be quite abundant at –2.0, and sometimes occurs as high as 0.0. Its variability partly accounts for the number of invalid species names applied to it. Most individuals are tumid, a little broader than long, and do not have much ribbing. The width is usually about 2 or 3 cm. A particularly attractive variant is common on Saltspring Island, in the Canadian San Juans, and perhaps elsewhere in the same general region. The shell is strongly ribbed, and the width is much greater than the length.

Chitons

The chiton *Katharina* (fig. 122), characteristic of zone 3, also occurs in zone 4; but it is overshadowed here by several other distinctive species. One of them, *Cryptochiton stelleri* (pl. 10), is the largest chiton in the world, frequently reaching a length of 20 cm. *Cryptochiton* may not be recognized for what it is because all eight of its shells are completely covered by the thick, gritty girdle. The genus name alludes to this feature; the species name, as in *Cyanocitta stelleri* (Steller's jay), commemorates Georg Wilhelm Steller, a naturalist on an early Russian expedition to Alaska.

Our most beautiful chiton is the lined chiton, *Tonicella lineata* (pl. 10). It is brightly colored, with dark brown lines zigzagging over a lighter background in which yellow, orange, pink, orchid, and lavender predominate. It attains a length of about 5 cm. *Tonicella* will generally be found close to the encrusting coralline alga *Lithothamnium*, on whose surface it grazes. It seems to eat the more superficial layers of the encrustations, and in doing so it also takes in the film of diatoms and other small organisms that happen to be in the way.

A smaller chiton most frequently found on the underside of rocks is *Lepidozona mertensii* (pl. 10). Its color, as the animal is seen from above, tends to be nearly uniformly brick red or reddish brown, but sometimes there are conspicuous blotches of white. Though the color varies, this species is unmistakable among intertidal chitons because the surface of its girdle is composed of tiny scales; other chitons with this same characteristic are essentially subtidal.

Three other chitons inhabiting this zone are the mopalias, which are characterized by hairs sticking out of the girdle. *Mopalia muscosa*, the mossy chiton (fig. 172), has the stiffest and thickest hairs, and is the species most likely to have barnacles or other settlers growing on its back. The other two mopalias have rather soft hairs, but *M. ciliata* (fig. 173) has a distinct cleft at the posterior end, whereas *M. lignosa* (fig. 174) does not; the girdle hairs of *M. lignosa*, moreover, generally originate in the center of light spots. Like nearly all chitons, mopalias are grazers. Their diet is not limited to plant material, however; they eat hydroids, bryozoans, and other low-growing animal organisms.

Snails and Limpets

Acmaea mitra, the whitecap limpet (pl. 11), is unusual for a member of its clan in having such a thick and conical shell. The height sometimes equals the length, which in exceptionally large specimens is a little more than 3 cm. *Acmaea*, like the lined chiton, *Tonicella*, is closely tied to the encrusting coralline red alga, *Lithothamnium*; it not only eats this alga, but its shell is almost always overgrown by it.

The keyhole limpets are rather close relatives of true limpets. In the latter group, however, water enters the mantle cavity on the left side, passes over the single gill, picks up wastes from the kidney and diges-

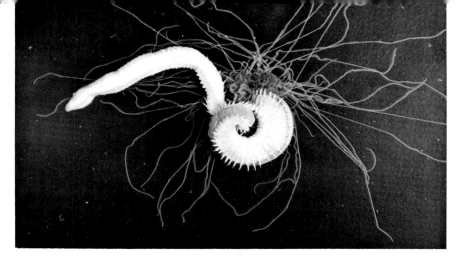

169. *Thelepus crispus*

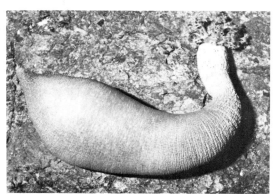

170. *Themiste pyroides*

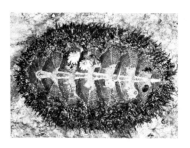 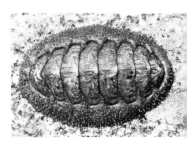

171. *Terebratalia transversa*, the usual form (*left*) and a variant with prominent ribs (*right*)

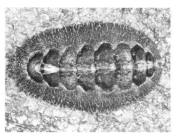

172. *Mopalia muscosa*, the mossy chiton

173. *Mopalia ciliata*

174. *Mopalia lignosa*

tive tract, and then flows out on the right side. In keyhole limpets, which are considered to be more primitive, there are two gills, one on each side of the mantle cavity. Water enters the mantle cavity on both sides of the head, passes over the gills, and flows out through the opening at the apex of the shell. The kidneys and digestive tract discharge their wastes not far from the exhalant aperture.

The only keyhole limpet likely to be found in the intertidal region—and then only in the lowermost zone—is *Diodora aspera* (fig. 175). Its shell reaches a length of about 5 cm. This species feeds mostly on encrusting sponges.

Almost every keyhole limpet will have a scaleworm, *Arctonoe vittata* (fig. 176), tucked away between the foot and mantle. The coloration of this polychaete—ivory, with a few dark transverse stripes—almost perfectly matches that of the mantle of its host. *Arctonoe* is associated with some other animals, including *Cryptochiton*, and its behavior with respect to its several hosts has been the subject of numerous investigations. Specimens taken from *Diodora*, if placed in an apparatus designed to test host preference, will tend to select *Diodora* over other molluscs; those from *Cryptochiton* will usually go back to *Cryptochiton*. As its host wanders over rock surfaces, *Arctonoe* nips off the heads of small, tube-dwelling polychaetes.

The northern abalone, *Haliotis kamtschatkana* (fig. 177; pl. 11), is sometimes found intertidally, but it becomes more abundant in the domain of divers. Its shell, which reaches a length of about 12 cm, is thinner than that of some species found on the coast of California, and much of the surface is wavy. The series of holes—the more recent ones, that is, which are still functional—serves in the same way as the single apical aperture of *Diodora*, to permit water that has passed over the gills to exit from the mantle cavity, taking with it the wastes from the excretory organs and digestive tract. Abalones are herbivores, using their large radulas to scrape plant material from rocks.

On the shores of the outer coast, there are several snails whose shells are more or less top shaped. In the Puget Sound region, however, only one is abundant intertidally. This is *Calliostoma ligatum* (pl. 12), whose whorls are sculptured spirally with alternating light ridges and pinkish brown furrows. The height of this species reaches a little more than 2 cm and is a bit greater than the width. There is no opening in the base of the shell near its center. *Calliostoma* feeds partly on plant material, partly on low-growing sessile animals, such as hydroids.

In the genera *Margarites* and *Lirularia*, which are closely related to *Calliostoma*, there is a distinct opening, or umbilicus, in the base of the shell; this opening goes up into the columella, the pillar around which the whorls are organized. *Margarites pupillus* (fig. 178), which reaches a height of 1.5 cm, is approximately as wide as it is tall. It is sculptured in much the same way as *Calliostoma ligatum*, but the fur-

175. *Diodora aspera*

176. A scaleworm, *Arctonoe vittata,* in the mantle cavity of *Diodora*

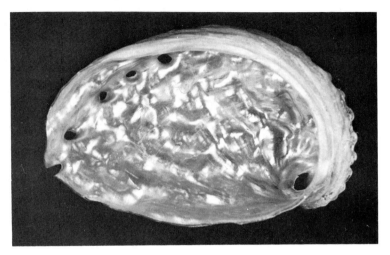

177. *Haliotis kamtschatkana*, the northern abalone, interior of shell

178. (*Above and right*) *Margarites pupillus*

179. *Homalopoma luridum*

180. *Fusitriton oregonensis,* the hairy triton

rows are almost as light as the ridges. The shell is also more likely than that of *C. ligatum* to show pearliness externally.

Margarites helicinus (pl. 12), up to about 6 mm high, has moderately convex whorls without any spiral sculpture. The two more common intertidal species of *Lirularia* are *L. lirulata* (fig. 239) and *L. succincta* (fig. 239; pl. 12). Both reach a height of about 6 mm, and both are most likely to be found clinging to the undersides of rocks or in coarse gravel between rocks. *Lirularia lirulata* is proportionately taller than *L. succincta*, and typically has prominent spiral ridges; some specimens, however, are nearly smooth. In *L. succincta*, spiral ridges are generally present, but they are so low as to be scarcely noticeable. On the base of the body whorl, just peripheral to the umbilicus, there is usually a shallow depression that runs to the inner lip of the aperture. This is perhaps the most distinctive feature of the species. When there are perceptible spiral ridges on the base, two or three of them occupy the depression.

The little snails of the genus *Homalopoma* resemble those of the genera *Margarites* and *Lirularia*, but they are distinctly different in that they have a thick, calcareous operculum for closing the aperture. *Homalopoma luridum* (fig. 179) is common in the Puget Sound region, as well as on the open coast. Its low-spired shell is up to about 8 mm in height and diameter and has rather prominent, regularly spaced spiral ridges. If the shell is not badly worn or overgrown by encrusting organisms, it is likely to be reddish, purplish, or gray.

A number of distinctly different groups of gastropods have limpet-like shells. The slipper shells of the genus *Crepidula*, for instance, are not at all close to true limpets, though they resemble them superficially. *Crepidula adunca* (pl. 12) may as well be mentioned at this point, because it is so commonly found on the shell of *Calliostoma*. (On the open coast, it is also on turban shells of the genus *Tegula*.) It has a definite beak on its posterior slope (when there is a pronounced beak in true limpets, as *Collisella digitalis*, it is on the forward side), and the color of the outside is brown. Inside, the shell has a well-developed white shelf. The largest specimens are only about 2 cm long.

The largest shelled gastropod commonly found in our region—other than the abalone—is *Fusitriton oregonensis* (fig. 180). It is more abundant subtidally than intertidally, but is nonetheless frequently seen in the infralittoral fringe. The shell has very distinct, rounded whorls, with spiral ridges as well as axial ribs. The copious brown periostracum is conspicuously hairy, and this gastropod is often referred to as the "hairy triton." Large specimens have shells about 10 cm long.

Fusitriton feeds on ascidians and some other invertebrates, including sea urchins. In attacking an urchin, it destroys the tissue on the outside of the test, and sometimes bores all the way through the test. At least some of the urchins showing blackish, tarlike discolorations are survivors of skirmishes with *Fusitriton*. The egg masses of this snail are always amazing—big sheets of what look like sawed-off translucent grains of corn packed into a spiral pattern.

Amphissa columbiana (fig. 181), about 3 cm long, at first may seem nondescript, partly because of the uninteresting brown or pinkish brown color of the shell. However, when the shell is examined carefully, it turns out to be rather nicely wrought. The almost elliptical aperture is bordered on its inner side by a conspicuous enameled area, and there is a distinct notch—almost a canal—through which the snail sticks out its long siphon. Externally, the whorls are marked by very fine spiral lines, which are intersected in the upper half of the shell by prominent longitudinal ridges. *Amphissa* is primarily a scavenger on dead animal tissue, and has good olfactory equipment for locating food.

Bittium eschrichtii (fig. 182) is the only really abundant snail with a slender, drill-shaped shell. This species is small, just a little over 1 cm long when full grown. The whorls are generally brown or gray and marked with closely spaced grooves. *Bittium* is usually found beneath rocks, and its shell is popular with very young hermit crabs.

The shell of *Ceratostoma foliatum*, the "leafy hornmouth" (fig. 183; pl. 13), reaches a length of about 8 cm. It looks heavier than it is because of the spiral ridges and three lengthwise frills with which it is ornamented. The frills vary from specimen to specimen, but they are generally discontinuous or so poorly finished that the shell looks as if it had been designed by a committee and then built by a succession of contractors. To the animal inside, however, the protective function of the shell matters more than its looks, and in this connection the frills are important. Most snails, if dislodged underwater by a predator, such as a fish, fall to the bottom with the aperture uppermost. *Ceratostoma* keeps spinning as it falls, and about half the time it lands with its aperture down. In that case it is less vulnerable to being picked at, for it does not have to expose itself much in order to become reattached.

The canal through which *Ceratostoma* extends its siphon is closed over, so that it is a tube instead of an open groove. This snail feeds on *Semibalanus cariosus* and *Balanus glandula*, and on various bivalve molluscs. (On the open coast, where there are plenty of boring and nestling clams, it attacks these.) If it has to, it can drill a hole through a shell with its proboscis, to get at the soft tissue. The big tooth on the outer lip of the aperture, near the base of the siphonal canal, is probably handy for gripping the substratum during feeding, and it can probably be hooked onto barnacles and certain bivalves.

Ocenebra lurida (fig. 184; pl. 13) is related to *Ceratostoma*, but lacks the leafy excrescences. It is only about 2 cm long. It might be confused with *Amphissa*, because its shell shows a similar mixture of fine spiral lines and axial ribs. It is, however, less slender than *Amphissa*, its canal is better developed, and its aperture is not at all the same shape, being oval rather than nearly elliptical. The yellow-brown or orange-brown coloration, and the fact that the axial ribs cross the body whorl, enable one to distinguish it from a small specimen of *Searlesia*.

A snail that almost never is found intertidally, but is so distinctive that it can hardly be neglected, is *Trichotropis cancellata* (fig. 185). It grows up to about 3 cm long, has a nearly round aperture, and is marked with both longitudinal and spiral lines, of which the latter are the stronger. The periostracum is light brown and elaborated into coarse hairs, as in *Fusitriton*. Specimens from deeper water, where *Trichotropis* is abundant, often have a tiny white-shelled snail, *Odostomia columbiana*, next to the aperture. This parasitizes *Trichotropis*, using its eversible proboscis, provided with a puncturing stylet, to suck the juices of its host. *Trichotropis* itself is a filter-feeder, using mucus and ciliary action to trap microscopic food and deliver it to the mouth. It seems not to move around a great deal. Once situated on a stone or empty shell and out of the way of clogging mud, it may stay there indefinitely. This immobility probably explains why *Trichotropis* is often overgrown by solitary ascidians and other sessile animals.

Petaloconchus compactus, the worm-shell (pl. 13), could easily be confused with a serpulid polychaete. Its shell, firmly cemented to a rock, sprawls instead of forming a tightly coiled spire. Typically, there are growth lines encircling the shell, especially at the aperture end, where the diameter is about 2 mm. The aperture is closed by an operculum when the animal withdraws. The operculum, by the way, is replaced occasionally. As a new one forms, the old one is shed. If this occurs in other gastropods, it is extremely rare.

Snails belonging to the worm-shell group collect microscopic food in mucus. *Petaloconchus* produces a mucous veil, and after this has become fairly well saturated with fine particles, the animal uses its toothed radula to pull the veil into the mouth. Some food is also captured by mucus in the mantle cavity, within which the gill is located. This mucus is constantly being moved to a place where it is rolled up into little balls. The radula then draws these into the mouth.

This *Petaloconchus* is extremely abundant in some places, especially on the west side of Vancouver Island. There it is often found in inlets where small rocks lie on a gravelly bottom, or even on a slightly muddy bottom. *Petaloconchus montereyensis*, found from central California southward, is similar, and may not deserve the status of a separate species.

Sea Slugs

The beauty of most of our sea slugs is usually apparent at first sight. Some of the smaller species may escape notice, however, because their coloration blends into that of the animals on which they live. *Doridella* (fig. 37) and *Corambe*, for instance, are not easily seen unless colonies of the bryozoan *Membranipora* on kelp are examined with the aid of a magnifier. *Eubranchus* (fig. 6), regularly associated with *Obelia*, like-

181. *Amphissa columbiana*

182. *Bittium eschrichtii*

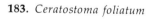

184. *Ocenebra lurida*

185. (*Right*) *Trichotropis cancellata*, with a small parasitic snail, *Odostomia columbiana*, perched on the lip of its aperture

183. *Ceratostoma foliatum*

186. *Dirona albolineata*

wise may be overlooked, although it is one of our more common species. All three of these sea slugs occur on rocky shores, but they have been discussed already in connection with the fauna of floating docks. *Rostanga* (pl. 1), whose color matches that of the red sponges on which it grazes, was considered earlier in this chapter.

The majority of the conspicuous sea slugs on floating docks may be expected in rocky intertidal situations. *Phidiana crassicornis* (pl. 16), *Aeolidia papillosa* (pl. 16), *Archidoris montereyensis* (pl. 14), and *Discodoris sandiegensis* (pl. 14) are probably the ones found with greatest regularity. *Archidoris odhneri* (pl. 14) is less common.

A dorid that is sometimes very abundant intertidally, especially during the late winter and early spring, is *Onchidoris bilamellata* (pl. 14). It has at least sixteen bushy gills around the anus, and the brown coloration of the upper surface is concentrated in a few bands. *Onchidoris* preys on barnacles, and is often found in zone 3.

Among the more stunning dorids are *Triopha catalinae* and *Laila cockerelli*. Both of these sea slugs are so brilliantly decorated that they seem almost unreal. In *Triopha* (pl. 14) the dorsal papillae, as well as the rhinophores and the gills, are tipped with orange; there are also spots of this color scattered over the otherwise white or yellowish white upper surface. *Triopha* reaches a length of about 6 or 7 cm. It eats bryozoans.

Laila (pl. 15) has an unusual feature for a dorid, namely, numerous long, fleshy processes that superficially resemble the cerata found on eolid nudibranchs such as *Phidiana*. These, and the rhinophores also, are tipped with orange, but there are no spots on the body surface and the gills are not colored. *Laila* is only 2 or 3 cm long.

Another dorid that was not mentioned in connection with floating docks, for it is only rarely found on them, is *Cadlina luteomarginata* (pl. 14). It is a relatively broad, flat species that does not often exceed a length of about 4 cm. The ground color is almost white, but all the way around the edge of the foot and the edge of the mantle there is a band of lemon yellow, and the low tubercles on the dorsal surface are tipped with this same color. *Cadlina* subsists on sponges.

Members of the genus *Dirona* look like eolids, for they have prominent cerata. They belong, however, to a separate group of nudibranchs called arminaceans. *Dirona albolineata* (fig. 186) is nearly translucent and usually almost colorless (or faintly pinkish or purplish), except for the internal organs that may show through the body wall. The flattened, sharp-tipped cerata are edged with brilliant white lines. This species eats small snails, whose shells it can crack with its jaws, and it also consumes ascidians and bryozoans. Large specimens are 5 or 6 cm long. *Dirona aurantia* (pl. 16) is similar to *D. albolineata* in size and form, but it is a dirty orange color, with white edges on the cerata and white spots scattered over the dorsal surface. It feeds on bryozoans and occasionally turns up in fair numbers around floating docks.

Janolus fuscus (*Antiopella fusca*) (pl. 16), also an arminacean, resembles *Phidiana crassicornis*, but it lacks the bright white or electric blue lines on the dorsal surface. Instead, there is a reddish mid-dorsal band and a reddish blotch between the rhinophores on the head. The cerata, below their white tips, have a colorless ring, then a ring of orange. Large specimens are about 6 cm long.

Bivalves

Our scallops are basically subtidal animals. Of the several species reported in this area, one—*Pecten caurinus*, the weather vane scallop—is huge, up to more than 15 cm in diameter. Although it will never be found intertidally, two of its relatives occasionally turn up in the course of shore collecting; they are extremely abundant on gravelly and shelly bottoms in deeper water. *Chlamys hastata* (figs. 187 and 188) and *Chlamys rubida* (fig. 189) are similar to one another, but the ribs of the former are rendered rasplike by the presence of little curved spines, whereas those of the latter are practically smooth. The shells of both reach a height of about 6 cm. Scallops normally lie with their right valves against the substratum, and they may be attached periodically, especially when they are younger, by means of a byssus, something like that secreted by mussels. Their valves are normally agape, so that they can process water for extraction of microscopic food. When they are in an aquarium and in their typical posture, the beautiful green eyes—which are iridescent and almost luminous—can be seen around the edge of the mantle in both valves. Sometimes spontaneously, and just about always when menaced by a predator, such as certain sea stars, they swim by a sort of jet propulsion, clapping the valves tightly together and forcing water out through openings on both sides of the hinge.

Chlamys hastata and *C. rubida* are regularly colonized—mostly on the left valve—by sponges that form thick coatings. *Myxilla incrustans* is generally yellow or yellow brown; *Mycale adhaerens* (Fig. 188) is usually light brown, gray, or violet. Color is not a fully reliable criterion for distinguishing the two species. One must examine the siliceous spicules with a microscope.

The purple-hinged rock scallop, *Hinnites giganteus* (fig. 190), is attached firmly to rocks by the right valve of its heavy shell. The left valve is generally somewhat irregular, and may be grotesquely misshapen. It is rather coarsely ribbed, and the ribs show some spinous or membranous excrescences. Both valves are white internally, except close to the hinge, where there is a large blotch of rich purple. The purple color penetrates deep into the shell, and as the area next to the hinge is the thickest part, it is the last to be worn away completely by erosion. Many of the purple bits of shell found on the beach can be traced to this species. The outside of the free valve is on the whole brownish, but when it becomes colonized by sponges, the coralline

187. *Chlamys hastata,* a live specimen showing the eyes near the free edges of the mantle

188. *Chlamys hastata,* a cleaned left valve and a specimen that is overgrown by a sponge, *Mycale adhaerens*

189. *Chlamys rubida,* left valve   **190.** *Hinnites giganteus,* the rock scallop

red alga *Lithothamnium*, and other encrusting organisms, it becomes varicolored.

The valves of the rock scallop are frequently partially eaten away by the boring sponge, *Cliona celata* (pl. 1). The presence of this sponge is evident at the surface as little yellow patches, but below the surface the shell may look something like a honeycomb. Evidently, certain amoeboid cells of *Cliona* are able to erode the calcareous substratum by etching out small portions until they are finally undercut and break off. The process of burrowing thus seems to be accomplished partly by mechanical means and partly by chemical means.

When *Hinnites* is young, it is free-swimming, after the fashion of real scallops, and the shell has the shape characteristic of a scallop. Even after the shell becomes thick, heavy, and irregular, the telltale "ears" remain as reminders of its relationship to scallops. The diameter of large specimens sometimes exceeds 15 cm.

The jingle shell or rock oyster, *Pododesmus cepio* (fig. 52), was described in Chapter 3, for it is rather common on floating docks. It also occurs intertidally, mostly in zone 4. As a rule, it is found on relatively smooth rocks.

Octopuses

We have two species of *Octopus* in shallow water. One of these, *O. dofleini*, with an arm spread of up to 3 m and a weight of up to about 100 pounds, is probably the largest anywhere. Divers encounter it frequently, and occasionally a small or medium-sized specimen is found under a ledge, in its den between rocks, or in a pool in the lowest part of the intertidal region. *Octopus rubescens* (pl. 13), whose body length (exclusive of the arms) is not over 6 cm, lacks the prominent skin folds that are characteristic of *O. dofleini*. Its skin is otherwise much rougher than that of *O. dofleini*, however. Baby octopuses found swimming at the surface, as around floating docks, could be the young of either species.

Octopuses feed to a large extent on crabs and generally eat heartily in captivity. In other respects, unfortunately, they are difficult to keep, as they require cold water and plenty of dissolved oxygen. Large tanks that have sea water running into them continuously are just about essential. Octopuses also have to be protected from their own bad judgment, for they will try to climb out of almost anything they are put into and will in the course of other acrobatics pull out standpipes that maintain the water level in their tanks. The moral of all this is that if you find a little octopus, it would be best to leave it in nature's care.

Barnacles

Semibalanus cariosus is usually plentiful in zone 4, and in some places there is the rather squat, smooth-shelled *Balanus crenatus*. The latter is common in subtidal situations and on floats, and some of its distinctive features have been described in Chapter 3. When found intertidally, it is likely to be on the undersides of smooth rocks.

Shrimps

Broken-back shrimps of the genus *Heptacarpus* (fig. 49) are common in tide pools, where they are usually hidden away in growths of algae. Occasionally they are shaken out of a mass of kelp that is lifted from rock for examination. The broken-backed look of these shrimps is due to a sharp bend in the body in the region of the third abdominal segment. They are sometimes so nearly transparent that the beating of the heart can be observed in the dorsal region. We have a number of species of *Heptacarpus* in our area, mostly ranging in length from around 2 to 3 cm; some of them are not found intertidally. (The closely related genera, *Spirontocaris*, *Eualus*, and *Lebbeus*, superficially indistinguishable from *Heptacarpus*, seem to be represented almost entirely by subtidal species.) The coloration varies greatly—from green through olive and brown to pink or red, sometimes complicated by opaque white bars or darker streaks—and frequently matches that of algae to which they cling. The coloration must depend to some extent on acquiring pigments of the seaweeds, either by eating them or the small animals that subsist on them. The few published observations on feeding by *Heptacarpus* and its relatives indicate that these shrimps are largely carnivores.

Crabs and Hermit Crabs

In zone 4 the predominant hermit crab is *Pagurus granosimanus*, a carryover from zone 3. *Pagurus hirsutiusculus* (fig. 117; pl. 20) is often present in fair numbers, and *P. beringanus*, which is chiefly subtidal, is also found here. In large specimens of *P. beringanus*—those around 4 cm long—the coloration of the claw of the second and third legs is distinctive: two orange bands separated by a white band. Younger individuals do not show this, but can be recognized by a red band at the joint below the claw. Iridescent green eyes are characteristic of all ages. In the intertidal region, *P. beringanus* mostly uses shells of *Nucella lamellosa*, *N. canaliculata*, and *Searlesia dira*. Shells of *Amphissa columbiana*, *Calliostoma ligatum*, and *Bittium eschrichtii* commonly house smaller hermit crabs of this species.

Clinging to kelp or hiding under it are two very common spider crabs. The larger of these is the kelp crab, *Pugettia producta* (fig. 191), which may have a carapace length of up to almost 10 cm. This crab is difficult to see, especially when the color of its slick carapace is an olive green that almost exactly matches that of *Egregia* and some of the other kelps on which it is found. Sometimes a bit of red or orange is worked into the coloration, especially underneath. *Pugettia gracilis* (fig. 358) is a smaller species, with a carapace length rarely exceeding 3 cm.

Its color is mostly reddish brown, but there are various subdued mottlings. The upper side of the carapace, unlike that of *P. producta*, has a few sharp spines. These help to hold bits of seaweed and other organisms that *P. gracilis* sticks onto its carapace. Both *P. gracilis* and *P. producta* are found in beds of eelgrass as well as on rocky shores, so they will be mentioned again in Chapter 7.

Oregonia gracilis, the decorator crab (fig. 192), is the most spidery of our intertidal spider crabs and the one most likely to have a really luxuriant growth of small seaweeds, hydroids, bryozoans, and other colonists. The carapace, broadest near the posterior end, is almost triangular and narrows anteriorly into two slender and nearly parallel rostral horns. The legs are very long and slender in proportion to the size of the body as a whole. The length of the carapace, including the rostrum, occasionally reaches 5 cm. The roughened surfaces of the carapace and legs probably encourage the settlement of foreign organisms, but *Oregonia* is an active decorator: some of the pieces of plant and animal material stuck to it are not permanently fixed to the exoskeleton, but are merely pressed into the matrix of other growths. The delicate pincers of the first legs are admirably constructed for handling the sort of decorations *Oregonia* likes. This crab is sometimes so heavily overgrown that the camouflage is perfect.

In *Scyra acutifrons*, the sharp-nosed crab (fig. 193), the shape of the carapace is about the same as that of *Oregonia*. The rostral horns, however, are relatively short and strongly flattened, and the legs are less spidery than they are in *Oregonia*. The roughened surfaces of the carapace and legs probably help colonizing organisms become well entrenched. In larger specimens, the carapace is about 3.5 cm. long.

The red crab, *Cancer productus* (fig. 357), is frequently taken on rocky shores, although it is more typically found in quiet bays, particularly where there are extensive beds of eelgrass (see Chapter 7). It is, in any case, a versatile animal. The carapace width of a large *C. productus* is about 15 cm. The coloration of the upper side of the body is on the whole a dark brownish red. The pincers are distinctive in being tipped with black. It is probably more common on shores strewn with rocks and boulders than on massive rock formations and reefs.

Cancer oregonensis (pl. 22) likes neat holes into which it can fit without much room to spare. This little crab is mostly dull red, but the tips of its pincers are nearly black; in both these respects it is similar to *Cancer productus*. It is much smaller, however, being at most only about 4 cm across, and the outline of the carapace is nearly circular. Below the intertidal zone, where the giant barnacle (*Balanus nubilus*) is abundant, it must be in seventh heaven, as many of the empty shells of this barnacle dredged from deep water are occupied by *C. oregonensis*.

The helmet crab, *Telmessus cheiragonus* (pl. 22), is a bristly, hairy species with a distinctly greenish look, especially when it is young. Older specimens generally have considerable red, orange, or brown worked into the coloration, but some of the greenish cast usually persists. The carapace, which in larger individuals may reach a width of about 6 cm, has six coarse teeth on either side; most of these have small secondary serrations.

The strangest crabs found in the intertidal region look little alike, but they belong to the same family (Lithodidae). Moreover, they are more closely related to hermit crabs and porcelain crabs than to true crabs.

Hapalogaster mertensii (pl. 20) is basically brown or red and brown, but the body is so thoroughly covered with golden brown bristles and hairs that the ground color may be mostly obscured. The fifth pair of legs is small and tucked out of the way in the gill chamber under the carapace. The abdomen is soft and cannot be folded up under the body. This species attains a length of about 3 cm.

The other crab in this odd series, *Cryptolithodes sitchensis* (the "hidden lithode from Sitka") (fig. 194; pl. 21) is quite weird looking. Its carapace extends outward after the fashion of an oblong saucer to cover the animal so completely that its legs cannot be seen from above. "Turtle crab" is a good common name for this species. In a large individual, the width of the carapace may exceed 5 cm. The rostrum is broad and abruptly truncate. As in *Hapalogaster,* the fifth pair of legs is out of sight, but the abdomen is more nearly like that of porcelain crabs and true crabs in being flat, bent under the carapace, and covered with several distinct, hard plates. The underside is generally almost white. The coloration of the upper side of the carapace varies extensively: sometimes it is almost completely red or purplish red (much the color of the coralline alga *Lithothamnium,* though duskier) but many specimens are predominantly gray, brown, or olive, with or without streaks or blotches.

Ascidians

The solitary ascidians found in the lower intertidal include some of those that colonize floats. *Pyura haustor* (fig. 60), with an ugly, wrinkled lower portion and gorgeous, nearly carmine-red siphons, is almost always present, especially in holes and at their edges. The wrinkled part of the tunic, which ranges from orange-brown to reddish brown in color, may be studded with bits of shell and other foreign material, and may have various small animals using it as a substratum. When the siphons of a large *Pyura* are extended, its height may be close to 5 cm.

Boltenia villosa (fig. 61) is not as common as *Pyura,* but it is easier to see and recognize because it is distinctly stalked, and its light orange-brown color and hairy tunic keep it from blending so easily into the background.

Cnemidocarpa finmarkiensis (pl. 28) may be hard to find because of its habit of living in holes, into which it sometimes fits so neatly that it

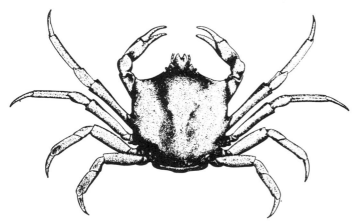

191. *Pugettia producta,* the kelp crab

192. *Oregonia gracilis,* the decorator crab

193. *Scyra acutifrons,*
the sharp-nosed crab

194. *Cryptolithodes sitchensis,* underside

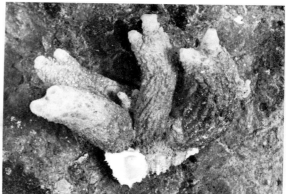

195. *Styela gibbsii*

will be unnoticed unless its siphons are extended. In spite of the fact that it looks as if it had just been skinned, it is a beautiful animal, with an almost pearly pinkish red look. The apertures of both its siphons are round when functioning, but they close down into the form of little crosses when the animal is disturbed. A large *Cnemidocarpa* is about 2.5 cm high.

Styela gibbsii (fig. 195) is not common intertidally, but it is abundant in deeper water, where it is attached to stones and shells, especially those of the snail *Trichotropis*. It frequently forms clumps and is often mixed with *Pyura*, *Boltenia*, and other ascidians. The tunic of *Styela* is wrinkled, like that of *Pyura*, but the body is rather slender and shaped like a cucumber. The color, on the whole, is tan or brown; the short siphons generally have a faint tinge of orange when they are expanded. The height of large specimens is about 4 cm.

Metandrocarpa taylori (pls. 21 and 28) is another species that is only occasionally seen at low tide. It is usually hidden away under ledges. *Metandrocarpa* is approximately hemispherical, and the largest specimens are not quite 7 mm in diameter. The color is typically orange red. This ascidian proliferates asexually to form groups of several to many nearly contiguous individuals. The young develop from short runners that are budded from the bases of adults. The connections between individuals are not permanent, but a few can usually be found in any large aggregation. In any case, *Metandrocarpa* fits the definition of a social ascidian.

Perophora annectens (pl. 28), whose yellowish green zooids are only 2 or 3 mm in diameter, is a decidedly social type, for the connections between zooids persist indefinitely. This species grows mostly on rocks, but is sometimes found on shells or seaweeds.

Intertidally, only a few compound ascidians are reasonably abundant in the region. *Distaplia occidentalis* (fig. 59; pl. 29), so common on floats and pilings, also grows on rocks. Its colonies range from club-shaped or mushroomlike masses, just 1 or 2 cm in diameter, to broad mounds several times as large as this. Characteristically, a number of colonies of various sizes and shapes form tight aggregations. The color varies greatly, from pale orange or tan to dark purplish red.

Colonies of *Aplidium* (pl. 29) form irregular slabs or cakes that may be more than 1 cm thick and more than 20 cm in diameter. Because of their form and consistency, they are often called "sea pork." The color varies, depending on the species; light tan, brownish orange, brownish pink, and brownish red are popular shades. Intertidally, members of the genus *Aplidium* are most likely to be seen on large rocks and reefs in situations where there is considerable wave action.

A rather different type of compound ascidian is one resembling white glove leather—the kind that shows little grayish pits in it. Ascidians of this type are sometimes mistaken for sponges, not only because of their appearance but because when they are teased apart and examined with a microscope, they show an abundance of calcareous spicules. The spicules, however, are globular and unlike those of any calcareous or siliceous sponges likely to be found here. Moreover, close examination of a colony will reveal the numerous tiny zooids characteristic of compound ascidians. There are apparently two genera in the Puget Sound region: *Didemnum* (pl. 5) and *Trididemnum*. They cannot be differentiated in the field, because the characters involved in identification require close attention to microscopic details.

Fishes

The small fishes of intertidal habitats fall largely into four groups: clingfishes, sculpins, pricklebacks, and gunnels. The pricklebacks and gunnels, taken together, are what most people call blenny eels, but they belong to separate families.

Oligocottus snyderi, the fluffy sculpin (fig. 196), resembles *O. maculosus*, the tidepool sculpin that is typically found at slightly higher tide levels. The easiest way to tell these two fishes apart is to look for clusters of small, fleshy outgrowths alongside the bases of both dorsal fins. If these outgrowths are present, you are probably looking at *O. snyderi*; if they are absent, the fish in hand is probably *O. maculosus*. Color is not completely reliable for distinguishing these fishes, but *O. maculosus* is likely to have dark gray bands on a light gray background, whereas *O. snyderi* is inclined to be green.

Oligocottus rimensis, the saddleback sculpin (fig. 197), is fairly abundant intertidally in some areas, especially in winter. It differs from both *O. maculosus* and *O. snyderi* in that much of its body is covered with tiny prickles, which are modified scales. (Neither *O. maculosus* nor *O. snyderi* have any scales.) Another feature that aids in the recognition of the saddleback sculpin is that the spine just in front of each gill cover has a single, acute tip, instead of a notched tip.

Members of the genus *Clinocottus*, also scaleless, are a little more stout than those of the genus *Oligocottus*, and have the anus located about halfway between the bases of the pelvic fins and the start of the anal fin. (In *Oligocottus*, the anus is immediately in front of the anal fin.) Three species are moderately common in the Puget Sound region. *Clinocottus globiceps*, the mosshead sculpin (fig. 198), has a rounded head. In *C. acuticeps*, the head is rather pointed. *Clinocottus embryum* also has a pointed head, but differs from *C. acuticeps* in having the anus located on a prominent tube, as does *C. globiceps*.

Ascelichthys rhodorus, the rosylip sculpin (fig. 199), is likely to be found only in situations where rocks are mixed with soft sediments. It is decidedly more abundant on cobble beaches than on rocky reefs. This species is unusual among sculpins in having no pelvic fins. There is sometimes red on the lips, as the common name indicates, and the spiny portion of the dorsal fin may have a red border.

Artedius lateralis, the smoothhead sculpin, differs from all of the pre-

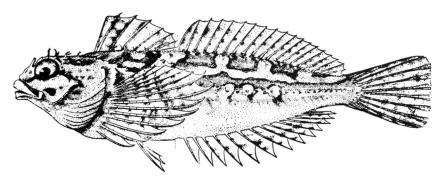

196. *Oligocottus snyderi,* the fluffy sculpin

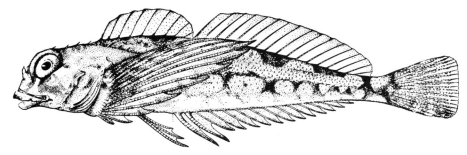

197. *Oligocottus rimensis,* the saddleback sculpin

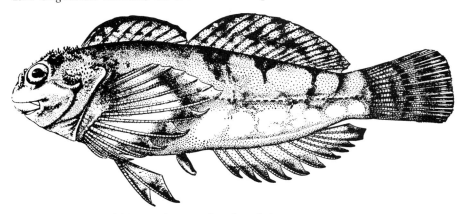

198. *Clinocottus globiceps,* the mosshead sculpin

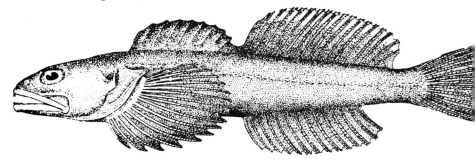

199. *Ascelichthys rhodorus,* the rosylip sculpin

ceding sculpins in having obvious scales. These are on the sides of the upper portion of the anterior half of the body, and are laid out in about 25 oblique rows.

The flathead clingfish, *Gobiesox maeandricus* (pl. 24), is the only representative of its group that one is apt to find in the intertidal region. It is common, however, especially beneath rocks that have smoothly rounded undersides. The basal portions of the pectoral and pelvic fins of the clingfish contribute to the formation of a surprisingly powerful sucker, by which the fish attaches itself.

The blenny eels—that is, the pricklebacks and gunnels—are also plentiful under rocks, slithering around like snakes when exposed. In gunnels, the soft extensions of the lower portions of the right and left gills are connected to one another across the ventral surface; in pricklebacks, on the other hand, there are no such connections. The cockscomb prickleback, *Anoplarchus purpurescens* (pl. 24), with a fleshy crest on the top of its head, is the most common species through much of the area, although in Puget Sound proper the penpoint gunnel, *Apodichthys flavidus*, may be more numerous in many situations; it is often bright green or orange yellow.

5

Rocky Shores of the Open Coast

The Puget Sound region, whose intertidal fauna and flora have been discussed in considerable detail in Chapter 4, is a relatively limited area. Its north-south axis is short compared with that of the stretch of coastline that extends from Vancouver Island to central California. Some of the marine invertebrates and seaweeds indigenous to the open coast of the region covered by this book are primarily northern species. They may be common on Vancouver Island and northern Washington, but drop out before they reach Oregon. Similarly, certain inhabitants of rocky shores in central California are near the northern limits of their ranges.

Nevertheless, a surprisingly large number of marine animals and plants that are to be dealt with in this chapter are found throughout the region under consideration. Another encouraging fact is that nearly all of the conspicuous organisms of rocky shores in Puget Sound and closely adjacent areas are present on the open coast, too. Thus there is no need to repeat here descriptions of species that were covered in Chapter 4.

ZONE 1: THE SUPRALITTORAL FRINGE

In central and northern California, the highest tides on the open coast reach 7 or 8 feet (2.1 to 2.5 meters) above mean lower low water (0.0). Farther north, the amplitude increases. At Port San Juan (Port Renfrew), on Vancouver Island, for instance, the highest tides reach a level of about 12.0 feet (3.7 meters). Thus the limits of the supralittoral fringe vary. In general, it may be said that its lower edge is at about 5.0 feet (1.8 meters) in California and at about 7 or 8 feet (2.1 to 2.4 meters), or perhaps a little higher, in Washington and on Vancouver Island.

The lichens of the splash zone—*Verrucaria, Caloplaca, Xanthoria, Physcia,* and others—are generally present, but they are not often so conspicuous as they are in the Puget Sound region. *Prasiola meridion-*

200. *Littorina keenae (L. planaxis)*

201. *Ligia occidentalis*

alis may be scarce except on rocks where droppings of sea birds are concentrated. This must not be interpreted as a cause-and-effect situation, because in the Puget Sound region *Prasiola* is abundant in many places where there are no bird droppings to speak of. *Enteromorpha intestinalis* is plentiful wherever there is seepage of fresh water, and the high tidepools, subject to severe fluctuations in salinity, generally have *Tigriopus,* at least during the summer months.

The checkered periwinkle, *Littorina scutulata,* is found on the open coast throughout the range of this book, but the Sitka periwinkle, *L. sitkana,* is not often seen south of the Oregon-Washington border. On the coast of California and in southern Oregon, its place is taken by the gray periwinkle, *Littorina keenae* (long known as *L. planaxis*) (fig. 200; pl. 11). The shape of the shell of this species, which is rare north of Coos Bay, is more or less intermediate between that of *L. scutulata* and *L. sitkana.* Most specimens have only three whorls and the surface is nearly smooth, except where it has been eroded. Typically, there is a narrow white band just inside the aperture, and the outside of the shell is usually purplish brown, with some light markings. There is no pronounced checkerboard effect, however. The height regularly reaches 1 cm, and in some specimens it may slightly exceed 1.5 cm. Although *L. keenae* and *L. scutulata* are found on the same rocks, the former occurs mostly at appreciably higher levels than the latter.

The barnacles *Chthamalus dalli* and *Balanus glandula* are routinely present; so is the limpet *Collisella digitalis. Notoacmea persona* should be expected under the lower edges of large boulders.

Ligia pallasii, the crevice-inhabiting isopod that one finds in the Puget Sound region, is abundant all along the open coast from Alaska to about the latitude of San Francisco. Here *L. occidentalis* (Fig. 201) makes its first appearance, and farther south it takes over the high-crevice habitat completely. Where the ranges of the two species overlap slightly, both may be found together. They occur, for instance, at Point Richmond, in San Francisco Bay, not only in natural rocky habitats but also on jetties and wharf pilings. Although *L. occidentalis* and *L. pallasii* are similar, the former is smaller. Its maximum length is about 2.5 cm; *L. pallasii* sometimes reaches 3.5 cm. The identification is most easily clinched by looking at the uropods, the two appendages that stick out backward at the hind end. If these appendages are nearly half the length of the body, then you have *L. occidentalis*. In *L. pallasii*, the uropods are short, and the basal pieces are scarcely longer than wide. Both species go through a long series of juvenile stages punctuated by molts, so not all specimens you pick up will look exactly like the ones illustrated.

ZONE 2: THE UPPER MIDLITTORAL ZONE

The lower limit of zone 2 on the open coast is at a tide level of about +3 or +4 feet (+0.9 or +1.2 meters). The upper limit varies from approximately +5.0 feet (+1.5 meters) to +7.0 or +8.0 feet (+2.1 or +2.4 meters) in Washington and on Vancouver Island. This portion of the intertidal region requires more detailed consideration than zone 1, partly because there are some striking differences in the assemblages of plants and animals found in the northern and southern sectors of the area covered by this book.

Of the algae common in zone 2 in the Puget Sound region, most are found at comparable tide levels and in comparable habitats on the open coast from Vancouver Island to central California. Among the red algae, the following are almost invariably present: *Endocladia muricata*, *Gigartina papillata* (and its encrusting "Petrocelis" phase), and *Hildenbrandia*. *Bangia fuscopurpurea* will be typical of smooth boulders. Various species of *Porphyra* occur, depending on the season. They all look much alike, and it seems best to leave the differences between them to specialized works.

Iridaea cornucopiae (pl. 35) is a strictly open-coast red alga. It does not resemble the large iridaeas that are characteristic of lower levels of the intertidal region. It generally grows in tight colonies, with several blades arising from each disklike holdfast. The blades are not often longer than 2 cm. It is the way some of them are rolled up into a "horn of plenty" that inspired the describers of the species to christen it *cornucopiae*. The plant is stiff and its usual color is olive green, so it is easy to mistake a colony of this alga for a mat of young *Fucus*. *Iridaea cornucopiae* is abundant on the west side of Vancouver Island and on the open coast of northern Washington. Farther south, however, it becomes less common, and it drops out altogether after reaching Mendocino County, California.

Fucus distichus, rockweed

Fucus spiralis

Hedophyllum sessile

Hedophyllum sessile, Egregia menziesii, and *Ulva*

Gigartina papillata (*above*) and its "Petrocelis" stage (*right*); both pictures also show *Littorina scutulata*

Pelvetiopsis limitata

Leathesia difformis

(*Far right*) Intertidal zonation on San Juan Island, Washington. Near the top are coatings of *Caloplaca* (yellow) and *Verrucaria* (dark gray). Just above the center is a narrow band of *Fucus spiralis*. Below this is *Fucus distichus* and some *Ulva*. The latter is at a tide level of about +2.0 feet (0.6 meter).

Plate 33

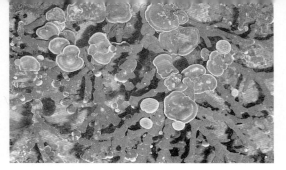

Mesophyllum conchatum on *Calliarthron*

Calliarthron tuberculosum

Bossiella orbigniana

Bossiella californica

Lithothrix aspergillum

Postelsia palmaeformis, the sea palm

Phyllospadix scouleri and *Laminaria setchellii* near Port Renfrew, Vancouver Island. The tide level is about −2.0 feet (−0.6 meter).

Plate 34

Cladophora columbiana (left) and Endocladia
muricata (right)

Rhodochorton purpureum

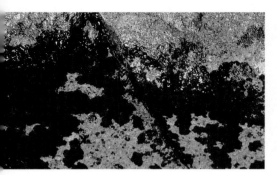

Hildenbrandia

Iridaea cornucopiae

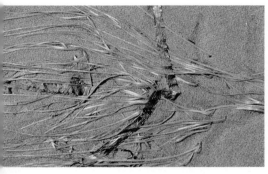

Zostera noltii with two decaying leaves of
Zostera marina

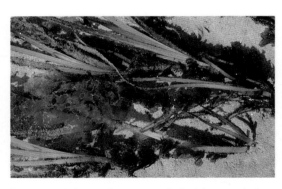

Zostera marina, eelgrass, with Smithora naiadum
(a red alga) and Kornmannia zostericola (a green
alga) growing on the leaves

(Far left) Ulva, Iridaea cordata
(large blades hanging down),
and Microcladia borealis (brownish red patches)

(Left) Halosaccion glandiforme

Plate 35

Ammophila arenaria, beachgrass, on a dune

Juncus lesueurii

Lathyrus japonicus, the beach pea

Lotus salsuginosus

Oenothera cheiranthifolia, the beach evening primrose

Lupinus arboreus, the bush lupine

Lupinus littoralis, the seashore lupine

Elymus mollis dunegrass

Plate 36

Mesembryanthemum chilense, the sea-fig

Abronia latifolia, the yellow sand-verbena

Mesembryanthemum edule, the hottentot-fig

Plantago maritima juncoides, the seaside plantain

Eschscholzia californica, the California poppy

Cakile edentula, the sea rocket

Polygonum paronychia, the knotweed

Rumex salicifolius, the willow dock

Plate 37

Erigeron glaucus, the seaside daisy

Agoseris apargioides

Senecio elegans

Ambrosia chamissonis bipinnatisecta

Tanacetum camphoratum, the dune tansy

Artemisia pycnocephala, the beach sagewort

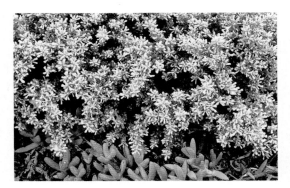

Baccharis pilularis pilularis

Haplopappus ericoides,
the mock heather

Plate 38

Jaumea carnosa

Salicornia europaea (left) and *S. virginica (right)*

A saltmarsh pool with a conspicuous growth of purple sulfur bacteria

A shallow lagoon. Most of the vegetation above the water line is *Salicornia virginica;* in the water are dark patches of *Lyngbya aestuarii* and growths of *Percursaria* and other green algae.

Cuscuta salina, the salt marsh dodder

Cuscuta salina

Frankenia grandifolia
(Right) *Salicornia virginica*, the pickleweed
(Far right) *Limonium californicum*, the sea lavender

Plate 39

Spergularia canadensis

Spergularia macrotheca

Spartina foliosa, cord grass

Tetragonia expansa, New Zealand spinach

Grindelia integrifolia, the gum plant

A narrow salt marsh in Willapa Bay, Washington. The vegetation in the foreground consists mostly of *Salicornia virginica* and *Triglochin maritimum;* dark green patches of *Vaucheria* can be seen; farther away are "islands" of *Spartina alterniflora.*

Baccharis pilularis consanguinea

Plate 40

The rockweed *Fucus distichus* (fig. 202; pl. 33) is regularly present and generally accompanied by one or two close relatives: *Pelvetia fastigiata* (fig. 202) and *Pelvetiopsis limitata* (pl. 33). The latter will be discussed first, because its range, extending from Vancouver Island to the Monterey Peninsula, corresponds almost exactly to that covered by this book. It is a strictly open-coast seaweed, and is not known to occur even on the more exposed shores of the islands in the San Juan Archipelago. It is light olive green and stands out brightly among most of the other algae around it. The stems are distinctly flattened and they fork several times in close succession, so that the growths of this species are rather compact. As in *Fucus,* the reproductive structures are concentrated on the appreciably swollen terminal portions of the stems. *Pelvetiopsis* generally grows to a length of about 6 or 8 cm; larger plants are occasionally encountered, however.

The range of *Pelvetia fastigiata* extends from southern Oregon to Baja California, but this seaweed is not especially abundant north of San Francisco. Its stems reach a length of 30 or 40 cm, and the intervals between the points where branching takes place are much longer than in *Pelvetiopsis.* Many of the branches, especially in the lower part of the plant, are nearly cylindrical. The color is less bright than that of *Pelvetiopsis,* and is often brownish. When *Pelvetia* and *Pelvetiopsis* are found together, the vertical distribution of the latter is in general a little higher.

The most obvious of the green algae is likely to be *Cladophora* (pl. 35), which forms mosslike tufts. If the beach is strewn with small stones that have been worn smooth, these may have what looks like a crop of green hair. This is produced by *Urospora penicilliformis* (pl. 31). Each of its filaments, up to 3 or 4 cm long, is just one cell wide, and there is no branching. A few of the cells in the basal portion of the filament send out delicate outgrowths that function as holdfasts. Luxuriant growths of this alga are extremely slippery when wet! *Urospora* may also be present on smooth stones in zone 1.

It is probably fair to say that *Tegula funebralis,* the black turban (pl. 12), is the most conspicuous snail of the upper midlittoral zone. Its range is from British Columbia to Baja California, but it is found only along the open coast. The organic periostracum that covers the shell is nearly black when wet, purplish black when dry. In most large specimens it is badly eroded, especially near the apex, so the pearly calcareous material shows through. The diameter reaches 2.5 cm and the height is sometimes a little greater than this.

The black turban feeds on algal coatings. As it gets larger, it may move to a slightly lower level in the intertidal region. Here it may get more food of the sort it likes, but it also is more likely to be eaten by the sea star *Pisaster ochraceus.* This snail can crawl with astonishing speed when it has to, and if it happens to be attached to a vertical or sloping surface, it can use another technique for escape: it simply detaches itself and tumbles away. *Tegula funebralis* often congregates, but the presence of numerous shells in a small pool or crevice does not mean that all of them belong to live snails. Some are likely to be occupied by hermit crabs.

Two small gastropods should be looked for on the shells of *T. funebralis*. One of them, *Collisella asmi* (pl. 12), is a true limpet. Its shell, up to 1 cm long and nearly 8 mm high, is almost uniformly gray brown or nearly black, but some specimens have a light band running around the inside of the aperture close to the lip. Externally, except where the shell is eroded, there are likely to be fine radial lines. *Collisella asmi* feeds on the microscopic algae that coat the shell of its host. Young specimens of other limpets are sometimes found on *T. funebralis*, but these are just temporary settlers, and none of them is likely to have such a proportionately high shell as *C. asmi*.

The other gastropod that is more or less regularly associated with *T. funebralis* is *Crepidula adunca*, the hooked slipper shell (pl. 12). It is mostly dark brown, or sometimes grayish brown, but the "deck" inside the shell is whitish. The apex is raised up well away from the margin. Large specimens are about 1.5 cm long. This *Crepidula* lives on other gastropods, including *Tegula brunnea*, *Calliostoma ligatum*, and *Searlesia dira*, typically found at lower levels. Like its free-living relatives, described under zone 4, it traps microscopic particles of food in mucus, instead of grazing the way true limpets do.

All four of the limpets commonly observed in zone 2 in the Puget Sound region are also found at comparable levels on the open coast throughout the range covered by this book. *Collisella digitalis*, as has already been explained in Chapter 4, is more typical of zone 1, and although it is present in zone 2, it tends to be concentrated at upper levels. *Collisella paradigitalis* is also likely to be most common in the higher reaches of zone 2. *Collisella pelta* and *Notoacmea scutum*, on the other hand, are abundant throughout zone 2, and generally plentiful in zone 3, too.

In California, a new face appears among the limpets of zone 2. *Collisella scabra*, the ribbed limpet (fig. 203), is most commonly noted on the tops of rocks that are relatively bare. It resembles *C. digitalis* in having stout radial ribs and a conspicuously scalloped margin, but its shell is not so tall and its apex is not so far forward. Even if the apical portion is eroded, the rest of the shell will be typical. Large specimens are about 2.5 cm long. The head and foot of the living animal are nearly white, but are peppered with tiny black flecks. *Collisella scabra* wanders freely at night and when its habitat is submerged, but it returns to its "home base," which is generally a noticeable depression. The range of this species extends to southern Oregon, but it is rarely seen north of Coos Bay.

Nucella emarginata and *N. canaliculata* may be extremely abundant in zone 2, but as a rule one or the other species predominates. On the

202. *Pelvetia fastigiata* (left) and *Fucus distichus* (right and upper left)

203. *Collisella scabra,* the ribbed limpet

204. (*Above and right*) *Acanthina spirata,* the angled unicorn

open coast of the Olympic Peninsula, for instance, there are places where *N. canaliculata* far outnumbers its relative. Farther south, however, it becomes scarce, and it is rarely seen in central and northern California, where *N. emarginata* may be abundant. As in the Puget Sound region, *N. lamellosa* is often found along with *N. emarginata* or *N. canaliculata* or both, but it is usually more plentiful at slightly lower levels. These snails, as has been explained in Chapter 4, drill through the shells of barnacles and mussels to get at the soft tissue.

Acanthina spirata, the angled unicorn (fig. 204), is also a predator on barnacles. It is common throughout much of California, but scarce in Oregon and Washington. It could be confused with *Nucella emarginata*, but it is unlike any species of *Nucella* in having a prominent spine on the outer lip of the aperture. The shell appears turreted because of the sharp angle at the "shoulder" of each whorl. The gray, brown, or greenish spiral bands on the whorls are interrupted, so they appear as a series of dark patches. The height of the shell reaches 3 cm.

As in the Puget Sound region, *Pagurus hirsutiusculus* is the common hermit crab of zone 2 on the open coast. It has been adequately described in Chapter 4. The other abundant hermit crabs are *P. granosimanus* and *P. samuelis*. One or both of these may be found with *P. hirsutiusculus*, but in general they are at lower levels, and they will be discussed in connection with zone 4.

Pachygrapsus crassipes, the lined shore crab (pl. 21), is common from southern Oregon to Baja California, and its vertical distribution is, on the whole, just a little higher than any of the other true crabs that inhabit rocky shores in the regions dealt with in this book. The coloration varies a great deal. Basically it is greenish, blackish, or reddish, with transverse stripes. The large pincers are sometimes red, or have red or purple lines. The body width of a large specimen is about 5 cm. This crab lives under rocks and in crevices, and if brought out into the open it moves sideways with speed and agility. It feeds to a considerable extent on algae (especially green algae such as *Ulva*), tearing these up with its pincers. It consumes some animal matter, too, and may even attack small crabs of other species. Generally it uses its right and left pincers alternately to bring the food to the mouth parts.

Pachygrapsus is not limited to rocky shores. It also inhabits bays (including San Francisco Bay), living under rocks or in burrows in firm clay. When found in salt marshes, its characteristic habitat is burrows in the sides of tidal channels. Some aspects of its life and associates in salt marshes are discussed in Chapter 7.

ZONE 3: THE LOWER MIDLITTORAL ZONE

Mussels, Goose Barnacles, and Organisms Associated with Them
The rocky shores of the open coast are almost invariably characterized by extensive beds of the California mussel (fig. 119; pl. 17) and the

goose barnacle (fig. 121; pl. 17). These sessile animals are generally concentrated at tide levels of from +2.0 to +4.0 feet (+0.6 m to +1.2 m). One or both species may be at considerably higher levels on nearly vertical cliffs or along surge channels. Typically, however, they are part of zone 3, which extends from about 0.0 to about +3.0 or +4.0 feet (+0.9 to +1.2 m).

Some of the attributes of the California mussel and goose barnacle have been given in Chapter 4. There is no need to cover these points again. It should be stressed, however, that these very characteristic inhabitants of zone 3 are typically open-coast dwellers, and that their presence in the San Juan Archipelago is restricted to the more exposed shores of only a few islands.

Mytilus edulis, the bay mussel or edible mussel, is not often seen on the open coast, except perhaps in situations where a shore turns inward into a quiet bay. Its young are known to settle in exposed situations, but they are simply unable to compete against the California mussel for space, and thus do not form persistent colonies.

As in the San Juan Archipelago, the beds of the California mussel are inhabited by a variety of other invertebrates. Either *Cucumaria pseudocurata* (pl. 27) or its look-alike, *C. curata,* is almost invariably present. Both of these little sea cucumbers are only about 3 cm long when fully extended, and they are so dusky that when they contract they resemble blobs of tar. Both also brood their young. Neither is strictly limited to mussel beds, but this habitat is where they are most likely to be found. To distinguish *C. curata* from *C. pseudocurata,* one must use a microscope to examine the perforated calcareous plates that are embedded in the body wall. If a bit of the body wall is placed in a drop of laundry bleach on a glass slide, the tissue will be dissolved, but the plates will remain. In *C. curata* the margins of the plates are smooth; in *C. pseudocurata* they are jagged. *Cucumaria pseudocurata* is found in Oregon, Washington, and British Columbia as well as in California; *C. curata* seems to be limited to central California. The distinction between the two is not especially clear, and some specialists have argued in favor of calling all of these blackish cucumbers *C. curata.*

Of the many polychaetes likely to be found in mussel beds, *Nereis vexillosa* is likely to be the most conspicuous. It has been described in Chapter 4.

The scavenging isopod *Cirolana harfordi* (fig. 205) is most appropriately dealt with here, for while it is more or less ubiquitous in zone 3 and lower, mussel beds are among its favored haunts. It is found all along the open coast from British Columbia to Baja California. It belongs to a group of isopods characterized by a "tail fan." This consists of the hindmost part of the abdomen (triangular in *Cirolana*) and the broad terminal pieces of the last pair of abdominal appendages. The color of *Cirolana* varies, but it is usually brown, with some darker markings that consist of tiny black specks. The length of large specimens is not quite 2 cm. *Cirolana* is attracted to almost any kind of dead animal matter.

Idotea wosnesenskii (pl. 19) is generally plentiful in beds of the California mussel and among algae, as well as under rocks. It has been discussed in Chapter 3 as well as in Chapter 4. It is, in any case, the most common of the larger isopods at moderate and lower tide levels. On the open coast, as in the Puget Sound region, the color varies. It is generally green, olive, or blackish brown, but specimens living among coralline algae are often mostly pink.

Idotea stenops (pl. 19) is the giant of the genus, sometimes reaching a length of 4 cm. Its usual color, olive green, matches that of kelps to which it clings. (It is especially partial to *Egregia*, found in zone 4 and lower levels of zone 3.) This species resembles *I. wosnesenskii*, but it bulges considerably at the sides, and the posterior end of the body has angular corners. Intertidally, *I. stenops* seems to be more common in California and Oregon than it is farther north.

The acorn barnacle *Semibalanus cariosus* is typical of zone 3, and there may be specimens of *Balanus glandula* that have escaped being eaten. In California, and occasionally in southern Oregon, there are places where *Tetraclita rubescens* (pl. 18) is common. This attractive species, which reaches a diameter of about 2 cm, has brick red streaks running up and down the wall plates. The red material is deposited within the plates, but erosion of the surface makes it visible. *Tetraclita* is an unusual acorn barnacle in that its wall consists of only four plates, instead of six.

The sea star *Pisaster ochraceus* (fig. 124; pl. 25) may as well be dealt with here. As in the Puget Sound region, it comes up into zone 3 to feed on mussels, barnacles, limpets, and other snails, and sometimes it moves even higher into the intertidal region. On the open coast it is more likely to live up to its specific name than it does in Puget Sound and closely adjacent areas. As a rule, about half the individuals in any population are ochre orange; the rest are purple, except for a few that are brown or reddish. The pudgy, stiff rays of this species, and the way the blunt spines on the upper surface are arranged in a networklike pattern, make it easy to identify. It is definitely the most obvious of the larger sea stars on the open coast.

Chitons

The black chiton, *Katharina tunicata* (fig. 122), and the much smaller *Lepidochitona dentiens* (pl. 9), are regularly present in zone 3 all along the coast. In central and northern California, *Nuttallina californica* (pl. 9) is also common. This species is occasionally found as far north as British Columbia, but it is not often seen north of Coos Bay. Unlike *Katharina*, which moves about to graze on algae such as *Hedophyllum*, *Nuttallina* is sedentary. It feeds on pieces of seaweed and other debris that settle around it. It is often entrenched in a pit, and if this pit is in hard rock and about 1 cm deep, it has probably been used by a long succession of individuals, each of which may have lived for more than twenty years. A large specimen of *N. californica* is about 5 cm long, but the body is relatively slender compared with those of most other chitons. The exposed portions of the valves are narrow and usually badly eroded and overgrown by other organisms. If they are not worn down, however, the valves resemble pleated fans because of radiating ribs that consist of raised granules. The girdle is light brown and covered with stiff bristles; most of these are dark brown, but a few may be whitish. Although *Nuttallina* is often situated close to colonies of mussels and goose barnacles, it is frequently noted at appreciably higher levels than those where mussels and goose barnacles are concentrated. In terms of its vertical distribution, it is the highest of our intertidal chitons.

Limpets and Snails

Collisella pelta (fig. 110) and *Notoacmea scutum* (fig. 111) are usually plentiful in zone 3, and there may also be some *C. paradigitalis* (fig. 109). All three of these are widely distributed along the coast. The next two species, however, are almost completely restricted to California. *Collisella limatula*, the file limpet (fig. 206), can generally be recognized with confidence because the radial ribs on its rather low shell appear to be scaly, due to the fact that they are intersected by concentric lines of growth. The outline of the shell, which may reach a length of about 4 cm, is oval, and the margin is serrated, unless the teeth have been worn away. The exterior is basically yellowish brown or greenish brown, but sometimes there are white specks. The head and the sides of the foot of the animal itself are dusky. Although the range of *C. limatula* extends from central Oregon to Baja California, this species is not really abundant north of the California-Oregon border. It is one of the more successful limpets in Tomales Bay, where it occurs on pilings as well as on rocks, and it is sometimes found in other small bays. Specimens from protected situations often have taller shells and coarser radial ribs than are characteristic of specimens from the open coast.

The natural history of this species has been extensively studied. Many of the specimens in a particular population exhibit homing behavior, returning to their accustomed spots after grazing, mostly on coatings that consist largely of diatoms and on encrusting algae such as *Hildenbrandia*. It will eat *Lithothamnium* and similar coralline algae if these are available, as they are on the open coast. *Collisella limatula* must be submerged or at least be thoroughly wet before it will feed.

Lottia gigantea (fig. 207; pl. 11) is called the owl limpet because the inside of the shell bears the image of an owl, the head of the bird being in the apical portion. This is our largest limpet and sometimes reaches a length of 9 cm. The exterior of the shell is almost always badly eroded, but radially arranged ribs are usually recognizable, and the margin is slightly scalloped. The apex is close to the anterior end. On the inside of the shell, the lip has a dark brown border. The owl pattern may be brown, too, or it may be white with brown around it. *Lottia* is generally found in bare spots between patches of mussels and goose barnacles. It is common south of San Francisco, but scarce north of the Golden Gate. Sharp-eyed and knowledgeable collectors have found a few specimens along the coasts of Oregon and Washington.

As in the Puget Sound region, *Nucella lamellosa* (fig. 116) is common at this level, where it has access to plenty of mussels and acorn barnacles. *Nucella emarginata* (figs. 112 and 114) and *N. canaliculata* (figs. 113 and 114) are also likely to be present. *Searlesia dira* (fig. 115), the scavenger, is abundant on the open coasts of British Columbia, Washington, and Oregon, but its occurrence in central and northern California is spotty.

Granulina margaritula (fig. 123) and the sluglike *Onchidella borealis* (pl. 16), both described in Chapter 4, are typical of zone 3 on the open coast. The former, however, may also occur at lower levels, and the latter may be at considerably higher levels, especially in caves.

Polychaetes

In the Puget Sound region, the blackish cirratulid polychaete *Dodecaceria fewkesi* (pl. 9) generally lives at low-tide levels, unless it is in a rock pool, and it forms relatively small colonies. On the open coast, however, there are places where it is abundant in zone 3, and where it forms huge colonies. The calcareous tubes of *Dodecaceria* may form a continuous sheet over the exposed surface of a large boulder. Only one worm is needed to start a colony, for this species can multiply by dividing in half. Within a single tube there may be several individuals in various stages of division and regeneration. *Dodecaceria* feeds by capturing microscopic organisms and other particulate matter on the two long, grooved palps that it sticks out of its tube. Ciliary activity on the palps moves the food in the direction of the mouth. The several pairs of more slender filaments behind the palps function as gills.

Phragmatopoma californica (fig. 208), a member of the family Sabellariidae, makes its hard tubes by cementing together sand grains. This is a gregarious worm, and a mass of its tubes may be more than 1 m across. The opening of each tube, about 3 mm in diameter, typically has a little rim around it. The worms themselves, when full grown, are about 5 cm long. The measurement includes what looks like a naked intestine doubled back against the main part of the body. It is not really naked; the body wall just happens to be very thin in this region. In any case, pointing the anus toward the mouth of the tube is a good adaptation, for it keeps fecal wastes from accumulating in the deepest part of the tube.

The blackish cone with which *Phragmatopoma* stoppers its tube

205. *Cirolana harfordi*

206. *Collisella limatula,* the file limpet. The specimen on the right, found in Tomales Bay, has a proportionately higher shell than is typical of specimens found on the open coast.

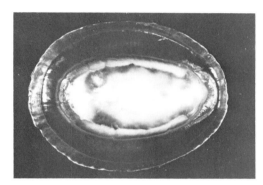

207. *Lottia gigantea,* the owl limpet, interior of shell

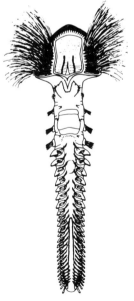

208. *Phragmatopoma californica.* The drawing at the right shows a specimen that has been removed from its tube.

when it withdraws consists of setae. They are on the expanded portion of a stalk that grows up from the first and second segments. The slender tentacles, concerned with trapping microscopic food and also with collecting sand used in tube construction, belong to the first segment. As food particles get stuck in mucus, they are moved by ciliary activity to the bases of the tentacles and then to the mouth. Sand grains are delivered to a pocket behind the mouth, where they are mixed with a cement that hardens quickly.

Phragmatopoma is found from northern California to Baja California. Some other sabellariids will be discussed later in this chapter, in connection with polychaetes of zone 4.

Crabs

Hemigrapsus nudus (pl. 21), discussed in Chapter 4, is characteristic of this zone, where its usual habitat is under rocks that are set on gravel. *Hemigrapsus oregonensis* (pl. 21) is not so abundant on the open coast as it is in more protected situations, but it does occur, especially in coves where there is some seepage of fresh water onto the shore.

Lophopanopeus bellus, the black-clawed crab (pl. 22), plentiful under rocks in the Puget Sound region, is also abundant on the open coast. At Monterey, it begins to give way to *L. leucomanus*, subspecies *heathii*. This crab resembles *L. bellus*, but it is a little smaller (maximum length less than 2 cm) and lacks the sparse hairs characteristic of the carapace and legs of the latter.

Two species of porcelain crabs of the genus *Petrolisthes* are found on the open coast. In Washington and on Vancouver Island, the common one is *P. eriomerus* (pl. 20), already described in connection with the fauna of the Puget Sound region. In Oregon and California, *P. cinctipes* (pl. 20) is the prevailing species. The two are so similar that it may be risky to identify them on the basis of photographs. Look carefully at the pincer-bearing first legs from above. In *P. eriomerus*, the article that comes just before the "hand" is about twice as long as wide, and has nearly parallel margins. In *P. cinctipes*, this article is about one and a half times as long as wide, and the margins converge appreciably toward the hand. Another point of distinction can be seen if the crab is turned over. The little fingerlike palps on the last pair of mouth parts (the third maxillipeds) are blue in *P. eriomerus*, orange red in *P. cinctipes*.

Sea Anemones

Anthopleura elegantissima (pl. 4) is an important component of the fauna of zone 3, and is often found in tidepools and water-filled crevices at slightly higher levels. As in the Puget Sound region, it reproduces asexually to form extensive beds, and is often partly covered by sand (fig. 125). Some aspects of its biology were discussed in Chapter 4.

Seaweeds

As in the Puget Sound region, green algae occupy much of the space in zone 3. The predominant types, especially in tide pools, are broad-bladed species of *Ulva*, especially *U. fenestrata*. *Ulva taeniata* (fig. 209), with ribbonlike blades about 3 cm wide, is plentiful in central California, and is sometimes found as far north as Oregon. *Acrosiphonia coalita* (fig. 126; pl. 31) is usually abundant on horizontal or gently sloping rock surfaces.

The brown seaweed *Hedophyllum sessile* (pl. 33), generally looking much less blistered than it does in the quiet waters of the Puget Sound region, is common along much of the open coast, but becomes scarce in California. *Leathesia difformis* (pl. 33) is likely to be present, from spring to fall, on surfaces that are nearly horizontal. It is almost invariably associated with *Halosaccion glandiforme*, one of the red algae, which will be mentioned later on.

Postelsia palmaeformis, the sea palm (pl. 34), also a brown alga, typically grows at about the same level as *Mytilus californianus* and *Pollicipes polymerus*, but only on rocks that sustain strong wave action. Its rubbery stalks, generally 20 to 40 cm tall, are topped by numerous blades that droop when the plant is out of water. When a wave strikes *Postelsia*, the plant bows down and touches the rock, but then it springs back to its nearly upright posture. Described in 1852, from specimens collected near Bodega Bay by a Russian expedition, *Postelsia* occurs as far north as Vancouver Island and as far south as San Luis Obispo County, California. The plants we see at the shore live only from early spring to late autumn or early winter. The little grooves visible on the blades of mature plants are sites of spore formation. After the spores have dripped off the blades, some of them develop into tiny plants of a sexual generation. The fertilized eggs develop into the sea palm phase. Young sea palms, in the spring, are usually greenish, but they become more nearly olive brown by the time they are fully mature.

The red alga *Gigartina agardhii* (fig. 210) looks much like *G. papillata* of zone 2, but it is more slender; the broadest blades are not likely to be more than 1 cm wide. On the whole, its vertical distribution is appreciably lower than that of *G. papillata*, but the two species do overlap. *Gigartina agardhii* occurs along the open coast from British Columbia to San Luis Obispo County, California, but it is not often found in the protected waters of the Puget Sound region, where *G. papillata* is common.

A few other species of *Gigartina* deserve to be mentioned. *Gigartina volans* (fig. 211) is most likely to be found on rocks that are scoured by sand. It has two phases. The one that reproduces asexually by spores is characterized by dichotomous branching and by relatively few outgrowths on the flat surface of the blades or at the margins. The sexually reproducing phase has a broad blade with a varying number of side branches and many outgrowths, but it is not dichotomously branched. Neither phase is conspicuously warty, so this species cannot be confused with *G. papillata* or *G. agardhii*. Large plants may be more than 20 cm high, and the color is typically dark, brownish purple. The range is from Oregon to Baja California.

Gigartina canaliculata (fig. 212) and *G. leptorhynchos* (fig. 213) may not, at first glance, appear to be related to the gigartinas that have already been discussed. This is because their branches are nearly cylindrical. *Gigartina canaliculata* is generally brownish green in its lower portion, turning to purplish higher up. Sterile plants branch repeatedly, mostly in one plane, and therefore have the look of fern fronds; reproductive plants branch less, and the ultimate branches are stubby and slightly smaller. Plants of both types are generally less than 25 cm high. The range is from southern Oregon to Baja California.

Gigartina leptorhynchos is brown to blackish brown, and forms slender growths characterized by many short, crowded branches. The thickness of some of the main stems may reach 5 mm, however. Large plants are about 20 cm high. The range of this species is from northern California to Baja California. There is some variability in the extent to which the main stems and branches are flattened; specimens from Mendocino and Humboldt counties are more likely than those from more southern localities to show appreciable flattening.

Cumagloia andersonii (fig. 214), found along the open coast throughout the region covered by this book, has an almost cartilaginous texture and is very slimy when wet. It is an annual, with several main stalks growing from a small holdfast. In the spring, when the stalks are young, they are cylindrical and may look as if they have been slightly inflated. As they get older, during the summer months, they tend to become flattened. The breadth of larger stalks is usually about 1 or 2 cm. The length commonly attains 30 cm, but it may exceed this. Most of the many side branches are short. The coloration ranges from olive or greenish red to purplish red.

Microcladia borealis (fig. 127; pl. 35) is generally common, its fronds making up much of the dark algal cover on the rocks. On flat-topped reefs and rocks that do not have steep slopes, there should be plenty of *Halosaccion glandiforme* (pl. 35). Its tall bladders, growing singly or in clusters, are usually mixed with the brainlike growths of the brown alga *Leathesia difformis*.

ZONE 4: THE INFRALITTORAL FRINGE

As in the Puget Sound region, the infralittoral fringe may be said to begin at about 0.0. In general, the lowest tides in central and northern California and Oregon are approximately –2.0 feet (–0.6 meter). On the west coast of Vancouver Island the lowest tides are about –2.5 feet (–0.8 meter).

209. *Ulva taeniata*

210. *Gigartina agardhii*

211. *Gigartina volans*

212. *Gigartina canaliculata*

213. *Gigartina leptorhynchos*

214. *Cumagloia andersonii*

Surfgrasses

There are two species of surfgrass, differing not only in leaf form but in geographic distribution. *Phyllospadix scouleri* (fig. 215; pl. 34), with thin leaves that are 2 to 4 mm wide, was discussed in Chapter 4, because it occurs on the more exposed shores of the San Juan Archipelago. Its geographic range is from Vancouver Island to southern California. In northern California, another surfgrass enters the picture. This is *P. torreyi* (fig. 216; pl. 11), whose leaves are more firm than those of *P. scouleri* and not over 2 mm wide. Its range extends to Baja California.

The two species do not regularly occur together in the region where their ranges overlap. On rocks where sand swirls about, or on rocks bordering sandy channels, *P. torreyi* is the prevailing surfgrass. *Phyllospadix scouleri* is more likely to be found on rocks where sand does not circulate to any great extent.

On the leaves of both *P. torreyi* and *P. scouleri* there is generally *Melobesia* (pl. 11), a coralline red alga that forms thin encrustations. From late spring to autumn, the red alga *Smithora naiadum* (pl. 35) and the green alga *Kornmannia zostericola* (pl. 35) are present. The blades of these reach a length of about 7 cm. *Kornmannia* looks like an *Ulva*, but its blades are only one cell thick, instead of two cells thick.

Of the more obvious animals that live on surfgrasses, the most remarkable is the little limpet *Notoacmea paleacea* (pl. 11). Its shell may reach a length of 1 cm, but even then it will not be more than 3 mm wide, so that the animal fits nicely on the narrow leaves. The color of the shell, except where there has been erosion, is brown externally, bluish internally. The apex is rather far forward and there are fine lines radiating from it. *Notoacmea paleacea* is rather regularly found on *Phyllospadix torreyi* in California. It is less common on *P. scouleri,* and although it occurs on this species as far north as Vancouver Island, it is rarely seen north of Oregon. Its food consists partly of diatoms and other small algae, partly of cells scraped out of the leaves themselves.

Little snails of the genus *Lacuna* may be extremely abundant on surfgrass leaves, but they are by no means limited to this habitat. They occur on various algae, and also crawl around on rocks. Lacunas, which are rather closely related to periwinkles, are called chink shells because of the groove that runs alongside the inner lip of the aperture. There are several species to contend with and they are not easy to separate. *Lacuna marmorata* (pl. 11) is common on surfgrass in California, and although its range extends to Alaska, it is seldom seen north of Oregon. Its shell, up to about 6 mm high, is basically brown, but generally has some white markings. The height of the aperture is two-thirds the height of the shell. All lacunas lay their eggs in gelatinous masses that look like little yellow life preservers; these are about 5 mm in diameter.

Clinging tenaciously to *Phyllospadix,* and feeding on the leaves, are several kinds of isopods belonging to the genus *Idotea*. One of them, *I. montereyensis* (fig. 217), about 1.5 cm long, has a wide geographic range—British Columbia to southern California. It is not restricted to *Phyllospadix*, and its color varies according to what it eats. Specimens found on *Phyllospadix* are green; those living on various red algae match these plants and some even show a banded pattern. The pigments are concentrated in the cuticle, and after each molt an *Idotea* must reestablish its characteristic color. If shifted from one alga to another, or from an alga to *Phyllospadix*, it will acquire the appropriate coloration soon after it molts. By matching its background, this isopod gives itself some protection from predation. Females of *I. montereyensis* are appreciably broader than males.

Other idoteas living on *Phyllospadix* are *I. kirchanskii* and *I. aculeata*. The former, about the same size as *I. montereyensis*, is apparently restricted to central California and to *P. scouleri*. It is basically green, but may have pink spots on the body and a pink suffusion on its antennae and legs. The best way to tell *I. montereyensis* and *I. kirchanskii* apart is to look at the little projection that extends forward from the anterior edge of the head. In *I. montereyensis* this is rather narrow and sharply acute; in *I. kirchanskii* it is blunt.

Idotea aculeata, which may be nearly 2.5 cm long, is found on seaweeds as well as on surfgrass. Its range covers nearly the entire coast of California. The telson has an obvious and rather acute terminal projection. The color is generally pink or reddish brown, and there may be white spots on the body.

Brown Algae

Although *Laminaria saccharina* and *L. groenlandica*, so common in the quiet waters of the Puget Sound region, occur on the open coast of Vancouver Island and Washington, neither is likely to be encountered in rocky intertidal habitats farther south. The genus is, however, admirably represented on the open coast by *L. setchellii* (fig. 218; pl. 34). At tide levels of −1.5 feet (−0.5 meter) and lower, one will see extensive forests of this distinctive species, which is called *L. dentigera* in some works on Pacific coast algae. Its blades, divided at the base into a number of strips, droop from the stiff, relatively long, and generally upright stipes.

Many of the other large brown algae characteristic of zone 4, and of the shallow subtidal region, are close relatives of *Laminaria*. Among them are *Costaria costata* (fig. 75), *Alaria marginata* (fig. 133), *Nereocystis luetkeana* (figs. 136 and 137), *Pterygophora californica* (fig. 132), and *Egregia menziesii* (fig. 131). All of these were described in Chapter 4, and all except *Costaria* are found intertidally throughout the range covered by this book. By the time it reaches California, *Costaria* becomes restricted to subtidal rocks.

Agarum fimbriatum (fig. 129) and *Cymathere triplicata* (fig. 130) are northern species. Neither is likely to be seen intertidally south of Washington.

Egregia should be examined for the presence of the seaweed limpet, *Notoacmea insessa* (fig. 219). This limpet rasps out scarlike depressions, and it may eventually destroy the kelp. The shell of *N. insessa*, dark brown inside and out, usually has a shiny surface, and is tall in proportion to its length and width. The height may, in fact, exceed the width. Large specimens are a little more than 1.5 cm long. This interesting limpet is abundant in central and northern California, and although its range extends to Alaska, it is not often found north of Oregon.

Lessoniopsis littoralis, Macrocystis pyrifera, and *M. integrifolia* are also allies of *Laminaria,* and each is remarkable in one way or another. Unlike the several species mentioned in the preceding paragraph, they are almost strictly open-coast kelps.

Lessoniopsis littoralis (fig. 220) is distinctive because its woody stalk branches several times in quick succession, and each ultimate branch produces several narrow blades that may be up to 1 m long. A single plant may have more than three or four hundred blades. The color of the plant as a whole is blackish brown. *Lessoniopsis* is found only where the surf is strong; it often lines the sides of surge channels. Its range extends from Alaska to central California.

Macrocystis integrifolia (fig. 221) is a large kelp that is attached to rocks in the lowest part of the intertidal region, and also subtidally. Each of the several main stalks it sends up from its creeping holdfast branches two or three times, sometimes more. Large growths may reach a length of 10 m. The blades, up to about 40 cm long, are rather narrow, slightly curved, and bordered by sharp teeth. At the base of each blade is a gas-filled float. The illustration shows how new blades originate by the splitting of the terminal blade. The range of this species extends from British Columbia to the Monterey Peninsula in California. It also grows on the Pacific coast of southern South America. It is sometimes found in relatively protected situations. There are, for instance, extensive beds of it near Sooke, at the south end of Vancouver Island, where there is little wave action, and in inlets in the region of Barkley Sound.

Macrocystis pyrifera (fig. 222) forms kelp beds offshore, in water up to 80 m deep, but large pieces of it wash up on the beach. It grows larger than *M. integrifolia,* and may reach a length of 40 m. Its holdfast does not creep, and typically produces a single main stem that forks several times. At the tip of each ultimate branch is a broad blade that keeps growing as it splits and leaves behind a series of progressively larger blades, each with its own basal float. The range of *M. pyrifera* in North America is from Alaska to Baja California. This species, like *M. integrifolia,* shows up again in cooler waters of the Southern Hemisphere.

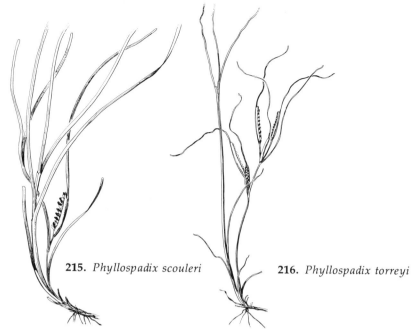

215. *Phyllospadix scouleri*

216. *Phyllospadix torreyi*

217. *Idotea montereyensis*

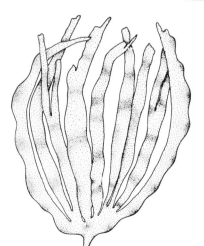

219. *Notoacmea insessa* on *Egregia menziesii*

218. *Laminaria setchellii*

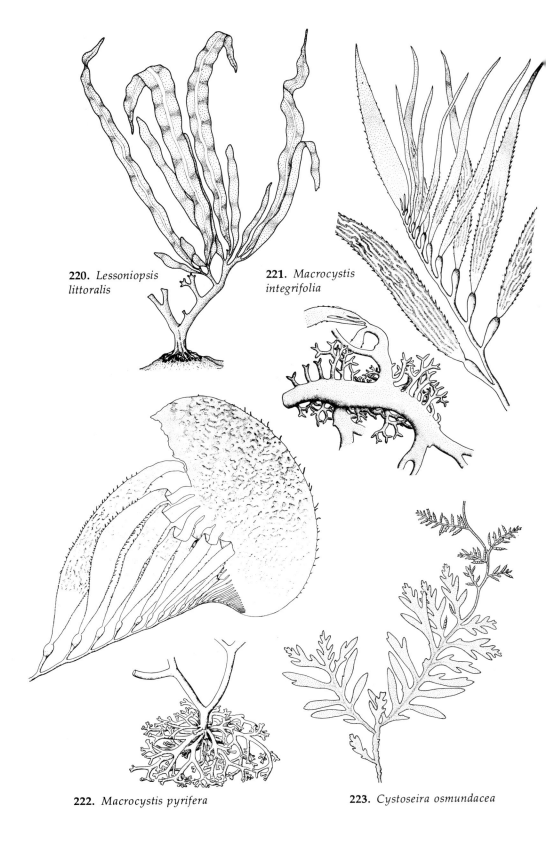

220. *Lessoniopsis littoralis*

221. *Macrocystis integrifolia*

222. *Macrocystis pyrifera*

223. *Cystoseira osmundacea*

Cystoseira geminata (fig. 139) is found in British Columbia and Washington. From northern Oregon to Baja California it is replaced by the larger and more beautiful *C. osmundacea* (fig. 223). The basal portion of each main branch of this species is flattened and divided into progressively smaller lateral lobes, so that it resembles a fern leaf. The rest of the branch, which commonly reaches a length of 2 m, and which is sometimes longer than 5 m, bears many groups of small, gas-filled bladders, arranged in series, like beads. In some places the plant produces bladders where one might expect it to produce flattened lobes, and *vice versa*. The color of this species is mostly light brown. Like *Cystoseira geminata*, it often has the saclike brown alga *Coilodesme californica* (fig. 140) growing on it.

Other common and widely distributed brown algae of the lowermost part of the intertidal region are *Desmarestia ligulata* (figs. 134 and 135) and *D. viridis* (fig. 76). The little blackish or olive-brown patches of *Ralfsia* (pl. 12), prominent at about mid-tide level, are also found in zone 4. *Scytosiphon lomentaria* (fig. 102) may be plentiful, too, although this species is not so noticeable here, where seaweeds really luxuriate, as it is at the edge of nearly bare shallow pools a little higher up on the shore.

Soranthera ulvoidea (fig. 151), epiphytic on *Odonthalia* and *Rhodomela* in the Puget Sound region, is found on these red algae all along the open coast, too. *Sargassum muticum* (fig. 138), introduced from Japan, is abundant in many places from Oregon northward, and has taken hold in a few places—especially protected situations—in California.

Green Algae

The more prominent green algae at low-tide levels are *Codium fragile* and *C. setchellii* (pl. 31). These were described in sufficient detail in Chapter 4, although they are rarely as abundant in the Puget Sound region as they are on the open coast. The concentrations of *C. fragile* are sometimes impressive, and many plants may be scattered through zone 3 as well as zone 4.

You may find some dark green bladders, up to about 1 cm in diameter (pl. 31), growing out of encrustations of the coralline red alga *Lithothamnium*. These represent the sexual stage ("Halicystis") of *Derbesia marina*, a green alga that has been discussed in Chapter 3. (Its filamentous, spore-producing stage is common on floats in the Puget Sound region.) When a bladder shows areas that are of a slightly different color than the rest of it, these mark the places where male or female gametes are being produced.

Red Algae

The number of red algae in zone 4 is large. There are many genera, and some of these are represented by two or more species that look very much alike. It will be best to concentrate here on the larger and more distinctive types. Some of the smaller species are important in terms of the space they occupy, either on rocks or on other seaweeds, but the distinctions between them are difficult to appreciate without recourse to microscopes and specialized treatises. Books that will enable the patient enthusiast to identify them are listed in the bibliography.

Every one of the red algae described and illustrated in connection with zone 4 of the Puget Sound region can be expected on the open coast throughout the range covered by this book. This must not be taken to mean that they will be found at low-tide levels everywhere, for some of them are specialized for living in particular situations. *Ahnfeltiopsis pacifica* (fig. 165), *Gymnogongrus linearis* (fig. 166), *Gracilaria sjoestedtii* (fig. 167), and *Sarcodiotheca gaudichaudii* (fig. 168), for instance, tend to be found on rocks where sand swirls about.

The conspicuous red algal associates of surfgrasses have been mentioned earlier in this chapter. One of them, *Melobesia mediocris* (pl. 11), is an encrusting coralline type; the other is *Smithora naiadum* (pl. 35), a close relative of the species of *Porphyra* that are typical of higher levels of the intertidal region.

There are several species of *Iridaea* on the open coast, but only two will be mentioned here. One is *I. cordata* (fig. 147; pl. 35) which occurs throughout the region covered by this book and which has been described in Chapter 4. The other is *Iridaea flaccida*, likewise found all along the coast. In most localities in California, it is the predominant species of the genus. The blades, usually less wrinkled at the margins than those of *I. cordata*, are several times as long as wide, and are largely greenish. Only the short basal stalk and the lower portion of the blade are likely to be purplish, unless the plant as a whole has been growing in a shaded situation. The length is usually about 30 cm, but sometimes it is considerably larger.

Gastroclonium coulteri (fig. 224), not found in the Puget Sound region, is easy to identify. Its main stems, about 3 mm thick, grow from a small perennial holdfast, and branch a few times in a dichotomous pattern. The many small side branches, each about 1 cm long, slightly resemble slender pickles. The color of the plant as a whole, which is not often more than 15 cm tall, is generally olive green. By late autumn or early winter, *Gastroclonium* dies back to a few short stubs. This alga is found from Vancouver Island to Baja California, but it is especially common in central and northern California.

Botryocladia pseudodichotoma (fig. 225) is easy to recognize. Its ultimate branches are swollen, fluid-filled sacs 1 or 2 cm long. The plant as a whole, usually brownish red, may therefore look like a bunch of grapes. Although this alga is sometimes seen at the shore in British Columbia and Washington, it is for all practical purposes a subtidal species. At Monterey, California, it is common on floating docks. This, of course, is a subtidal situation, for the plants are never out of water. It is odd, however, that *Botryocladia* does not seem to grow on floats in the Puget Sound region, where it is abundant subtidally. It should be mentioned that the growths of *Botryocladia* at Monterey provide a substratum for various attached invertebrates, particularly *Ascidia ceratodes* and the small serpulid polychaetes of the genus *Spirorbis*. Two other larger red algae that stand out on floats at Monterey are *Prionitis lanceolata* and *Cryptopleura lobulifera*.

The next two species, both deep red and about 20 or 30 cm high, are attractive because of their pattern of branching, which resembles that of delicately divided fern fronds or certain mosses. *Ptilota filicina* (fig. 226) is found from Alaska to Baja California. The range of *Neoptilota densa* (fig. 227) is from northern California to Baja California. The photographs should enable one to distinguish them. There are some other species of *Neoptilota*, however, and the trained algologist will make sure of his determinations by looking at certain microscopic details.

Sponges

Of the many siliceous sponges found intertidally on the open coast, a few are especially common and distinctive. *Ophlitaspongia pennata* (pl. 1) is almost everywhere that there is rock. It is not the only bright red sponge, but if the encrustation is thin, it is likely to be of this species. Wherever it occurs, one should also expect the little dorid nudibranch, *Rostanga pulchra* (pl. 1), which eats it. *Plocamia karykina* is perhaps the second most common red sponge, especially in California, but it is often more than 2 cm thick, and its color is not always really red; it may be pinkish, pinkish orange, or some other color between salmon and red.

Halichondria panicea (pl. 1) and a species of *Haliclona* (perhaps *H. permollis*) (pl. 1), both dealt with in Chapter 4, are abundant almost everywhere. They will not be described again here, but in summary, it may be said that a violet or grayish encrusting sponge whose oscula are on prominent, volcanolike eminences is likely to be *Haliclona*. *Halichondria* is generally greenish or yellowish, and its oscula are usually aligned along ridges. When bruised, it gives off an odor resembling that of exploded gunpowder.

The skunk sponge, *Lissodendoryx firma*, is also yellowish, but is not likely to be confused with *Halichondria*. Its encrustations may be nearly 5 cm thick, and there are no prominent oscula. When bruised or broken open, this species gives off a disagreeable odor. *Lissodendoryx* is more abundant in central California than it is father north. Its typical habitat is on the undersides of rocks, including those partly buried in sand.

Other siliceous sponges, some thin and some thick, could be mentioned here. They are either less common than those that have already been discussed or are impossible to identify without going into minute details of their spicule types.

There are relatively few calcareous sponges occurring intertidally in the region covered in this book. The most distinctive species is *Leucilla nuttingi* (fig. 228). It forms vase-shaped structures, grayish white or pale tan in color, set on slender, dark stalks. The height reaches 3 cm. *Leucilla* is fairly abundant on rocky shores of central California, but farther north it is primarily subtidal, although it is sometimes found on floats in the Puget Sound region.

Leucosolenia eleanor is the only other calcareous sponge that will be mentioned. It is a little more delicate than the *Leucosolenia* that was described in Chapter 3, in connection with the fauna of floats. Its tubes are only about 1 mm in diameter and they unite with one another much more freely than do those of the float-inhabiting species. A large colony may be more than 5 cm across.

Hydroids and Hydrozoan Corals

There are many hydroids, not only on rocks, but also on shells, worm tubes, and seaweeds. Many of them are too small to show off their distinctive features in the field. Only a few that are especially conspicuous and also easily recognized will be discussed here.

Obelia geniculata (figs. 7 and 8) was described in Chapter 3, in connection with the fauna of floats. On rocky shores, this thecate hydroid is most likely to be found on seaweeds, forming a dense, whitish fuzz about 1 cm high. One should not jump to the conclusion that all fuzzy looking hydroids are of this species. If, however, microscopic study shows that the club-shaped reproductive polyps release medusae of the type shown in Figure 8, then the colony is almost certainly an *Obelia*.

Some other thecate hydroids that can be identified to genus without much bother are *Aglaophenia* (pl. 2), *Abietinaria* (pl. 2), and *Plumularia* (pl. 2). All of these branch in a featherlike pattern. The first two were described in Chapter 4. *Aglaophenia* is distinctive because of its corbulae—the little baskets within which reproductive polyps develop. *Abietinaria* lacks corbulae and differs from *Aglaophenia* also in having feeding polyps on both sides of its side branches. *Plumularia* is more nearly similar to *Aglaophenia* than to *Abietinaria*, for its feeding polyps are on one side of the branches. It has no corbulae, however—its reproductive polyps are scattered among the feeding polyps—and it is much more delicate than *Aglaophenia*. The plumes come up from a stolon that is tightly bonded to a rock, shell, or stalk of a kelp. Scattered among the feeding polyps and reproductive polyps are still tinier polyps in which batteries of stinging capsules are concentrated. These are probably primarily for defense (*Aglaophenia* has these special

224. *Gastroclonium coulteri*

225. *Botryocladia pseudodichotoma*

226. *Ptilota filicina*

227. *Neoptilota densa*

228. *Leucilla nuttingi*

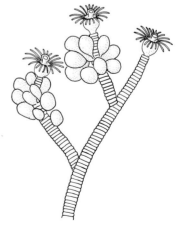

229. (*Right*) *Eudendrium californicum*, a small portion of a colony, magnified

polyps, too). *Plumularia setacea*, whose plumes are generally 3 to 4 cm high, is the most common species along the coast.

All three of the hydroids just mentioned retain their medusae within the reproductive polyps. The fertilized eggs develop into swimming larvae. These emerge, and if successful in finding a suitable place to settle, they become the founders of new colonies.

Sertularia (pl. 2) slightly resembles *Abietinaria*, because it has feeding polyps on both sides of its branches. The feeding polyps on a particular branch are arranged in such a way, however, that they are directly opposite one another, rather than alternating as they do in *Abietinaria*. In *Sertularella* (pl. 2), whose feeding polyps alternate, the branching is irregular, and there is no tendency to form featherlike plumes. Both *Sertularia* and *Sertularella* are small and delicate compared with *Abietinaria*.

The largest athecate hydroid likely to be found on intertidal rocks is *Tubularia marina* (fig. 11). The characteristics and life history of this species, which occurs on floats in the Puget Sound region, are described in Chapter 3.

Garveia annulata (pl. 2) is a distinctive athecate type because its feeding polyps and reproductive polyps are bright orange. The colonies are much branched, and the short stems that support the feeding polyps appear to consist of many contiguous rings stacked one on top of the other. The globose reproductive polyps, growing out of the thick main stalks, do not release the medusae that develop inside them.

Eudendrium californicum (fig. 229) is similar to *Garveia*, but much larger; it sometimes grows to a height of more than 10 cm. In general, the colony is brownish, but the feeding polyps are pinkish, with white tubules. All of the stems are noticeably ringed. The reproductive polyps are borne on the basal portions of the feeding polyps. The medusae remain inside them. The eggs that develop within female medusae are orange.

The hydroid stages of one or more species of *Sarsia* (fig. 10), described in Chapter 3, may also be expected, but they are less likely to be noted on rocks or seaweeds that are exposed at low tide than on floats or in a pool where they are submerged and expanded.

Most corals—that is, cnidarians which secrete a calcareous skeleton—belong to the Anthozoa, the group that includes sea anemones and sea pens. There is, however, one subdivision of the Hydrozoa that consists of corals. The genus found in the region for which this book has been written is *Allopora*, and from Vancouver Island to central California the only species likely to be seen intertidally is *A. porphyra* (pl. 2). It forms thin encrustations over rocks and shells, and is usually purplish pink, sometimes truly purple. Surrounding each pit occupied by a feeding polyp are several notches, each with a little pore from which a single tentacle—actually a specialized, nonfeeding polyp—is extended. Within the limy skeleton there are tubes of tissue that connect the polyps. There are also chambers within which medusae are produced. These medusae do not leave the colony. After the eggs are fertilized, they develop into ciliated larvae, which emerge from the colony by way of the mouths of the feeding polyps. If a larva is successful in finding a suitable place to settle, it flattens out and becomes the first polyp of a new colony.

Some subtidal alloporas form lumpy colonies, or colonies in which the encrustations are raised up into erect, branching fingers. The extent to which a single species may vary needs to be studied. In other words, not all of the distinctly different growth forms necessarily belong to separate species.

Sea Anemones and Their Allies

Of the low-intertidal anemones described in Chapter 4, *Anthopleura xanthogrammica* (pl. 4), *Urticina crassicornis* (pl. 4), *U. coriacea* (pl. 4), and *Epiactis prolifera* (fig. 346) occur on the open coast throughout the range of this book. *Anthopleura artemisia* (pl. 4), described in Chapter 7 in connection with the fauna of quiet bays, is sometimes found in sand-filled or gravel-filled pools on rocky shores.

Cnidopus ritteri (pl. 4) looks a little like *Epiactis,* but it has fewer and proportionately larger tentacles than are typical of *Epiactis,* and it does not brood its young externally. There are no radiating white lines on the oral disk, and when radiating lines occur on the edges of the base, they are not especially distinct. The height of this anemone, even when the animal is fully expanded, is much shorter than the diameter. The oral disk of a large specimen is about 4 cm across. The column is nearly smooth, but it does have some small tubercles and it accumulates sand and bits of shell. The young are brooded within the gut until they are more or less fully developed little anemones, and they are then released through the mouth. *Cnidopus* is found mostly under rocks, and its range extends from Alaska to central California.

Aulactinia incubans (pl. 4) resembles *Epiactis* even more than *Cnidopus* does, for it has radiating white lines on its disk and has about the same body proportions. It is fairly common in the San Juan Archipelago, and has been collected in a few places on the open coast of Alaska and British Columbia. A description of it has been given in Chapter 4.

Urticina lofotensis (pl. 4) resembles *U. coriacea,* but its column is more nearly scarlet than red, and has white tubercles arranged in rather neat lengthwise rows. This species does not accumulate bits of shell the way that *U. coriacea* does, and it is usually attached to vertical rock faces instead of being tucked away in gravel-filled crevices or pools.

Cornyactis californica (pl. 5) is distinctive because of its delicate appearance and knobbed tentacles. The knobs contain high concentrations of stinging capsules. This species generally grows under rock ledges and tends to be in clusters. Large individuals are about 2 cm high. The color varies from nearly white to pink, red, pale blue, and lavender. *Cornyactis* is fairly common in central California, and although its range extends to British Columbia and includes the San Juan Archipelago, it is rarely encountered intertidally north of Oregon. It is not, by the way, a true sea anemone. It belongs to the Corallimorpharia, a group of cnidarians that may be described as corals that lack skeletons.

Of the two close allies of anemones mentioned in Chapter 4, *Balanophyllia elegans,* the orange cup coral (pls. 5 and 28) occurs throughout the region. *Epizoanthus scotinus* (pl. 5), though found intertidally in the San Juan Archipelago and Strait of Georgia, is primarily subtidal. It is, in any case, a northern species, and probably does not reach California, or perhaps even Oregon.

So-called soft corals are mostly subtidal, but two genera barely get into the intertidal region. A soft coral has spicules of calcium carbonate within it, so it is moderately firm, but it does not have a completely calcified skeleton like that of reef-building corals of warmer seas, or even like that of the cup coral of our coast. The polyps of soft corals have eight tentacles, each with delicate side branches. This establishes their relationship to sea pens and to most of the colonial reef-building corals.

Clavularia (pl. 5)—the species is uncertain—forms colonies in which the polyps, each less than 1 cm high—are joined together by stolons. As new polyps are formed from the stolons, the colony enlarges. The color is usually pale orange, pale pink, or cream. A large cluster is about 10 cm across.

Gersemia rubiformis (pl. 5) forms a lumpy colony, sometimes 10 or 15 cm in diameter, whose color ranges from cream through orange to deep pink. The lumps, when the polyps have withdrawn, slightly resemble raspberries or blackberries, which belong to the genus *Rubus;* hence the specific name *rubiformis.* Extended, the individual polyps stick out about 5 mm beyond the lump to which they belong.

Flatworms

Most of the flatworms that are large enough to be noticed in the field belong to the group called polyclads. Even these cannot usually be identified without careful study of microscopic details. *Kaburakia excelsa* (pl. 6), already discussed in Chapters 3 and 4, is distinctive because of its large size. Fully extended specimens may measure 8 by 5 cm, sometimes a bit larger. The color is mostly light brown, with darker dashes. Besides the eyespots that are concentrated near the brain in the head region, there are eyespots all around the margin of the body. These will have to be seen with a microscope.

On the undersides of rocks, in mussel beds, and in similar situations, there are likely to be pale brown or gray polyclads that are about 2 or 3 cm long. Some of them are so thin that they could be mistaken for slimy coatings. They glide rapidly, however, and change shape a little as they move along. Most of these worms belong to one or another species of the genus *Notoplana*. In central and northern California, *N. acticola* (pl. 6) is an especially common species.

Nemerteans

All of the more conspicuous nemerteans found on rocky shores or floats in the Puget Sound region also occur along the open coast. They will be listed here but not described again: *Micrura verrilli* (pl. 6); *Tubulanus polymorphus* (pl. 6) and *T. sexlineatus* (pl. 6); *Emplectonema gracile* (pl. 6); *Amphiporus imparispinosus* (pl. 6), *A. formidabilis*, and *A. bimaculatus* (pl. 6). *Paranemertes peregrina* (fig. 335) occurs in rocky areas, especially in California, but in the Northwest it is more characteristic of bays where there is sandy mud. It is dealt with in Chapter 7.

Polychaetes

With polychaetes, of which there are many species, one hardly knows where to begin and where to stop. Nearly all of the ones that will be mentioned are relatively large and construct tubes that are partly or completely exposed. Most of the polychaetes that were discussed in Chapters 3 and 4 occur on the open coast, but the north-south distribution of some of them needs to be commented upon.

The family Serpulidae is represented by *Serpula vermicularis* (pl. 7) and various species of *Spirorbis* (pls. 7 and 12). There are plenty of sabellids, too. *Potamilla occelata* (pl. 7) is found throughout the range covered by this book, and is especially characteristic of rocky shores that are somewhat protected. *Eudistylia vancouveri* (pl. 7) and *Schizobranchia insignis* (pl. 7) are common in the Northwest, but neither is as abundant in California as *Eudistylia polymorpha* (pl. 7). The latter, with prostomial cirri that are reddish brown or maroon and tipped with orange (but without green bands typical of *E. vancouveri*), was described in Chapter 3. Its range extends to the Northwest, but its place is largely taken there by *E. vancouveri* and *Schizobranchia*.

Thelepus crispus (fig. 169) is probably the most common larger terebellid on the open coast. As in the Puget Sound region, its tubes are coated with sand grains and are generally found on the undersides of rocks and in crevices. *Neoamphitrite robusta*, whose tubes are made of clay particles, is likely to be found under rocks that rest on mud. It is about the same size as *T. crispus*—15 cm long when full grown. The easiest way to distinguish *Neoamphitrite* from *Thelepus* is to look, with a strong magnifier, at the arrangement of hooklike setae on the swollen anterior portion of the body. In *Thelepus*, the first four sets of these setae are arranged in single rows, and the others form open rings. In *Neoamphitrite*, these setae, on the few segments that have them, are in two closely spaced rows, so they look much like the teeth in a zipper.

Pista elongata (pl. 7), also a terebellid, builds a tube whose exposed portion, sticking out of a crevice, is an almost globular network. This part of the tube may, in fact, look like an accumulation of plant fibers that some animal has cemented together to make a house for itself. The worm extends its tentacles through the openings in the network and feeds in the same general way as *Thelepus* and other terebellids do. A large specimen of *P. elongata* is about 15 cm long.

Sabellaria cementarium (pl. 9), a member of the family Sabellariidae, has hard tubes made of what looks like dark gray concrete. The material consists of small sand grains mixed with a secretion that hardens soon after it is applied. The tubes, attached to rocks and large shells, may be aggregated and may form large masses. The openings, however, are not so regularly spaced as they are in *Phragmatopoma*, the sabellariid that was described in connection with zone 3.

The body of *Sabellaria* is organized in much the same way as that of *Phragmatopoma*, there being a slender posterior portion, resembling a naked intestine, doubled back against the ventral side. The numerous tentacles that arise from the first segment function as collectors of microscopic food and also of sand grains. The latter are delivered to a sac on the ventral side of the body just behind the mouth, where they are mixed with the cement that forms the matrix of the tube. The trapdoor consists of three circles of stout, yellow setae. The length of a large specimen, if the slender caudal portion is included in the measurement, is about 7 cm.

Sabellaria cementarium is found along the coast from Alaska to southern California, as well as in Japan. It is plentiful in the Puget Sound region, but there it is almost strictly subtidal. A smaller species, *S. gracile*, is a rarely seen component of the low intertidal fauna in California. *Idanthyrsus ornamentatus*, about the same size as *S. cementarium* and with a similar geographic distribution, has only two circles of setae in its trapdoor. It is inclined to be solitary.

The parchmentlike tubes of *Phyllochaetopterus prolifica* (fig. 230), generally about 1 mm in diameter and usually in dense clusters, may be found sticking out of crevices that have accumulated a little sand or gravel. This worm, a member of the family Chaetopteridae, collects food in mucus that it secretes on the dorsal side of its body, behind the head region, and also in mucus that coats the two long palps it extends from its tube. Special ciliary tracts move the mixtures of food and mucus to the mouth.

Phyllochaetopterus reproduces asexually by dividing, as well as by eggs and sperm that it releases into the water. In populations that consist primarily of asexual individuals, it is not uncommon to find that a single tube contains several small worms, all derived from the same parent. In time they form tubes of their own, some of which may be branches of the original tube.

Over most of its range, which extends from British Columbia to southern California, *Phyllochaetopterus* is much more abundant sub-

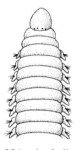

231. *Arabella iricolor,* anterior portion

230. *Phyllochaetopterus prolifica*

tidally than intertidally. At Monterey, however, it is one of the more conspicuous colonizers of pilings and floats in the harbor. On the floats, in fact, it forms nearly pure stands close to the surface of the water. More detailed information about chaetopterid polychaetes, based on what has been learned about certain larger species that live in muddy sand, is given in Chapter 7.

Scaleworms of the family Polynoidae are often associated with other animals. *Halosydna brevisetosa* (fig. 32), the most common species on rocky shores, inhabits the tubes of various polychaetes, especially larger terebellids such as *Thelepus crispus*, *Neoamphitrite robusta*, and *Pista elongata*, but it is known to have a few molluscan hosts, and it may also be free-living. *Harmothoe imbricata* (fig. 33) seems to be basically free-living, although it is often hidden away in clumps of sessile animals, such as sponges and mussels. *Arctonoe vittata* (fig. 176) was mentioned in connection with the keyhole limpet, *Diodora aspera*, but it also lives in the mantle cavity of *Cryptochiton stelleri* and in the ambulacral grooves of certain sea stars, including *Dermasterias imbricata*. There are several other fairly abundant intertidal species, especially on sea stars, sea cucumbers, polychaetes, and molluscs. As a group, polynoids are carnivores, but they do not feed on the animals with which or on which they live. Their association with certain hosts puts them in the right situation for capturing food.

Arabella iricolor (fig. 231) resembles various species of *Lumbrineris* (fig. 329), so common in muddy sand (see Chapter 7). It is distinctive, however, in having four eyes on the dorsal side of the prostomium, the anteriormost unit of the segmented body. This polychaete is most likely to be found in crevices where sediment has accumulated, in muddy gravel, or among roots of *Phyllospadix*.

Sipunculans

Phascolosoma agassizii (pl. 9) is common under rocks and in gravel, as well as in crevices, empty shells, and holdfasts of kelps. *Themiste pyroides* (fig. 170) is usually tucked away in empty burrows of *Pholadidea penita* and other rock-boring bivalves, but it also occupies crevices. Both of these sipunculans were described in Chapter 4.

Themiste dyscrita is more slender than *T. pyroides*, and does not become so swollen posteriorly when it contracts. It is often abundant in crevices or between tight-fitting rocks on the open coast. A distinctive feature of this species, which may grow to a length of more than 15 cm, is a purplish ring at the anterior end of the body, where the bushy tentacles originate.

Sea Stars

Pisaster ochraceus (fig. 124; pl. 25) is common almost everywhere on rocky shores within the range covered by this book. Because of its importance as a predator on mussels and barnacles, it has been mentioned in connection with zone 3, not only in this chapter but in the preceding one. Four other sea stars described in Chapter 4—*Leptasterias hexactis* (pl. 25), *Dermasterias imbricata* (pl. 26), *Henricia leviuscula* (pl. 26), and *Pycnopodia helianthoides* (pl. 25)—are found all along the open coast, too.

In California, one should watch for *Leptasterias pusilla*, which broods its eggs and young in the same general way as *L. hexactis*. Its diameter does not often exceed 5 cm, and its rays remain rather slender to their very bases, instead of becoming thick, as do those of *L. hexactis*. The color of *L. pusilla* is usually greenish or deep red, with yellow mottling.

Patiria miniata, the bat star or webbed star (pl. 25), is unmistakable because of its proportionately large disk and nearly sandpaperlike texture. It is found along much of the California coast and is incredibly abundant in some places on the western shore of Vancouver Island. On Vancouver Island, in fact, it occurs in inlets where much of the substratum is muddy. It is rarely if ever seen in Oregon or Washington, however. The color of the upper surface is often orange red, but brownish, purplish, or greenish individuals are also common. This is an unusual sea star in that it feeds mostly on seaweed. Nearly every *Patiria*, if examined carefully, will have one or more specimens of a little brown polychaete, *Ophiodromus pugettensis* (fig. 336), living in the groove on the underside of each ray. It probably eats other small worms, which is its custom when it occurs in a free-living state in sandy or muddy lagoons (see Chapter 7).

Evasterias troschelii (pl. 25), common in the Puget Sound region, is plentiful on the open coast of Vancouver Island and Washington, but scarce farther south. Most specimens seen intertidally in California and southern Oregon belong to an especially attractive red color phase.

Orthasterias koehleri (pl. 25) is even rarer than *Evasterias* in Oregon and California. It is a largely subtidal species, anyway, even in Washington and British Columbia.

Solaster stimpsoni (pl. 26) is moderately abundant intertidally from Oregon northward, but not often encountered in California. A less colorful relative, *S. dawsoni*, which has twelve to sixteen rays, does occasionally turn up in California, although it is almost strictly subtidal throughout its wide range, which extends to Alaska and includes Puget Sound. The diet of *S. dawsoni* includes other sea stars, and it will even attack *S. stimpsoni*, pinning it down arm for arm.

Brittle Stars

Ophiopholis aculeata (pl. 26) is fairly abundant throughout the region, but specimens from the southern sector are a little different from those of the Puget Sound area and the open coast of Washington and Vancouver Island. The spines on the rays are on the average a little longer, and the disk itself often has spines.

In California, *Ophiothrix spiculata* (pl. 26) is a common species in tidepools and among algal holdfasts. In body form it resembles *Ophiopholis aculeata*, but its arm spines are especially long and glassy, and each one has a number of small thorns on it. The color is extremely variable, but it is generally greenish brown, sometimes tinged with blue, and the rays are often marked with orange bands; there may be some orange on the disk, too. In spite of all the color variation, this species is unmistakable because of its thorny spines. The geographic range of *O. spiculata* seems not to reach the Oregon-California border.

Amphipholis squamata (pl. 26), the small brittle star that broods its young, is present all along the coast, and is especially common under rocks set on gravel. It has been adequately described in Chapter 4.

Amphiodia occidentalis (fig. 354), characterized by exceptionally long rays, lives buried in sand, but it is often exposed when rocks embedded in sand are lifted up. It is dealt with more extensively in Chapter 7, for it is regularly found among roots of eelgrass and in other sandy situations in quiet bays.

Sea Urchins

The purple sea urchin, *Strongylocentrotus purpuratus* (pl. 24), absent from Puget Sound proper and found on only a few of the more exposed shores of the San Juan Archipelago, is abundant on the open coast. As explained in Chapter 4, the purple urchin's spines will abrade soft rock. Many of the specimens in a dense bed are likely, therefore, to be ensconced in depressions, some of which are as deep as the urchins themselves. The red sea urchin, *S. franciscanus* (pl. 24), is usually fairly abundant at very low tide levels, too, and its numbers generally increase in the shallow subtidal region. The green sea urchin, *S. droebachiensis* (pl. 24), the most common of the intertidal species in Puget Sound and adjacent inland waters, occurs also on the open coasts of northern Washington and Vancouver Island, but seems not to be found in Oregon or California. It should be noted that when the purple sea urchin is only 1 or 2 cm in diameter, it is greenish and could be mistaken for *S. droebachiensis*.

Sea Cucumbers

Stichopus californicus (pl. 27), *Cucumaria miniata* (pl. 27), and *Eupentacta quinquesemita* (fig. 56), the three more common species found at low tide in the Puget Sound region, occur on the open coast of Vancouver Island, Washington, and Oregon. In California, however, *Stichopus* is almost strictly subtidal, and the other two species are not so common intertidally as they are farther north.

Psolus chitonoides (pl. 27) and *Psolidium bullatum*, both mentioned in Chapter 4, are mainly subtidal and primarily northern, but *Psolus* has been collected by divers and by dredging in central California.

Lissothuria nutriens (pl. 27) is similar to *Psolus* and *Psolidium* in having a flattened "sole" that it applies to the rock surface. It has no externally visible calcareous plates, however. The color is usually bright red, and the maximum length is about 2 cm. As a rule, this species carries an accumulation of algal fragments on its exposed surfaces, and females also brood their young on their backs. *Lissothuria* is common in some places around Monterey, but is not likely to be found any farther north.

On the coast of California, one often finds a wormlike sea cucumber in the sand beneath stones, and also in sand-filled crevices. This is *Leptosynapta albicans*, which also occurs in sand flats in quiet bays. It is almost indistinguishable from *L. clarki* (fig. 288) of sandy bays in Puget Sound and adjacent regions. Females of the latter species brood their young in the ovary during the autumn and winter months, but *L. albicans* does not do this. The length of a large specimen of *L. albicans*, when fully extended, is about 5 cm. The body is whitish and translucent. As in most other sea cucumbers, there are branched tentacles at the anterior end. These are modified tube feet used for collecting detritus and shoving it into the mouth. There are no tube feet elsewhere, however. Leptosynaptas have microscopic, anchor-shaped ossicles projecting from nearly all parts of the body surface. These will cling to the skin of one's fingers.

Bryozoans

There is a rich variety of bryozoans, and a diligent search of any rocky shore will probably turn up at least twenty species. Unfortunately, most of them cannot be identified without careful study of microscopic details. Therefore, only a few distinctive types will be mentioned here. One species or another of *Bugula* (figs. 34, 35, and 36) will almost certainly be present, and some related genera that form bushy growths similar to those of *Bugula* should be expected. *Membranipora membranacea* (figs. 37 and 38) grows on blades of kelp, especially *Macrocystis*. *Dendrobeania lichenoides* (fig. 39), so common on floats in the Puget Sound region, is not especially abundant in rocky intertidal areas, but it does occur, and there are some look-alikes.

A large proportion of the bryozoans found intertidally on rocks, shells, or seaweeds are calcified encrusting types. One of the few of these that can positively be recognized without a great deal of work or the help of an expert is *Eurystomella bilabiata* (pl. 23). Its color—rose red, orange red, or a mixture of one of these colors with brown—helps narrow down the field of candidates. The identification can then be clinched if the opening through which each zooid extends its lophophore has the shape of a narrow-brimmed derby hat. Large colonies may reach a diameter of 4 or 5 cm.

Heteropora magna (pl. 23), solidly calcified and with upright, cylindrical branches up to 5 mm in diameter, is often mistaken for a coral. A large colony may reach a height of 5 cm. The terminal portions of the branches, where the zooids are alive, are pale yellow; other parts of the colony are generally greenish, the discoloration probably being due to unicellular algae. This bryozoan is moderately common from Vancouver Island to southern Oregon, but is almost never seen intertidally in California.

Heteropora pacifica is substantially the same as *H. magna*, but characteristically at least some of its branches unite. Some experts consider *H. pacifica* to be just a form of *H. magna*.

Phidolopora pacifica (pl. 23) is distinctive in that its zooids, all firmly calcified, form a network. The regularly spaced perforations allow water to move freely through the colony. This flow-through arrangement could be a distinct advantage in situations where there are strong currents. It probably also increases the efficiency with which the zooids collect food, for water that has already been driven through the lophophores by ciliary activity can move away through the holes and not interfere with currents approaching the lophophores. The color of *Phidolopora* is usually pinkish orange. Large growths may reach a diameter of more than 10 cm. The geographic range of this species extends from British Columbia to South America. It is uncommon intertidally, however, and is mentioned here only because it is so unusual.

A bryozoan that may at first glance look like a seaweed is *Flustrellidra corniculata* (pl. 23). Students working with algae sometimes fool around with it for a while until they finally get a tip that what they are looking at is an animal, not a plant. The texture of *Flustrellidra* is something like that of leather or cartilage. The colonies branch at the base, then the main stems may branch again. All over the surface are rather firm, brownish spines that break up into several sharp prongs. The color of the colony as a whole is more or less tan, and the length of the larger stems may reach 10 cm. The lophophores are extended through slitlike apertures that are less distinct than those of most bryozoans whose zooecia are glassy or hardened by calcium salts.

Chitons

Of the chitons mentioned in Chapter 4, in connection with low-tide levels of rocky shores in the Puget Sound region, the following occur on the open coast throughout the range covered by this book: *Cryptochiton stelleri* (pl. 10), *Tonicella lineata* (pl. 10), *Lepidozona mertensii* (pl. 10), *Mopalia muscosa* (fig. 172), *M. ciliata* (fig. 173), and *M. lignosa* (fig. 174). It will not be especially useful to add to this list all the other low-intertidal chitons that occur on the open coast, for most of them will not be encountered except by those who have the time and opportunity to make thorough searches of many areas. The ones that will be mentioned are those that are rather regularly encountered.

Mopalia hindsii resembles both *M. ciliata* and *M. lignosa*. It is especially similar to *M. ciliata*, for it has a prominent posterior cleft. The hairs on its girdle do not branch as they do on *M. ciliata*. *Mopalia hindsii*, which may reach a length of 7 cm, is the chiton most likely to be found in shallow bays and other somewhat protected situations. It is often noted in places where there is more silt than most chitons can stand.

Lepidozona cooperi (pl. 10), found from northern Washington to southern California, resembles *L. mertensii* in size and general appearance, but its coloration is different. Instead of being reddish, it is largely olive brown or blackish brown. The scales on the girdle are appreciably smaller than they are in *L. mertensii*.

Ischnochiton regularis (pl. 10), common in central and northern California, is usually gray or bluish gray, sometimes olive, occasionally bright blue. It is closely related to the species of *Lepidozona* and is similar to them in having a scaly girdle. The lateral portions of its valves, however, do not have such strongly developed rows of small, wartlike protuberances as is typical of the intertidal lepidozonas.

Two chitons of the genus *Stenoplax* are typically found under smooth rocks that are partly embedded in sand. They are of a distinctive appearance because they are almost three times as long as wide. *Stenoplax heathiana* (pl. 10), which ranges from northern California to Baja California, may be slightly larger than 6 cm. The ground color is light— usually cream—with greenish, brownish, or grayish markings. *Stenoplax fallax* is found from Vancouver Island to Baja California, but is uncommon in central California, where *S. heathiana* prevails. Its maximum length is about 5 cm, but most specimens are smaller. The coloration includes much dark red or reddish brown.

Placiphorella velata, the veiled chiton (pl. 10), is unmistakable because of the way its fleshy girdle is enlarged anteriorly to form a kind of head flap. The hairs on the girdle are sparse, but they are relatively large and prominent. They often have a distinctly reddish color. In young specimens, in fact, much of the girdle has reddish blotches. The length of *P. velata*, which is less than twice the breadth, reaches 5 cm. This species is disinclined to move around much. It is usually on the underside of a ledge or overhang, where it sits waiting for a small crustacean to come under its raised-up flap. Then the flap comes down and the prey is worked into the mouth. The range extends from British Columbia to Baja California.

Keyhole Limpets and Abalones

Diodora aspera (fig. 175), the common keyhole limpet of the Puget Sound region, occurs all along the open coast of the region covered by this book. It is, however, a little less common in California than it is from Oregon northward. There is a scaleworm, *Arctonoe vittata* (fig. 176), in the mantle cavity of nearly every specimen.

The shell of *Fissurella volcano*, the volcano limpet, is similar to that of *D. aspera* in outline and approximate size (the length is up to about 3.5 cm). The opening at the top, however, is about three times as long as wide, and there is generally a distinctive coloration. The exterior is pinkish, with darker, reddish black rays; the interior is greenish. This species is found from northern California to Baja California, but it is uncommon north of Monterey.

In *Megatebennus bimaculatus* (pl. 11), the firm tissue of the mantle, brown to dingy orange in color, generally covers the shell completely. The shell itself, with an oval opening and nearly parallel sides, reaches a length of about 1.5 cm. This species is primarily an inhabitant of the open coast, but it is abundant in some places along the Strait of Juan de Fuca where there is relatively little surf. It is usually associated with sponges and compound tunicates, and it seems to feed on both. The geographic range extends from Alaska to Baja California.

The northern abalone, *Haliotis kamtschatkana* (fig. 177; pl. 11), the only member of this genus likely to be found in the Puget Sound region, occurs on the open coast of Vancouver Island and Washington. Farther south it becomes strictly subtidal.

Haliotis walallensis (fig. 232) is a relatively small species whose range extends from British Columbia to southern California. It seems to be more common in Oregon and northern California than elsewhere. The outline of its shell is almost elliptical and there are usually four to eight holes. The exterior is brick red and has low ribs intersected by delicate, raised striations. The inside is generally pink, with green reflections, and there is no obvious muscle scar. The body of the animal is yellowish with brown or greenish mottlings. Shells of this species

232. *Haliotis walallensis*

233. *Haliotis rufescens,* the red abalone

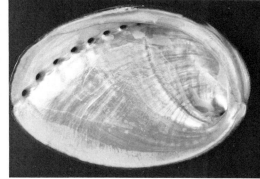

234. *Haliotis cracherodii,* the black abalone

may reach a length of 17 cm, but specimens larger than 10 cm are rare. In any case, this species is not often found intertidally.

The red abalone, *Haliotis rufescens* (fig. 233), is the largest member of the genus in the area; the length of its shell may exceed 25 cm. The geographic range extends from central Oregon to Baja California, and attempts have been made to establish it in Washington, especially in the San Juan Archipelago and along the Strait of Juan de Fuca. It is uncommon north of Monterey, however. Unless eroded or overgrown by algae and other organisms, the bumpy outside of the shell is pinkish red. The inside of the lip of the aperture has a narrow border of the same color, but otherwise the interior of the shell is pearly and highly iridescent. The muscle scar is prominent. The shell of the red abalone usually has only three or four open holes.

The black abalone, *Haliotis cracherodii* (fig. 234), has about the same range as the red abalone. It is primarily an intertidal species and is moderately abundant in central and southern California, but scarce north of Mendocino County. The nearly smooth shell, greenish black to blue black on the outside and generally free of encrusting organisms, may reach a length of 20 cm, but specimens larger than 12 cm are rarely seen. The interior of the shell is silvery, with some green and pink reflections, and has no obvious muscle scar. There are usually five to nine holes, and the edges of these are flush with the exterior of the shell. The body of the living animal is black.

Limpets

Acmaea mitra (pl. 11) is abundant on all shores where there are coralline algae for it to feed upon. *Collisella pelta* (fig. 110) and *Notoacmea scutum* (fig. 111) are also present, even if they are not so much characteristic of this zone as of higher levels. The former is found not only on rocks and shells, but also on kelps, including *Laminaria setchellii* and *Egregia menziesii*. Its shell form varies a great deal, and one must be careful not to confuse kelp-inhabiting specimens of *C. pelta* with *Notoacmea insessa*, which is restricted to *Egregia* (it was discussed earlier in this chapter), or *C. instabilis*, which will be described in the following paragraph.

Collisella instabilis (fig. 235) is called the unstable limpet because its shell, if placed on a flat surface, can be rocked back and forth. The reason for this is that the shell is shaped something like a saddle, its lateral margins being extended downward so as to fit tightly around the cylindrical stipe of a kelp. Externally, the shell is usually dark brown, the interior is bluish brown. Large specimens reach a length of about 2 cm. In California and southern Oregon, this species is fairly common intertidally on *Laminaria setchellii*, but farther north it is more likely to be found on *Pterygophora californica*.

The low shell of *Collisella ochracea* (fig. 236) rarely exceeds a length of 2 cm. The apex is about a third of the way back from the anterior

235. *Collisella instabilis,* on a stipe of *Pterygophora californica*

236. *Collisella ochracea*

end. The outside of the shell, sculptured with fine radial lines, is generally olive, buff, or tan, and often has angular white spots. The interior is bluish white, with irregular brown markings in the region of the apex. The body of the living animal is almost white. This limpet, an especially active crawler, is most likely to be found beneath smooth rocks. Its range extends from Alaska to Baja California, but the species is more common in California than it is in the more northern portions of the region covered by this book.

Notoacmea fenestrata (pl. 11) varies considerably in shape and coloration. The shell of a young specimen is likely to be rather flat and dark gray brown. As it grows, it becomes proportionately higher, so that it may resemble the shell of *Collisella pelta.* It will be broader than *C. pelta,* however, and its interior will have considerable brown between the dark band along the lip and the dark scar in the apical portion. The external surface is smooth and the margin is not scalloped as it is in some specimens of *C. pelta.* The apex is usually about two-fifths of the way back from the anterior end. The shell of a full-grown specimen is about 2.5 cm long. The species name *fenestrata* refers to "windows," or light spots on the exterior of the shell, but these spots may be obscure or absent. *Notoacmea fenestrata* is an open-coast limpet and is generally found on relatively smooth rock surfaces. Boulders next to sandy areas seem to be a favored habitat. The species is common in California, but becomes gradually scarcer farther north, even though its range extends to Alaska.

Other Snails

Of the several species of *Tegula* that occur at lower levels of the intertidal region, only three are reasonably common. The periostracum of these snails is usually some shade of brown, so they are not likely to be confused with the black turban, *T. funebralis,* which lives higher on the shore. The shell of *Tegula brunnea,* the brown turban (pl. 12), has rather convex whorls, and although the umbilicus is closed, there is a pitlike remnant of it. This species, which reaches a height of about 3 cm, is abundant along the coast of California, but is scarce north of the Oregon–California border. *Tegula montereyi*, about the same size as *T. brunnea* but with flat whorls and an open umbilicus, is rare north of Marin County. *Tegula pulligo* (pl. 12) is the only member of the triumvirate that is regularly found along the open coast of Oregon, Washington, British Columbia, and Alaska. Its range extends to southern California, but it is primarily a northern species. The whorls of *T. pulligo* are nearly as flat as those of *T. montereyi*, but its umbilicus is partly closed by a callus.

The purplish red crust that covers shells of *Tegula brunnea, T. pulligo,* and *T. montereyi* is *Peyssonelia meridionalis* (pl. 12), one of the red algae. This sometimes grows on rocks, and then it is difficult to distinguish it from *Hildenbrandia* without studying microscopic details. The latter, however, is more nearly brownish red than purplish red, and it does not form coatings on the shells of tegulas.

The topshell, *Calliostoma ligatum* (pl. 12), is about as plentiful on the open coast of Oregon, Washington, and Vancouver Island as it is in the Puget Sound region. In rocky intertidal areas in California, it does not stand out the way it does farther north, but it is often common in kelp beds offshore. The channeled topshell, *C. canaliculatum* (fig. 237), characterized by flat-sided whorls and light brown special grooves, grows to a little larger size than *C. ligatum* (its height may reach 3.5 cm), also occurs in kelp beds in central California, and is sometimes found on rocky shores of that area. It is scarce north of San Francisco, although its range extends to southern Alaska.

Calliostoma annulatum, the ringed topshell (pl. 12), is the most beautiful of our calliostomas. Unfortunately it is almost never found intertidally. It is like *C. canaliculatum* in having flat-sided whorls. The basic color of the rather thin shell, which may reach a height of 3 cm, is golden yellow, but there is considerable purple, especially on the body whorl. The colors fade after the animal has died. The body of the living animals is mostly pinkish orange. This snail, whose range extends from Alaska to Baja California, is plentiful subtidally in many places along the coast, including the San Juan Archipelago, and it is sometimes fairly common in kelp beds offshore.

The various species of *Margarites, Lirularia,* and *Homalopoma* are all smaller than any of our tegulas and calliostomas. *Homalopoma* is distinctive, anyway, because it has a thick, calcareous operculum. One species, *H. luridum* (fig. 179), described in Chapter 4, is found throughout the range covered by this book, although it seems to be more common in the Northwest than in California. South of San Francisco, the prevailing species is *H. baculum* (fig. 238). That is not to say that this species is limited to California, for it occurs as far north as Alaska. It is a little smaller than *H. luridum*, reaching a height and diameter of about 5 mm. The spiral ridges characteristic of *H. luridum* are lacking, so the shell is nearly smooth; there are, however, fine spiral lines that can be seen with a strong magnifier. The color of the shell is usually gray, reddish gray, or brown.

Margarites pupillus (fig. 178) and *M. helicinus* (pl. 12), described in Chapter 4, are primarily northern snails. Neither is likely to be found intertidally as far south as California. *Margarites salmoneus*, which does occur in California, is so similar to *M. pupillus* that some regard it as a subspecies of the latter. Its color—orange or reddish brown—seems to be a main point of distinction between it and *M. pupillus*.

Lirularia succincta (fig. 239; pl. 12), common under rocks and in gravel between rocks, is found throughout the region covered by this book, and is the prevailing species of *Lirularia* in California. *Lirularia lirulata* (fig. 239) is common in British Columbia and Washington, but is not likely to be seen intertidally south of Washington. The distinctions between these two lirularias have been explained in Chapter 4.

Astraea gibberosa, the red turban (fig. 240), is found from central California to Baja California, and also on Vancouver Island. It is rarely if ever encountered in northern California, Oregon, or Washington, however, so its distribution—intertidally, at least—is similar to that of the bat star, *Patiria miniata*. It is a striking snail, with a conical, brick-red shell that sometimes reaches a height of 5 cm and a diameter of 6 cm. A prominent ridge runs along the base of each whorl, next to where it is sutured to the succeeding whorl, and there are also low axial ribs running obliquely over the whorls. The operculum is thick and calcareous. A similar species in southern California is *Astraea undosa*, the wavy topshell, whose height may exceed 10 cm. In *A. undosa* the spiral ridge is more wavy than it is in *A. gibberosa*, and the periostracum is light brown instead of brick red.

Bittium eschrichtii (fig. 182), abundant under rocks in the Puget Sound region, also occurs on the open coast. There are other species of the genus to be reckoned with, however, especially in California. *Bittium attenuatum* is perhaps the most common of the look-alikes. Unlike *B. eschrichtii*, in which spiral lines form the only sculpture, *B. attenuatum* has both spiral lines and axial ribs; these intersect to form a pattern of squares. The two species are about the same size—a little over 1 cm high.

A group of snails called "wentletraps"—the name comes from a Danish word for a spiral staircase—are specialized for preying on sea anemones. They bite off tentacles or pieces of the column. Several species, in two genera, are found at low-tide levels in the region covered by this book. *Opalia chacei* (fig. 241), found from British Columbia to southern California, reaches a height of about 3 cm, and its spire has seven or eight turns. A characteristic feature of this species is the inequality of the six to eight axial ribs on each whorl. The color is white, unless there is a grayish discoloration. *Epitonium tinctum* has 9 to 13 axial ribs on each whorl, and its basal portion is broader in proportion

237. *Calliostoma canaliculatum*   **238.** *Homalopoma baculum*

 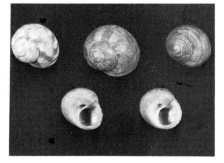

239. *Lirularia lirulata (left)* and *Lirularia succincta (right)*

240. *Astraea gibberosa,* the red turban   **241.** *Opalia chacei*

242. *Barleeia haliotiphila*

to the height of the shell than is true of *O. chacei*. The largest specimens collected intertidally are not likely to be larger than 1.5 cm, but specimens found subtidally may reach 3 cm. The range of this species extends from British Columbia to Baja California.

Tiny snails of the genera *Alvinia* and *Barleeia* are apt to be present on almost all rocky shores. Because of their small size—the height is not likely to exceed 4 mm—they are often overlooked. In both genera the shell is brown or at least brownish. Species of *Alvinia*, usually found in fine gravel, have sculpturings that run both axially and spirally, but those of one set may be weaker than those of the other. *Alvinia compacta*, up to 2.7 mm high, occurs from Alaska to Baja California; other species appear south of San Francisco. The genus *Barleeia* is characterized by a lack of sculpturing and by an operculum that has a peglike projection on its inner side. A low-power microscope is necessary to see this latter feature. The shell is also usually a little more slender than it is in *Alvinia*. At least three species should be expected within the range covered by this book. *Barleeia haliotiphila* (fig. 242), up to 3 mm high, is especially common. *Barleeia subtenuis* is a little smaller, up to 2.7 mm high; *B. acuta* may reach 4 mm. The distinctions between the three species had best be left to experts.

Gastropods of the next two genera may look like limpets, but they belong to a more advanced group, the one that includes periwinkles. In one of the genera, *Crepidula*, the shell has a horizontal shelf in its posterior portion. For this reason crepidulas are called slipper shells. These molluscs are filter feeders that use mucus secreted within the mantle cavity to trap fine particles of food. The mixture of food and mucus is delivered to the mouth by way of a ciliated tract. *Crepidula adunca*, which is attached to the shells of various snails, has been discussed earlier in this chapter, and also in Chapter 4. The more common species attached to rocks or to the insides of the apertures of empty, large snail shells (or shells inhabited by hermit crabs) are *C. perforans* and *C. nummaria*. A favorite habitat for both is the wall of a tunnel bored into rock by a pholad or some other bivalve.

Both species reach a length of at least 4 cm, and the shell of both is basically white. *Crepidula nummaria* (fig. 243), however, typically has an almost shaggy periostracum of a yellowish brown color; *C. perforans* (fig. 244) has a periostracum, too, but it is so smooth as to be scarcely noticeable. The shell shape varies greatly, for as it grows it has to fit the situation where the young animal has settled. Thus many specimens are convex ventrally, concave dorsally. In general, shells of *C. nummaria* are almost oval in outline, whereas those of *C. perforans* are rather elongated, at least in the case of specimens taken from borer holes. The systematics of these crepidulas need to be straightened out better than they have been, and even professionals are advised to be wary when making an identification. Both species occur throughout the range covered by this book, and both occur in the Puget Sound region, but there they are almost completely subtidal.

Hipponix cranioides (fig. 245), fairly common in California, scarce farther north, is not much for looks, but once its structure and biology are appreciated it is captivating. The shell, up to about 2 cm across, is nearly circular, although the apex is near one edge. It is thick, wrinkled, and has a brownish periostracum. So far the animal is nothing but homely. After detaching it from the rock, however, one finds that it has been sitting on a calcareous slab. This is not properly part of the shell, but a secretion of the foot. Nevertheless, when the animal clamps down, the slab fits tightly into the shell, so the effect is essentially the same as that achieved when a clam pulls its valves together.

Hipponix generally occurs in groups, and is most likely to be found under rocks, under ledges, or in crevices. It feeds by extending its proboscis and grabbing detritus and bits of algae. It is practically omnivorous.

The leafy hornmouth, *Ceratostoma foliatum* (fig. 183; pl. 13), is abundant throughout the geographic range under consideration in this book. As explained in Chapter 4, it is a predator on various bivalves and also on barnacles. Where it has access to bivalves that bore into rock or that nestle in borer holes after the original inhabitants have died, it feeds on them. It sinks its foot into a hole in such a way that the foot helps guide the proboscis. The proboscis is then inserted into the tissue through the gape between the valves of the shell, or through an opening drilled by the snail. The extent to which the frills on the shell are developed depends on the amount of wave action. Specimens from Puget Sound and subtidal situations along the open coast tend to be more elaborately frilled than specimens from wave-swept rocks.

Ocenebra lurida (fig. 184; pl. 13), described in Chapter 4, is common all along the open coast. *Ocenebra interfossa* (fig. 246), with sharper axial ribs, often occurs with it. In *O. circumtexa* (fig. 247), which is uncommon north of Monterey, the spire is not as tall in proportion to the body whorl as it is in *O. lurida* and *O. interfossa*. The shell therefore appears to be more plump. The spiral ridges are generally prominent and separated by narrow grooves, and the axial ribs are so low that they may be indistinct, at least on the body whorl. The basic color is whitish, but there are usually two discontinuous brown bands running around each whorl. The siphonal canal is typically open. The height of the shell reaches 1.5 cm.

Amphissa columbiana (fig. 181), so common in the Puget Sound region, is abundant on the open coast of Oregon, Washington, and Vancouver Island. It also occurs in California, but from Sonoma County southward it is outnumbered by *A. versicolor* (pl. 13). The latter is a little smaller than *A. columbiana*—its height does not exceed 1.5 cm. The axial ribs are relatively coarse and set at a distinct angle to the long axis of the shell, so that the shell may look as if it has been twisted slightly. The color varies considerably. Most specimens have brown or dark gray markings against a lighter background, but a few are almost uniformly reddish brown or orange. Though abundant in central California, *A. versicolor* is not often seen north of Mendocino County.

Alia carinata (*Mitrella carinata*), the keeled dove-shell (pl. 13), is common on rocks and seaweeds. (It also occurs in beds of *Zostera* in some bays.) The shell, up to 1 cm high, is generally dark brown with lighter markings, but sometimes much or all of it is bright orange. A particularly good feature by which this species can be identified is the ridge that runs around the top of the body whorl; it gives the body whorl a distinct "shoulder." The body of the live animal is white with black speckles. Though small, this snail is an active crawler, and it keeps its siphon extended well out in front. The empty shells of *Alia* are much used by young hermit crabs.

Other species of *Alia*, without a ridge running around the top of the body whorl, are also found within the range covered by this book. Among them are *A. tuberosa*, with nearly flat whorls on which the periostracum is raised up into delicate frills that run lengthwise on the shell, and *A. gouldi*, whose whorls are decidedly convex and smooth.

Sea Slugs

Many of the sea slugs found in the Puget Sound region are also residents of rocky shores of the open coast. Nearly all of the dorids described in Chapters 3 and 4 have wide ranges, although some are more common in certain areas than in others. One may, in any case, expect *Archidoris montereyensis* (pl. 14), *Onchidoris bilamellata* (pl. 14), *Cadlina luteomarginata* (pl. 14), *Triopha catalinae* (pl. 14), and *Laila cockerelli* (pl. 15). *Rostanga pulchra* (pl. 1), is likely to be found on or near sponges, and the delightful little *Doridella steinbergae* (fig. 37), and its close relative *Corambe pacifica*, should be looked for wherever the bryozoan *Membranipora membranacea* is growing on kelp. In general, however, these last two dorids are more likely to be found in kelp beds offshore than they are in rocky intertidal areas subjected to strong wave action.

Triopha maculata (pl. 15) is not often found within the region covered by this book, but it is fairly common from Monterey southward. It is much like *Triopha catalinae* in having the head region broadened into a "veil" that is fringed by branched tentacles. The color of the animal varies according to age. Younger specimens tend to be reddish and to have pale blue spots; older specimens, which may be more than 7 cm long, are usually brownish, with crowded patches of pale blue.

Hopkinsia rosacea (pl. 15) is moderately plentiful at Monterey, but is not likely to be seen much farther north, although a few specimens have been collected in southern Oregon. It is small—only 1.5 cm long when full grown—but of arresting beauty. The color of the animal as

243. *(Above and right) Crepidula nummaria*

244. *Crepidula perforans*

245. *(Above and right) Hipponix cranioides*

246. *Ocenebra interfossa*

247. *Ocenebra circumtexta*

a whole is an almost luminous rose pink, with the gills around the anus usually being a little darker. The upper side of the body has many slender outgrowths that superficially resemble the cerata of eolid nudibranchs; these do not, however, have branches of the gut extending into them. This species feeds, at least in part, on certain bryozoans.

Both of the next two dorids are striking and worth watching for, although neither is likely to be found north of Monterey. *Hypselodoris californiensis* (pl. 15) is dark blue with two oblong, orange-yellow spots on each side, plus some similar spots in the head region. The length reaches 6 cm. *Chromodoris macfarlandi* (pl. 15) is basically purple and a little lighter than *H. californiensis*. Instead of spots, it has three yellow stripes running lengthwise; the outer of these meet behind the gills. The margins of the mantle have an orange or reddish border. The length is up to 6 cm.

Among the larger eolid nudibranchs, *Phidiana crassicornis* (pl. 16) is probably the most nearly ubiquitous species all along the coast. The anemone-eating *Aeolidia papillosa* (pl. 16) is also abundant. The tiny *Eubranchus olivaceus* (fig. 6) will probably be found on *Obelia* wherever this hydroid occurs. There are a number of other small eolids, all associated with hydroids or other cnidarians.

Flabellinopsis iodinea (pl. 15) is an especially striking eolid, almost entirely purple except for its orange cerata and rose red rhinophores. The length is generally about 3 or 4 cm. This species swims vigorously when it has to, bending first to one side, then the other. Its food consists mostly of hydroids, but it has been observed to eat compound ascidians. Although this species is found from Vancouver Island to Baja California, it is not often seen intertidally north of California.

The arminacean nudibranchs are represented by four conspicuous species. *Dirona albolineata* (fig. 186) and *D. aurantia* (pl. 16), as well as *Janolus fuscus* (pl. 16)—the one that is a look-alike of the eolid *Hermissenda crassicornis*—have already been described in Chapter 4, for they are common in the Puget Sound region. *Dirona aurantia* is a northern form, not likely to be found in California. *Dirona albolineata* and *J. fuscus* do occur in California, however, and are joined there by the more southern *D. picta*. This species is basically greenish, grayish, or brownish, but is speckled with dots of pink, pale yellow, or pale green, and it also has a reddish spot on each ceras. It is smaller than either *D. albolineata* or *D. aurantia*, reaching a length of about 2 cm.

The brown sea hare, *Aplysia californica* (pl. 16), is found from Humboldt Bay to Baja California, but it is rarely seen north of Monterey. In places where it is abundant, specimens 20 cm long are not unusual, and individuals more than 40 cm long may occur. The prevailing coloration of the sea hare is usually reddish or grayish brown, but it may be slightly greenish, and there are typically black spots and fine dark lines. The posterior half of the body is raised up into a hump, within the dorsal part of which a platelike internal shell is buried. The hump, and the gill on the right side of it, are largely covered by a pair of lateral folds.

Aplysia is a herbivore whose exact diet depends to a considerable extent on where it lives. It is most commonly found on seaweed covered rocks in somewhat protected situations, and in this type of habitat it consumes a variety of algae, including the peppery tasting *Laurencia*. In muddy or sandy bays, it eats considerable eelgrass. It is, therefore, a rather versatile animal. As homely as it is, the sea hare is extremely attractive to biologists, especially those who specialize on the nervous system and sense organs. The fact that many of the cells in the brain and other ganglia are large and well marked makes the sea hare valuable for certain types of experimental work aimed at understanding how nerve cells function and identifying those that are involved in specific behavioral responses.

When a sea hare is poked or handled roughly, it may discharge a purple ink from a tubelike structure, or "siphon," that is formed by the lateral folds at the rear of the dorsal hump. The ink, secreted by large glands located beneath the skin in the hump region, is derived from phycoerythrin, the red pigment characteristic of red algae.

Sea hares belong to the order Anaspidea, a group of gastropods that also includes *Phyllaplysia taylori,* common on leaves of eelgrass in quiet bays (Chapter 7). Though *Aplysia californica* is the only species of its genus that can be expected in the region covered by this book, there is another one in southern California. This is the black sea hare, *A. vaccaria,* which may be the largest gastropod in the world. Specimens about 75 cm long and weighing more than 15 kilograms (33 pounds) have been recorded.

Bivalves

The purple-hinged rock scallop, *Hinnites giganteus* (fig. 190), is generally common on the open coast. As in the Puget Sound region, its shell is often ravaged by the sponge *Cliona celata* (pl. 1). *Ostrea lurida*, the native oyster (fig. 309), not often found on the open coast of Vancouver Island, Washington, or Oregon, is sometimes plentiful in California. It is probably most common, however, in parts of San Francisco Bay, as at Point Richmond.

In the same family as oysters are the chamas. These have a thick, nearly boxlike shell, one valve of which is cemented to a rock. The shell of *Chama arcana*, the agate chama (fig. 248), is translucent. The texture is rough, however, because of frills that develop along the concentric lines of growth. Off-white is the usual color, but there may be tints of pink or orange. Exceptionally large specimens are 6 cm across. This species occurs from southern Oregon to Baja California, but it is not often seen north of San Francisco.

In *Pseudochama exogyra*, the reversed chama (fig. 249), which reaches a diameter of about 5 cm, the shell is only slightly translucent, and the frills are less conspicuous than in *C. arcana*. Its range is about the same as that of the latter. If there is any question about which species you have, orient the shell so that the hinge is uppermost and the beaks are pointing away from you. In *C. arcana*, the right valve is the one that is attached to the substratum; in *P. exogyra*, it is usually the left valve that is cemented down.

Septifer bifurcatus, the branch-ribbed mussel (fig. 250), grows to a length of about 4 cm. It can easily be distinguished from a small *Mytilus californianus* or *M. edulis* by the numerous closely spaced ribs, most of which divide once as they radiate toward the broad end of the shell. The exterior of the shell is blackish, the interior purplish. The geographic distribution of this species extends from near the Oregon-California border to Baja California. In the northern part of its range, it is generally found attached to the undersides of rocks at low-tide levels, but from about Monterey southward it starts to show up in zone 3, in mussel beds and in crevices between rocks.

Glans carpenteri, the little heart clam (fig. 251), is typically found on the undersides of rocks. Like a mussel, it attaches itself with organic byssus threads. If the threads break or come loose, *Glans* extends its foot and crawls about until it finds a suitable place to settle. The shell of this species attains a length of 1.5 cm and a height of 1 cm, and is characterized by beaded ribs that radiate away from the beaks. There are brown or pinkish markings against a whitish or tan background. The young develop in the mantle cavity and are released as fully formed clams that are a little less than 1 mm long. These may attach themselves temporarily to the shell of the parent or to that of another mature individual nearby.

Mytilimeria nuttallii, the sea-bottle clam (fig. 252; pl. 17) is a thin-shelled bivalve that becomes overgrown by a compound ascidian. As a rule, only the siphons of the clam are visible. The shape of the shell varies considerably, but its height, which reaches 4 cm, is generally greater than the length. A number of species of ascidians are capable of growing on *Mytilimeria*, but *Cystodytes lobatus* is perhaps the one that is most commonly associated with this bivalve.

Where the rock is shale or some other relatively soft, sedimentary material, it is likely to show deep holes made by burrowing clams. The fact that a burrow is occupied does not mean that the clam that made it is still alive and well. In our fauna of bivalves there are several species that make burrows, and others that settle in burrows left vacant by the death of the original inhabitants. These are called "nestlers," and they often develop within the empty shells of their predecessors. There may be a succession of nestlers of the same or a different species. It is not unusual to find a live nestler enclosed by the still-intact shells of at least two bivalves, one of which may have been the original proprietor of the burrow.

248. *Chama arcana,* the agate clam

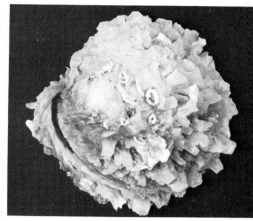

249. *Pseudochama exogyra,*
the reversed chama

250. *Septifer bifurcatus,*
the branch-ribbed mussel

251. *Glans carpenteri,*
the little heart clam

252. *Mytilimeria
nuttallii,* the
sea-bottle clam

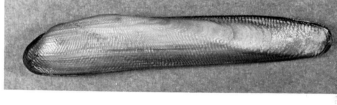

254. *Adula falcata*

253. *Penitella penita,* the flap-tipped piddock

Not all of the primary rock borers of one region will be discussed, but the following account covers all that are likely to be encountered. They fall into two main groups: those in which the shell is rasplike, and those in which the shell is smooth but has a tough, shiny periostacum.

Penitella penita, the flap-tipped piddock (fig. 253), is the most common representative of the first group. Its shell reaches a length of about 7 cm, and its usual habitat is soft rock, especially shale. The foot, projecting from the gap between the valves, is attached to the rock like a suction cup. By moving its valves and also pressing them against the wall of the burrow it has started, the clam works its way deeper into the rock. Eventually, it may be 15 cm beneath the surface. The roughenings in the rasplike anterior portion of the shell are worn away as a consequence of their being used in the abrasive activity, but the shell continues to enlarge and new roughenings are formed. In time, growth and burrowing cease. When that happens, the foot is pulled in permanently and the gap between the valves is sealed with a calcareous deposit. A distinctive feature of this species is the pair of leathery flaps at the posterior end. In order to pump water into and out of its mantle cavity, the clam must extend its siphons—which are fused—to the small external opening of the burrow. The range of *P. penita* is from Alaska to Baja California. It is almost strictly limited to the open coast.

Parapholas californica, the scale-sided piddock, reaches a length of 10 cm, and its burrows may be more than 25 cm deep. It is likely to be found only in large rocks at low-tide levels. The animal does not have leathery flaps at the posterior end of its shell, but it does make a chimney of cemented particles around the basal portion of its siphon. As in *P. penita*, the gap through which a younger specimen extends the foot eventually becomes sealed. The range of this handsome piddock is from northern California to Baja California.

The borers of the other group—those with smooth shells—are in the same family as mussels. Like mussels, they use byssus threads in order to maintain tight contact with the soft rock into which they burrow by the persistent rubbing action of the valves. Their shells are relatively slender and coated with a shiny, finely striated periostracum which is of a dark reddish brown color. This is tough and generally is not worn away except at the "beaks" of the valves, where the shell is widest. As in piddocks, boring is achieved by mechanical action of the valves. *Adula californiensis* (pl. 17), with a shell up to about 3 cm long, is the most common species in the range covered by this book. It is found all along the open coast from Alaska to central California. *Adula falcata* (fig. 254) found from southern Oregon to Baja California, may be up to 8 cm long, and is proportionately more slender and more markedly curved.

Adula diegensis, found from Oregon to Baja California, is not a burrower; it lives under rocks, often in small colonies. Its shell, not often more than 2 cm long, is proportionately more plump than that of *A. californiensis*.

Lithophaga plumula, the date mussel (fig. 255), bores into calcareous substrata, such as limestone, conglomerates of shell fragments, and thick shells of molluscs. It uses its shell valves abrasively, as the adulas do, but the mucus it secretes is acidic, and this also promotes the burrowing activity. The specific name *plumula* refers to the fuzzy periostracal outgrowths on much of the posterior half of the shell. Elsewhere, the periostracum is dark brown and shiny. The shell length of a large specimen is about 5.5 cm. This species is fairly common in some places along the coast of southern California, and its range extends to Peru. Although it has been found in Mendocino County, it is seldom encountered north of Monterey.

Petricola carditoides, the rock dweller (fig. 256), occupies holes made by borers such as *Penitella* and *Adula*. No two specimens have shells that are exactly alike, for this clam grows to fit the hole in which it nestles. The chalky shell is rather thick and has fine lines radiating from the beaks. There are also fine concentric lines; these are sometimes raised into ridges. *Petricola* could be confused with *Hiatella arctica* (fig. 257) another nestler, but the latter has a thinner shell, a more persistent periostracum, and crimson siphon tips. (In *Petricola*, the siphon tips are purplish.) The length of a *Petricola* shell may reach 4.5 cm, that of a *Hiatella* about 3 cm. Both clams are found throughout the area covered by this book.

Kellia laperousii (fig. 258) is a nestler that usually lives in empty shells of other clams, including those of pholads that have burrowed into rock. *Kellia* is rather plump and has a faintly yellowish green periostracum. Large specimens are about 2 cm long. In live animals, the translucent mantle lobes are extended in such a way as to almost cover the valves, and the siphons point in nearly opposite directions. The range is from the Bering Sea to Baja California.

Various animals other than clams inhabit the burrows made by rock borers. Among them are the sipunculans *Phascolosoma agassizii* and *Themiste pyroides*. These are not obligatory nestlers, for they may also be found under rocks and in crevices. Large specimens of *Themiste*, however, may seem to be the perfect nestlers, for they generally fit old burrows so tightly that there is no room to spare. A few facts about the biology of *Phascolosoma* and *Themiste* were given in Chapter 4.

Barnacles

Semibalanus cariosus (fig. 108) is generally the most common barnacle in zone 4. At least some of the specimens that have reached a diameter of 5 or 6 cm are probably more than ten years old. Occasionally one finds the smooth-shelled and smaller *Balanus crenatus* (fig. 51), which is primarily a subtidal species. As in Puget Sound, *B. crenatus* tends to occur on the undersides of rocks, although it also colonizes pier pilings. In deeper water, it is attached to bottles, shells, soggy wood, and kelp, as well as to rocks.

Balanus nubilus (pl. 18), which reaches a diameter of slightly more than 10 cm, is almost strictly subtidal in the Puget Sound region, but there are places on the open coast where it is common at low tide, even on pilings. It is a rough-shelled barnacle, generally much eroded, often honeycombed by the boring sponge *Cliona*, and encrusted by a variety of organisms. Two of the four closing plates are sharp tipped and strongly curved. When *B. nubilus* extends its cirri, the lips of soft tissue that surround the opening show attractive tints of orange and yellow. The geographic range of this species extends from Alaska to southern California; and north of San Francisco it is the only really large barnacle. At about the level of San Francisco, a look-alike, *B. aquila*, appears. It is sometimes mixed with *B. nubilus*. The opening at the top of its shell is proportionately smaller than that of *B. nubilus*, and the "beak" formed by its closing plates resembles that of an eagle; hence the specific name *aquila*.

Megabalanus californicus (*Balanus tintinnabulum californicus*), about the same size as *Semibalanus cariosus*, is found all along the coast of California and much of Mexico, but it is not often seen as far north as San Francisco. It is distinctive for a large barnacle in that it has alternating red and white lines on the outside of the shell, so that it slightly resembles the much smaller *Tetraclita rubescens*, described under zone 3.

Shrimps

In tide pools and among seaweeds there are generally plenty of shrimps. Most of them are of the "broken-back" type—various species of *Heptacarpus* (fig. 49) and *Spirontocaris*. The distinctions between the numerous kinds that occur along the open coast should be sought in specialized treatises.

Crabs

Of the spider crabs that are common intertidally in the Puget Sound region, *Pugettia producta* (fig. 191) is the species most often seen on the open coast. It is almost ubiquitous, clinging to kelps such as *Egregia*. Healthy specimens rarely have anything growing on them, so if the carapace is overgrown by seaweeds or hydroids this is an indication that the crab has not been able to molt normally. If you turn it over, you are likely to find a lump in the abdominal region. This is not a tumor; it is part of *Heterosaccus californicus*, a remarkable parasite related to barnacles. Much of the tissue of the crab is pervaded by rootlike growths of *Heterosaccus;* the protruding portion consists primarily of an egg sac, but there is also a chamber within which a dwarf male lives. The early part of the life history of *Heterosaccus* is much like that of a typical barnacle, in that there is a series of free-swim-

255. *Lithophaga plumula,* the date mussel

256. *Petricola carditoides,* the rock dweller, nestling in burrows made by *Penitella penita.* (The tip of a siphon of *Penitella* shows in the photograph at right.)

 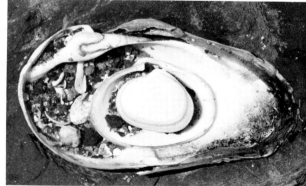

257. *Hiatella arctica*

258. *Kellia laperousii,* nestling in empty shells of *Pholadidea penita* and another *Kellia*

ming larval stages. If the infective stage becomes attached to *Pugettia* in just the right place, its soft tissues migrate into the crab and growth of the parasite begins. The hormonal balance of the crab is upset because certain tissues are destroyed by the parasite. Molting is therefore suppressed, and if the crab is a male, it will soon start to resemble a female. After *Heterosaccus* has grown to the point that it is evident externally, a male larva enters it. This is a cozy arrangement that insures fertilization of eggs. Individuals of *Pugettia* parasitized by *Heterosaccus* are fairly common in the Monterey area and in southern California, but they are rare north of San Francisco.

Pugettia gracilis (fig. 358) also occurs throughout the region covered by this book, but it is more common intertidally in the northern part. There is also *P. richii*, which resembles *P. gracilis* and is about the same size (length up to 3.5 cm). Its carapace, unlike that of either *P. gracilis* or *P. producta*, is decidedly wider posteriorly than anteriorly. It generally has algae and other organisms attached to it.

Mimulus foliatus (pl. 22) looks a little like a *Pugettia*, but the length of its carapace, which may reach 3 cm, is equaled or even slightly exceeded by the width. (In all of our pugettias, the carapace is distinctly longer than it is broad.) *Mimulus* is often overgrown by sponges, bryozoans, and small hydroids. It is found along the more exposed shores of the Strait of Juan de Fuca as well as on the open coast throughout the range covered by this book.

Scyra acutifrons (fig. 193) and *Oregonia gracilis* (fig. 192) are relatively rare intertidally in California and Oregon. Both are fairly common on exposed shores of Washington and on Vancouver Island, as well as in the Puget Sound region.

Cancer productus (fig. 357) and *C. oregonensis* (pl. 22), both abundant in the Puget Sound region, are also found on the open coast. The former is abundant throughout the range covered by this book; the latter, though common from British Columbia to southern Oregon, is scarce in California.

Cancer antennarius (pl. 22), a rock crab common in California, resembles *C. productus*, but its carapace is not so wide in proportion to length. The part of the carapace between the eyes, moreover, is not appreciably extended forward. The red spots scattered all over the pale yellow underside of *C. antennarius* are a distinctive feature of the species. The maximum width of the carapace does not often exceed 10 cm, whereas large specimens of *C. productus* are about 15 cm wide. The range of *C. antennarius* extends from British Columbia to Baja California, but this crab is not often seen north of Oregon.

Telmessus cheiragonus (pl. 22), common in the Puget Sound region, is rare on the open coast. It is, in any case, a northern type and is not likely to be found intertidally south of Washington.

Hermit Crabs and Their Relatives

Pagurus granosimanus and *P. samuelis* (pl. 20) are the prevailing hermit crabs in zone 4. Both are found from Alaska to Baja California. The former has been discussed in Chapter 4, for it is common in the Puget Sound region. *Pagurus samuelis* is almost completely restricted to the open coast. The two species are similar in that their antennae are reddish. In *P. samuelis*, however, the anterior end of the carapace, between the eyes, forms a rather sharp, triangular projection; this projection is lacking in *P. granosimanus*. Another distinctive feature of *P. samuelis* is the blue or white ring that encircles the article next to the claw of each walking leg. This species reaches a length of about 4 cm.

Pagurus hemphilli, another open-coast hermit crab found throughout the range covered by this book, has reddish antennae and the triangular projection at the anterior end of the carapace. It lacks the blue or white rings on the walking legs, but generally has a white spot at the tip of the claw of each walking leg.

The next two species, with soft abdomens, belong to the family Lithodidae. They are probably derived from hermit crabs that gave up the habit of living in shells. As in hermit crabs, the legs of the fifth pair are reduced and tucked up under the carapace.

Hapalogaster mertensii (pl. 20), common in the Puget Sound region, is a northern type, and its intertidal occurrence is largely limited to the area north of the Strait of Juan de Fuca. In central and northern California there is a related species, *H. cavicauda*, not quite so large as *H. mertensii* and with shorter hairs. It is primarily subtidal, but is occasionally found under rocks at very low tide.

Oedignathus inermis (pl. 20) is moderately common along the open coast from Oregon to Alaska. It is not often seen in California, though its range extends at least as far south as Monterey. It is rare in the San Juan Archipelago, and is not found at all in Puget Sound. The favorite habitats of this warty little crab are holes and crevices into which it can fit tightly. The body, up to about 2 cm long, has a fleshy abdomen. The legs are stout; the ones with pincers are unequal. This species may look soft and helpless, but be advised that its pincers are strong. They also have sharp, slightly in-curved tips, so they can focus a lot of pain on one spot.

Cryptolithodes sitchensis (fig. 194; pl. 21) and *C. typicus* (pl. 21) are lithodids, too, but their abdomens are firm and pressed tightly to the underside of the cephalothorax, as in true crabs. The carapace, as explained in Chapter 4, is expanded laterally so that the legs can be hidden away completely. Both species occur on the open coast, but only *C. sitchensis* is likely to be seen intertidally in California.

The so-called porcelain crabs (family Porcellanidae), also with reduced fifth legs, are represented by the genera *Petrolisthes* and *Pachycheles*. Two species of *Petrolisthes* were discussed in connection with zone 3. Our representatives of the genus *Pachycheles* are more plump than those of *Petrolisthes*, and their pincer-bearing first legs are unequal and warty. The article next to the palm is about as wide as it is long in *Pachycheles*, whereas in *Petrolisthes* it is decidedly longer than wide. *Pachycheles rudis*, the thick-clawed porcelain crab, occurs from British Columbia to Baja California, and is the prevailing species in central and northern California. *Pachycheles pubescens* (pl. 20) ranges from British Columbia to central California, but in general it is more common in the northern sector. It is abundant in parts of the Puget Sound region, where *P. rudis* rarely occurs. In both, the carapace is up to about 1.5 cm in length and width, and the color is rather light. The "hands" of the pincers of *Pachycheles pubescens* are more hairy than those of *P. rudis*. A sure way to tell the two species apart is to look at the nearly triangular terminal portion of the abdomen, which is folded back under the body. If this consists of seven plates (two are small), the crab is *P. pubescens*; if there are only five plates, then the crab is *P. rudis*.

Ascidians

Four solitary ascidians—*Pyura haustor* (fig. 60), *Boltenia villosa* (fig. 61), *Styela gibbsii* (fig. 195), and *Cnemidocarpa finmarkiensis* (pl. 28)—have been mentioned in the two preceding chapters. All of them occur on floats or in rocky habitats in the Puget Sound region. They are found on the open coast, too, but *Pyura* is the only one that is at all common intertidally south of Oregon. The others are primarily northern species, and in California one must hunt for them diligently at very low tides. They are abundant subtidally, however.

The long-stalked sea squirt, *Styela montereyensis* (pl. 28), is the most conspicuous solitary ascidian all along the coast, from British Columbia to southern California. It reaches a length of about 12 cm. The siphons are red, but the rest of the animal is pale tan. The lengthwise grooves, which mark thinner places in the body wall, become especially prominent when the animal is contracted. Although primarily an inhabitant of rocks and pilings in the open coast, this species is found in some protected harbors. At Neah Bay, Washington, for instance, it is common on floats and pilings. It should not be expected in Puget Sound or the San Juan Archipelago, however.

Styela truncata, abundant in California but rare farther north, looks more like *S. gibbsii* than like *S. montereyensis*, for it has no stalk. It is hemispherical, egg-shaped, or nearly globular, and up to about 3 cm high. Its tunic is smoother than that of either *S. gibbsii* or *S. montereyensis*.

The more common social ascidians are *Metandrocarpa taylori*, *Perophora annectens*, and *Clavelina huntsmani*. The first two, which occur intertidally in the San Juan Archipelago and perhaps elsewhere in the Puget Sound region, have been described in Chapter 4; all three are illustrated in Plate 28.

Clavelina huntsmani, whose clustered zooids are up to about 3 cm tall, is distinctive because of its relatively large size and two almost luminous orange-pink lines that show through the transparent tunic. One of these lines runs along the "floor" of the pharynx; the other is on the opposite side of the pharynx. At Monterey, *Clavelina* prospers during the summer and early autumn. It then deteriorates, so it is not likely to be seen again until the following summer. The range of this species extends to British Columbia, but it is almost strictly subtidal north of Monterey Bay.

Metandrocarpa dura should also be expected. It is especially common on Vancouver Island. The zooids are almost indistinguishable from those of *M. taylori,* but they are packed so tightly together that the colony as a whole resembles that of a compound ascidian.

The open coast has a rich intertidal fauna of compound ascidians. Of the many species present, some will look alike to a beginner. It seems best to mention just a few of the especially common and distinctive types.

Species of *Aplidium* (pl. 29), found sparingly in the Puget Sound region, are just about everywhere at low-tide levels. Their slippery encrustations, often more than 1 cm thick, are usually tan or dull orange brown, sometimes reddish. The distinctions between the species are based mostly on microscopic details. Colonies of certain aplidiums, as well as of species in related genera, characteristically form bulbous or club-shaped elevations, and they may also accumulate considerable sand on the surface or within the matrix. *Ritterella pulchra* (pl. 29),which makes tight clusters of bulbous lobes that may be more than 4 cm high, is widespread and can be identified in the field. Its zooids are typically orange.

Distaplia occidentalis (fig. 59; pl. 29) is moderately common along the open coast, but it is not nearly so abundant as it is on floats and pilings in the San Juan Archipelago and adjacent inland waters.

Compound ascidians of the *Didemnum–Trididemnum* type (pl. 5) are likely to be plentiful, just as they are in the San Juan Archipelago. It was pointed out in Chapter 4 that these ascidians are distinctive because they form thin encrustations that resemble white glove leather. The whiteness is due to the light-reflecting properties of the globular calcareous spicules that are deposited within the colonies. The little grayish pits mark the location of the zooids.

6

Sandy Beaches

Much of the shoreline along the outer coast consists of sandy beaches that are pounded by the surf. Relatively clean sand also predominates in many protected coves and shallow bays. As a rule, however, the substratum in sheltered situations is decidedly muddy. In most bays, in fact, one can see muddy sand change gradually to mud. In some places, moreover, gravel and pebbles make up more than half the volume of the sediment. The coarse material strongly influences the nature of the substratum, and many organisms are found only in gravelly muds.

The finer the hard particles, the more water the substratum can hold by capillary action. The type and amount of organic matter also influence the water-retaining capacity of the substratum, as well as the extent to which the particles cohere to one another. On exposed sandy beaches, most of the hard particles—generally of quartz or its variants, as found in granitic rocks—have a diameter larger than 0.1 mm, and the amount of organic detritus is low. Water percolates rather freely through the sand, but the sand is not especially effective in retaining water in its interstices. In mud flats, the substratum contains high proportions of silt and clay. In silt, the particle size ranges from about 0.06 mm down to 0.004 mm; in clay, it is below 0.004 mm. The fine grain size and corresponding capillary force of the surface sediments, and the cohesive property of organic matter and microorganisms, encourage the peristence of shallow pools. These pools are typical not only of mud flats but also of many situations in which very fine sand predominates.

When the substratum retains considerable water, at least near the surface, it tends to liquefy when walked upon. This is an entertaining property of many of our gooey mud flats, which makes mushing through them quite strenuous. On sandy beaches, the substratum simply packs down when it is stepped upon.

In mud, the microbial flora concerned with decomposition of organic matter is apt to be rich, and the rotten-eggs smell of hydrogen sulfide may be strong. Digging down into mud, one will generally encounter a black layer just a few centimeters below the surface. This marks the zone at which compounds of iron, especially iron oxide, react with hydrogen sulfide and become converted into sulfides. Conditions in the mud above this black layer are aerobic; that is, most of the organisms conduct their biological activities in the presence of oxygen. Below the black layer, conditions are anaerobic, and energy-releasing life processes involve various chemical pathways that do not require free oxygen. On exposed sandy beaches, and even in protected bays where the particle size is coarse enough to facilitate circulation of water and oxygen dissolved in it, a black layer may not be encountered anywhere near the surface. It will almost certainly be there, however, if one digs deep enough.

In muddy and sandy substrata, the food habits of the animals are diversified, just as they would be in any other ecological situation. There are suspension feeders, which process the water flowing over the substratum to collect diatoms, other microscopic organisms, and fine detritus. A number of bivalve molluscs, such as cockles and littleneck clams, and certain polychaete annelids are in this category. Another type, deposit feeders, is either somewhat selective or almost completely unselective. The former includes clams of the genus *Macoma*, which sweep the surface with the incurrent siphon to pick up lighter particles; it also includes terebellid polychaetes, which utilize ciliary tracts along their extensile tentacles to bring microscopic food to the mouth. A good example of an unselective deposit feeder is the lugworm, which extracts what nourishment it can from mud in its burrow. Deposit feeders are generally restricted to muddy habitats, whereas suspension feeders are present in both sandy and muddy areas.

Scavengers on animal or plant material include many of the crabs, isopods, amphipods, and polychaetes. Finally, there are out-and-out carnivores, such as the nemertean *Cerebratulus*, certain polychaetes (including *Nephtys*), the moon snail, and most of the fishes and birds.

This chapter is concerned with the organisms typically found on beaches that consist of sand which is stirred up by surf. Most such beaches are on the outer coast. Some of them are subject to strong wave action; others are protected to a certain extent. There will also be a discussion of the vegetation commonly found on the backshores and dunes of sandy beaches. Chapter 7 will deal with bays where sand, mud, and gravel are present in varying amounts, and it will also deal with the salt-marsh habitat. The user of this book must realize, however, that the distributions of animals and plants depend on many factors, and that one type of habitat may pass so gradually into another that it is unwise to draw up hard and fast rules and expect the animals and plants to adhere to them.

The extensive sandy beaches found in certain areas of the outer coast provide, in terms of substratum, an unstable habitat. Depending on tides, currents, and weather, the sand shifts a great deal from season to season and from year to year. Moreover, at any given time the sand is stirred by the beating of breaking waves and by the subsequent rush of receding water. Thus the only large animals able to live on the portion of a beach that sustains heavy wave action burrow at least a few inches into the sand, or move up and down the beach as the tide level fluctuates. Sand is not at all suitable as a substratum for attachment of seaweeds, so the only plants likely to be found in this kind of environment are diatoms and other microscopic forms that live attached to sand grains or between them. The sand grains tend to absorb at least a little organic material, which is populated by a variety of bacteria.

The microscopic plants and bacteria provide food for some of the very small animals that live in this situation. These animals consist predominantly of ciliated protozoans, turbellarians, nematodes, annelids, and copepod crustaceans. Representatives of other groups also occur, however, and of the more remarkable and previously unsuspected organisms discovered in recent years, a large proportion have been found in sandy beaches. The small animals and plants living on and between sand grains are referred to as the interstitial fauna and flora. On the Pacific coast, studies on these interstitial organisms have hardly begun, so some rewarding opportunities await those who may wish to investigate them.

For a discussion of the more obvious elements of the fauna of sandy beaches, it seems easier to begin at a low-tide level and to work gradually up the slope to the fringes of the marine environment, dealing primarily with the animals that actually live in or on the sand, rather than with jellyfishes or other pelagic organisms that just happen to be washed up on the beach.

The animal most people associate with wave-swept sandy beaches of the exposed outer coast, from Alaska to central California, is the razor clam, *Siliqua patula* (fig. 259). It is an important article of food, and the sport of digging it provides pleasant recreation for many who live in the region covered by this book. Normally, the razor clam is found only on the lowermost part of the beach—the region exposed by tides of about −1.0 foot and lower. It is usually rather close to the surface and is sometimes washed out of the sand by the action of the surf. Most clam diggers look for little dimples in the sand or for a shimmering, which indicates some activity beneath the surface. A quick thrust with the spade may bring instant reward, or it may lead to frantic digging to keep from losing the rapidly retreating clam. Too often, however, a little olive snail or some kind of polychaete worm just beneath the surface is all the clam digger gets for his trouble.

The astonishing capacity of the razor clam to burrow is due to intense muscular effort which is linked to changes in the shape of the foot caused by displacement of body fluids. As the foot is extended and fluid is squeezed out of it, it pushes into the sand. Its tip then swells up, the foot as a whole contracts, and the animal is pulled deeper into the substratum.

On cleaning his day's catch, the happy digger may find what looks like a leech, up to about 2 or 3 cm long, in the mantle cavity. This is *Malacobdella*, a short-bodied, highly specialized nemertean. It is attached to the wall of the mantle cavity, usually close to the siphon, by its posterior disklike sucker. It feeds upon microscopic and nearly microscopic organisms, including small crustaceans which the clam brings into the mantle cavity through its incurrent siphon. *Malacobdella* is indeed an unusual nemertean; almost all of its relatives are slender, free-living worms that subdue relatively large prey.

The Pismo clam, *Tivela stultorum* (fig. 260), barely gets into the region for which this book has been written. Although it has been found in the sandy beach at Half Moon Bay, about 40 kilometers south of San Francisco, it is not often encountered north of Monterey Bay. The heavy shell of *Tivela* reaches a length of 15 cm, and often shows radiating dark lines or bands. The periostracum, usually yellowish, tan, or greenish, is so glossy that the shell appears to have been varnished. The siphons are short, so the animal must live close to the surface of the sand. It is oriented vertically, with its hinge facing the ocean.

At one time, the Pismo clam was common and had considerable commercial importance, but now it is rather scarce intertidally. It cannot be denied that clam diggers put a great deal of pressure on it, but shorebirds, sea otters, and some other predators also attack it, especially when it is small. We may have little control over the natural phenomena that encourage or discourage the reproduction and growth of the Pismo clam, but it would be wise to consider giving the species a little more protection. Perhaps large populations will eventually become re-established, at least on certain beaches.

Olivella biplicata, the purple olive snail (fig. 261; pl. 13), is a beautiful little gastropod that plows through the sand, searching for animal matter upon which to scavenge. It is one of the few snails on the Pacific coast that has such a highly polished shell and such a proportionately long aperture. The length of the shell of a large specimen is about 2 cm. The coloration is primarily a mixture of gray and purple, with some dark lines defining the edges of the whorls or crossing them lengthwise. The trail of *Olivella* is generally right at the surface, so that the shell is at least partly exposed. Sometimes, however, *Olivella* is completely buried, and creates a little dimple or shimmering of the sand that may bring false hope to a clam digger. The olive snail occupies a rather wide band on the beach and thus is commonly found at levels considerably higher than those to which the razor clam is restricted.

Olivella baetica (fig. 262), about the same height as *O. biplicata* but more slender, is not likely to be found on wave-swept beaches. It is primarily subtidal, and its occurrence intertidally is usually restricted to sandy bays.

Digging in the sand of an exposed beach, at around the level of midtide or lower, will turn up several kinds of worms. Among the larger species, two types will probably be most frequently noticed. One is a nemertean, *Cerebratulus* (fig. 263), which is smooth, much flattened, very extensile, and very fragile. Large specimens may be about 1 cm wide and 30 cm long, but they tend to break up into pieces when handled. Several species of *Cerebratulus* occur along the Pacific coast. All of them show conspicuous slits on either side of the head and have a little cirrus at the tail end, but this cirrus is apt to break off. *Cerebratulus* feeds largely on polychaetes that burrow in the sand. It has a huge proboscis which, when called into action, emerges from a pore at the front end. This proboscis is not armed with piercing stylets, characteristic of nemerteans such as *Paranemertes* and *Emplectonema*, which are described elsewhere in this book. The sticky mucus on the proboscis, however, helps to immobilize the prey. The way in which the proboscis of a large *Cerebratulus* can wrap itself in a spiral around one's finger, by turning itself inside out until it is completely everted, is impressive. The mucus holds so firmly that the proboscis may have to be peeled away like a strip of tape.

The other worm frequently found in the same general habitat is *Nephtys* (fig. 264), a predaceous polychaete. It may at first look something like a *Nereis*, but its eversible pharyngeal equipment is altogether different, and there are no long tentacles on the head region.

Shrimps belonging to the genus *Crangon* (pl. 19) may be abundant in shallow water, especially at lower tide levels. If dislodged from the sand by a wave, they swim for a while, then dig back in.

Almost invariably present are the crustaceans called mysids, or "opossum shrimps," the females of which carry their young in a brood pouch under the thoracic region. These animals are up to about 2.5 cm long and may be caught in large numbers by running a net or kitchen sieve through the water in the surf zone. Another way of getting them is to dig a hole that will quickly fill with water. If there is sunshine, the shadows of the mysids will be seen before the animals themselves, because they are nearly transparent. They soon settle down into the sand again. There are several species in our area. The differences between them are microscopic and it seems best not to attempt to describe them here. The most widespread species, and the one al-

259. *Siliqua patula,* the razor clam

260. *Tivela stultorum,* the Pismo clam

261. *Olivella biplicata,*
the purple olive snail

262. *Olivella baetica*

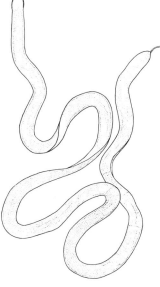

263. *Cerebratulus*

264. *Nephtys*

265. *Archaeomysis grebnitzkii*

most invariably found in Washington and British Columbia, is *Archaeomysis grebnitzkii* (fig. 265).

Cumaceans are often found in the surf zone, especially at lower tide levels. They are distinctive crustaceans in that they have a relatively broad cephalothoracic region and a slender, very flexible abdomen. The total length does not often exceed 1.5 cm. Most cumaceans feed by cleaning organic material from sand grains. A typical one is shown in Figure 266.

Some other crustaceans that are dislodged as water sloshes over the sand, or that can be found by digging holes, are the unusual amphipods of the family Haustoriidae. They are plump and their appendages are fringed by abundant long hairs, some of which are featherlike. Thus haustoriids have a furry appearance. *Eohaustorius washingtonianus* (fig. 267), up to about 8 mm long, is common on beaches in the Northwest, but there are other species within the range covered by this book.

Amphipods of the family Phoxocephalidae are also characteristic of sandy beaches. As a rule, they are less obviously hairy than haustoriids, and are more nearly like typical amphipods in having bodies that are deeper than they are wide. The species illustrated—*Grandifoxus grandis* (fig. 268)—is found on the open coast and also on some of the more exposed beaches of the Puget Sound region.

Emerita analoga, the mole crab (pl. 21), is a relative of hermit crabs, porcelain crabs, and lithodid crabs, a few of which were discussed in Chapters 4 and 5. It is almost ovoid, and its length may reach 4 cm. The color of the back and sides is gray or bluish gray; beneath, the animal is whitish. Eggs carried by a female mole crab are orange. In general, *Emerita* lives at about mid-tide level, but it migrates up and down the beach to some extent, for its method of obtaining food depends on the backwash of waves. After a wave breaks and the water moves up the slope of the beach, the crab may be jostled a little, but it quickly digs back into the sand, hind end first, until little more than its eyes and feathery antennae are exposed. The antennae form a V, and as the water moves back down the beach, the bristles on the antennae strain out organic detritus. This is scraped off by the mouth parts and swallowed. Mole crabs generally live in groups, and the presence of a colony may be detected by little V-shaped ripples where the eyes and antennae have caused a deflection in the runoff of water.

The mole crab is found from Vancouver Island to South America, but most of the populations north of the Oregon-California border do not persist indefinitely. They appear if larvae originating farther south have been carried in by currents and have found a favorable place to settle and mature. After a population has died out, it may be several years before another batch of larvae arrives.

More or less following the tide are little isopods of the genus *Excirolana.* Like *Cirolana harfordi* of rocky shores, they are scavengers on animal matter, such as dead mole crabs (where this species occurs), dead fishes, and so on. The efficiency with which a few dozen *Excirolana* can pick a small fish skeleton clean makes these isopods marine counterparts of carrion beetles of the terrestrial environment. Walking barefooted in places where *Excirolana* is abundant invites these crustaceans to nip at one's toes and ankles, and their bites are like pricks of a pin. The common species in the Puget Sound region and along the open coast from British Columbia to Oregon is *E. kincaidi* (fig. 269). It is about 8 mm long, and the posterior portion of its telson is bluntly pointed and forms an angle of about 120°. *Excirolana chiltoni*, found in Oregon and California, is about 1 cm long, and the posterior portion of its telson forms an angle of about 90°. *Excirolana linguifrons*, so far known only from central California, is about 4 mm long. The posterior portion of its telson is rounded and bordered by blunt teeth.

Not far above mid-tide level there will probably be a large population of the bloodworm, *Euzonus mucronatus* (pl. 8). Sometimes a strip of crowded, small holes is an indication that bloodworms are present, but the only sure way to find them is to dig a trench up the beach to intersect the narrow band in which *Euzonus* is concentrated. The band is generally less than a meter in width, but there may be more than a hundred worms in an area 10 by 10 cm. *Euzonus* is small—about 3 or 4 cm long—and of a purplish red color (the color is due to a rich supply of hemoglobin in the blood). It burrows through the sand, moving down to a depth of 10 or 20 cm when the tide is out. It actually eats the sand grains, obtaining nourishment from the organic matter and microorganisms attached to them.

On beaches in the vicinity of Tomales Bay, there are two other bloodworms that look much like *E. mucronatus*. For those who wish to tell them apart, the following diagnostic features, visible with a low-power microscope or strong magnifying glass, are offered. In *E. mucronatus*, the dorsal gills that arise on both sides of nearly every segment have two branches, but these are not divided again. In *E. dillonensis* (pl. 8), each branch has numerous branches on one side of it, so that it resembles a comb. The gills of *E. williamsi* are divided into two or three main branches, one or more of which may have a few side branches.

Having nothing directly to do with sandy beaches, the goose barnacles of the genus *Lepas* are sometimes washed up on them during storms. Unlike *Pollicipes polymerus* (Chapter 4), which is fixed to rocks on wave-swept shores, the species of *Lepas* are pelagic. One of them, *L. fascicularis* (pl. 18), secretes material at the base of its stalk, contributing to a common float shared by several to many individuals. The other species—*L. anatifera* (fig. 270) is the most abundant of them— are attached to floating timbers or stalks of kelps. The colonies they form are sometimes massive, and various other kinds of sessile and semisessile organisms may be hidden away in them. Some of these

266. A typical cumacean

267. *Eohaustorius washingtonianus*

268. *Grandifoxus grandis*

269. *Excirolana kincaidi*

270. *Lepas anatifera,* a pelagic goose barnacle that is attached to floating timbers

271. *Alloniscus perconvexus*

272. *Velella velella,* the "by-the-wind sailor," in drift on a sandy beach

goose barnacles must surely travel widely before they have the misfortune to get too close to shore. If the weather is cool, they may be very much alive even after a day or two out of water. The same timbers that are colonized by *Lepas* may also be riddled by the shipworm, *Bankia setacea* (see Chapter 3).

Velella velella, the "by-the-wind sailor" (fig. 272; pl. 3), is an open-ocean dweller that is often washed up on beaches, especially in late spring and early summer. Specimens that drift into quiet bays may stay alive for a few days if they remain immersed. The elliptical float, pervaded by tubes containing air, has a sail set at an angle to its long axis. The length is usually from 4 to 6 cm. Hanging down from the underside of the float is a central feeding polyp and a marginal fringe of tentacles, plus polyps that bud off medusae and that also act as supplementary feeding devices. The prevailing color of the animal's tissues is blue, but the float is colorless. After a *Velella* has been washed up on the beach and the tissue rots away, all that is left is the nearly transparent float, which has the texture of parchment or soft plastic.

In modern schemes of classification, *Velella* is placed close to hydroids of the genus *Tubularia*. The polyp of a *Tubularia*, with its central mouth fringed by tentacles, with another fringe of tentacles around the margin, and with branches in between that produce medusae, certainly does bear some resemblance to *Velella*. Another *Velella*-like feature of *Tubularia* is the fact that its gut is broken up into many small tubes. Unlike most species of *Tubularia*, however, *Velella* releases its medusae. These are tiny and lack tentacles, and they are of a golden color because of the symbiotic dinoflagellates in their tissues.

In, under, and around the decomposing seaweed on the upper reaches of a sandy beach, the more obvious animals are amphipod crustaceans, commonly called beach hoppers or sand fleas. (If you use the latter term, remember that they are not fleas, and not even insects.) When a mass of seaweed in which beach hoppers are scavenging is lifted, hundreds of them will usually start to jump in what looks like aimless behavior. It is nevertheless amazing how quickly they disappear back into the seaweed and wet sand.

Several kinds of beach hoppers are found on the open coast, but two are prominent. *Megalorchestia californiana* (*Orchestoidea californiana*) (pl. 19), our largest species, attains a length (exclusive of the antennae) of about 2.5 cm. The coloration of the body is basically grayish white or ivory, but the long antennae are a gorgeous pinkish orange. It is found only on exposed beaches, usually in the vicinity of decaying seaweed. During the daytime, it is hidden away in burrows in the sand, from which it emerges after night falls. Where *M. californiana* is really common, the beach is a pretty lively place after dark, with many of the hoppers moving down the slope to scavenge closer to the water's edge. They are able to orient themselves with reference to the moon, and thus manage to find their way back to the upper part of the beach before daybreak.

Traskorchestia traskiana (*Orchestia traskiana*) (pl. 19) is a smaller species, with a maximum length of about 2 cm. It is usually dark gray, and its antennae are not distinctively colored. *Traskorchestia* is typically found at the borders of bays, estuaries, and salt marshes, but it does occur on somewhat protected beaches of the open coast.

Still farther landward than the beach hoppers, in a zone where the driftwood is almost never disturbed except during periods when there are high tides and wild storms, is *Alloniscus perconvexus* (fig. 271). This isopod resembles its completely terrestrial relatives, the sow bugs and pill bugs. It is most often found under pieces of wood resting on just slightly moist sand, but sometimes its presence out in the open is revealed by little telltale ridges in the sand. Large specimens are a little more than 1 cm long.

Once this far up the beach, one starts running into insects that burrow in the sand or that like to hide beneath debris. The more obvious of these are beetles. Rove beetles (family Staphylinidae) (fig. 273), characterized by small wing covers, but substantial wings, are especially abundant. They come out at night to wait for their prey, mostly other insects and amphipods. (The robust *Thinopinus pictus*, nearly 2 cm long, feeds primarily on the large beach hopper, *Megalorchestia californiana*.) The powerful jaws pierce the armor of the prey and the juices are then sucked out.

The Backshore and Dunes

When sand that has been washed high up on a beach dries out, it may be blown landward by winds. This leads to the formation of a sandy "backshore" above the level reached by the highest tides. Under certain conditions, an extensive area of sand dunes may develop. In that case, there is likely to be a moderately well-stabilized foredune close to the shoreline, then a region of rolling dunes in which bare sand predominates. The rolling dunes may extend inland for a distance of several kilometers, as they do between Florence and Coos Bay, in Oregon. Finally there is usually a hinddune, often higher than the other dunes. There is much variation in the layout, however.

The stability of the backshore depends on a number of factors, including the extent to which it is colonized by vegetation, the type of vegetation, the amount of clay and organic matter in the soil, and wind velocity. Dunes are especially prone to disturbances. If the vegetation on a dune is uprooted by a strong wind, the sand of that dune may be blown away and may menace plants growing on other dunes.

The following account deals with most of the flowering plants characteristic of backshores and dunes of our region. It does not cover components of the coastal forest that have colonized ancient dunes, or

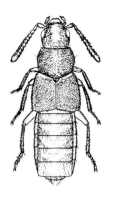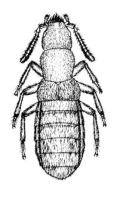

273. Three rove beetles: *Emplenota arenaria* (*left*), *Diaulota densissima* (*center*), and *Thinopinus pictus* (*right*)

species that grow in freshwater ponds or bogs that may be nestled among the dunes. Not all of the plants mentioned are strictly limited to backshores and dunes, by the way; some of them grow on sandy bluffs high above the shore, and a few occur in inland situations.

Grasses and Grasslike Plants

Among the many true grasses (family Gramineae) found on dunes, two large species stand out. These are the dunegrass, *Elymus mollis* (pl. 36), and the beachgrass, *Ammophila arenaria* (pl. 36). *Elymus* is a native, and it was the chief sand binder on Pacific coast dunes before *Ammophila* was introduced from Europe about a hundred years ago. *Ammophila* is more effective than *Elymus* in binding sand, and this seems to be the reason that foredunes in most parts of the region under consideration are higher than they once were. Low foredunes are still found in a few places, as in an area just south of Trinidad Head in northern California. In southern California, where *Ammophila* does not grow as exuberantly as it does farther north, low foredunes are the rule.

Both *Elymus* and *Ammophila* are perennials that have creeping rhizomes. Both are also relatively large grasses, their flowering spikes reaching a height of more than 1 m. They are readily distinguished from one another, however. The leaf blades of *Elymus* are usually about 1 cm wide, and the plants as a whole have a decidedly grayish tinge. The leaf blades of *Ammophila* are rarely more than 4 mm wide, and the plants are mostly yellowish green.

Rushes (family Juncaceae) are typical of low spots where the water table is not far below the surface. *Juncus lesueurii* (pl. 36) is probably the most regularly encountered species on the Pacific coast. It is sometimes found in situations that seem to be almost bone dry, but excavation will generally reveal appreciable moisture around the roots and creeping rhizomes. In dunes, this species reaches a height of about 25 cm.

Many species of sedges (family Cyperaceae) are found in freshwater habitats and some occur in slightly brackish marshes. Two species are limited to sandy situations along the coast. *Carex pansa* (fig. 274), with leaves up to 3 mm wide, raises its flower spikes to a height of about 20 cm; the spikes themselves, about 2 cm long, usually consist of both pollen-producing and seed-producing flowers. The plants are joined together by rhizomes that generally creep in a nearly straight line. The range of this species is from southern Washington to central California. *Carex macrocephala* (fig. 275) has leaves up to 8 mm wide, and its flower spikes are scarcely if at all raised above the leaves. As the name *macrocephala* implies, the flower spikes are large—usually about 4 or 5 cm long. As a rule, pollen-producing and seed-producing flowers are in separate spikes in this species, whose range on the coast extends from Alaska to northern Oregon.

Knotweed Family (Polygonaceae)

Knotweed, *Polygonum paronychia* (pl. 37), ranges from near Monterey to British Columbia. It is an unimpressive sprawler whose stems radiate away from a woody root. The narrow leaves, with downcurved and inrolled margins, are about 2 cm long. The flowers are inconspicuous, but they are worth a look with a magnifying glass because their white or pale pink sepals (there are no petals) are attractively marked with featherlike green "veins." A conspicuous feature of this plant is the papery sheaths that cover the leaf buds; these persist even after the leaves are fully developed.

Rumex salicifolius, called willow dock (pl. 37), is a close relative of rhubarb and several weedy species of dock that grow in gardens, fields, and along roadsides. The stems may be floppy or upright, but they are generally under 1 m long. The leaves, with blades from about 6 to 13 cm long and 2 cm wide, grow from the stems in groups. The small greenish or whitish flowers are crowded into oblong clusters that arise from among some of the leaves. This plant grows on dunes and in other sandy or gravelly maritime situations from southern California to British Columbia. It is not limited to coastal areas, however, and its distribution includes much of North America. It is an extremely variable species, and in some books dealing with the flora of the Pacific coast, the seaside form, with rather fleshy leaves, is called *R. crassus,* or *R. salicifolius* variety *crassus*.

Goosefoot Family (Chenopodiaceae)

Atriplex leucophylla (fig. 276), one of the plants called saltbushes, is a grayish, mat-forming perennial with crowded, sessile leaves. The leaf blades are broadly oval, sometimes nearly circular, and usually about 2 cm long. The flowers are small. The ones with pollen are packed into

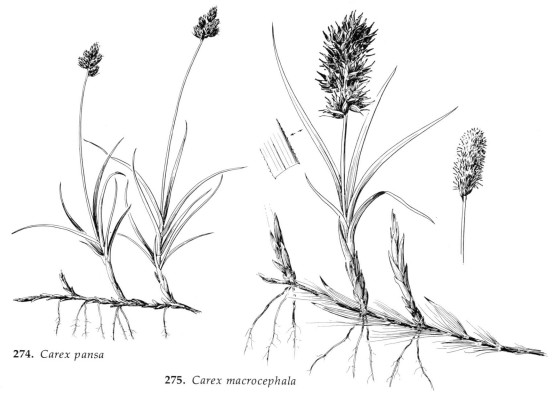

274. *Carex pansa*

275. *Carex macrocephala*

276. *Atriplex leucophylla*

277. *Abronia umbellata,* the pink sand-verbena

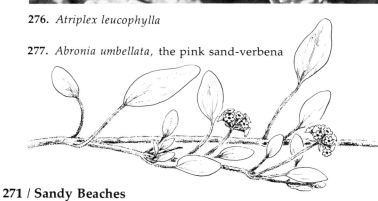

terminal spikes; those that produce seed are in clusters set into the axils of the leaves. The range of this species is from San Francisco to southern California.

Four-o'clock Family (Nyctaginaceae)

Sand-verbenas are not really verbenas; they belong to the same family as cultivated four-o'clocks. Only one species is widespread within the range covered by this book. This is the yellow sand-verbena, *Abronia latifolia* (pl. 37). Although found primarily along the outer coast, from Vancouver Island to southern California, it occurs in suitably sandy situations in the San Juan Archipelago and even in Puget Sound. It is a prostrate perennial that spreads into large mats. The flower heads, about 3 cm across, are produced in profusion throughout the summer. The bright yellow color of the individual flowers, each about 5 mm across, resides in the trumpetlike calyces; there are no petals. The whole plant is rather gummy and generally has considerable sand sticking to it.

The pink sand-verbena, *Abronia umbellata* (fig. 277), is abundant in southern California, where it occurs together with a crimson-flowered species, *A. maritima*. Although *A. umbellata* has been found along the open coast as far north as Vancouver Island, it is not often really abundant north of San Francisco. Its leaves are much less fleshy than those of the yellow sand-verbena.

Pink Family (Caryophyllaceae)

Honkenya peploides, sea purslane (fig. 278), is a rather succulent, mat-forming perennial with opposite leaves that are mostly 1 to 2 cm long. The small flowers are borne singly in the leaf axils. They generally have five petals, which are whitish and inconspicuous because they do not stick out beyond the sepals. The fruit is almost globular. The range of this plant, which commonly grows to a height of about 20 cm, is from Alaska to northern Oregon.

Carpetweed Family (Aizoaceae)

The sea-fig, *Mesembryanthemum chilense* (pl. 37), is found along nearly all of the California coast. In the past, it has been looked upon as a possible or probable native, but the consensus now is that it was introduced. In any case, it is an effective sand binder, and is much used for controlling erosion on road cuts and steep hillsides. The fleshy leaves, up to about 5 or 6 cm long and 1 cm thick, are triangular in cross section. The flowers, with magenta petals and white-and-yellow centers, are about 4 cm across.

Mesembryanthemum edule, the hottentot-fig (pl. 37), forms the same sort of dense mat as *M. chilense*, but it has yellow petals that turn pinkish or reddish when they wither. This species was definitely brought from South Africa, whose seacoast areas have the world's greatest concentration of mesembryanthemums and related plants.

Mustard Family (Cruciferae)

Sea rocket, *Cakile edentula* (pl. 37), is an annual that was introduced from the Atlantic coast during the nineteenth century. It is now found on dunes and backshores of sandy beaches throughout the range covered by this book. It is an almost succulent plant that forms much-branched, sprawling growths that are often more than 1 m across. Its membership in the mustard family is confirmed by the following combination of flower characters: four petals, six stamens (two of which are shorter than the rest), and a seed pod that originates above the bases of the petals rather than below them. The petals, about 6 mm long, are pale purple. The seed pods are fleshy and pinched into unequal halves by a slight constriction. The larger leaves, generally 4 to 6 cm long, have wavy margins.

Cakile maritima, a closely related European species, has become established on the coast of central and northern California. Its petals are 8 to 10 mm long, and its larger leaves are so deeply cut that there are a number of lobes on both sides of the midrib. The seed pod is distinctive in that it has a pair of pronounced protuberances at about the level of the constriction that divides it into two parts.

Poppy Family (Papaveraceae)

The California poppy, *Eschscholzia californica* (pl. 37) is a variable species. The maritime form, found on backshores of beaches from Mendocino County to Santa Barbara County, is typically rather small and characterized by a stout taproot, nearly gray foliage, and petals that are yellow except for an orange spot at the base. The petals, incidentally, are not often more than 2 cm long, so the flowers of this form are smaller than those of plants in most inland populations of the species.

Rose Family (Rosaceae)

The beach strawberry, *Fragaria chiloensis* (fig. 279), resembles the cultivated strawberry and native inland species. It hugs the sandy ground in which it is rooted, however, and is not likely to raise its flowers more than about 3 cm. The leaflets are dark green and shiny above, silky below. The flowers are of two types: those that have only stamens for producing pollen, and those that have only pistils that collectively form the fruit. As a rule, the pistillate and staminate flowers are on separate plants. The beach strawberry has a wide geographic distribution. Besides being found from central California to Alaska, it occurs on the Pacific coast of South America (its specific name alludes to the fact that an early collection came from the island of Chiloe, in

278. Two views of *Honkenya peploides*, the sea purslane

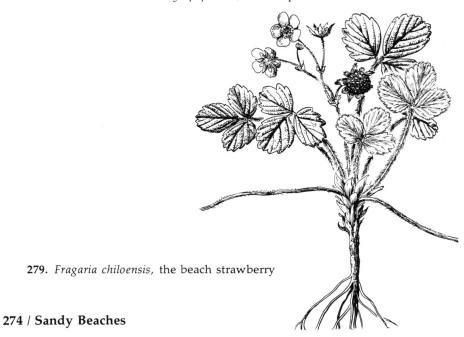

279. *Fragaria chiloensis*, the beach strawberry

Chile), and also in Hawaii. It has figured in the parentage of some strains of the cultivated strawberry.

Pea Family (Leguminosae)

The beach pea, *Lathyrus japonicus* (pl. 36), occurs throughout the range covered by this book. It is found in Puget Sound, in the San Juan Archipelago, and in other relatively protected situations, as well as along the open coast. Its favorite habitat is the backshore of a beach where there is a fair amount of driftwood for it to clamber over. The leaves have up to a dozen leaflets in addition to the tendrils. The flowers, of which there are generally several, are about 2 cm long and typically deep pink suffused with purple.

Another kind of beach pea, *Lathyrus littoralis*, is abundant in many places along the open coast. It is unmistakable because its leaves are so hairy as to be nearly silky, and there are no tendrils. The flowers, usually pink, sometimes white, are not often more than 1.5 cm long.

The bush lupine, *Lupinus arboreus* (pl. 36), is a shrubby species native to the region between southern California and central Oregon. It has been introduced farther north, however, and is now common in some places around Puget Sound and in the San Juan Archipelago. It grows not only on backshores and sand dunes, but also a little farther back from the beach. This species is regularly about 1 m high, and the typical yellow-flowered form is a lovely sight when it is in full bloom in late spring or early summer. There are forms with pale blue or pale lilac flowers, and these could be confused with another coastal beach lupine, *L. chamissonis*. This species differs from *L. arboreus*, however, in having hairs on the back of the upper petal, which is called the "banner." It is more characteristic of what may be called "real dirt" than of sand dunes.

Lupinus littoralis, the seashore lupine (pl. 36), is a low creeper found from northern California to British Columbia. It is not restricted to the open coast, and there are nice colonies of it on sandy beaches and bluffs in the San Juan Archipelago. This species is perennial, but it dies back each autumn. The leaves have five to nine leaflets, and these, like almost all parts of the plant, are rather hairy. The blue or lilac flowers, mostly about 1 cm across, are concentrated in dense, upright spikes. The seed pods reach a length of about 3 cm. This is the only lupine, other than the much larger *L. arboreus*, that is likely to be found on sandy beaches right next to salt water.

Lotus salsuginosus (pl. 36) is an annual that radiates from a central stem. This plant is not strictly limited to the dunes habitat, but when it is found in this situation its branches are usually pressed tightly against the sandy soil. The yellow flowers are generally not quite 1 cm across, and the seed pods are about 1.5 cm long. The leaves typically have five leaflets, sometimes seven. The range of this species extends from central California to Baja California.

Evening Primrose Family (Onagraceae)

The beach evening primrose, *Oenothera cheiranthifolia* (or *Camissonia cheiranthifolia*) (pl. 36) is a common perennial of dunes and sandy soils along the open coast. From a crown of basal leaves, it sends out several to many stems that may spread out to form a mat that is more than a meter across. The flowers, with four bright yellow petals, are generally about 1.5 cm in diameter. They open in the morning, instead of in the evening the way many other species of *Oenothera* do. As the flowers age, the petals usually become reddish.

Parsley Family (Umbelliferae)

Glehnia leiocarpa (fig. 280) is a compact, slightly succulent plant. Its leaves, up to about 15 cm long, are deeply divided into several leaflets, each of which may have secondary lobes. The bases of the leaf petioles, often buried in sand, clasp the main stem. The foliage is rather hairy or woolly, especially on the underside. The numerous small flowers are packed into several tight clusters that collectively form a nearly flat-topped inflorescence of the type that is characteristic of the carrot and its allies. The flower stalk sticks up only a few centimeters above the leaves. *Glehnia* is common on the backshores of sandy beaches from British Columbia to southern Oregon, but it gradually drops out in northern California. It apparently does not grow as far south as San Francisco.

Morning-glory Family (Convolvulaceae)

The beach morning-glory, *Convolvulus soldanella* (fig. 281), is one of the more distinctive species of the genus to which it belongs. It is fleshier and more compact than most morning-glories, and its leaves, up to about 5 cm across, are rounded at the tip instead of being pointed. The flowers, in which the petals are fused to form a wide funnel, are generally broader than the leaves and are pink or purplish pink, with lighter stripes on the upper face. The beach morning-glory is a perennial and is found along much of the open coast from southern California to Washington, but its distribution is not continuous. In northern California, for instance, its occurrence is spotty. Although apparently native in our region, it is found in other parts of the world, including Europe and South America.

Borage Family (Boraginaceae)

Heliotrope, *Heliotropium curassavicum* (fig. 282), belongs to the family that also claims the wildflowers called fiddleneck and popcorn flower and the garden herb called comfrey. It is not restricted to maritime situations, for in California it is sometimes common in moist inland areas. At the borders of salt marshes it is inclined to grow coarser and taller—up to about 30 or 40 cm high—than it does on the backshores of

280. *Glehnia leiocarpa*

281. *Convolvulus soldanella*, the beach morning-glory

282. *Heliotropium curassavicum*, heliotrope

283. *Ambrosia chamissonis*, the silvery beachweed

beaches, where it hugs the sand. Regardless of where it grows, it is an evergreen perennial and its foliage is rather fleshy, smooth, and grayish green. The flowers, crowded into slightly curved clusters, are about 5 or 6 mm across. The five petals are white at their extremities, but the throat of the tube into which they are fused has considerable yellow in it.

Plantain Family (Plantaginaceae)

Seaside plantain, *Plantago maritima* subspecies *juncoides* (pl. 37), occurs at the edges of salt marshes, along sandy beaches, and on cliffs and bluffs close to the shore. It is an evergreen perennial with narrow, fleshy basal leaves whose shape and length vary according to the exact habitat. In general, however, the leaves are 5 to 15 cm long and at least five times as long as wide. As in the weedy plantains introduced from Europe, the greenish, four-petaled flowers are concentrated in spikes raised up on leafless stalks. This species occurs throughout the range covered by this book, and is found as far north as Alaska.

Aster Family (Compositae)

Seaside daisy, *Erigeron glaucus* (pl. 38), is an evergreen perennial with elongated leaves, most of which are basal. Characteristically, this plant forms rather low mounds in which the flower heads are raised to a height of 15 or 20 cm. The ray flowers, about 1.5 cm long, are pale violet to lavender; the central disk, which consists of tubular yellow flowers (not all of these necessarily open at the same time), is usually about 2 cm across. The seaside daisy has a narrower range than some of the other plants discussed in this section. It occurs along the open coast from central California to northern Oregon.

A specialty of the backshore in the vicinity of Golden Gate Park in San Francisco is *Senecio elegans* (pl. 38). It was introduced from South Africa, but is beautiful and not so aggressive as to be objectionable. Its ray flowers are magenta and its disk flowers are bright yellow. The heads are about 2.5 cm across, and the plant grows to a height of approximately 30 cm.

Agoseris apargioides (pl. 38) is a native dandelion whose range extends from southern Washington to Santa Barbara County. It has a number of named subspecies, some of which are almost strictly limited to coastal areas. When found growing on sandy backshores, this plant tends to be short-stemmed and all of its leaves hug the ground. The flower heads, about 2 or 3 cm across, are light yellow and lifted up on stems 5 to 10 cm long. The leaves, mostly 8 to 12 cm long, are woolly at first, but they usually become smooth as they mature. Sometimes they are divided into a number of lateral lobes, but in many populations the margins of the leaves are just slightly wavy.

Silvery beachweed, *Ambrosia chamissonis* (*Franseria chamissonis*) (fig. 283), is a mat-forming perennial whose crinkly edged leaf blades, up to about 4 cm long, are so densely clothed with silky hairs that they are almost white. The heads of seed-producing flowers are situated in the axils of the upper leaves, and their bracts are spiny enough to form burs. The heads in which the pollen-producing flowers are concentrated are in a terminal spike. The range of this species extends from central California to British Columbia, but it seems to be more common between Santa Cruz County and the Oregon-California border than it is farther north.

Growing with *A. chamissonis*—or replacing it completely in some areas, especially along the coast of Oregon, Washington, and British Columbia—is a subspecies called *bipinnatisecta* (pl. 38). Its leaves are mostly gray green, for they are less hairy than those of silvery beachweed, and they are divided into leaflets that are divided once and sometimes twice again. The organization of the flower heads is substantially the same as in *A. chamissonis*, so this plant is now considered to be a variety rather than a distinct species. (In the past it has been called *Franseria bipinnatifida*.) It grows from Baja California to British Columbia, and is almost continuously present on sandy beaches throughout this range. It is not limited to the open coast, either; there are robust stands of it in Puget Sound, the San Juan Archipelago, and other somewhat protected areas.

Beach sagewort, *Artemisia pycnocephala* (pl. 38), is generally common on sandy backshores and dunes from northern Oregon to Monterey County, California. It is a bushy and somewhat woody plant that grows to a height of about 40 cm. The stems and foliage are covered with silky hairs, and the plant as a whole is therefore silvery gray. The leaves, up to about 2.5 cm long, are divided into many slender lobes. The inconspicuous flowers are concentrated in upright spikes.

The dune tansy, *Tanacetum camphoratum* (pl. 38), is characterized by fernlike leaves, a strong aroma of camphor, and yellow flowers concentrated in buttonlike heads about 1.5 cm across. There are no ray flowers. On new growth, the stems and foliage are woolly—sometimes almost white—because they are covered with long, cobwebby hairs. Many of the hairs are shed as the shoots mature. This plant forms clumps up to about 50 or 60 cm high. Its range is limited to the region around San Francisco. Farther north, from Humboldt County to British Columbia, there is *T. douglasii*, the northern dune tansy. It is similar to *T. camphoratum*, but it has distinct ray flowers, and its foliage is not so woolly.

Haplopappus ericoides, called mock heather (pl. 38), would be rather nondescript if it were not for the fact that it produces its small, orange-yellow flower heads in such profusion. The plant as a whole, up to about 1 m high, is shrubby and its older stems are woody. The slender leaves, which are crowded together in groups, resemble those of a heather in being nearly cylindrical; the largest of them are about 6 mm long. The flower heads are approximately 1 cm high and 1 cm across when the several rays are spread out. This plant is found on dunes in central and southern California.

Baccharis pilularis subspecies *pilularis* (pl. 38), called chaparral broom, is common in central and northern California. This dune-inhabiting shrub is almost prostrate and sometimes forms extensive mats. The leaves, up to about 2 cm long, are slightly sticky, and are characterized by a few rather indistinct marginal teeth. The flowers, concentrated into heads about 1 cm high, are whitish; none of them has rays. A different subspecies, *consanguinea*, is more widely distributed than the one that grows on dunes. It is discussed in Chapter 7 because of its occurrence in dry ground around salt marshes.

PROTECTED SANDY BEACHES

In the Puget Sound region, and in many bays and coves located along the outer coast, there are sandy beaches that sustain almost no wave action. These beaches generally have a rich variety of microscopic organisms that live between sand grains, and they are also likely to have mysids, cumaceans, the little scavenging isopods of the genus *Excirolana*, and furry amphipods of the genus *Eohaustorius*. One or another species of *Crangon* may be common, too, but since "swash" pools of the type characteristic of exposed beaches are not usually present on protected beaches, these shrimps may have to be looked for in shallow water of the surf zone. A little digging at various tide levels may turn up some large nemerteans of the genus *Cerebratulus* (fig. 263), and also polychaetes of the genus *Nephtys* (fig. 264).

In the San Juan Archipelago and a few other places in the Northwest, there are protected sandy beaches that support large populations of the lugworm *Abarenicola claparedi oceanica*. This polychaete is concentrated at mid-tide level, or a little lower. Its cake-decorator fecal castings are similar to those of its relatives that live in bays where there is considerable mud, but they are larger and appreciably sandier. Lugworms and their interesting life style will be discussed in more detail in Chapter 7.

Certain of the more conspicuous invertebrates of exposed sandy beaches are rarely seen on beaches that do not have considerable wave action. The absence of the razor clam and mole crab will be especially conspicuous, and a search for bloodworms higher up on the beach will almost certainly be futile. The purple olive snail, however, is more consistently associated with slightly protected beaches than with those that are fully exposed. The drift zone, where decaying seaweed accumulates, will have a joyful population of beach hoppers, but the species that predominates will be *Traskorchestia traskiana* (pl. 19), not *Megalorchestia californiana*. *Traskorchestia* is smaller, with a body length under 2 cm, and is drab compared with its beautiful open-coast cousin. The isopod *Alloniscus perconvexus*, so common under pieces of driftwood left by the highest tides on exposed beaches, is only occasionally found on protected sandy beaches.

The backshores of protected beaches are rarely extensive. At least a few of the flowering plants described in connection with backshores and dunes of exposed beaches should be present, however. Dune-grass, the yellow sand-verbena, and sea rocket are perhaps the most regularly occurring species in sheltered situations.

7

Quiet Bays and Salt Marshes

Larger bays, including those located along the outer coast, are relatively protected and have little wave action except during storms. Many of them are estuaries into which substantial rivers and streams empty. In such situations, there is usually an abundance of fine silt brought down from the land, and the salinity at the surface of the substratum is apt to vary extensively from season to season and according to tidal fluctuations. Within the muddy sand, mud, and clay, however, the salinity tends to remain rather stable in the face of fresh water flowing over the surface. This buffering capacity of fine-particled substrata thus protects burrowing animals against changes in salinity. This is not to say that the salinity of the substratum throughout a bay is always like that of sea water. Any estuary will show a gradient from sea water to fresh water, with daily or seasonal fluctuations all along the way. Nevertheless, in areas that are inundated by the sea daily, the substratum will tend to retain its salinity even when the tide is out and there are strong rains or runoff from a stream.

In the San Juan Islands and other places where there are few freshwater streams of any consequence, the fine silt that accumulates in quiet bays is largely a result of erosion around the margins of the bays. Since wave action is so slight, this silt tends not to be stirred up and washed out to sea. The salinity generally remains remarkably constant, although there are places where seepage from the land reduces it somewhat.

The character of the substratum in most bays ranges from fine sand, which is only slightly muddy, to real mud and finally to hard-packed clay. There may be gravel worked into the substratum, and rocks of moderate to large size may be scattered about, especially at higher tide levels. There are many variations on the theme, and any one bay may have several rather different but intergrading substrata within it. Thus the fauna and flora may be diversified, with many of the organisms being more or less restricted to certain areas.

A few of the principal ecological situations found in quiet bays will serve as the structure for discussing some of the animals and plants identified with each one. It must be remembered, however, that as long as there are intergradations in the size of the sand particles, the amount and nature of the organic matter, and other variables, it is neither possible nor desirable to make the classification of substrata rigid. To complicate matters even further, in a particular bay one kind of substratum is apt to be at a different tide level than it would be in another.

RATHER CLEAN SAND

What can definitely be called sand, as distinct from muddy sand, is likely to be found at lower tide levels (about 1.0 foot [0.3 meter] and lower) and only near the mouths of bays. The particles will ordinarily be smaller, on the average, than those of more exposed sandy beaches and will be packed rather tightly. The sand will shift to some extent from season to season and from year to year as a result of currents, and sand bars may alternate with depressions. The bars will be free of any obvious vegetation; but the depressions—shallow pools at low tide—may have extensive growths of the eelgrass, *Zostera*. By forming thick colonies, with a system of creeping rhizomes and roots, *Zostera* helps to stabilize the substratum and to provide shelter for a variety of organisms. Eelgrass and the animals and plants commonly associated with it will be discussed in some depth later in this chapter.

The two most eye-catching animals found plowing through the surface of rather clean sand are sand dollars and moon snails. Sand dollars are echinoderms closely related to sea urchins, but their tests are flattened and their tube feet and spines are relatively small. The mouth is situated near the middle of the underside; but the anus, instead of being close to the middle of the upper side, is displaced to a position on the underside near the margin. The madreporite, through which some water may enter and leave the water vascular system, is slightly off-center on the upper side; and the five sets of tube feet radiating from this are of unequal size. The specific name of our sand dollar, *Dendraster excentricus* (fig. 284), was given in allusion to this off-center look. *Dendraster excentricus* reaches a diameter of about 8 cm, and its color ranges from gray to blackish red. As it pushes its way through the sand, generally partially exposed, fine particles of detritus that fall onto the surface between the spines are carried by tracts of cilia to the margins, and then other tracts on the underside convey them to the mouth. Sand dollars have an Aristotle's lantern similar to that of sea urchins, but it is modified for processing smaller particles of food that enter the mouth instead of for scraping and for chopping up larger pieces. These animals release their eggs and sperm into the water. A fertilized egg develops into a bilaterally symmetrical, free-swimming larva which eventually, if it is lucky enough to find a suitable substratum, settles and metamorphoses into the adult.

The moon snail, *Polinices lewisii* (fig. 285), is our most massive intertidal snail. Its shell, which may reach a height of about 12 cm, is composed almost entirely of the body whorl; the rest of the whorls (about five) form a low but distinct spire. The periostracum is very smooth, and the color is generally a soft brownish gray. The aperture is large and closed tightly by an operculum when the animal withdraws. While the animal is extended and working its way through the sand, its mantle is enormous and covers most of the shell; it is always something of a surprise to see that it can pull all of this soft tissue into the shell. (A lot of water is squeezed out in the process, of course.) The moon snail is a pure carnivore, feeding on clams by drilling a neat hole in one of the valves (fig. 299) and then sucking out the tissue. Moon snails are less abundant intertidally during the winter months, when they seem to move out into deeper water, than they are during the spring and summer. After they appear in large numbers on the sand flats, they commence to lay their eggs in very characteristic collarlike configurations. The eggs are sandwiched between two layers of sand cemented together by mucous secretions. They hatch in midsummer, and the young go through a free-swimming stage before they settle down.

The channeled basket-whelk, *Nassarius fossatus* (fig. 286), is sometimes found on sandy flats, but it is more common subtidally. The shell of this species, which may reach a height of 4.5 cm, has low spiral ridges. Where these ridges are intersected by small axial ribs, little "beads" are formed. An especially distinctive feature is the deep furrow on the body whorl, just above the siphonal canal. There is a prominent "callus" on the columella, and this is often tinged with orange. The rest of the shell is pale grayish brown or ash colored.

Nassarius mendicus, the lean basket-whelk (fig. 287), is smaller and more slender than *N. fossatus*. The shell is usually dark gray or grayish brown, and the height may reach 2 cm. Both species of *Nassarius* mentioned here are scavengers that feed on dead animal material. Their empty shells are favorites of hermit crabs and often turn up in situations where the living snails do not occur.

The holes at the surface belong mostly to clams, a variety of polychaete worms, and a burrowing sea cucumber. Digging into the sand will expose some worms and other invertebrates that do not have permanent burrows.

The burrowing sea cucumbers, *Leptosynapta clarki* (fig. 288) and *L. albicans*, live within a few inches of the surface. They do not look much like typical sea cucumbers because they have no tube feet, except for the pinnately branched tentacles that encircle the mouth. These tentacles are used in processing the sand that the animal swallows to get the food value tied up in the organic coating on the grains and in the

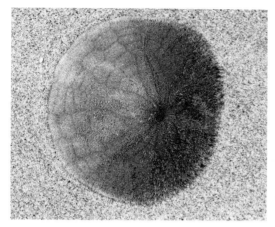

284. *Dendraster excentricus,* the sand dollar

285. (*Above and right*) *Polinices lewisii,* the moon snail

286. *Nassarius fossatus,*
the channeled basket-whelk

287. *Nassarius mendicus,*
the lean basket-whelk

associated detritus. Both species are mostly whitish, although they may be tinted with brown or orange. Large individuals, fully extended, are about 10 cm long. When handled, these cucumbers may cling to one's fingers, because numerous microscopic, anchorlike hooks projecting from the body wall engage the skin. The anchors undoubtedly serve the cucumbers in their natural environment by providing traction as the animals contract and elongate. In the Puget Sound region, *L. clarki* is the prevailing species. It is distinctive in that females brood their young in their ovaries during the autumn and winter. *Leptosynapta albicans*, common in California, not only in sand flats but also under rocks and in sand-filled crevices, does not brood its young.

In places where one finds the sand dollar, or at least the moon snail and *Leptosynapta*, there are apt to be several species of bivalve molluscs. Most of them—including the cockle and bent-nosed clam—are more abundant in a muddier habitat and will be considered in the following section. One species, however, seems to require rather clean sand. This is *Macoma secta*, the sand clam (fig. 289). When compared with other members of the genus found locally, it is large, sometimes reaching a length of 10 cm, and its hinge is very short. It is also much neater than most macomas, since its periostracum is light and thin. As in all species of *Macoma*, the incurrent and excurrent siphons are completely separate. The incurrent siphon is very mobile and is used much like a vacuum-sweeper hose to pick up detritus from the surface of the sand. *Macoma secta* is usually buried at least 20 cm deep. The number of live specimens encountered in the course of intensive digging is much smaller than one might expect to find on the basis of the number of empty shells found on the surface.

Tellina bodegensis (fig. 290), though not strikingly marked, is an attractive clam because of its polished shell and regular growth lines. The color is close to ivory. The shape is elongated, the length being more than twice the height. The narrow siphonal end is bent slightly toward the right. Large specimens are nearly 6 cm long. *Tellina bodegensis* burrows to a depth of about 10 cm, and its preferred habitat is relatively clean sand just inside the mouth of a bay that opens on the outer coast. Its method of feeding is similar to that of *Macoma*. Its range extends from British Columbia to Baja California.

On sand flats, wherever there are pools or depressions that hold at least a little water at low tide, two fishes are usually encountered (excluding, of course, the fishes that move into the bay and out again during periods of high tide). Both of these are apt to surprise one when they dart off, as they may be difficult to see until they move. The sand sole, *Psettichthys melanostictus* (fig. 291), flattened like soles and flounders of our fish markets, reaches a length of about 60 cm, but most specimens seen in pools at low tide are smaller than 20 cm. Both eyes are normally on the right side, which is thus uppermost. The generally gray color of *Psettichthys* is complicated by some salt-and-

288. *Leptosynapta clarki,* the burrowing sea cucumber

289. *Macoma secta,* the sand clam

290. *Tellina bodegensis*

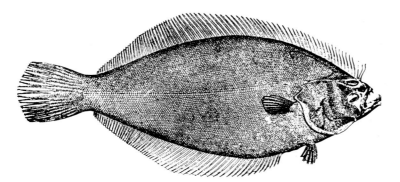

291. *Psettichthys melanostictus,* the sand sole

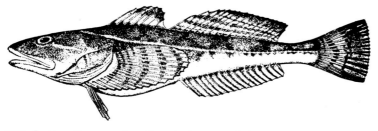

292. *Leptocottus armatus,* the staghorn sculpin

pepper effects, and these, coupled with the transparency of the fins and the fact that the fish often is at least half buried, makes it difficult to see this species until it moves.

The other fish is the staghorn sculpin, *Leptocottus armatus* (fig. 292). It looks like sculpins in general, but is on the whole a rather slender species. It is also large compared with the sculpins found intertidally on rocky shores, sometimes attaining a length of about 25 cm. Its coloration above consists mostly of grays of varying degrees of darkness, but the underside is very light, with a weak yellow tint. *Leptocottus* is found also on mudflats and is one of the more common fishes of estuarine situations where the salinity is low on account of runoff from a river or stream. It is frequently taken with hook and line, though not intentionally.

Muddy Sand, Mud, and Gravel

As the amount of organic material increases, the fauna generally becomes richer. Mud and muddy sand support large populations of animals, and if you spread out a little of the surface sediment and sort through it with a low-power microscope, you will find an astonishing diversity of invertebrates, some of which are restricted to this type of situation. Diatoms and certain other small plants will also be abundant. When the microscopic organisms are discounted, the animals fall into three principal groups: polychaete annelids, bivalve molluscs, and crustaceans. Evidence that these are numerous can be seen as holes to burrows, as little piles of sand or mud around some of the openings, and as fecal castings. A person really familiar with the mudflat fauna can usually tell which clams, shrimps, and worms have made the various kinds of burrows, and which worms have deposited the several obvious types of fecal castings.

Since the character of the substratum in most bays changes so gradually, and since the faunas considered typical of particular situations tend to overlap, it seems best to develop the discussion largely around groups of animals. This method will obviate considerable repetition, as well as prevent one from associating certain animals too definitely with very specific habitats.

Bivalve Molluscs: Clams, Cockles, Mussels, and Oysters

Where the sand is rather muddy, two medium-sized clams reach their peak of abundance. The bent-nosed clam, *Macoma nasuta* (fig. 293), has a maximum length of about 5 cm and its valves are bent rather sharply to the right near the posterior end. This species is generally about 10 or 15 cm beneath the surface, lying with its left valve down. Its siphons, completely separate as in all macomas, are directed upward through the flexed portion. The orange coloration of its siphons is another distinguishing feature. The periostracum, usually most prominent near the lower edge and near the siphonal end of the valves, is dirty brown; the valves are otherwise white, and chalky where they have been eroded.

Macoma inquinata (fig. 294) is of about the same size and appearance as *M. nasuta*, but its valves are not bent and the shell is slightly more inflated. The siphons are barely yellowish, and definitely not orange. Both of these clams would be attractive as food if their mode of feeding did not bring considerable sand into the mantle cavity.

Another species of *Macoma*, whose shell rarely exceeds 1.5 cm in length, is also apt to be found in muddy sand, living close to the surface. This is *M. balthica* (pl. 17). Its shell is more nearly oval in outline than that of either *M. nasuta* or *M. inquinata*, and there is no appreciable amount of periostracum; moreover, it is often pink, blue, yellow, or orange. It seems not to be as abundant in Puget Sound or in the San Juan Archipelago as it is in San Francisco Bay and bays that front on the open coast of the Northwest.

The largest bivalves that a clam digger can expect to gather from tide flats of quiet bays are the gaper clams or horse clams of the genus *Tresus*. They generally live in sandy mud, or in mud that has gravel and bits of shell mixed with it, but they are sometimes found in stiff clay. The depth at which they lie depends to some extent on the character of the substratum; in clay, specimens are usually less than 30 cm below the surface; but in mud they may be deeper, down to nearly 50 cm. The valves of the shell may attain a length of about 20 cm. The periostracum, where it persists, is a dull brown color, and the rest of the shell is chalky white, unless blackened by sulfides. The siphon, though large, can be retracted almost completely into the shell.

The common gaper clam of central and northern California is *Tresus nuttallii* (pl. 17). Its shell is generally more than one and a half times as long as it is high, and its umbones are typically near the end of the anterior quarter. The tip of its siphon has a pair of large, leathery plates; these are frequently colonized by small barnacles, hydroids, and delicate red algae such as *Polysiphonia*. The wrinkled, brown periostracum on the siphon is persistent and prominent.

Tresus capax (fig. 295) is the species likely to be seen in Oregon, Washington, and British Columbia. Its shell is generally about one and a half times as long as high, and the umbones are typically near the end of the anterior third. The siphon has little periostracum, and the leathery plates at the tip of the siphon are small and not very distinct. The species does often have organisms growing on its siphons, but not to the extent characteristic of *T. nuttallii*. *Tresus capax* and *T. nuttallii* coexist in Humboldt Bay and in some places in Oregon and Washington, but in general one can count on gaper clams dug in the Northwest to be *T. capax*.

Almost every gaper clam will have a pair of small, soft-bodied crabs in its mantle cavity. Actually, three species of crabs are known to be associated with gaper clams: *Pinnixa faba* (fig. 296), *P. littoralis,* and *Fabia subquadrata.* In all of these, the female is larger than the male and is also less inclined to move around, generally staying put in one place. The mantle tissue may appear irritated or blistered in the area of her residence. Although several immature crabs of this sort may be found in a particular clam, no more than one female and one male are left after the crabs mature. The female seems to feed unselectively on the diatoms and other material brought in with the feeding currents produced by the clam, and also on strings of mucus. Just what the male lives on is not clear, as it has not been observed to feed actively.

Younger stages of *Pinnixa* and *Fabia* are known to occur in various other species of clams, such as *Mya arenaria, Clinocardium nuttallii, Saxidomus giganteus,* and *Saxidomus nuttalli.* Apparently they can later move from these hosts into gaper clams.

The geoduck (pronounced "gooey duck"), *Panopea generosa* (fig. 297), is larger than the gaper clam: the shell of a really huge specimen may be 20 cm long, and its siphon, even after it has contracted as much as it can, may hang out about 25 cm. The total weight occasionally exceeds 20 pounds. The geoduck is much prized but not often dug, for it is rather scarce intertidally and older individuals are generally at least 75 cm below the surface. It is, moreover, a specialty of the Northwest, although it is sometimes taken in certain bays in California. The valves of the shell, as viewed from one side, are nearly rectangular and gape widely. The periostracum is yellowish, rather than brown as in *Tresus.* The siphon has no leathery pads at the tip.

The heart cockle, *Clinocardium nuttallii* (fig. 298), seems to prefer those portions of quiet bays in which the substratum consists of muddy fine sand. Beds of eelgrass growing on mud often support large populations. This cockle is versatile, however, and is sometimes plentiful in rather clean sand. Its vertical distribution is likewise extensive, for it is found from rather high levels in the intertidal region to deep-water situations. Since its siphon is very short, the heart cockle lives with the posterior end of its shell just below the surface of the substratum.

The shell of *Clinocardium* attains a length of about 10 cm. Viewed from the right or left side, the valves have a shape something like a triangle with rounded corners; viewed from one end or the other, they have a heart-shaped profile. There are about thirty-five strong ribs radiating from the umbo. The coloration of young specimens is characteristically a warm brown, with some mottling; older specimens tend to be a monotonous darker brown. Although appearing to be rather sedentary, cockles have a powerful and very extensile foot, and specimens lying in a pan of water will sometimes push themselves around or even flip over. This activity will become remarkably purposeful if the arm of a sunflower star, *Pycnopodia,* is applied to the edge of the mantle, so that the tube feet actually touch the tissue: the cockle will flip itself violently to get out of reach.

293. *Macoma nasuta,* the bent-nosed clam

294. *Macoma inquinata*

295. *(Right) Tresus capax,* the gaper clam

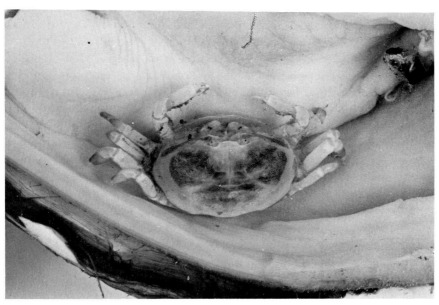

296. *Pinnixa faba,* a pinnotherid crab living in the mantle cavity of *Tresus capax*

In protected situations where the substratum is composed largely of gravel mixed with sand or mud, certain clams reach their peak of abundance. First in order of importance, at least in the lower reaches of the intertidal region, is the littleneck clam, *Protothaca staminea* (fig. 299). The shell of this common species is moderately heavy and reaches a length of about 6 cm. The valves are sculptured with both radiating and concentric ridges. Younger specimens often have some brown markings that look like the outlines of teepees, or like squares in a checkerboard, but older individuals tend to be rather uniformly pale brown, sometimes with a pinkish cast. The interior of the valves is practically white. A distinguishing characteristic of this species is the filelike sculpturing of the valves just inside the ventral margins. The fused siphons are extremely short, so the posterior end of the clam is just at the surface. The population density of this species is sometimes so heavy that several specimens will be turned out in a single shovelful of gravel. Actually, it is hardly necessary to dig for this species, for it can be scratched out.

Protothaca tenerrima, the thin-shelled littleneck clam (fig. 300), attains a length of nearly 10 cm. As its common name implies, its valves are proportionately thinner than those of *P. staminea*; they are also more shallow. Externally, the valves are grayish white, without any dark markings, and the only prominent sculpturing consists of rather sharp concentric ridges; the lines radiating from the umbo are very fine. Internally, the valves are nearly pure white. *Protothaca tenerrima* is sometimes found in association with *P. staminea*, but it prefers beaches in which there is considerable sand in proportion to pebbles. In any case, it is never common.

Tapes japonica, the Japanese littleneck clam (or Manila clam) (fig. 301), is about the same size as *P. staminea*, but it is more graceful because of its slightly more elongated shape. The radial ridges of the shell are decidedly more prominent than the concentric ridges, and they are proportionately better developed and more widely spaced than those of *P. staminea*. The color is usually grayish, greenish, or brownish, and distinct darker or lighter markings regularly form designs resembling mountain ranges, maps, or graphs. Internally, the valves are typically yellowish, with a purple suffusion near the posterior margin. This species was originally imported with seed oysters coming from Japan and has become well established in the Puget Sound region, in San Francisco Bay, and in suitable places elsewhere. It may be found together with *P. staminea*, but on the whole it tends to reside at slightly higher tide levels.

A thick-shelled bivalve that is common in sandy and gravelly muds in British Columbia, Washington, and Oregon is the butter clam or Washington clam, *Saxidomus giganteus* (fig. 302). Its shell, commonly 10 cm long and sometimes a little larger, is basically whitish, though it may have blackish discolorations owing to the presence of iron sul-

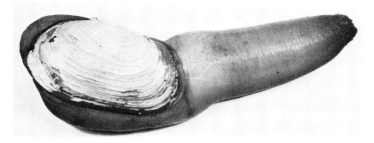

297. *Panopea generosa,* the geoduck

298. *Clinocardium nuttallii,*
the heart cockle

299. (*Upper right and right*)
Protothaca staminea, the littleneck
clam; the specimen on the right has
been drilled by *Polinices*

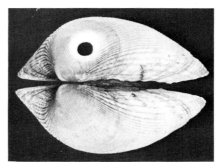

300. *Protothaca tenerrima,*
the thin-shelled littleneck clam

301. *Tapes japonica,*
the Japanese littleneck clam

fide. The surface is marked only by raised concentric growth lines and grooves. The more conspicuous grooves reflect the deceleration of growth in winter. The hinge is very thick. When the valves are tightly closed, there is practically no gape at the siphonal end. This species may be buried as deep as 30 cm, but it is often much closer to the surface. The flesh, on the whole, is rather rubbery, but it makes a superb chowder, and this species is extensively exploited commercially. *Saxidomus giganteus* is found from Alaska to San Francisco Bay, but it is rarely seen south of Humboldt Bay.

The shell of *Saxidomus nuttalli* (fig. 303) resembles that of *S. giganteus*, but the growth lines are more prominently raised, and the interior of the valves, near the siphonal end, are stained with purple. The length may reach 15 cm. This is the prevailing species of *Saxidomus* in California, where it usually inhabits sandy mud.

Mercenaria mercenaria, the quahog (fig. 304), is native to the Atlantic coast. Large quantities of it are shipped to seafood markets in the west, and most of the live specimens picked up in San Francisco Bay and a few other places probably have been discarded or have fallen out of holding pens. In Humboldt Bay, and also in Colorado Lagoon, near Long Beach, there are reproducing populations that have persisted ever since they were introduced many years ago.

The shell of the quahog (pronounced "kó-hog"—it is a shortened version of the Indian name "poquahock") may exceed a length of 10 cm. It is thick and solid, and the ligament that holds the valves together is substantial. When the valves are pulled tightly together, there is no appreciable gape. The interior of the shell is mostly white, but the lower edge of each valve has a purple border; the outside is generally grayish, with a light brown periostracum. Between the obvious concentric growth lines visible on the shell, there are many microscopic lines. Careful analysis of these has enabled experts to correlate the rate of shell growth with tidal cycles and seasons. Extension of these studies to fossil clams, and to calcareous skeletons of some other fossil invertebrates, has brought forth evidence that a month is about two days shorter than it was 500 million years ago.

The soft-shell clam, *Mya arenaria* (fig. 305), is typically found in mixtures of sand and mud, or mud and gravel, where the salinity is reduced by influx of considerable fresh water, either from a stream or by seepage. It is usually about 20 cm below the surface. The shell may exceed a length of 10 cm. It is rather thin and fragile, hence often cracked when the clam is dug. In outline, it is rounded anteriorly and somewhat truncately pointed posteriorly. The color is basically whitish or chalky gray, and the brownish periostracum tends to be restricted to the edges of the shell. Internally, the left valve is characterized by a very large, shelflike excrescence, called the chondrophore. The hinge ligament, being internal, cannot be seen from the outside of the shell. The soft-shell clam, found in appropriate habitats throughout the region, was almost certainly imported from the Atlantic coast, for it is not present in old Indian shell mounds. It is a common species in Europe, especially in areas with low salinity such as the Baltic Sea.

Jackknife clams resemble the razor clam in general form and in having a glossy shell, but they are more slender. The only one likely to be encountered in the range covered by this book is *Solen sicarius* (fig. 306). Its shell, up to 12 cm long, is slightly curved, and the hinge is close to one end. The foot usually shows considerable dark pigment. Intertidally, this species is found in sandy mud, but subtidally it is often in thick, stiff mud. It digs a permanent burrow in which it can move rather freely up and down. Its range is from British Columbia to Baja California. *Solen rosaceus,* not likely to be found north of Point Conception, is similar, but its shell is straight. In *Tagelus californianus,* which is fairly common in southern California but scarce north of Monterey, the shell is less slender than it is in the solens, and the hinge is close to the middle.

The ribbed horse mussel, *Geukensia demissa* (fig. 307), is an Atlantic species that was first noted in San Francisco Bay in 1894. It was probably brought in with oysters. It is now extremely abundant, and it has also become established in Los Angeles Harbor and Newport Bay. Like other mussels, it secretes byssus threads for attachment to firm objects—pebbles, sticks, shells, grass stems, and other individuals of its own kind. It sometimes forms huge clumps in which there are more than a hundred specimens of various sizes. This species is easy to recognize because the shell has many distinct ribs radiating away from the umbones; the ribs are most prominent on the broader posterior portion of the shell. The periostracum is dark brown. The flesh is unusual in that it is yellow. The length reaches 10 cm.

Another kind of horse mussel, *Modiolus modiolus* (pl. 17), is occasionally found intertidally in quiet bays in the Puget Sound region. It tends to form aggregates in which several to many individuals are attached to one another or to empty shells. At least some of the specimens in a cluster are likely to be partly buried in mud. In younger specimens, the periostracum is a rather warm, shiny brown and is elaborated into soft, yellowish brown hairs at the broader end of the shell. Older specimens tend to be more nearly blackish brown and to lack the hairs. This bivalve is primarily a subtidal species, and is especially common on muddy bottoms that have a substantial accumulation of shells. The length reaches 15 cm.

The Japanese oyster, *Crassostrea gigas* (fig. 308), was introduced to many areas on the Pacific coast long ago and is now so well established in some places that it looks like part of the natural fauna. It is, as oysters go, a giant: the length of very large specimens may exceed 25 cm. Normally, the left valve, which is deeper than the nearly flat right valve fitting into it, is partly or almost completely cemented to a hard substratum. Since this species tends to settle on shells of its own kind, sizable clumps are sometimes built up. The shells are often grotesquely twisted and deformed, and no two specimens are quite alike. The fluting of the external surface is almost always prominent.

When summer water temperatures are favorable for spawning and normal development of larvae, the Japanese oyster reproduces naturally. Many commercial growers, however, periodically restock their beds in spring by importing young oysters ("spat") that have settled on empty shells ("cultch"). These shells, on arrival, are strung out from racks or floats in suitable situations, usually muddy tidal flats. In some places, conditions are not regularly favorable for both spawning and normal development of young, so annual importations of spat are essential to insure future crops. The Japanese oyster will tolerate a salinity considerably lower than that of normal sea water, so it grows well in estuaries.

To those who take oysters seriously, the Japanese oyster just about has to be fried, stewed, or worked into a casserole dish to make it acceptable. It is generally concluded, even by those who put on no airs, that it is far from being the equal of the European oyster or Atlantic oyster when eaten raw. Neither of these much-esteemed species has been coaxed into really successful cultivation on the Pacific coast, though both have been introduced, and small colonies of the Atlantic oyster (*Crassostrea virginica*) seem to be reproducing in some estuarine situations in our area. The shell of the Atlantic oyster rarely exceeds a length of about 10 cm and is relatively smooth; it is marked by concentric lines, which do not become fluted. A distinctive characteristic of the species is a dark blue blotch found on both valves at the point where the adductor muscle is attached.

Our native oyster, *Ostrea lurida* (fig. 309), fulfills most of the taste requirements of learned sophisticates. Unfortunately, although it is widely distributed in our region, and along the Pacific Coast in general, it is not often found in abundance. It is common on loose boulders in some parts of San Francisco Bay, but would-be gatherers of it seem to be discouraged by pollution. Moderately successful cultivation of this species is at the basis of a rather esoteric industry, and it yields an expensive delicacy. The native oyster lives on the undersides of rocks, except in muddy places, where it will usually be on the upper sides of rocks. It is small, the length rarely exceeding 5 cm. The shell may be gnarled and eroded, but it does not often show flutings like those on the Japanese oyster. Externally, it is grayish, and internally it is usually a shiny grayish green or grayish olive color, with a touch of mother-of-pearl.

Snails

Nearly all of the common snails found on mudflats and in oyster beds have been introduced from the Atlantic coast or from Japan. The first

302. *Saxidomus giganteus,* the butter clam

303. *Saxidomus nuttalli*

304. *Mercenaria mercenaria,* the quahog

305. *Mya arenaria,* the soft-shell clam

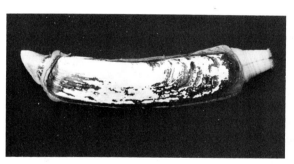

306. *Solen sicarius,* a jackknife clam

307. *Geukensia demissa,*
the ribbed horse mussel

309. *Ostrea lurida,* an oyster
native to the Pacific coast

308. *Crassostrea gigas,*
the Japanese oyster

two that will be discussed are a menace as far as oyster growers are concerned. *Urosalpinx cinerea,* the oyster drill (fig. 310), is now established in Tomales Bay, Willapa Bay, and a number of other places where culture of the Atlantic oyster has been attempted in the past. It is perfectly content to bore holes in the less delectable but more adaptable Pacific oyster that was brought from the Orient. It also feeds on barnacles. The shell of *Urosalpinx* resembles that of a rocky-shore *Nucella* or *Ocenebra.* It has fairly strong axial ribs as well as finer spiral ridges. The color is usually gray, and the inside of the aperture is stained with purple. Large specimens are about 2 cm high. The oyster drill is found only in bays, and is not likely to be seen in winter, when it buries itself in mud.

Ceratostoma inornatum (Ocenebra japonica), the Japanese oyster borer (fig. 311), was introduced with the Pacific oyster. It is now moderately common in parts of Tomales Bay and Willapa Bay. It is rather similar to *Ceratostoma foliatum* of rocky shores, but smaller (up to about 3 cm high) and less conspicuously ornamented. Its mode of feeding, by drilling a hole in an oyster and then sucking out the soft tissue, is like that of *Urosalpinx.*

Two common species of slipper shells, which feed by filtering diatoms and other microscopic particles from sea water, were brought in with the Atlantic oyster. *Crepidula convexa* (fig. 312) is now abundant in San Francisco Bay and Tomales Bay. It can be found on *Mytilus edulis* and shells of *Ilyanassa obsoleta* that are occupied by hermit crabs, as well as on oysters. The shell of *C. convexa,* which is more elevated than that of the two common native species found on rocks on the open coast (see Chapter 5), is generally pale, translucent brown, with reddish brown streaks and spots. Large specimens are about 2 cm long.

Crepidula fornicata (fig. 313) also has a markedly convex shell, the apex of which is sharply turned to one side and fused to the margin. The color is generally a dull, leaden gray, but sometimes there are brownish markings. Large specimens may reach a length of 4 cm. The species name *fornicata* alludes to the fact that this *Crepidula* tends to settle on shells of other members of the species, forming an asymmetrical pile in which the bottom specimen, originally a male, is now a female, and in which the other individuals are in various stages of changing their sex from male to female. *Crepidula fornicata* is abundant in some parts of Puget Sound and Willapa Bay, and should be expected elsewhere, too.

Cerithidea californica, the California horn shell (fig. 314), found on mudflats from Marin County to Baja California, is a native. The number of individuals one can see is sometimes almost unbelievable. Bolinas Lagoon, in Marin County, is one of the places where there is always a huge population. This snail feeds on diatoms and other components of the film of organic matter that coats the mud. The shell of *Cerithidea* is slate colored or brownish gray. It reaches a height of about

310. *Urosalpinx cinerea,* the oyster drill

311. *Ceratostoma inornatum,*
the Japanese oyster borer

312. *Crepidula convexa*

313. *Crepidula fornicata*

314. *Cerithidea californica,*
the California horn shell

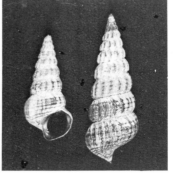

315. *Batillaria attramentaria*

316. *Ilyanassa obsoleta*

317. *Nassarius fraterculus*

3 cm and may have up to ten turns. There are axial ribs as well as spiral ridges, but sometimes the sculpturing is faint.

Batillaria attramentaria (fig. 315), introduced from Japan, is similar to *Cerithidea* in size, appearance, and habits. It is common in some muddy bays in California and in the Northwest. It has neat spiral ridges, but lacks axial ribs. The apertures are also different. The "spout" is more prominent in *Batillaria* than it is in *Cerithidea*, and it is directed outward nearly at a right angle to the long axis of the shell.

Ilyanassa obsoleta (fig. 316) is probably the least attractive snail dealt with in this book. Its shell, up to about 2.5 cm high, is often badly proportioned because the upper part of the spire is missing, and the blackish brown periostracum is usually cracked. The greenish color of some specimens is due to a microscopic alga that is concentrated in the periostracum. This snail is a close relative of the species of *Nassarius* that are occasionally found on sandy flats, and that were mentioned earlier in this chapter. It is, in fact, placed in *Nassarius* by some specialists. It was introduced from the Atlantic coast, and is now especially abundant in San Francisco Bay and in Willapa Bay. *Ilyanassa* is a deposit feeder that skims organic material from the surface of the mud through which it plows. Wherever it occurs, one will also see its egg clusters attached to sticks and stones.

Nassarius fraterculus (fig. 317), introduced from Japan, occurs on a few muddy beaches near Anacortes, Washington, and may soon turn up elsewhere in the Puget Sound region. It is up to 1.3 cm high—thus smaller than *N. fossatus* (fig. 286) and *N. mendicus* (fig. 287), which usually live in relatively clean sand. The axial ribs are strong, but the spiral lines are scarcely apparent.

Burrowing Crustaceans

The ghost shrimp, *Callianassa californiensis* (pl. 19), burrows in very muddy sand with enough clay and organic matter to make the substratum reasonably cohesive and to provide the animal with material for lining its tunnels. The appearance of *Callianassa* is indeed ghostly, but the delicate coloration—waxy pale pink and orange—is beautiful. Out of water, the animals are flabby and helpless, and it is unfortunately nearly impossible to dig for them without damaging some specimens in the process. Normally, however, they are rarely exposed to predators, and the largest specimens, with a body size of about 10 cm exclusive of the appendages, are probably at least ten years old.

Callianassa burrows by means of the chelate first and second legs, which loosen the substratum and pull it backward. A pushing movement of the third legs, aided by a raking activity of the mouth parts, causes accumulation of the material in a sort of receptacle formed by the last pair of mouth parts (third maxillipeds). The animal then crawls backward, reverses itself in a special turnaround chamber, and moves to the mouth of the burrow to dump its load. Eventually the burrow will have a number of branches and turnaround chambers, with at least two openings to the surface, which provide for some circulation of sea water through the system of tunnels. The openings to *Callianassa* burrows are typically in the middle of little piles of sand or of sand mixed with small pebbles (fig. 318).

The ghost shrimp obtains much of its food from detritus in the mud that it handles. It collects the very fine particles on the hairs on its legs, allowing the coarser material to fall through. The hairs on the third maxillipeds scrape the prospective food off the legs and pass it to the forward mouth parts, which then deliver it to the mouth. When the burrow is under water at high tide, *Callianassa* fans water through the tunnel it happens to be in by means of its leaflike abdominal appendages (pleopods). When the tide is out, the animal is believed to slow down all of its activities.

The burrows of *Callianassa* are populated by a wide variety of organisms that profit in one way or another by their association with the ghost shrimp. There are small pea crabs (mostly of one species, but as many as three species are reported); a scaleworm, *Hesperonoe complanata;* and a small clam, *Cryptomya californica* (fig. 319), whose siphons open into the burrow instead of to the surface. Most interesting of the animals loosely associated with *Callianassa* is the little goby, *Clevelandia ios* (fig. 320). This fish is not restricted to burrows, and is occasionally observed in pools in the same general area, but it is nevertheless rather regularly found with *Callianassa.*

Living under the carapace of *Callianassa* is a reddish copepod, *Clausidium vancouverense.* It is only about 2 mm long, but it can easily be seen through the translucent portion of the carapace that covers the gills. A related species, *Hemicyclops thysanotus,* may also be present. If the carapace in the gill region is bulging, this is a sign that there is a parasitic isopod, *Ione cornuta,* underneath. The fat, asymmetrical female, up to about 2 cm long, is accompanied by a small, slender male.

The blue mud shrimp, *Upogebia pugettensis* (fig. 321), generally lives where the substratum is even muddier than that occupied by *Callianassa,* but the two species are often found together. *Upogebia* is much more hairy than *Callianassa,* and its coloration is a mixture of gray, brown, and bluish tones. It makes burrows similar to those of *Callianassa,* but usually does not heap up sand around the openings. Like *Callianassa,* it uses its pleopods (swimmerets) to fan water through its tunnels, feeding on detritus that it thus strains out.

Upogebia is frequently parasitized by an isopod, *Phyllodurus abdominalis.* The female, attached to the pleopods, is about 1 cm long, and is accompanied by a much smaller male. The copepods *Clausidium* and *Hemicyclops* are less often noted on *Upogebia* than on *Callianassa.* An interesting commensal clam, *Orobitella rugifera* (fig. 322), is attached to the anterior part of the underside of the abdomen of some specimens; it secretes a byssus, something like that of mussels, to moor itself tightly

318. Opening of a burrow of *Callianassa californiensis* at the surface of muddy sand

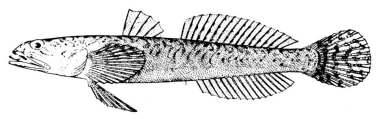

319. *Cryptomya californica*   **320.** *Clevelandia ios*

321. *Upogebia pugettensis,* the blue mud shrimp

322. *Orobitella rugifera,* a small clam that lives attached to the underside of the abdomen of *Upogebia*

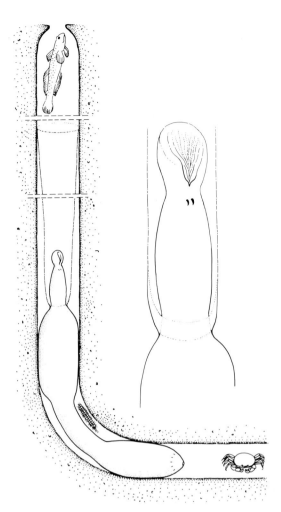

323. *Urechis caupo,* the innkeeper, and some of the animals associated with it

to its host. It benefits from its relationship with *Upogebia* by enjoying the protection of a burrow while having access to currents of water containing the sort of microscopic food it requires.

An Echiuran

The phylum Echiura consists of stout, generally sausage-shaped worms. They are not segmented, and they have a broad, nonretractable proboscis. This is used for collecting detritus and other microscopic food, or for secreting a mucous net in which food particles are trapped. The only species likely to be found intertidally in the region covered by this book is the "innkeeper," *Urechis caupo* (fig. 323). It occurs in Humboldt Bay, Bodega Bay, Tomales Bay, and a few other California localities where there are flats of muddy sand. When contracted, this remarkable animal is shaped like a frankfurter, so some call it the "weenie worm." The length of a large specimen may exceed 30 cm, and the color is usually pale pink. The proboscis is a tonguelike flap, and the mouth is located at its base. *Urechis* occupies a burrow that is approximately U-shaped. The openings are generally about 40 to 80 cm apart.

Urechis fits rather snugly in the tunnel it has made for itself, but it can move forward or backward by contracting and relaxing muscles of its body wall. Rhythmic contractions of this type also serve to create a current of water moving through the burrow, as long as the sand flat is covered by the tide. This current is needed not only to bring in oxygen and carry away wastes, but also to deliver food particles. The worm's method of trapping the food is remarkable. From glands on its proboscis, it secretes some mucus and sticks this to the wall of the burrow. As it backs down deeper, it continues to secrete mucus, so that a funnel of mucus is formed. This funnel is actually a net with openings so fine that bacteria and even smaller particles are trapped. After the net has become clogged, the animal moves upward and swallows it. Some larger particles are rejected, but the bacteria and most of the other fine organic particles are taken into the gut. The animal of course also gets back its own mucus and can recycle this.

Urechis is called the "innkeeper" because its burrow is home for a variety of other animals. The little fish *Clevelandia ios* (fig. 320), the scaleworm *Hesperonoe adventor,* and two species of small pea crabs, *Pinnixa franciscana* and *Scleroplax granulata,* are free in the burrow. The little clam *Cryptomya californica* (fig. 319) lives in the sand off to one side, but its siphons open into the burrow and it collects food from the water current created by its host. *Clevelandia, Pinnixa, Scleroplax,* and *Cryptomya* also live in association with the mud shrimp and ghost shrimp, discussed above. The *Hesperonoe* found with these crustaceans, however, is a different species.

A Sea Anemone

The sea anemone *Anthopleura artemisia* (pl. 4), when found in muddy sand, is attached to a buried shell, pebble, or substantial rock. This is a fairly large species, and its column may have to stretch to a length of 15 or 20 cm to bring the oral disk and tentacles to the surface. When the crown of tentacles is fully expanded, it may be more than 5 cm in diameter. The column is warty, as in *A. elegantissima* and *A. xanthogrammica* of rocky shores, but the warts are limited to the upper two-thirds. The prevailing coloration is usually white or pale pink, although there is dark gray on the upper third of the column, and sometimes the tentacles are bright pink, orange, green, or blue. This anemone also occurs on rocky shores, where it is likely to be in pools in which the bottom is covered by sand or gravel, or in holes made by boring clams. *Anthopleura artemisia,* like *A. elegantissima* and *A. xan-*

thogrammica, has symbiotic algae in its tissues, but these are limited to the upper portion of the animal, which can be exposed to light.

Polychaete Annelids

Where the substratum consists of rather hard-packed, muddy sand, there will usually be some brittle, sandy tubes, about 3 mm in diameter, sticking up. If dug out carefully, down to a depth of at least 15 cm, and then picked away, the worms that make the tubes may still be intact. They will probably turn out to be bamboo worms, *Axiothella rubrocincta* (pl. 8), which are polychaete annelids belonging to the family Maldanidae. The maldanids as a group are characterized by having segments that are much longer than wide; moreover, the areas where segments join one another tend to be somewhat swollen. *Axiothella* does indeed resemble a cane of bamboo, prettily banded with dull red. The anterior end, which looks as if it had been sliced off obliquely, is directed downward in the tube; the posterior end, elaborated into a fringed funnel, effectively plugs the tube below the opening. This species, like most maldanids, swallows detritus and small sand grains that are coated with nourishing organic material.

Wherever there is *Axiothella*, there is also likely to be *Owenia fusiformis* (fig. 324). The tube of this polychaete, though composed of sand grains and bits of shell, is flexible. It reaches a length of 10 cm, tapers at both ends, and does not ordinarily project noticeably above the surface. The worm itself is about 5 cm long, and is slightly similar to *Axiothella* in that some of its segments are much elongated. In *Owenia*, however, the mouth is surrounded by six lobes, each of which is further divided into stubby tentacles. Much of the anterior portion of the worm is a lovely pale green color. By extending its tentacular crown from its tube, *Owenia* can collect fine particles of food and direct these to the mouth along ciliated tracts. It can also bend down and touch the sediment, picking up detritus on a pair of lips that are next to the mouth.

Pista pacifica (fig. 325), a large terebellid found from British Columbia to southern California, makes a sandy tube that is buried vertically. Above the surface of the substratum, the tube flares out into a fringed, hoodlike structure. When the tide is in, the worm spreads its grooved, ciliated tentacles over the sand to collect microscopic food particles. Large specimens of *Pista* reach a length of more than 30 cm.

If you find an exposed tube that is about 8 mm in diameter, parchment-like, and coated with fine sand grains, it almost certainly belongs to *Mesochaetopterus taylori*, a polychaete of the family Chaetopteridae. The range of this species extends from British Columbia to Tomales Bay, California. The tube usually sticks up out of the sand for 3 or 4 cm, and tapers a little toward the opening (fig. 326). The worm itself reaches a length of about 30 cm. If it happens to be in the upper part of its tube, a quick stab with a shovel may get a substantial piece of it. Trying to get an entire tube, with the worm still intact, is nearly futile, because the tube goes straight down to a depth of 1.5 or 2 m. The deeper one digs, the tougher the digging gets, because watery sand keeps filling up the bottom of the hole.

The body of *Mesochaetopterus* and its relatives consists of three main regions. The anterior portion bears a pair of prominent palps, and sometimes also a pair of shorter tentacles; the middle portion has a few large, fanlike flaps, which are modified parapodia used for circulating water, and it is also the region where much mucus is secreted for trapping microscopic food particles; the hind portion is longer and a little more slender than the more anterior regions. Much of what we know about chaetopterids has been learned from *Chaetopterus variopedatus*, found in Europe and Asia and on the Atlantic coast of North America, as well as along much of the Pacific coast from Monterey south. *Chaetopterus* builds a U-shaped tube, and the flaps on its midbody region move water in a backward direction past the worm. Thus one opening of the tube is inhalant, the other exhalant. One pair of flaps is specialized for secreting mucus for a net that collects food as water goes through it. After the net has become clogged, it is rolled up by the action of cilia that line a little dorsal cup. When the ball of mucus mixed with food reaches a diameter of about 1 or 2 mm, the animal temporarily stops pumping water and ceases to secrete mucus for the net. During the interlude, it moves the ball forward along a ciliated dorsal groove until it reaches the anterior end and can be taken into the mouth. Then the pumping of water and secretion of mucus are resumed. A single cycle of collecting food and passing it to the mouth lasts about 20 or 30 minutes.

Because *Mesochaetopterus* makes a long vertical tube with only one opening at the surface, the worm must pump water forward as well as backward. It appears, moreover, to secrete two mucous nets, at least part of the time. The palps, much longer than those of *Chaetopterus*, collect some food, and are also concerned with rejecting unsuitable particles.

Spiochaetopterus costarum (fig. 327), another chaetopterid, may be found in the relatively clean sand where *Mesochaetopterus* typically occurs, but it is sometimes common in places where there is considerable mud or gravel, or both. This is a widely distributed species, found in Asia and Europe and on both the Atlantic and Pacific coasts of North America, as well as in other areas. Although common in appropriate situations in British Columbia, it is scarce in Oregon and seems not to have been reported from California. Its shiny, gray tubes are about 2 mm in diameter. They project above the sand for 1 or 2 cm, but they go down to a depth of 20 or 30 cm, sometimes more. They are distinctive in that they have regularly-spaced, ringlike thickenings. The animal itself is about 10 cm long, but in some parts of the world specimens 50 or 60 cm long have been reported. Like *Mesochaetopterus,* this chaetopterid has long palps.

Tube-inhabiting polychaetes of the family Spionidae are abundant in sandflats and mudflats, and some are found on wave-swept sandy beaches. These worms, mostly under 2 cm long, have two long palps, and in this respect they resemble chaetopterids; their bodies are not organized into three distinct regions, however. The identification of the several genera and numerous species found on the Pacific coast requires careful attention to microscopic details. A typical spionid, removed from its tube, is illustrated in Plate 9.

Cirriformia spirabrancha (pl. 8), a member of the family Cirratulidae, is sometimes so abundant that there are more than a thousand individuals per square meter. Its body, up to about 10 cm long and generally yellowish green, is permanently buried, but the many filaments characteristic of the worm are extended so that they spread over the substratum. The filaments are of two types. The reddish ones, which arise on most segments, are gills. The others, dark green in color and appreciably thicker than the gills, originate on a few segments close to the anterior end; they are grooved and are concerned with collecting microscopic food, thus serving the same function as the anterior tentacles of a terebellid polychaete. This species is limited to California and Baja California. Particularly impressive beds of it are found on the clam flats of Tomales Bay and Bodega Bay. It is an important part of the diet of several shorebirds. A related species, *C. luxuriosa,* with reddish orange feeding tentacles, is abundant on rocky shores, where it lives mostly in sand-filled crevices and among the roots of surfgrass.

Almost every quiet bay, from Humboldt Bay northward, has an extensive area near its inner margins where the muddy sand is ornamented by coiled fecal castings (fig. 328), which look as if they have been squeezed out of a cake decorator. These are produced by the lugworm, *Abarenicola pacifica* (pl. 8). If you observe a group of castings for a while, you may see one of them suddenly get longer.

Lugworms belong to a family of polychaete annelids called the Arenicolidae. They excavate J-shaped burrows and are oriented with their posterior ends close to the surface, so that ejection of the fecal castings is simplified. Lugworms swallow sand and mud, which adhere to mucus secreted on the proboscis. When the proboscis is inverted, the material sticking to it is pulled into the digestive system. As the mud passes through the gut, at least much of the usable organic detritus is digested. Lugworms often reach a high population density—perhaps fifty per square meter—and play an important role in turnover of organic matter in mudflats.

When a lugworm is first dug out, it may not appear to be a particularly attractive animal. Its general coloration is a rather unpleasing mixture of yellow, green, and brown; however, after it has been washed off and placed in a dish of clean sea water for examination, it becomes more interesting. From its thicker anterior portion arise several pairs of branched gills. These are supplied with blood vessels, and the hemoglobin in the blood makes the expanded gills a very beautiful bright red. Lugworms irrigate their burrows, to bring in fresh sea water with sufficient oxygen for respiratory activities, by pulsating movements of the body.

Another lugworm in the northern sector is *Abarenicola claparedi*, which tends to be restricted to rather clean sand and is thus generally found near the mouths of bays and in sandy coves. The situation is further complicated by the fact that specimens of *A. claparedi* in bays and those in coves where there is at least a little wave action belong to slightly different subspecies; these are called, respectively, *A. claparedi vagabunda* and *A. claparedi oceanica*.

A lugworm found in California from Humboldt Bay southward is *Arenicola cristata*. It has sixteen to eighteen pairs of gills, whereas neither of the two species of *Abarenicola* discussed above is likely to have more than thirteen pairs. Its fecal material, moreover, spreads out in small sheets, instead of cohering in coiled castings. In San Francisco Bay there are a few localities where *Arenicola brasiliensis* is abundant. This widely distributed species, found mostly in warmer parts of the world, does produce coiled castings, but it has only eleven pairs of gills.

There are so many borrowing polychaetes in muddy sand that it would be best to concentrate on those that are relatively large or at least long enough to be easily noticed. Almost always present in muddy sand and mud are *Lumbrineris*, *Notomastus*, and *Hemipodus*. The several species of *Lumbrineris* (family Lumbrineridae) (fig. 329) in the region superficially resemble very slender earthworms, not only because of their general size (length up to about 15 cm) but also because the head region is unadorned by tentacles. The parapodia—the flaps of tissue on either side of each segment, on which the bristles are borne— are small compared with those of most polychaetes, but the bristles themselves are fairly large. The jaws are specialized for tearing algae. The beauty of a *Lumbrineris* will probably not become apparent unless the worm is examined in bright light and with the help of a magnifier: the iridescence of its surface, rich in luminous blue and green tones, changes constantly as the worm crawls and bends.

The most common obvious worm in many muddy situations is *Notomastus tenuis* (pl. 8), a member of the family Capitellidae. When it is really abundant, as is evident from the presence of numerous fine, blackish fecal castings at the surface, a shovelful of mud may contain a hundred. Most of them will be broken, for *Notomastus* is so slender (about 20 cm long and only about 1 mm wide when extended) that it does not stand the strain of being stretched. *Notomastus* is much like *Lumbrineris* in having rather small parapodia and no tentacles of any kind on the head. Its prostomium (the first segment), however, has

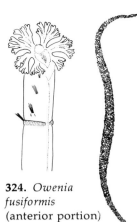

324. *Owenia fusiformis* (anterior portion) and its tube

325. The exposed portion of the tube of *Pista pacifica*

326. The exposed portion of the tube of *Meso-chaetopterus taylori*

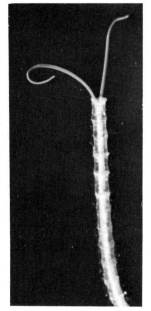

327. *Spiochaetopterus costarum*

328. Fecal castings of a lugworm, *Abarenicola pacifica*

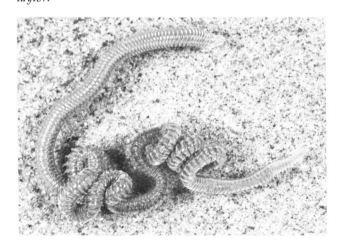

329. *Lumbrineris*

two patches of little blackish eyespots. It feeds by ingesting sediment.

Hemipodus borealis (pl. 8) measures up to about 8 cm long. Its color is usually a slightly purplish red. The prostomium is long and pointed, with four tiny tentacles at its tip. Periodically, *Hemipodus* will evert its large, club-shaped proboscis, which has four hooklike black jaws. Polychaetes with this general type of prostomium and proboscis belong to the family Glyceridae, of which we have a number of species, all apparently carnivores. Most of our glycerids that are larger than *Hemipodus* are in the genus *Glycera*. Some of them may be expected along with *Hemipodus* in mudflats, or in sandy or gravelly habitats.

Tongue Worms

Tongue worms, or enteropneusts, belong to the small phylum Hemichordata. Their bodies are not segmented, but they are divided into three regions. The anterior portion looks like a tongue or an acorn. The next part forms a kind of collar, and the mouth is located on the ventral surface just in front of this. The last part is proportionately long and generally so fragile that it breaks while the worm is being separated from the mud.

The tongue is used in burrowing; it also produces mucus that traps small particles of food and sand grains that are coated with organic matter. This material is moved to the mouth by the action of cilia and perhaps also by muscular undulations. In the course of feeding, considerable water is taken into the gut, too, but much of it is eliminated through the numerous pores, generally called gill slits, located on both sides of the body behind the collar. The food is therefore concentrated to some extent before it gets into the part of the gut where most of the digestion takes place.

Tongue worms live in more or less permanent U-shaped or J-shaped burrows. Periodically they discharge coiled fecal castings that resemble those of lugworms, although they are usually more slender. The mucus exuded by these animals contains a pungent compound of bromine that may cling to one's skin for several hours or longer. The odor is not disagreeable, however, and some of us zoologists, who do not often get to see tongue worms, like it because it reminds us of a pleasant field experience.

The tongue worms of the Pacific coast are poorly known. The ones likely to be found intertidally within the range covered by this book belong to the genus *Saccoglossus*, but they have not been given species names. Most of them are about 15 or 20 cm long. There are great concentrations of one species (fig. 330) in sandy mud in parts of Willapa Bay, at tide levels of about +1.0 foot (0.3 meter) and lower. In some places there may be more than 150 burrows per square meter. Chuckanut Bay, not far south of Bellingham, and the northernmost of the three small bays of Cape Arago, Oregon, are other localities where

Saccoglossus (not necessarily the same species as that in Willapa Bay) can be found.

Phoronids

Members of the small phylum Phoronida superficially resemble sabellid polychaetes, partly because of their general form and partly because they secrete parchmentlike tubes in which sand grains and other foreign particles are usually embedded. The tentacles of phoronids, however, are unbranched and are arranged in a double row, in the pattern of a horseshoe whose free ends are spirally coiled. Collectively, the tentacles constitute what is called the lophophore. They function in a type of ciliary-mucous feeding similar to that practiced by sabellids and serpulids. Small food particles trapped in a film of mucus on the tentacles are moved by the action of cilia down to a groove between the two rows and then toward the mouth. The digestive tract of a phoronid is U-shaped, so that the anus is at the same end as the mouth, though it is situated on a little papilla outside the lophophore.

In our region, there are two species of phoronids that live in muddy sand or muddy gravel. Neither is apt to be found in situations where the salinity is significantly lower than that of full-strength sea water. *Phoronopsis viridis* (pl. 24), with pale green tentacles, is extremely abundant in a few bays in California. Its habitat is muddy sand, and where conditions are to its liking, it has a rather wide vertical range: from about +3.0 feet to below the level reached by the lowest tides. In parts of Tomales Bay, *P. viridis* is so crowded that the tentacular crowns of neighboring individuals, each spread out to a diameter of about 8 mm, nearly touch one another. When the tide is out, specimens in shallow pools may keep their lophophores expanded after the tide has gone out, unless the sunshine becomes too bright. Even after the worms have withdrawn, their presence can be detected by the fecal castings on the sand (fig. 331). The tubes go straight down to a depth of about 10 cm, and are rather brittle. They consist mostly of sand grains that have been cemented together. If *P. viridis* is removed from its tube, one can see a few of the more prominent blood vessels. They show up well because the blood contains hemoglobin, and is therefore red. The hemoglobin, incidentally, is in corpuscles, just as it is in the blood of vertebrate animals.

In the Northwest, at least as far south as Coos Bay, the place of *P. viridis* is taken by *P. harmeri*. This species is not often found in huge numbers, but it seems to tolerate more varied conditions than does *P. viridis*. There are places in Puget Sound, for instance, where it grows in mixtures of mud, coarse sand, and gravel. When this is the case, its tubes tend to grow crooked, and they may have grains 3 or 4 mm in diameter adhering to them. *Phoronopsis harmeri* is about the same size as *P. viridis*, but its tentacles are whitish.

Algae

Muddy sand is generally coated by a rich variety of diatoms, especially during the summer months. Patches of olive-brown scum consist primarily of these organisms, which provide food for many of the invertebrates that inhabit sheltered bays.

The larger algae—mostly green and red types—are also important sources of food for microorganisms and for herbivores, especially certain polychaetes, amphipods, and crabs. Among green algae, *Ulva fenestrata* (pl. 32) is likely to be common. It is often attached to shells, pebbles, rocks, or pieces of wood, and it probably always starts out this way. In quiet bays, however, it may float around, except when it has been left behind by a receding tide. Floating specimens, in fact, tend to grow larger than those that are attached; the blades sometimes reach a length of 1 m, and they are often extensively perforated, particularly from Oregon northward. The species name, *fenestrata*, alludes to the holes, or "windows," in the blades.

Enteromorpha linza (fig. 69) was discussed in Chapter 3, for it is common on floats. On muddy sand or muddy gravel, however, its growths are much larger than they are on floats, and they may be tubular only at the base, where they are attached to a shell, pebble, or some other firm object. Some specimens reach a length of 30 or 40 cm, although they are not likely to be more than 10 cm wide. They may be twisted and ruffled, but are not normally perforated.

One or more other species of *Enteromorpha* may contribute to green mats in protected bays. Most of them are tubular for a major portion of their length, if not throughout. *Enteromorpha flexuosa, E. prolifera,* and *E. clathrata* are the ones most likely to be encountered. Of these, the last two are typically branched. The distinctions between most species of *Enteromorpha* and *Ulva,* as well as of the closely related genera *Ulvaria, Blidingia, Monostroma,* and *Kornmannia,* require microscopic study, and should be sought in specialized treatises. The fact that experts keep changing their minds about their determinations tells us that the taxonomy of these algae is not stable. It is not the fault of the algae; we simply do not know enough about them.

Several smaller green algae are found in shallow pools and lagoons at higher tide levels. To identify them, one will need a microscope. *Percursaria percursa* (fig. 332) is perhaps the most easily recognized because its filaments, which are about 20 micrometers (0.02 mm) wide, consist of a double row of cells. The color is pale green. The filaments of *Rhizoclonium implexum* (fig. 333) are about the same thickness as those of *Percursaria* and consist of a single row of cells, most of which are about two to three times as long as wide. The color is yellowish green. *Chaetomorpha aerea* (pl. 32) has much thicker filaments than either of the foregoing species. They are usually 300 to 400 micrometers (0.3 to 0.4 mm) in diameter. The individual cells, arranged in a single row, are mostly just a little longer than wide, and they tend to

330. A tongue worm, *Saccoglossus* (a part of the fragile hind portion is missing), and the fecal castings made by this species in Willapa Bay

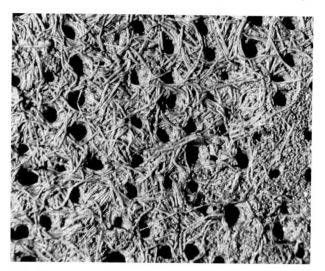

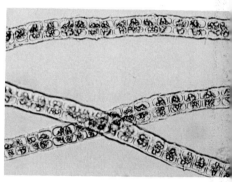

332. *Percursaria percursa;* photomicrograph

331. Fecal castings of *Phoronopsis viridis*

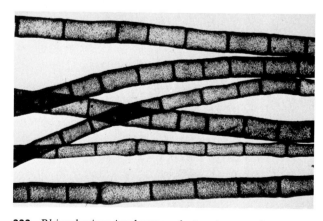

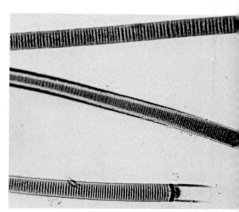

333. *Rhizoclonium implexum;* photomicrograph

334. *Lyngbya aestuarii,* a blue-green alga; photomicrograph

bulge in the middle. This alga, when abundant, sometimes looks like excelsior that has been soaked in a greenish dye.

In shallow pools where there are *Enteromorpha* and filamentous green algae such as *Chaetomorpha*, one may find a small sacoglossan sea slug, *Aplysiopsis smithi* (pl. 32). Like the sacoglossans described in connection with *Codium* (see Chapter 4), this species slits open algal cells with the single large tooth of its specialized radula, then sucks out the protoplasm. There are numerous dorsal cerata. The color pattern consists of greenish or blackish brown blotches on a pale yellow background. The length of a large specimen is about 2 cm.

Vaucheria (pls. 32 and 40), which forms nearly black, feltlike mats, belongs to a separate group called the yellow-green algae. It will be discussed later in this chapter in connection with salt marshes, where it is almost invariably present. It often occurs, however, at high-tide levels on flats of mud or muddy sand, especially where there is a seepage or runoff of fresh water.

The most common red alga on mudflats and sand flats, other than *Smithora*, which grows on eelgrass leaves, is *Polysiphonia* (fig. 78). There are several species, all of them delicate and finely branched. One should not be too casual about identifying even the genus without looking at the plant with a low-power microscope. The distinctive features of *Polysiphonia* were described in Chapter 3. In bays, it is common to see tufts of one species or another attached to pebbles or waterlogged sticks embedded in mud or muddy sand, and also on tips of the siphons of gaper clams of the genus *Tresus*.

Blue-green algae are apt to be present in shallow pools and lagoons where the salinity is reduced by an influx of fresh water. If abundant enough to form an obvious coating on the substratum, this growth is apt to be nearly black and to cohere, and it may have a nearly gelatinous texture. Large pieces are likely to become detached and float up to the surface. These generally turn yellow or brown in time. *Lyngbya aestuarii* (fig. 334; pl. 39), common in some places in the Puget Sound region and Coos Bay, has filaments about 10 micrometers (0.01 mm) thick. This is large for a blue-green alga.

THE SURFACE SEDIMENT ON MUDDY SAND AND MUD

In areas where a substratum of muddy sand or mud has an oozelike superficial layer and is covered by patches of *Ulva* and *Enteromorpha* (these algae tend to die back in winter), there is usually a characteristic assemblage of organisms. Crawling on the surface, unless forced by bright sunlight to retreat, is the nemertean *Paranemertes peregrina* (fig. 335). A large specimen, fully extended, may be more than 15 cm long.

The upper surface is uniformly dark brownish purple, relieved only by a narrow white border around the anterior part of the head region; the underside is pale yellow. The body of *Paranemertes* is soft, but it is at the same time highly muscularized, so the worm is capable of lengthening and shortening itself to an amazing extent. Its locomotion is accomplished in part by muscular activity, and in part by the beating of cilia which cover the body. *Paranemertes* feeds on several species of small and medium-sized polychaetes, but its favorite food seems to be *Platynereis bicanaliculata*, which is only about 2 cm long. *Platynereis* builds little tubes on *Ulva*, using bits of the alga in construction of the tubes; it also feeds on the *Ulva*.

As *Paranemertes* glides along on its track of slime, it evidently cannot recognize prey from any distance. However, when it bumps into *Platyneresis* or another suitable prey organism, it recoils for a moment, then everts its large, whitish proboscis, which is provided with a sharp stylet and venom-producing glands. The prey soon becomes quiet, and *Paranemertes* then proceeds to swallow it whole. *Paranemertes* can find its way back to its burrow by following its own slime trail. The burrow is probably not permanent, and it cannot be dug out intact.

In this habitat there will almost always be a polychaete, about 2 cm long, that swims or scurries by undulating, then rests. This is *Ophiodromus pugettensis* (fig. 336), the only member of the family Hesionidae that is common in our region. The tip of its tail generally bears a white mark of some sort, but its color is otherwise a rich dark brown. *Ophiodromus* is not always free-living. It is sometimes commensal with other invertebrates, especially the bat star, *Patiria miniata*. This sea star is abundant on rocky shores in central and northern California, and in some places on the open outer coast of Vancouver Island, but it is either absent or exceedingly rare on the coasts of Washington and Oregon.

In the same general habitat, especially if the pebbles are rather numerous, one of the more common polychaete annelids is *Eupolymnia heterobranchia* (fig. 337). It is similar in size and appearance to *Thelepus crispus* (fig. 169), but its color is dark brown or greenish brown. Like other members of the family Terebellidae, it is characterized by numerous extensile tentacles originating from the anterior end. *Eupolymnia* resides in a parchmentlike tube and extends its tentacles through and over the surface of the substratum. Each tentacle has a ciliated groove, along which food enmeshed in mucus is passed toward the mouth. The diet of *Eupolymnia* probably consists largely of detritus and diatoms, but this species is reported to scavenge on decaying polychaetes and crustaceans, and it has been observed to grab with its tentacles at living polychaetes. The little hesionid polychaete *Ophiodromus* is sometimes commensal in the tube of *Eupolymnia*.

During the spring and summer, a mollusc that looks like a flattened blackish slug may become abundant on soft mud and very muddy sand. Although it has no external shell, *Melanochlamys diomedea* (*Aglaja diomedea*) (fig. 338), which reaches a length of about 2 cm, does not belong in the same group as "true" sea slugs, or nudibranchs. Its closest intertidal relatives are the bubble shells of the genus *Haminoea* (see "Beds of Eelgrass" section). In *Melanochlamys*, as in *Haminoea*, the anterior part of the dorsal surface is set apart as a head shield. There is a shell, but this is much reduced and strictly internal. The posterior end of the mantle is drawn out into a siphonlike structure. *Melanochlamys* moves through the surface sediment by ciliary activity; mucus secreted at the anterior end of the body helps to consolidate the otherwise loose particles of the substratum and thus facilitates progression. *Melanochlamys* has neither a radula nor jaws, but it is equipped with a large, muscular pharynx that produces suction strong enough to seize prey organisms and swallow them whole. It feeds on various small animals in the sediment. The gelatinous, ovoid egg masses of *Melanochlamys* (fig. 338), attached to the substratum by a slender, short stalk, are usually more abundant than the slugs themselves.

Rictaxis punctocaelatus (fig. 339), the striped barrel snail, belongs to the same general group of gastropods as *Melanochlamys* and *Haminoea*. It has a prominent external shell, however. This is rather solid, reaches a height of about 1.5 cm, and has a distinct spire. Each of the two broad, gray bands that spiral down the whorls consists of several parallel lines. When the animal is actively plowing through the sand, a considerable part of it is extended out of the shell. It probably feeds on small polychaete annelids. This species, like *Melanochlamys*, lays eggs in gelatinous masses that are anchored in the sand. The range of *Rictaxis* extends from Alaska to Baja California, but it is not often found intertidally north of the Oregon-California border. Its populations come and go. In some seasons or in certain years, it may be rare or absent in places where it previously had been seen in large numbers.

Under algae, and especially among small stones that are impressed into the substratum, there may be numerous individuals of a small brittle star, *Amphipholis squamata* (pl. 26). This species, which reaches a diameter of only about 3 cm, has been described in Chapter 4. It feeds on diatoms and detritus and broods its young in little pockets on the disk. The young are released when they are about 2 mm in diameter.

The surface sediment covering the habitat of the animals discussed in this section contains many kinds of small organisms that cannot be appreciated without the aid of a microscope. There is almost always a nice assortment of diatoms, numerous protozoans (especially ciliates and foraminiferans), and a splendid variety of turbellarian flatworms. Some of the turbellarians are herbivores that feed primarily on diatoms, but there will also be carnivorous types whose food consists mostly of small crustaceans, such as ostracodes and harpacticoid copepods. Other crustaceans likely to be present are isopods, amphipods, cumaceans, and tanaids.

The most common intertidal tanaid deserves special mention. This is *Leptochelia dubia* (fig. 340), which is often present in enormous num-

335. *Paranemertes peregrina*

336. *Ophiodromus pugettensis*

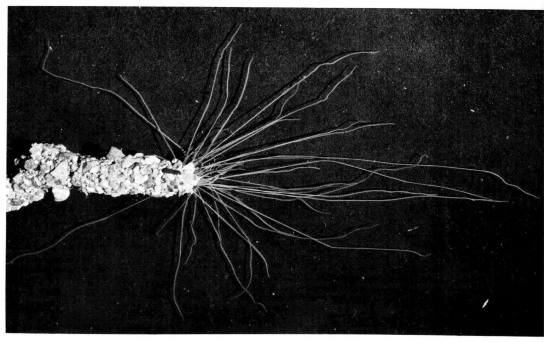

337. *Eupolymnia heterobranchia*

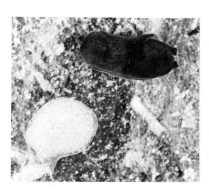

338. *Melanochlamys diomedea* and one of its egg masses

339. *Rictaxis punctocaelatus,* the striped barrel snail

341. *Nebalia pugettensis*

340. *Leptochelia dubia,* a tanaid

bers in mud, muddy sand, or muddy gravel. It looks like a slender-bodied isopod, but the first legs are pincerlike; this is one of several features that distinguishes tanaids from isopods. *Leptochelia* reaches a length of about 5 mm and is usually whitish, but it may be decidedly greenish, and some specimens are tinged with orange. Like amphipods of the genus *Corophium*, with which it may be associated, *Leptochelia* makes tubes by cementing together particles of detritus, and in this way it helps to stabilize the substratum. The food of this interesting little crusteacean consists mostly of diatoms and detritus, but it has been observed to scrape tissue from tiny sand dollars less than 0.5 mm in diameter. In males, the pincers are larger and more graceful than they are in females. There is equality among the sexes, however, in the sense that many young females in a population are likely to become transformed into males before they reach maturity.

In addition to the animals already mentioned, surface sediment generally contains tiny polychaetes and other invertebrates that will not be dealt with here. All of them are interesting—some are astonishing—but the scope of this guide includes only the more conspicuous elements of the fauna and flora. Anyone who wants to study the sediment will find it teeming with many kinds of organisms, some of which are restricted to this type of habitat.

In pools in sandy and muddy bays where seaweed and other detritus accumulate and decay, one often finds *Nebalia pugettensis* (fig. 341). It belongs to a group of crustaceans called the Leptostraca, which has only a few species in the entire world. Leptostracans are in the same general assemblage as isopods, amphipods, shrimps, and crabs, but they have some distinctive features. The carapace, which is somewhat inflated, covers the thoracic segments, but is not fused directly to them. There is an adductor muscle that enables the animal to pull the right and left flaps closer together. The head is partly covered by a little rostrum that is hinged to the carapace. The appendages of the thorax are leaflike and used for creating currents of water from which small food particles are strained out; there is a ventral groove along which the food is moved to the mouth parts.

Nebalia pugettensis, at most about 1 cm long, is silvery, sometimes with a tinge of orange. The eyes are brick red. The situations where it is plentiful generally show signs of being foul when they are stirred up. The easiest way to collect this interesting crustacean is to agitate the accumulated detritus, thereby getting some specimens to the surface where they become trapped and can be skimmed off. *Nebalia* is usually accompanied by a variety of scavenging amphipods of about the same general size.

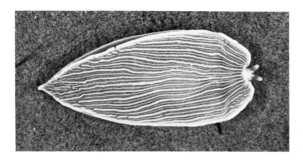

342. *Armina californica*

In Deeper Water

The sea pen, *Ptilosarcus gurneyi* (pl. 5), is almost completely subtidal, but in Puget Sound it is sometimes seen at the shore when the tide is very low. It is so frequently displayed in public aquaria that mention of it cannot be avoided. It is decidedly one of our most beautiful marine animals, and a nicely established group of fully expanded sea pens seen in nature or in a large aquarium tank is not easily forgotten. The color of *Ptilosarcus* ranges from a pale to a rather rich orange. Large specimens are about 50 cm long when extended. The lower half is almost completely buried in muddy sand; the upper half is elaborated into a series of leaflike branches, each bearing numerous little feeding polyps which capture small animals. Opening onto the surface of the main stem are less conspicuous polyps whose function is to conduct water into and out of the system of canals that ventilates the colony. When a sea pen is stimulated to contract, water is forced out of the colony, and it may be some time before it becomes inflated again. Sea pens belong to the same general group of Cnidaria as the sea anemones, but the fact that their polyps are small and organized into a featherlike colony obscures the kinship to some extent. *Ptilosarcus*, like most sea pens, is beautifully luminescent, yielding a rather strong greenish light when stimulated mechanically by stroking.

One of the predators on *Ptilosarcus* is a very unusual nudibranch, *Armina californica* (fig. 342). It is a large species, sometimes about 7 cm long, and is strikingly marked with alternating longitudinal white and brown stripes which converge anteriorly. *Armina* differs from all other nudibranchs of our area in several respects. It has neither the branched gills characteristic of dorids nor the fleshy dorsal processes characteristic of eolids. Instead, it has a series of flaplike gills on either side of the body, in a groove between the foot and an overhanging fold of skin. The two rhinophores of *Armina* seem to come from a common base and to be directed forward, instead of arising separately and pointing almost straight upward as they do in most nudibranchs. *Armina* only occasionally wanders into shallow waters of quiet bays.

Mediaster aequalis (pl. 26), an orange-red sea star, is also a predator on sea pens, and is occasionally seen close to shore. Its disk is proportionately broad, and the rays taper abruptly. A distinctive feature of this species is the series of large plates that abut one another all around the margins of the animal. A large specimen is about 15 cm across. A faint odor similar to that of exploded gunpowder is often detectable when this sea star is brought close to one's nose.

BEDS OF EELGRASS

Eelgrass, *Zostera marina* (pl. 35), is found at lower levels of the intertidal region, as well as subtidally, growing on substrata that range from rather clean sand to mud. Wherever it is successful, its spreading rhizomes and abundant roots form tangled mats that have a binding effect on the substratum and thus help to provide a stable habitat for many kinds of small animals. The leaves support a wide variety of organisms, many of which go unnoticed because they are microscopic or nearly so. A heavy growth of eelgrass also provides an excellent cover for some larger, mobile animals, such as crabs and fishes. Although it is a perennial plant, its abundance in a particular place varies considerably according to season. Colonies of eelgrass tend to build up in spring and summer, and then to regress during the fall and winter.

Eelgrass is a flowering plant and belongs to the same family (Zosteraceae) as *Phyllospadix*, the surfgrass found on rocky shores. The flowers, borne in spikelike clusters, are relatively inconspicuous. The thin leaves, 3 to 10 mm wide, are sometimes more than 1 m long.

A dwarf eelgrass, *Zostera noltii* (*Z. nana*) (pl. 35), has been introduced from Europe. Its leaves are about 15 cm long and not quite 2 mm wide. There are now substantial colonies of this species in muddy habitats in Willapa Bay, as well as near Bellingham and at other localities in Washington and British Columbia. As a rule, it seems to be most abundant at tide levels appreciably higher than those where *Z. marina* grows best. In any case, the following account of organisms associated with eelgrass refers to *Z. marina*.

The fauna and flora on leaves of eelgrass vary from place to place and from season to season; in general, they are richer and more interesting in late spring and summer. In a particular situation, the fauna and flora on eelgrass tend to follow the same pattern each year. A number of the more common and more distinctive animals and plants found on eelgrass leaves will be discussed here, but the user of this book will have to find the situations where they actually occur.

In certain places, especially during the summer months, the leaves of eelgrass become colonized by a variety of essentially microscopic plant organisms. Most obvious among these are the diatoms, which, if present in large numbers, constitute a furry, olive-brown coating. If some of the diatoms present are of the chain-forming type, a good deal of the coating will seem to consist of fine filaments. Bacteria will also be plentiful, and once the biological ball starts to roll, detritus tends to become incorporated into the film.

The diatoms, bacteria, and detritus, as well as the decaying tissue of eelgrass leaves themselves, are food souces for many protozoans, microscopic worms (especially certain turbellarians), and small crustaceans. These in turn are eaten by other protozoans, other turbellarians, nemerteans, hydroids, and jellyfishes.

Several small algae other than diatoms are here or there associated with leaves of eelgrass. *Smithora naiadum* (pl. 35) stands out in particular because it is almost invariably present during the spring and summer, and is conspicuous in color as well as size. It is closely related to species of *Porphyra* common on rocky shores. The very thin blades of *Smithora*—they are a single cell-layer thick—are purplish red, and when fully developed are several centimeters long. They are usually joined to the eelgrass leaf by a narrowed, stalklike portion. *Smithora* also grows on *Phyllospadix*.

A green alga often found on the leaves of *Zostera*, and also on *Phyllospadix*, is *Kornmannia zostericola* (*Monostroma zostericola*) (pl. 35). It is about the same size as *Smithora*. As in all species of the *Monostroma-Ulvaria-Kornmannia* complex, the blades are just one cell thick. In California, this seaweed starts growing in early winter, and is usually gone by summer. Farther north, its growing season is a little later.

A wide assortment of animal organisms is found on eelgrass leaves. Others live buried in the sand or mud among the roots, or use eelgrass beds as a refuge. Before going into the conspicuous animals associated with this plant, it is important to point out that there are many more or less microscopic animals living in the coating of diatoms and bacteria on the leaves. The herbivores are represented mostly by certain ciliated protozoans, a few turbellarian flatworms, and copepods. The carnivores include some of the ciliates, most of the turbellarians, and all of the nemerteans, hydroids, and jellyfishes. Among the small crustaceans that provide food for carnivores are copepods, ostracodes, and amphipods, including the bizarre caprellids (fig. 343). The crustaceans available to hydroids and jellyfishes are not limited to those crawling on the leaves, for these animals can capture swimming or drifting organisms that have the misfortune to come into contact with their tentacles. The sessile jellyfishes, *Haliclystus* and *Thaumatoscyphus*, feed mostly on caprellids, which are sometimes found by the millions on eelgrass.

Hydroids, Jellyfishes, and Sea Anemones

Hydroids are common on eelgrass. Some of them, especially *Obelia dichotoma* (fig. 6), form conspicuous growths, but most species are small and creeping and may be overlooked completely.

Gonionemus vertens (pl. 3) is a hydrozoan jellyfish that usually has a

343. A caprellid amphipod on eelgrass

diameter of about 1.5 cm and a height slightly less than this, so it is a bit broader than tall when relaxed. The manubrium, on which the mouth is situated, and the extensively crinkled gonads on the four radial canals are rather opaque and impart most of the color that the jellyfish shows. In males this color tends to be buff or light brown; in females it is more nearly pale orange. The tentacles are numerous, fairly long—some are longer than others—and have a ringed appearance because of the way the stinging capsules (nematocysts) are arranged. A particularly distinctive feature is their adhesive pads, located nearer the tips of the tentacles than their bases; the tentacles are sharply angled at the points where the pads are inserted. With the aid of its sticky pads, *Gonionemus* can cling very tightly to the leaves of eelgrass, and also to seaweeds on rocky shores. If it becomes detached by vigorous mechanical stirring of the eelgrass, it swims much like any other jellyfish of the same general type until it manages to get a foothold again. *Gonionemus* feeds largely on small crustaceans. It is locally abundant during the summer months, from Puget Sound to Alaska, the Kamchatka Peninsula, and Japan.

During the late spring, summer, and early autumn, one should watch for attached medusae of the genera *Haliclystus* and *Thaumatoscyphus*. These are scyphozoans, more closely related to *Cyanea* and *Aurelia* than to most of the other jellyfishes found in the region covered by this book. They are affixed to eelgrass—and sometimes to seaweeds—by a stalk on the aboral surface. They do not move around much, and they cannot swim if they are detached. They are characterized by eight marginal lobes, each tipped with a cluster of knobbed tentacles; the little knobs are batteries of stinging cells for subduing prey, which consists almost exclusively of the caprellid amphipods abounding on eelgrass leaves. In color, they are generally greenish or olive, sometimes reddish brown, and the diameter of large specimens is about 2.5 cm.

Thaumatoscyphus may be distinguished from *Haliclystus* by the cushionlike swellings that are located at the bases of at least its outer tentacles. It is also more slender than a *Haliclystus*. The only known species of *Thaumatoscyphus* in our area is *T. hexaradiatus* (fig. 344); it is sometimes abundant in the Puget Sound region. The genus *Haliclystus* is represented by at least two species: *H. salpinx*, which has stalked cups between its tentaculate lobes; and *H. stejnegeri* (fig. 345), in which structures corresponding to the cups of *H. salpinx* are neither cuplike nor distinctly stalked.

A sea anemone regularly found on the leaves of eelgrass, especially in the Puget Sound region, is *Epiactis prolifera* (fig. 346). In color, it is usually brown to greenish brown, more rarely almost green, blue, or purple. (Red or pinkish red specimens are sometimes found on rocky shores, but are rare on eelgrass.) The oral disk is typically marked with radiating white lines, and there are generally white lines on the pedal disk and column also. It is an unusual anemone because of its habit of brooding young on its pedal disk. To one not acquainted with the life history of *Epiactis*, it might appear that the young are in the process of differentiating from buds formed at the base of the column. The true story is far more interesting than that, however. These young are derived from eggs liberated into the digestive cavity and fertilized there. The embryos develop into motile planula larvae, which escape through the mouth, glide down the column, and become embedded in the pedal disk, to remain there until they are fully formed little anemones ready to migrate away and to begin life on their own. Usually they leave the parent by the time they are about 5 mm high, but there seems to be no particular deadline.

Snails, Sea Slugs, and Smaller Clams

Almost invariably, eelgrass leaves support large numbers of a small snail, *Lacuna variegata* (fig. 347), called the chink shell. The height of its shell does not exceed 7 mm. The color is usually pale brown, with chevron-shaped markings. The aperture is about half as high as the shell. This species might be confused with *Littorina scutulata*, but it is more plump. It also has a very distinguishing feature: a deep slit between the aperture and the first whorl above the aperture. The habitats of *Lacuna* and *Littorina* are, moreover, very different, for *Lacuna* is never found in the upper reaches of the intertidal region, and *Littorina* does not inhabit eelgrass. Wherever *Lacuna* occurs, its eggs (fig. 347), which look like little yellow life preservers about 5 mm in diameter, will perhaps be noted before the snails themselves. *Lacuna* is by

345. *Haliclystus stejnegeri*

344. *Thaumatoscyphus hexaradiatus*

346. *Epiactis prolifera,* the brooding sea anemone

347. *Lacuna variegata,* the chink shell; the photograph at right shows a live snail and its egg masses.

no means restricted to eelgrass, for it is found on a variety of sea-weeds, both in bays and on rocky shores. On eelgrass, however, it is especially conspicuous.

Alia carinata (pl. 13), common on rocky shores of the open coast, is often found in eelgrass beds. This small carnivorous snail was described in Chapter 5.

A nudibranch gastropod sometimes found in beds of eelgrass, as well as in kelp beds offshore, is the remarkable *Melibe leonina* (fig. 348). It must be among the "top ten" of curiosities brought to marine biologists, or described over the telephone, for identification. For a sea slug, *Melibe* is fairly large—up to about 10 cm long—and almost color-less and transparent. It has just a few cerata on the dorsal surface, but these are large and flat and have dark branches of the digestive gland ramifying through them. Single cerata that have been detached and found out of context have brought grief to many a student who has tried to fit them into the phylum Platyhelminthes. But the most aston-ishing feature of *Melibe* is its oral hood, fringed with numerous slen-der tentacles. The hood and tentacles work together to trap small crus-taceans, especially amphipods. If *Melibe* is separated from eelgrass or whatever it is crawling on, it usually begins to swim by thrashing movements. It can also trap air in its oral hood, thus becoming buoy-ant and drifting for some time.

A number of nudibranchs other than *Melibe* are found on eelgrass; there are many uncommon species, but two are rather abundant: the almost ubiquitous *Phidiana crassicornis* (pl. 16) and *Aeolidia papillosa* (pl. 16). For detailed descriptions of these nudibranchs see Chapter 3. In eelgrass beds *Phidiana* seems to subsist mostly on hydroids, and *Aeolidia* preys on sea anemones.

A sea slug that is restricted to eelgrass is *Phyllaplysia taylori* (fig. 349). Mature specimens, when extended, are about 4 cm long and just a little wider than the leaves of eelgrass. When closely examined, the color pattern of *Phyllaplysia* may not seem to match that of the leaves particularly well, for the yellow-green color is rather bright and the blackish brown longitudinal streaks are so distinct. In a bed of eel-grass, however, *Phyllaplysia* certainly does not stand out. This sea slug is not a nudibranch; it is more closely related to the sea hares of the California coast.

The bubble shells, members of the genus *Haminaea*, are sometimes abundant during the summer months in places where eelgrass grows on mud. The sluglike bodies of these relatives of *Melanochlamys* (dis-cussed earlier in this chapter) are 2 to 3.5 cm long. The shell is propor-tionately large, but only a little of it can be seen at the top of the hump just behind the middle of the body. The color of the animal itself is usually greenish gray or yellowish, with some scattered light and dark flecks. There is a pair of conspicuous eyespots on the head. In *Haminaea vesicula* (figs. 350, 351) the shell reaches a height of 2 cm, and the aperture, at the place where the shell is widest, is about one-third the total width of the shell. In *Haminaea virescens* (fig. 351), the aperture at the widest part of the shell is about half the total width of the shell, and the shell is generally less than 1.5 cm high.

Transennella tantilla (fig. 352) is a tiny clam—about 5 mm long—found scarcely buried in rather clean sand, especially where roots and rhizomes of eelgrass or deposits of shells help to stabilize the substratum. It is not at all restricted to eelgrass beds, however, and will be found widely distributed in sandy areas of quiet bays. The umbo of *Transennella* is almost midway between the anterior and posterior margins; and the valves of the shell, as viewed from the side, have the outline of a rounded isosceles triangle. About a third of the shell, nearest the end from which the siphons emerge, is stained purplish brown, inside as well as outside. This is one of several species of small Pacific coast clams that brood their young. The females carry their tiny offspring—sometimes thirty or forty of them in various stages of development—in the mantle cavity. Release of the little clams takes place mostly during the summer months. This species is found from Alaska to Baja California.

A closely-related species, *T. confusa*, is known to occur from Coos Bay, Oregon, to central California. It is about the same size as *T. tantilla*, but lacks the prominent stain. (When there is a small blotch of brown, it is on the side opposite the end from which the siphons emerge.)

Gemma gemma (fig. 353), similar to the transennellas in size and general appearance, and also in its habit of brooding its young until they are fully-formed, was introduced to the Pacific coast from the Atlantic. It is now common in muddy situations in a number of bays. The easiest way to distinguish *Gemma* from a *Transennella* is to open up the shell and look, with a strong magnifier, at the inside of the lower margin of one of the valves. In *Gemma*, there is a series of minute teeth, or "crenulations," along this margin; *Transennella* does not have them.

The bent-nosed clam, *Macoma nasuta* (fig. 293) and its close relative *M. inquinata* (fig. 294), are usually present in eelgrass beds. Both of these species have been discussed in connection with muddy sand, where they are among the numerically dominant animals.

Sea Stars, Brittle Stars, and Sea Cucumbers

The little six-rayed sea star, *Leptasterias hexactis* (pl. 25), so abundant in rocky habitats, also turns up in beds of eelgrass. During the daytime low tides, it may go unnoticed unless one pokes around the tight mass of rhizomes. In the fall and winter, however, when the best low tides come at night, *Leptasterias* becomes a very conspicuous feature of the eelgrass fauna, moving with some agility among the leaves, even at the surface. Its food here consists to a large extent of the little snail

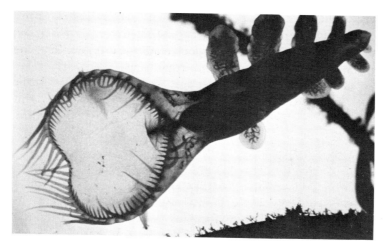

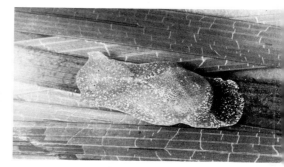

348. *Melibe leonina*

349. *Phyllaplysia taylori*

350. *Haminaea vesicula*

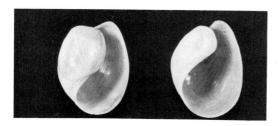

351. Shells of *Haminaea vesicula* (left) and *H. virescens* (right)

352. *Transennella tantilla*

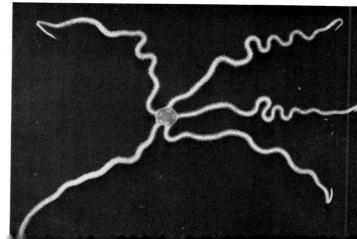

353. *Gemma gemma*

354. *Amphiodia occidentalis*

Lacuna (fig. 347), which is a good choice, for it seems to be a nearly inexhaustible resource for a carnivore to feed upon.

Pisaster brevispinus (pl. 25) resembles *P. ochraceus* of rocky shores, but it is flabbier and its color is usually pink or purplish pink. The diameter may exceed 50 cm. This is primarily a subtidal species, but in inlets along the west coast of Vancouver Island it can be found at the shore during extremely low tides. In Tomales Bay, California, a small variety—not often larger than 25 cm across—is fairly abundant in beds of eelgrass. This variety has been given the subspecific name *paucispinus* because it has fewer spines than its deepwater counterpart. The food of *P. brevispinus* consists of clams.

Amphiodia occidentalis (fig. 354) is a long-rayed brittle star that lives buried in muddy sand, especially where there are colonies of eelgrass. It often forms dense populations. In order to collect food, it extends the tips of its rays to the surface of the sand. In a large animal whose rays are outstretched, the diameter may reach 12 cm, but the disk is only about 6 mm across. The rays are fragile, and in many specimens at least one will probably be in the process of regenerating a new tip. The range of *A. occidentalis* is from Alaska to southern California.

If the substratum is decidedly sandy, the little burrowing sea cucumber, *Leptosynapta*, will probably be just as common as it is in sandy situations where there is no eelgrass.

Isopods and Crabs

An isopod that blends in beautifully with eelgrass is *Idotea resecata* (fig. 355). A distinguishing characteristic of this species is the way in which the tip of its telson—the terminal piece of its abdomen—is cut off concavely. Large specimens are about 4 cm long, about the width of an eelgrass blade, and of a translucent green color. It is easiest to find *I. resecata* by pulling the leaves of eelgrass through one's fingers, since the animal clings very tightly to the leaves by means of its seven pairs of clawed legs. Once detached, however, it swims with grace, using its flattened abdominal appendages as paddles.

Idotea wosnesenskii (pl. 19), which has been adequately described in the chapters dealing with floating docks and rocky shores, is generally common on eelgrass, too. There may also be other species of *Idotea*.

Cancer magister (fig. 356), the Dungeness crab of our markets, is taken commercially with traps set on a sandy bottom in rather deep water. It is sometimes found, however, at low tide in sandy and muddy bays where there is a good growth of eelgrass. It can burrow backward into the substratum so that little more than its antennae and eyes protrude. The Dungeness crab feeds largely on small clams, which it can open by chipping away at the shell with its heavy pincers. Large specimens may have a carapace 20 cm (8 inches) wide. (The minimum size for crabs of this species taken for food is 6½ inches, and only males can be kept.) The color of the dorsal side of the carapace is grayish brown, sometimes with a purplish tinge.

The red crab, *Cancer productus* (fig. 357), is not exploited commercially because it is not as large as the Dungeness crab and because its shell is so heavy in proportion to the body. It is much more abundant intertidally than the Dungeness crab, occurring in most sandy, muddy, and gravelly bays, especially where there is eelgrass; it even occurs in rocky situations. Its carapace rarely attains a width of 15 cm, and the general coloration of the upper side of the body is a dark brownish red. The pincers have black tips, and the spines on the anterior part of the carapace are less sharp than the corresponding spines of the Dungeness crab.

Cancer gracilis, the graceful crab (pl. 22), is primarily a subtidal species, but it is moderately abundant at low tide levels in some bays, especially in the Puget Sound region. It resembles *C. magister*, but the upper surface of its carapace is smooth rather than bumpy, and its legs are relatively slender. The color ranges from grayish brown to brownish red. The breadth of the carapace does not often exceed 7 cm, although some males are a little larger than this.

Three other crabs are rather regularly associated with eelgrass. These have already been considered in connection with rocky shores, where they are typically found hiding in or under kelp. In beds of eelgrass, they are not so inclined as the *Cancer* crabs to stay on the bottom, and are usually seen clinging to the stems and leaves.

The most common of the three, and the one most likely to bask right at the surface, is *Pugettia gracilis* (fig. 358). It is one of the so-called spider crabs and, like some of its relatives, it sticks small seaweeds, sponges, and other organisms on its carapace. The basic coloration of the animal varies, but it is usually dark reddish brown. The carapace has sharp spines on its dorsal side, as well as large teeth along its lateral margins. A carapace length of about 3 cm is maximum.

Pugettia producta (fig. 191), abundant on rocky shores all along the coast, is found on eelgrass in the Puget Sound region, and perhaps elsewhere. It cannot be said, however, to be a regular associate of eelgrass. Its carapace, which may attain a length of 10 cm, is perfectly smooth above. The color of the dorsal side is generally olive-green, but it may have some reddish or orange tones, and there is typically considerable red on the underside.

More closely related to the species of *Cancer* than to spider crabs is the helmet crab, *Telmessus cheiragonus* (pl. 22), common in the Puget Sound region. Its carapace, characterized by six jagged teeth on both sides, attains a maximum length of about 5 cm, which is slightly less than its width. Both the carapace and the legs are intensely hairy. The basic coloration is greenish or yellowish green, but there may be considerable red, orange, or brown worked into this.

355. *Idotea resecata*

356. *Cancer magister,* the Dungeness crab

357. *Cancer productus,* the red crab

358. *Pugettia gracilis*

Extensive intertidal deposits of stiff clay are not common in the region with which this book is concerned. Some of them are covered with a layer of sand or mud, so they do not become apparent until after one has done a little digging. Others are exposed at the shore. A good example of a thick clay stratum can be seen at the base of cliffs at Goose Point and neighboring areas along the east shore of Willapa Bay (fig. 359). About 120,000 years ago, when the sea level was a little higher than it is now, fine particles of clay that had been washed down to the sea accumulated in a tidal flat, forming a deposit that now rises for about 1 m above the high-tide line. Overlying the clay is a layer of slightly coarser sediment, similar to the mixture of sand and mud that is characteristic of most quiet bays. Shells of mudflat clams, including species of *Macoma*, and a few gastropods have been preserved in this upper layer, and there are distinct traces of burrows that belonged to the mud shrimp or ghost shrimp, or both.

The clay at Goose Point is so firm that larvae of *Balanus glandula* settle on it and develop into perfectly normal barnacles. There is, in fact, a broad and nearly continuous band of *B. glandula* near the high tide line. One may expect that the clay is worn away more rapidly than rock, so the barnacles that colonize it probably do not live for more than a year or two. (On rock, *B. glandula* may live for at least seven years.)

At a tide level of about +3 feet (0.9 m), the clay is riddled by a small polychaete, *Polydora proboscidea* (*Boccardia proboscidea* in some accounts). This is a member of the Spionidae, one of several families characterized by two long palps originating from the head end. The palps are extended from the burrow, or from a distinct tube in other species, and are used for collecting microscopic particles of food. *Polydora proboscidea* is widespread along the Pacific coast, and can make burrows in shale as well as in clay. Some other spionids, including other species of *Polydora*, have similar habits. There are also species that burrow into shells of snails or barnacles, and many that form upright tubes in mud or sand. As a matter of fact, almost any small, two-palped polychaete will prove to be a spionid. The distinctions between the various genera and species will be revealed only by careful microscopic study. A typical spionid, removed from its tube, is shown in Plate 9.

Petricola pholadiformis (fig. 360) is a clay-boring clam that was brought to Willapa Bay and San Francisco Bay many years ago, along with Atlantic oysters. The oysters did not become established, but *Petricola* has persisted in a few places where the substratum is suitable for its life style. At Goose Point, it is most abundant at tide levels of about 0.0 to +2 feet (0.6 meter). The way in which it bores is somewhat similar to that used by piddocks such as *Penitella penita*, which forms permanent burrows in soft rock (see Chapter 5), and *Zirfaea pilsbryi*, a clay-inhabiting species that will be described next. *Petricola* extends its foot, anchors it, then contracts. The rasping ridges on the blunt anterior end of the shell rub away a little clay and thus the burrow is made deeper.

Although the shell of *P. pholadiformis*, which reaches a length of about 5 cm, resembles the shell of a piddock, it is important to appreciate that the clay-boring habit of this bivalve evolved independently of the boring habit of piddocks. *Petricola* belongs, in fact, to a family that is closely related to the one which includes littleneck clams, the Pismo clam, and eastern quahogs. Another species of the genus, *P. cardi-toides*, is a nestler in burrows of deceased piddocks; it was discussed in Chapter 5.

Zirfaea pilsbryi, the rough piddock (fig. 361), is found mostly at tide levels of below −1.0 foot (−0.3 meter). It can dig into soft shale as well as into clay and sticky mud, and is sometimes encountered in situations where the substratum in which it makes its permanent burrows is covered by a layer of sand. When this is the case, the animal must extend its siphons all the way to the surface of the sand.

The shell of *Zirfaea* reaches a length of more than 10 cm. Although the rasping ridges are largely concentrated on the anterior half of the shell, this portion is not so sharply demarcated from the rest of the shell as it is in *Penitella penita* and other rock-boring species. Moreover, no matter how large *Zirfaea* gets, the gape where the short foot emerges does not become closed over by a callus. The method of boring is similar to that employed by *Penitella*. The suckerlike foot is attached to the substratum and the shell is slowly rotated.

UNDER AND ON ROCKS AND OLD WOOD

Many quiet bays have loose rocks scattered around, especially near their margins. There may also be massive boulders, and even rock islands to which one can wade at low tide. The fauna and flora associated with rocks in sandy and muddy bays will vary according to the position of these objects with respect to tide levels, as well as with respect to the nature of the substrata on which they lie or in which they are embedded.

Substantial pieces of soggy wood, including remnants of old pilings, also provide surfaces that certain organisms can colonize. Some animals, moreover, are commonly found under wood that is pressed tightly against mud.

The Puget Sound Region

In the Puget Sound region, and elsewhere in the northern part of the range covered by this book, the common invertebrates found on rocks in bays are mostly species that are found on typical rocky shores. The

359. A thick stratum of clay in a cliff in Willapa Bay. Much of the portion in which burrows of *Polydora* are concentrated appears as a broad, dark band.

360. *Petricola pholadiformis*

361. *Zirfaea pilsbryi,* the rough piddock

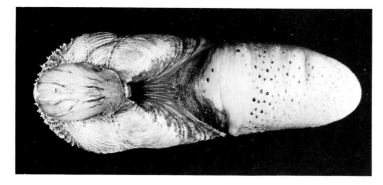

periwinkles, *Littorina sitkana* (fig. 95; pl. 11) and *L. scutulata* (figs. 96, 97, and 103), are generally abundant at higher levels. The barnacles *Balanus glandula* (fig. 99; pl. 11), *Semibalanus cariosus* (fig. 108), and *Chthamalus dalli* (figs. 97 and 98) are also more or less routinely present, along with their predators, *Nucella emarginata* (figs. 112 and 114) and *N. lamellosa* (fig. 116); *N. canaliculata,* however, is rare in bays. *Mytilus edulis,* the bay mussel (pl. 17), sometimes forms masses that occupy much of the available space.

Three limpets are likely to be found on scattered rocks that are uncovered by the tide much of the time. *Collisella digitalis* (fig. 97) and *Collisella paradigitalis* (fig. 109) will be on the upper sides, whereas *Notoacmea persona* (fig. 101) will tend to be stuck under the edges, close to where the rocks meet the sand or mud. *Collisella pelta* and *Notoacmea scutum* are not especially common in muddy bays, but they do occur, generally at tide levels at least slightly lower than those where *C. digitalis* and *N. persona* are prevalent.

The scavenging snail *Searlesia dira* (fig. 115) may be abundant at the edges of rocks, but the shells that move too jerkily and too quickly to be snails will be found to have been appropriated by hermit crabs, mostly *Pagurus granosimanus. Pagurus hirsutiusculus* (fig. 117; pl. 20) may also be common, but is more likely to be in shells of periwinkles or of *Nucella emarginata* than in those of *Searlesia* or *N. lamellosa.*

Nereis vexillosa (fig. 120) is the most nearly ubiquitous of the larger nereid polychaetes. It is often found in mussel beds and is generally abundant under rocks and pieces of wood in quiet bays. It also burrows, but is usually close to the surface. The coloration is variable, but almost always consists largely of bluish, greenish, and grayish tones. In the sexually mature phase of this species, the fleshy parapodia become expanded into paddlelike structures for swimming, and periodically during the summer the ripe males and females swarm at night near the surface. The swarming behavior can be seen from floating docks if the area is illuminated. The posterior part of the body of the female is characteristically redder than that of the male. The worms do not survive long after their nocturnal orgy, during which they simply spew out their eggs or sperm through openings that develop in the body wall. *Nereis vexillosa,* like most other nereids, uses the heavy jaws on its eversible pharynx for tearing the algae it consumes.

Occasionally, worm watchers get a special treat when the huge *N. brandti* (pl. 9) swarms. This species is regularly 30 or 40 cm long, and really gigantic specimens are 80 or 90 cm long; so when a few dozen of these start to thrash around near the surface it is a pretty exciting spectacle. The nonswarming stage of *N. brandti* is fairly common in mudflats, especially where the mud is stiff; but it burrows deeply and is not encountered as frequently as *N. vexillosa.*

If the substratum on which loose rocks are lying is gravelly, the crab *Hemigrapsus oregonensis* (pl. 21) and the isopods *Idotea wosnesenskii* (pl.

19) and *Gnorimosphaeroma oregonense* (fig. 118) are usually plentiful. *Gnorimosphaeroma oregonense* is especially abundant if there is considerable seepage of fresh water from the shore.

The anemone *Haliplanella lineata* (pl. 3) is thought to have been introduced to North America from the Orient. It is now widespread along both the Atlantic and Pacific coasts, especially in estuarine situations. This is a small species, not often more than 1.5 cm tall when fully extended. Its olive-green column is marked lengthwise with stripes of orange or white. *Haliplanella* is a fairly close relative of *Metridium*, the anemone that is so common on floats and pilings. Like *Metridium*, it responds, when poked or prodded, by extruding acontia—delicate threads in which stinging capsules are concentrated. *Haliplanella* has a fairly wide vertical range, but it is found mostly at rather high levels. It grows on wood, shells, and rocks, and its basal portion is often buried in sediment. Sometimes it congregates in crevices or in shallow depressions on the top sides of rocks.

The small variant of *Metridium senile* (fig. 26) described in Chapter 3 is often abundant. Its habit of budding off new individuals from the base is conducive to the formation of substantial aggregations. As in the case of specimens on floats, the prevailing color of intertidal specimens is generally brown, but the tentacles are usually grayish or whitish, and there is sometimes a light ring around the mouth.

The larger algae on scattered rocks are not particularly varied. The sea lettuce, *Ulva* (pls. 32 and 35), predominates on some, and the rockweed, *Fucus distichus* (fig. 202; pl. 33), may almost completely cover others.

Islands of rock that are well out from the shore in muddy and sandy bays generally have diversified faunas and floras of the sort one associates with rocky habitats. There will be sponges, anemones (probably at least *Metridium senile* and *Anthopleura elegantissima*), some ascidians, and representatives of other groups not likely to be found on or under rocks just scattered around near the margins of the bay. Chapter 4 should cover such situations adequately, although there are bound to be some distinctive elements in the fauna and flora, because the water will be relatively quiet and the rocks will tend to collect more silt than they would if they were exposed to considerable wave action or to strong currents running parallel to the shore.

Two species of the small phylum Phoronida were discussed earlier in this chapter, in connection with the fauna of muddy sand and gravel. A different species, *Phoronis vancouverensis* (pl. 24), should be looked for at low tide levels (about 0.0) on rock where silt accumulates. A large colony of *P. vancouverensis*, which may be more than 5 cm across, is a beautiful sight when the lophophores are expanded. These are practically transparent and colorless, and about 5 or 6 mm in diameter. The individual tubes, often twisted around one another, are about 2 or 3 cm long. Attached to a firm substratum (usually a slab of sandstone, a pebble, or a shell), they then come up through the accumulation of silt. This phoronid is not limited to such a habitat, however. It turns up unexpectedly in a variety of situations: wooden floats and pilings, trees that have fallen into muddy lagoons, and occasionally on somewhat exposed rocky shores, provided that there is at least a small accumulation of silt. In quiet portions of Monterey Bay, wharf pilings and boulders at low tide levels along the shore have massive populations of this species.

San Francisco Bay, Tomales Bay, and Other More Southern Bays

In general, California bays do not have much natural rock scattered over the surface of mud or muddy sand. In some places, however, rocks have been hauled in for causeways, jetties, and other man-made structures. Those shaded by wharves tend to be colonized by animals and algae that live on the pilings. Some of the organisms inhabiting such situations are discussed in the portion of Chapter 3 that deals with San Francisco Bay.

Rocks that are in the open provide habitats comparable to those afforded by rocks that lie on mud and muddy sand in the Puget Sound region. Some of the animals are the same, too. On the exposed surfaces there will be the checkered periwinkle, *Littorina scutulata* (but not *L. sitkana*, whose range does not extend to California, and not *L. keenae*, which is found on the open coast but which disdains the bay habitat); the barnacles *Balanus glandula* and *Chthamalus dalli* (but not *Semibalanus cariosus*); and the bay mussel, *Mytilus edulis*.

The limpets *Collisella digitalis* and *C. pelta* are sometimes abundant on large boulders, and they are more or less routinely present on massive rock formations and on jetties. *Notoacmea scutum* is less common, and *N. persona* is rarely seen in bays of central and northern California. The file limpet, *Collisella limatula*, occurs on rocks and pilings in parts of Tomales Bay, but very few specimens have been seen in San Francisco Bay. Snails of the genus *Nucella* are scarce, but this does not mean that the barnacles are safe from predation, for the unicorn snail, *Acanthina spirata*, is sometimes present.

The native oyster, *Ostrea lurida*, is common in some places. The ribbed horse mussel, *Geukensia demissa*, attaches itself to just about any solid object available to it over a rather wide vertical range. The little Asiatic anemone, *Haliplanella lineata*, is abundant on remnants of pilings and other wooden structures, as well as on rocks and pieces of concrete.

Beneath rocks that are simply resting on the mud, one should expect to find the crabs *Hemigrapsus oregonensis* and *Pachygrapsus crassipes*, and the isopod *Gnorimosphaeroma oregonense*. The only hermit crab likely to be present is *Pagurus hirsutiusculus*. The snail shells this species occupies may have washed in from other habitats.

Nearly all of the larger bays and river mouths on the Pacific coast are bordered by salt marshes. These are inundated by sea water only during the highest tides, and they are typically almost level except for some shallow pools and meandering ditches (fig. 362) that are formed by the erosive action of tidal flow. These ditches are especially prominent in extensive salt marshes.

Unfortunately, many areas once occupied by salt marshes have been "reclaimed" with a view to creating farmland, airports, and industrial property. The "improvements" have generally been started with the construction of dikes to keep out the sea, or with the dumping of garbage and other fill material in order to raise the ground level. Discharge of noxious effluents into bays and rivers has also affected some of our salt marshes. Collectively, the changes have endangered or eliminated certain native species, and they have favored the spread of aggressive opportunists that have been quick to move into modified habitats. In spite of what has just been said, there are still many fine salt marshes in Puget Sound, San Francisco Bay, Coos Bay, Willapa Bay, and elsewhere.

In general, it may be said that more than half the sediment in a salt marsh consists of particles less than 0.004 mm in diameter. Thus the soil is essentially a kind of clay. The roots of salt marsh plants, and also fragments of decaying vegetation, help to stabilize the sediment. As more sediment is carried in and consolidated, the marsh expands and encroaches on the tidal flats of the bay it borders.

The salinity of the soil in a salt marsh varies according to the amount of tidal flooding, rainfall, runoff of fresh water, and evaporation. South of San Francisco, where evaporation more or less cancels out rainfall, the salinity remains nearly constant across the marsh. North of San Francisco, higher rainfall and a lower rate of evaporation conspire to produce a continuous decline in salinity as one moves landward.

Brackish Marshlands

At the borders of many salt marshes there are mucky areas rarely touched even by high tides. Owing to a considerable influx of fresh water from the landward side, the salinity of the mud is persistently low. These situations support vegetation of a type characteristic of inland marshes. A few of the more striking components of such habitats will be described, but it must be understood that the concentrations in which they occur and the extent to which they spread in the direction of salt water vary according to a number of factors, salinity being one of them.

The three most conspicuous elements of brackish-water marshlands are cattails, bulrushes, and sedges. Cattails, familiar to everyone, need no description. It will suffice to say that they are basically freshwater

362. A tidal ditch in a salt marsh at El Cerrito, on the east shore of San Francisco Bay

363. A portion of Bolinas Lagoon, in Marin County, California. The tall, grasslike plant in the foreground, where the ground water is of low salinity, is the bulrush, *Scirpus robustus*. The low vegetation in the salt marsh proper consists mostly of *Salicornia* and *Jaumea*. Farther out, in the mudflat, there are "islands" of *Spartina foliosa*.

plants and are likely to be found only where the salinity is extremely low. The bulrushes, or tules, which are sedges of the genus *Scirpus*, seem to tolerate decidedly saline conditions and are often found adjacent to beds of genuine salt marsh plants (fig. 363). They generally form dense stands and may reach a height of more than 1 m. The upright stems, which are like those of most sedges in being triangular, bear grasslike leaves at intervals and are topped by a few short leaves and bunches of egg-shaped flower clusters. *Scirpus robustus* (fig. 364) is the prevailing species in coastal marshes of California and Oregon. In Washington and British Columbia its place is taken by a closely related species, *S. maritimus*.

The hardstem bulrush, *Scirpus acutus* (fig. 365), is basically a freshwater plant, but it is mentioned here because it is commonly present in shallow ponds and seeps that border salt marshes. The usual height is about 1.5 or 2 m, but in some populations, such as those around Bolinas Lagoon in California, the height may reach 3 m. All of the tall portions are flowering stems, the ensheathing leaves being short and partly covered by mud and water. The largest of the few bracts that originate beneath a flower cluster is sharp-tipped and points straight up as if it were an extension of the stem. *Scirpus acutus* is found in much of North America, and certainly throughout the region covered by this book.

The Salt Marsh Proper

The most characteristic flowering plant in salt marshes is the pickleweed or saltwort, *Salicornia virginica* (pl. 39). This is a member of the goosefoot family, Chenopodiaceae, which has many representatives in saline situations, inland as well as along the coast. Pickleweed forms spreading mats and reaches a height of about 25 cm. Its stems are jointed and its leaves are reduced to little scales. The flowers are organized into clublike spikes at the tips of the branches. This species is a perennial, but it is inclined to die back during the winter. Smaller bays, especially those with a fairly steep profile at the shore, may lack *Salicornia*, or may have just a narrow strip of it in the zone of transition between the marine and terrestrial environments.

Salicornia europaea (pl. 39) is an annual species of pickleweed, about 15 cm high. It generally grows in crowded colonies among plants of *S. virginica*, and is often reddish throughout.

Wherever *S. virginica* grows, it is likely to be parasitized by the salt marsh dodder, *Cuscuta salina* (pl. 39). This is an aberrant member of the family Convolvulaceae, to which morning-glories and sweet potatoes belong. Its wirelike stems, orange or yellow in color, wind around pickleweed and are attached to it by connections that penetrate the tissue. The leaves of dodder are so much reduced as to be nearly nonexistent, and the plant has no roots and no chlorophyll of its own. Its life as an independent plant is limited to a very short period after the

364. *Scirpus robustus*

365. *Scirpus acutus* (an especially tall form found near Bolinas Lagoon)

seed germinates. Its small flowers do not look much like those of morning-glories, but have basically the same structure.

Spergularia canadensis (pl. 40), one of the so-called sand-spurreys, is an annual belonging to the family Caryophyllaceae, which includes carnations and pinks. It tends to be concentrated at a level slightly above that where *Salicornia* is most abundant, but it may be mixed with the latter. The five-petaled flowers, about 7 mm across, are white or pale pink. The leaves, strictly opposite and mostly about 2 cm long, are only about 1 mm wide, and they are slightly fleshy. The whole plant, in fact, is somewhat succulent. The height does not often exceed 15 cm. This species occurs from Alaska to northern California. A closely related species, *S. macrotheca* (pl. 40), typically inhabits drier ground; it will be discussed later in this chapter.

On the substratum beneath growths of *Salicornia* or other plants, dark patches of algae usually become prominent in late spring and summer. These generally consist of a variety of microscopic forms, including diatoms, blue-green algae, and green algae. When the growths resemble felt, one can be fairly certain that the predominant alga is *Vaucheria* (pls. 32 and 40). Under the microscope, the branching filaments of *Vaucheria*, which are not divided up into cells, resemble those of certain green algae. Some peculiarities in the structure, reproduction, pigments, and food-storage products of *Vaucheria* have led botanists to place it in a separate group called the yellow-green algae.

Of the small animals characteristically associated with mats of *Vaucheria*, the most engaging is a greenish sea slug about 5 mm long. This is *Alderia modesta* (pl. 32), which looks much like an eolid nudibranch because of the cerata on its back. It is not, however, a nudibranch, but a type of sea slug called a sacoglossan. Sacoglossans suck juices from seaweeds, using a sharp tooth on the radula to puncture the cells. *Alderia* subsists entirely on *Vaucheria*.

Jaumea carnosa (pl. 39), a creeping perennial of the aster family, Compositae, is characteristically mixed with *Salicornia*, but only at levels where it is not likely to be covered by the tide. This plant has a fleshy consistency similar to that of *Salicornia*. The leaves, opposite and nearly cylindrical, are about 2 to 4 cm long. The flower heads, about 1 cm across, have yellow rays of inconsistent length.

The most prevalent of the true grasses is saltgrass, *Distichlis spicata* (fig. 366), which reaches a height of about 20 cm. It spreads by runners and forms dense stands wherever it grows.

Arrow-grass, *Triglochin maritimum* (fig. 367; pl. 40) belongs to a related family, Juncaginaceae. Its distinctive flowering stems, frequently more than 50 cm tall, tower above the other vegetation. The slender, fleshy leaves are concentrated in a basal rosette. *Triglochin concinnum*, represented in our coastal areas by the variety *concinnum*, is similar, but its flowering spikes are rarely more than 30 cm tall. Its leaf blades

366. *Distichlis spicata*, saltgrass   **367.** *Triglochin maritimum*, arrow-grass

are only about 1 mm wide, whereas those of *T. maritimum* are commonly 3 to 5 mm wide.

The pickleweeds, *Jaumea*, saltgrass, and arrow-grass are found throughout the range covered by this book. The two plants that follow, however, do not grow north of the California-Oregon border.

Frankenia grandifolia (pl. 39) is our only representative of the small family Frankeniaceae. Its range extends from Sonoma County, California, to Baja California, and it is common around much of San Francisco Bay. It forms rather dense patches, and although it is seldom more than 30 cm tall, it is somewhat shrubby. The small leaves are paired, but two or more pairs are generally crowded together, so it may look like the leaves are arranged in whorls. The rose-pink flowers, about 1 cm across, are odd in that they do not consistently have the same number of petals; some flowers have six, others have five.

Sea-lavender, *Limonium californicum* (pl. 39), is one of two native species of the Plumbaginaceae, or leadwort family, found on the Pacific coast of North America. (The other is thrift, *Armeria maritima*, discussed in connection with the vegetation of the spray zone on rocky shores.) Sea-lavender is found at the edges of salt marshes throughout most of California. Its large, somewhat fleshy leaves are concentrated at the base of the plant, which grows to a height of about 50 cm. The small flowers, with pale violet petals, are on the upper sides of the ultimate branches. The blooming season usually extends from July to December. Sea-lavender may not be beautiful, but it confers an interesting quality upon salt marshes where it grows. One of its European relatives, called statice, is widely cultivated for its papery "everlasting" flowers, and has established itself as an escape in some coastal areas.

Cord grass, *Spartina foliosa* (pl. 40), is not, strictly speaking, a salt marsh plant. It grows at an appreciably lower level than *Salicornia* and the other plants of the salt marsh, and it is rather regularly submerged at high tide. It forms large "islands" and may reach a height of about 1 m. *Spartina* is a true grass and is a perennial that spreads by rhizomes below the surface of the mud. The foliage dies down in late autumn and new growth does not appear until spring. The range of this species extends from northern California to Baja California.

Spartina alterniflora (pl. 40), native to the Atlantic coast and Gulf of Mexico, is similar to *S. foliosa* in appearance and in the way it spreads. It was introduced to Willapa Bay, in southern Washington, many years ago, and is now firmly established there. It occupies substantially the same habitat as the native *S. foliosa* does in California.

If you notice a pale pink coating on the bottom of a salt marsh pool (pl. 39), this is likely to consist, in part, of so-called purple sulfur bacteria. In addition to various carotenoid pigments that give them their characteristic color, these bacteria have a type of chlorophyll that enables them to absorb light (especially in the infrared portion of the spectrum) and carry out photosynthesis, just as algae and other plants do. Their photosynthetic process is unusual, however, in that the hydrogen they incorporate into the organic products comes not from water, but from hydrogen sulfide. This is the "rotten egg gas" that results from decay of animal and plant material. The odor of hydrogen sulfide is often noticeable in the vicinity of salt marshes and mudflats, particularly during periods of low tide.

There are also green photosynthetic bacteria in salt marsh pools. Like the purple sulfur bacteria, they get the hydrogen they need for photosynthesis from hydrogen sulfide.

Dense white coatings generally turn out to consist of bacteria, too. These bacteria are interesting because they oxidize hydrogen sulfide and sulfur, using the energy reieased in this way for synthesis of organic material from inorganic compounds. In other words, by chemically "burning" hydrogen sulfide and sulfur, they achieve what plants and photosynthetic bacteria accomplish by trapping light energy.

The subject of salt marsh and mudflat microbiology is complex, and only an infinitesimal part of it has been explored here. It is important to appreciate, however, that besides the many kinds of bacteria that bring about decay or cause disease, there are some that are photosynthetic or chemosynthetic.

Nematostella vectensis (fig. 368) is a small anemone, rarely more than 1.5 cm long, that is common in shallow pools in salt marshes, in the mud of estuaries, and other situations where salinity fluctuates or is persistently below that of full strength sea water. It has been found, however, in salt marsh pools where the salinity is abnormally high because of evaporation during dry periods. *Nematostella* can reproduce by dividing or by budding off pieces that become whole anemones, and thus it may form dense populations. There are generally sixteen tentacles, but these are so slender and so nearly transparent that the anemone may be completely overlooked even where it is abundant. Anyway, most of the body is buried, and of course if the anemone is touched or jarred it quickly contracts and disappears.

An interesting feature of *Nematostella* is the presence, in the gut cavity, of little spheres called nematosomes. These can be seen through the body wall if the animal is examined with a low-power microscope. They consist in part of ciliated cells, and this accounts for the trembling movements of the spheres. The remaining cells are concerned with production of stinging capsules similar to those used by the tentacles in capturing tiny crustaceans. *Nematostella* has been found in San Francisco Bay, Coos Bay, and in the San Juan Archipelago, and should be expected in Puget Sound and many other places. It is an Atlantic species, and the exact date of its introduction into our region is unknown.

Two small snails are strictly limited to the salt marshes. They will be found under driftwood and other debris, as well as on the soil under mats of *Salicornia* and other plants. One of them, *Ovatella myosotis* (fig. 369), has a chestnut brown shell up to about 8 mm long; it is a lung breather, apparently more closely related to lung-breathing pond snails than to land snails and slugs. The other species, *Assiminea californica* (fig. 369), is only about 2 mm long, and it is a gill breather. Like most of its relatives, it can close its aperture with an operculum.

Littorina sitkana (fig. 95; pl. 11), characteristic of the upper reaches of rocky shores and also found on rocks scattered near the high-tide mark in muddy and sandy bays, is sometimes abundant in salt marshes in the Northwest. *Littorina scutulata* is less likely to be seen in this type of habitat.

Algamorda newcombiana (*Littorina newcombiana*) (fig. 370) has been found with *Salicornia* and other salt marsh plants from Humboldt Bay, California, to Grays Harbor, Washington. It is a poorly known snail that has probably been mistaken for *Littorina scutulata*. Its shell is distinctly thinner, however, and has no pronounced markings. The color is usually almost uniformly brown or grayish brown. The height reaches 7 mm.

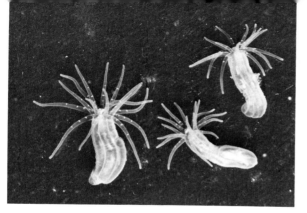

368. *Nematostella vectensis*

369. *Ovatella myosotis*
(the larger snail)
and *Assiminea californica*

370. *Algamorda newcombiana*

371. Burrows of *Hemigrapsus oregonensis* in the bank of a tidal ditch

372. *Halobisium occidentale,*
a pseudoscorpion

The common amphipod under mats of *Salicornia*, decaying algae, and pieces of driftwood is *Traskorchestia traskiana* (pl. 19). This species, generally dark gray or olive gray, reaches a length of about 2 cm. It is common under decaying algae at the high tide level of sandy and muddy bays, and it has been discussed in Chapter 6.

The only crabs likely to be found are *Hemigrapsus oregonensis* (pl. 21), *H. nudus* (pl. 21), and *Pachygrapsus crassipes* (pl. 21). These have been discussed in some detail in Chapters 4 and 5, for they are important components of the fauna of rocky shores. All three are primarily vegetarians that feed on seaweeds, especially *Ulva* and related green algae. By day, they remain hidden under debris or in burrows that they have excavated. The burrows are especially noticeable in the muddy banks of tidal ditches (fig. 371). *Hemigrapsus oregonensis* is to be expected in salt marshes throughout the range of this book, and in California it is often found side by side with *P. crassipes*. *Hemigrapsus nudus* is common in some salt marshes in the Northwest, and it may even be the prevailing species. In California, however, it is scarce in salt marshes, even though it is abundant on rocky shores.

Pseudoscorpions, because of their pincerlike appendages, would look like real scorpions if they had a long tail and sting. Away from the seashore, they are found under bark of dead trees, in humus, under peeling wallpaper, and comparable situations. They prey on other small animals. There seem to be only two common maritime species along the Pacific coast. *Halobisium occidentale* (fig. 372), about 4 mm long (not counting the pincers), is often abundant under rocks and driftwood around bays, especially those bordered by salt marshes. The places where it lives will be touched by salt water only during extremely high tides. Its range extends from Alaska to central California.

Garypus californicus is a little larger than *H. occidentale*. It, too, is found under loose rocks and driftwood above the usual high-tide line, but mostly on open beaches, rather than around bays. It occurs from northern California to Baja California, but is rarely encountered north of Monterey.

Landward from the Salt Marsh

The relatively dry land that borders a salt marsh generally has a characteristic assemblage of flowering plants, not all of which are necessarily limited to this habitat. Most of the ones that will be mentioned may also be found on bluffs that overlook the protected shores of bays, and certain of them are successful in suitable habitats some distance from the sea.

Gumplant, *Grindelia integrifolia* (pl. 40), is a member of the aster family. It is essentially a small shrub, although little of it is really woody. Its yellow flower heads, resembling those of sunflowers, are up to about 4 cm across and are produced in great profusion. The toothed, more or less oval leaves clasp the stems. Both the foliage and

373. *Atriplex patula,* saltbush

the curved bracts that surround the bases of the flower heads are res-
inous. The taxonomy of grindelias has been kicked around a great deal
ever since the first few species were described. The plants called *G.
humilis* and *G. stricta* in books dealing with the flora of California seem
to be very similar to *G. integrifolia* of the Northwest. All three occur
around salt marshes and on coastal bluffs.

Baccharis pilularis, subspecies *consanguinea* (pl. 40), called chaparral
broom, is a decidedly woody shrub, and is sometimes more than 1.5
m high. It, too, is a member of the aster family, but its flower heads,
about 1 cm high and 5 or 6 mm wide, have no rays. The many tiny
flowers in each head are whitish. The slightly sticky leaves, more or
less oval, are up to about 2 cm long, and have a few teeth at their
margins. This plant, found from northern Oregon to southern California, is not as strictly limited to maritime situations as the subspecies
pilularis. The latter, discussed in Chapter 6, is a low shrub that inhabits dunes and backshores of sandy beaches. Its range does not extend
as far north as that of the subspecies *consanguinea.*

New Zealand spinach, *Tetragonia expansa* (pl. 40), is a fleshy annual
that is now well established in California and southern Oregon. It is
most likely to be found at the edges of salt marshes and bay shores,

but decidedly above the high-tide mark. It sprawls to some extent, but at least the tips of the stems are more or less upright. The nearly triangular leaf blades are usually 3 or 4 cm long and have a velvety appearance. The flowers, borne singly in the leaf axils, lack petals, but have four small, yellow sepals. The firm fruits, about 1 cm in length and diameter, are almost flat-topped. This plant, cooked and eaten like spinach, does grow in New Zealand, but is by no means limited to that country; its natural range probably includes parts of Australia and Southeast Asia. It belongs to the Aizoaceae, the carpetweed family, which also includes the genus *Mesembryanthemum*, discussed in connection with sand dunes.

Spergularia macrotheca (pl. 40) resembles *S. canadensis*, described earlier, in connection with the salt marsh proper. It is, however, a perennial that produces a stout taproot, and it is also rather hairy. The flowers, not quite 1 cm across, have five petals and ten stamens. The petals are usually bright pink, but in some populations most or all of the plants have white flowers. The range of this species extends from British Columbia to Baja California. It is found not only close to salt marshes, but also on bluffs that overlook the sea.

Saltbush, *Atriplex patula* (fig. 373), a member of the goosefoot family, has many varieties spread over North America and parts of the Old World. Certain of them, particularly the variety *hastata*, are characteristic of drier portions of coastal salt marshes. The younger stems and foliage of *A. patula* have a mealy look, owing to the scaly outgrowths that cover them. These usually fall away after a while. The outlines of the leaves resemble those of arrowheads, but they are extremely variable. The pistillate flowers are generally in the same spike as the staminate flowers, but below them. The two types of flowers are rarely on separate plants. In any case, the flowers are small, and the pistillate ones are sandwiched between pairs of bracts that resemble the leaves. *Atriplex patula* is an annual and grows to a height of about 50 cm.

Glossary

Abdomen. The posterior part of the body, if the body is divided into distinct regions

Aboral. Opposite the end or side on which the mouth is located

Actinula. A young cnidarian polyp, already provided with tentacles

Adductor muscle. In bivalve molluscs, a large muscle that pulls the valves of the shell together

Alternation of generations. In the life cycle, alternation of a phase that reproduces sexually with one that reproduces asexually

Antenna (pl. antennae). In arthropods, one of a pair of joined sensory appendages on the head (crustaceans have two pairs of antennae, whereas insects have only one pair)

Anterior. At or near the front end of the body

Anus. The posterior opening of the digestive tract

Aristotle's lantern. A group of five teeth and some accessory structures associated with the mouths of sea urchins and sand dollars, used for breaking up food

Article. A unit of an appendage on an arthropod

Avicularium (pl. avicularia). In bryozoans, a type of individual that has two jaws and resembles the beak of a bird

Axial. Along the midline of the body or of some other structure

Bilateral symmetry. A type of symmetry in which the body can be divided, down the midline, into two equal halves

Bullations. Blisterlike areas on the blades of some brown algae

Byssus. In bivalve molluscs, organic material, generally in the form of threads, secreted by a gland at the base of the foot and used for attachment

Calcareous. Composed of calcium carbonate; limy

Carapace. In crustaceans, a hard portion of the exoskeleton that covers the head and thorax

Carnivorous. Eating other animals or the flesh of animals

Cerata. In sea slugs, fleshy projections of the upper surface, usually with a branch of the digestive tract going up into each

Cilia (sing. cilium). Vibratile microscopic projections of cells, important in locomotion, creating water currents, and feeding (structurally the same as flagella)

Ciliated. Provided with cilia

Cirrus (pl. cirri). A soft appendage, usually fingerlike or tentaclelike

Coelom. A body cavity lined by an epithelial layer of cells, the peritoneum

Colloblasts. Sticky cells ("glue cells") on the tentacles (and sometimes other parts of the body) of ctenophores, used in the capture of food

Commensalism. A type of association between two species in which one (the commensal) lives on, in, or with the other, obtaining some benefit from the relationship, but neither harming nor benefiting its host to any appreciable extent

Corbula (pl. **corbulae**). In certain hydroids, a basketlike structure, composed of extensions of the perisarc, within which the reproductive polyps develop

Ctene. In a ctenophore, one of the paddlelike aggregations ("combs") of large cilia serving to propel the animal

Ctenidium. In molluscs, a "true" gill, usually resembling a comb or feather (often lacking, or replaced by other structures having a respiratory function)

Cypris. In barnacles, the larval stage that succeeds the nauplius and metamorphoses into the adult; characterized by six pairs of thoracic appendages and a bivalved shell

Detritus. Finely divided organic matter derived from the disintegration of animals and plants

Diatoms. A group of one-celled plants characterized by cell walls that contain silica

Dorsal. Referring to the back or upper surface of the body

Ecto-. A prefix referring to something that is external (an ectoparasite, for instance)

Endo-. A prefix referring to something that is internal

Exoskeleton. An external skeleton, as in crustaceans and other arthropods

Flagella (sing. **flagellum**). Vibratile, microscopic projections of cells, important in locomotion, creating water currents, and feeding (structurally the same as cilia, but the term flagellum is applied when there is only one or a few)

Foot. In molluscs, the organ used for crawling, digging, and some other functions

Gonophore. In some cnidarians (especially hydroids), a reproductive polyp in which the medusa stage (or an abortive counterpart of the medusa) is produced

Host. An organism that provides a home—in its burrow, or on or within itself—for another species

Introvert. In sipunculans, a portion of the body that can be retracted by being pulled back into itself

Lateral. At the side; to one side of the midline

Lophophore. In phoronids, bryozoans, and brachiopods, a circular or horseshoe-shaped ridge that bears ciliated tentacles used in feeding and respiration

Madreporite. A perforated calcareous plate ("sieve plate") on the aboral surface of sea stars and sea urchins that permits water to enter the water-vascular system

Mantle. In molluscs, an outer sheet of tissue that secretes the shell and also encloses the cavity within which the true gills (if present) are located

Manubrium. In jellyfishes, a stalk on which the mouth is located

Median. Referring to the midline of the body or of some structure

Medusa. A jellyfish

Mesogloea. In cnidarians and ctenophores, the "middle jelly," a largely noncellular layer between the cellular layers that line the digestive cavity and the outer surface of the body

Mutualism. A type of association between two species that is of mutual benefit to both

Nauplius. The first larval stage of many aquatic crustaceans, characterized by three pairs of appendages corresponding to the first antennae, second antennae, and mandibles of the adult

Nematocyst. In cnidarians, a stinging capsule

Notochord. In the vertebrates and other chordates, a firm, elastic rod, composed of cells and lying between the digestive tract and the dorsal nerve cord (it may not persist to the adult stage of the animal)

Operculum. A trap door, as used for closing the shell of a snail after the animal withdraws

Oral. Referring to the mouth, or to the end or side of the body on which the mouth is located

Osculum. In sponges, an opening through which water passes out of the body

Ossicle. In echinoderms, a small calcareous plate or spine

Pallets. Calcareous, featherlike structures secreted by the mantle of shipworms (bivalve molluscs burrowing in wood), used for closing the opening of the burrow

Papilla. A small, fleshy projection of the body wall

Parapodium (pl. parapodia). In polychaete annelids, a fleshy flap of tissue on each side of most segments (the bristles are set into the parapodia); in some sea slugs, a winglike flap on each side of the body

Parasite. An organism that lives on or in another organism, obtaining nourishment from it

Pedicellaria (pl. pedicellariae). In sea stars and sea urchins, a small, pincerlike structure on the body surface

Pelagic. Living in the open sea

Perisarc. In some hydroids, a protective covering

Periostracum. In molluscs, the organic material, often fibrous, on the outside of the shell

Peritoneum. The layer of cells lining a coelom, or body cavity

Pinnate. Branched in a featherlike pattern

Plankton. The organisms, mostly small in size, that are suspended in the water and either drift with the currents or swim only weakly

Planula. In cnidarians, a ciliated larva developing from the fertilized egg

Pleopod. In crustaceans, an abdominal appendage, used for swimming, respiration, holding egg clusters, and other functions

Podium (pl. podia). In echinoderms, a "tube foot," used for locomotion and feeding

Polyp. In cnidarians, an individual (in colonial types, it may serve only for feeding or be specialized for reproduction or some other function)

Posterior. At or near the hind end of the body

Proboscis. An extensile organ used in feeding

Prostomium. In annelids, the anteriormost segment of the body, in front of the mouth

Pseudopodium (pl. pseudopodia). A lobe or strand of protoplasm extended by amoebae, foraminiferans, and some other protozoans, which functions in locomotion and feeding

Radial symmetry. A type of symmetry in which the structures of the body are arranged around a central point, so that the animal can be divided into several equal parts (as in jellyfishes, sea stars, and sea urchins)

Radula. In chitons and gastropods, a ribbonlike band of teeth that can be protruded through the mouth and used for scraping; sometimes modified into a venom-injecting apparatus

Rhinophores. In sea slugs, a pair of tentacles, often elaborate, on the upper surface of the head

Rhopalium. In scyphozoan jellyfishes, a structure concerned with equilibrium, consisting of a fleshy outgrowth of the margin, weighted by a mass of crystals, that contacts a sensory lobe

Rostrum. In crustaceans, a forward prolongation of the carapace

Scyphistoma. The sessile polyp stage of scyphozoan jellyfishes

Sessile. Fixed tightly to the substratum and ordinarily not capable of moving

Siliceous. Composed of, or containing, silica

Spicules. Small calcareous or siliceous structures that stiffen the body or certain parts of the body of some animals (such as sponges)

Statocyst. An organ of balance, in which a small crystalline mass makes contact directly or indirectly with sensory cells

Stolon. A "runner," creeping over or through the substratum, from which new individuals (as in some hydroids, hydrozoans, and ascidians) are budded

Stylet. In nemerteans, a needlelike structure located on the eversible proboscis

Symbiosis. A constant association between two species of organisms (includes parasitism, mutualism, commensalism)

Telson. The terminal segment ("tail") of the abdomen of a crustacean

Test. In sea urchins and sand dollars, the hard shell against which the spines articulate and through which the tube feet are extended

Thorax. In crustaceans and other arthropods, the middle portion of the body, between the head and the abdomen

Transverse. At right angles to the long axis of the body

Trochophore. The first larval stage of some molluscs, annelids, and certain related groups, generally more or less ovoid in shape, and characterized by an apical tuft of cilia at the anterior end and by bands of cilia encircling the body

Tube feet. In echinoderms, extensile projections, sometimes with cuplike tips, used for locomotion and feeding

Tunic. The outer covering, often rather thick, of a solitary or social ascidian, and the matrix in which the several to many zooids of a compound ascidian are embedded; composed to a large extent of a material chemically related to plant cellulose

Umbo (pl. **umbones**). In bivalve molluscs, the oldest part of each valve, near the hinge, often elevated or somewhat beaklike

Umbilicus. In gastropod molluscs, a pit at the base of the shell, leading into the pillar around which the whorls are spiraled

Veliger. A larval stage of molluscs, succeeding the trochophore and eventually metamorphosing into the adult, characterized by ciliated lobes for swimming and usually provided with a shell

Velum. In certain jellyfishes, a circular membrane extending inward from the margin of the bell

Ventral. Referring to the underside of the body

Zooecium. In bryozoans, the boxlike or tubelike "house" secreted by a zooid

Zooid. In bryozoans and compound ascidians, an individual member of a colony

Suggestions for Further Reading

General References

Barbour, M. G., R. B. Craig, F. R. Drysdale, and M. T. Ghiselin. *Coastal Ecology: Bodega Head.* Berkeley and Los Angeles: University of California Press, 1973. Relationships of marine and maritime species to one another and to their environment; covers freshwater and saltwater marshlands, dunes, and grasslands, as well as the intertidal habitats of a small area in northern California.

Carefoot, T. H. *Pacific Seashores: A Guide to Intertidal Ecology.* Vancouver: J. J. Douglas, Ltd.; Seattle and London: University of Washington Press, 1977. Provides an excellent introduction to ecological relationships in rocky intertidal regions and also in sand dunes. Most of the examples discussed are found on the Pacific Coast. Includes an extensive bibliography on ecology and natural history of intertidal organisms.

Defant, A. *Ebb and Flow: The Tides of Earth, Air, and Water.* Ann Arbor: University of Michigan Press, 1958. A rather easy-to-understand discussion of tides.

Hedgpeth, J. W. *Introduction to Seashore Life of the San Francisco Bay Region and the Coast of Northern California* (California Natural History Guides, 9). Berkeley and Los Angeles: University of California Press, 1962.

MacGinitie, G. E., and N. MacGinitie. *Natural History of Marine Animals.* 2nd ed. New York: McGraw-Hill Book Co., 1968. A compendium of observations, many of them original, on marine animals, especially those of the California coast; not intended to be a guide for identification.

Ricketts, E. W., and J. Calvin. *Between Pacific Tides.* 4th ed., revised by J. W. Hedgpeth. Stanford, Calif.: Stanford University Press, 1968. More useful on the California coast than in regions farther north, but contains much of general interest on natural history, ecology, tides, and intertidal zonation; has an extensive bibliography.

Southward, A. J. *Life on the Seashore.* Cambridge, Mass.: Harvard University Press, 1965. A small book, but one that provides good coverage of marine environments and the ways in which animals and plants are adapted to them; the examples are drawn mainly from British shores.

Stephenson, T. A., and A. Stephenson. *Life between Tidemarks on Rocky Shores.* San Francisco, Calif.: W. H. Freeman & Co., 1972. A nearly cosmopolitan review of the subject of intertidal zonation, based largely on the authors' own observations; one chapter deals with the Pacific coast of North America.

Identification Guides

Invertebrates

Abbott, R. T. *American Seashells*. 2nd ed. New York: Van Nostrand Reinhold, 1974.

Behrens, D. W. *Pacific Coast Nudibranchs*. Los Osos, Calif.: Sea Challengers, 1980.

Cornwall, I. E. *The Barnacles of British Columbia*. 2nd ed. Handbook 7, British Columbia Provincial Museum, Victoria, 1969.

Griffith, L. M. *The Intertidal Univalves of British Columbia*. Handbook 26, British Columbia Provincial Museum, Victoria, 1967.

Hart, J. F. L. *Crabs and Their Relatives of British Columbia*. Handbook 40, British Columbia Provincial Museum, Victoria, 1982.

Kozloff, E. N. *Keys to the Marine Invertebrates of Puget Sound, the San Juan Archipelago, and Adjacent Regions*. 2nd ed. Seattle and London: University of Washington Press, 1984.

Lambert, P. *The Sea Stars of British Columbia*. Handbook 39, British Columbia Provincial Museum, Victoria, 1981.

McDonald, G. R., and J. W. Nybakken. *Guide to the Nudibranchs of California*. Melbourne, Florida: American Malacologists, Inc., 1980.

Morris, R.H., D. P. Abbott, and E. C. Haderlie (with 31 text contributors). *Intertidal Invertebrates of California*. Stanford, Calif.: Stanford University Press, 1980. A detailed compendium of knowledge about several hundred invertebrates known to occur in California. Nearly every species mentioned in the text is illustrated. Advanced students will find the bibliographies to be useful.

Quayle, D. B. *The Intertidal Bivalves of British Columbia*. Handbook 17, British Columbia Provincial Museum, Victoria, 1960.

Rice, T. *Marine Shells of the Pacific Northwest*. Edmonds, Wash.: Ellison Industries, 1971.

Smith, R. I., and J. T. Carlton, eds. *Light's Manual: Intertidal Invertebrates of the Central California Coast*. 3rd ed. Berkeley and Los Angeles: University of California Press, 1975. Consists mostly of technical keys for identification, and indispensable in the region for which it has been written; valuable all along the Pacific coast for its detailed bibliographies.

Fishes

Carl, G. C. *Guide to Common Marine Fishes of British Columbia*. Handbook 23, British Columbia Provincial Museum, Victoria, 1971.

Hart, J. L. *Pacific Fishes of Canada*. Bulletin 180, Fisheries Research Board of Canada, 1973. The definitive work on marine fishes of the Northwest.

Miller, D. J., and R. N. Lea. *Guide to the Coastal Marine Fishes of California*. Fish Bulletin 157, California Department of Fish and Game, Sacramento, 1972.

Somerton, D., and C. Murray. *Field Guide to the Fish of Puget Sound and the Northwest Coast*. Seattle and London: University of Washington Press, 1976.

Seaweeds

Abbott, I. A., and C. J. Hollenberg. *Marine Algae of California*. Stanford, Calif.: Stanford University Press, 1976. Although concerned primarily with algae of California, most of the species described are found as far north as British Columbia. Excellent illustrations and a detailed bibliography. Indispensable to the advanced student and to the amateur who is willing to master the rather complex vocabulary used in algal classification.

Scagel, R. F. *Guide to Common Seaweeds of British Columbia*. Handbook 27, British Columbia Provincial Museum, Victoria, 1971.

Waaland, J. R. *Common Seaweeds of the Pacific Coast*. Seattle, Wash.: Pacific Search Press, 1977.

Index

Bold-face numerals refer to pages on which text figures are located.